SOUL'S COMPASS

An Awakening Odyssey Beyond Earth

ALSO BY TREY RATCLIFF

Under the Influence—How to Fake Your Way Into Getting Rich on Instagram:
Influencer Fraud, Selfies, Anxiety, Ego, and Mass Delusional Behavior

The CAA Parking Structure or: How I Learned to Stop Worrying About Humans and
Become Sentient

A World in HDR

Light Falls Like Bits: The Photography of Trey Ratcliff

SOUL'S COMPASS

An Awakening Odyssey Beyond Earth

Trey Ratcliff

Cover design by Stephan Bollinger
www.stephanbollinger.com

Interior layout and design by www.writingnights.org
Book preparation by Chad Robertson
Edited by Chad Robertson

ISBN: 979-8-9909132-1-9
LIBRARY OF CONGRESS CATALOGING-IN-PUBLICATION DATA:
NAMES: Ratcliff, Trey., author
TITLE: Soul's Compass – An Awakening Odyssey Beyond Earth / Trey Ratcliff
DESCRIPTION: Through the Crown Chakra Press, Flower Mound, Texas, 2024
IDENTIFIERS: ISBN 979-8-9909132-1-9 (Perfect bound) |
ISBN 9798990913233 (Perfect bound in color) | ISBN 9798990913226 (eBook)
SUBJECTS: | Reincarnation | Personal Transformation | Spiritual Awakening |
Transcendence |
CLASSIFICATION: Pending
LC record pending

Through the Crown Chakra Press
Printed in the United States of America.
Printed on acid-free paper.

24   23   22   21   20   19   18   17   8   7   6   5   4   3   2   1

Dedicated to my family of souls, those seen and unseen.

"Laughter was the true applause you offered to the world for being beautiful."

—Patrick Rothfuss, *The Narrow Road Between Desires*

CONTENTS

INVITE TO THE COMMUNITY FOR A FREE BOOK TWO!

TREY'S READING NOOK—FACEBOOK COMMUNITY

In the test readings of this book, I have found that so many people want to share comments, thoughts, and their own experiences, that I decided to make a Facebook community for us. Now, I'm not the biggest fan of Facebook, and I usually consider it equal to staring into the fridge when you are not even hungry. However, they do have a pretty good community area, and I believe that people that would enjoy this kind of book, are the kind, loving sort of people that will make for a beautiful community.

FB Community Link—Trey's Reading Nook
https://www.facebook.com/groups/treyratcliffsreadingnook/

There will be many fun discussions in the community as well as a bunch of fun bonus things. For example, I know the Kindle version of this will convert all my beautiful and colorful pictures in the book into a yesteryear black & white. So, I'll add a special area where you can see all the pictures and their captions in their true glory in case you are a visual person like me.

BOOK ONE AND BOOK TWO

Book One is, well this! It recounts my unexpected passage beyond the physical realm into the spirit world and the heartfelt shifts in reality that ensued. There's no need for me to summarize what you are just about to read about in the introduction. I don't like books when I have to read the same thing twice in a row, or even two times in a row, if even for a third time in a row.

Book Two delves into the aftermath of the saga, including a generous helping of introspection and wisdom gleaned from a library's worth of literature that has nudged my compass needle in wonderful ways. It serves as a blend of a subsequent bizarre series of scenes that could only have been directed by Steven Spielberg in a surreal mashup with David Lynch. Far from ordinary, this section details my experiences with lucid dreaming, astral projection, otherworldly encounters, mind-shattering revelations, and encounters with entities.

SPECIAL THANKS

Helen Amelsberg, Kenneth Adkins, Aaron Applebaum, Yitz Applebaum, Hannah Auckram, Joe Azure, Geno Barassa, Marissa Lianne Bakker, Jason Bennett, Cliff Baise, Hana Black, Justin Boreta, Steve Brooks, Beat Bucher, Jerry Bunger, Vikki Bouett, Sherry Cavalier, Francesca Chalmers, Tim Chang, Korey Cayetano, Lisa Clark, Joy Christine, Marisa Depaulis-Hawn, Kat delaney, Stu Davidson, Debra DePalo, Barna Zoltán Bereczki, Kevin Dunseath, Amanda Dunn, Doug Ebbert, Ray Edwards, Lisa Eve, Ariane Firouzian, Hugo Forte, Mark Frey, Edward Shea, Tanya McDouall, Tara Feilmeier, Ted Driver, Trevor Gribble, Theresa Roberts, Tim Keir, Trent North, Trish Speed, Troy Testa, Vicki Runyan, Suzy McCanny, Andrea Garnier, Danny Garcia, Martin Herlinghaus, Graham Hart, Jason Harris, Halfdan Skjerning, Jesse Houk, Hugh Howey, Neil Jacobstein, Carol Jackson, Gavin Jackson, Chris Madison, Jack Madison, Jaime Madison, Beth Madison, Randal Jaffe, Dorothee Johnson, Dorothy Robertson, Ross Johnston, Erlyn Lucas, Sue Marriott, Isaac Marston, M McCarty, Debralee Merchant, John Mitchener, Michael Moen, Alma Mayor, Matt Mullenweg, Paul Melde, Joseph Mina, John Potter, Jonathan Pabalate, Oprea Claudiu, Orit Mey, Parag Mahalley, Paul Sommers, Peggy Kohn, Michelle Pianika, Bridget Porter, Jackie Pride, Miranda Spary, Mr.

Mikey, Jeff Spolarich, Mark Stephens, Ryan Steele, Karen Stannard, Ryan Young, Sarsha Hope, Aftaab Sandhu, Alina Seufert, Angelique, Ankur Sharma, Xavier Maczulajtys, Kelly Hohneck, Kelly Sample, Kelly Smith, Kathleen Kerndt, Kathy Russell, Keith Van Tassel, Kevin Kelly, Joe Ip, Jacquelyn Wheeler, Jessica Winkle, Jon Parker, Lorna Kroepfl, Lynn Snow, Ray Moss, Rick Schwartz, Rick Wiemholt, Carlo Tanganelli, David Hera, Dale Stockton, Doug Bear Stroud, DrWil, Beth Bracle, Berry Davis, Billie Rich, Claire Wilkins, Stacy LeClair, Steven Roberts, W. Julian Gancarz, T.J. Klapprodt, Mike Towers, Racael Holderness, Marsha Jones, Helena Maack, Lindsey Schofield, Kylie Hanson, Josh Whiton.

INTRODUCTION

"Laughter was the true applause you offered to the world for being beautiful."
—PATRICK ROTHFUSS, THE NARROW ROAD
BETWEEN DESIRES

Let me tell you a story.

It begins unexpectedly: in one moment, I was surrounded by the familiar landscapes of Scotland; in the next I found myself involuntarily saying twenty-four magical words then collapsing. My body switched off but my soul shot upwards, flying through space, eventually reaching the Spirit Realm. I spent some time there, understanding everything while being showered with love from my soul family in our true home. I felt like I had completed "Mission: Planet Earth."

Obviously, I was sent back into my body because there is more to the mission. An important note is they failed to tell me what it is.

Since then, I've been figuring out what exactly happened to me, diving deep into the nature of reality. What's actually going on here? I've come to understand what happens after we die, the eternal nature of our souls, and some of the bigger philosophical questions we all have. And it's amazing.

In the wake of this experience, I am remembering more and more as I encounter breakthroughs and elegant synchronicities. Writing it down chronologically has been my way of reordering the chaos and piecing together a mosaic that blends my life's studies in science with spirituality. Following an education at an all-boys Jesuit school (yes, I spent the vast majority of my life as an atheist) armed with skepticism and reason. I hope my wild journey serves as a beacon, igniting a part of you that may be dormant or just stirring to an awakening. Following the event in Scotland, my life tumbled. Afterwards it erupted forth like a flash flood, inundating me with one cliff-hanger after another.

Besides being in three different ambulances, four medical facilities, pinned down in solitary confinement by six big guys as they ripped down my pants to give me an injection, roughed up by cops, restrained by handcuffs multiple times, enduring two mental hospitals on two continents in two weeks, being strapped down to a hospital bed, screaming silently into the void under a vorpal blade— yes, regardless of all that undignified stuff it was an experience of a lifetime where I learned so many things. Ninety-five percent of the experience was some of the most transcendent and incredible journeys I've had in my life.

The realizations and epiphanies that followed were like navigating through a storm of entropy, as I endeavored to map the intricate web of events and insights that unfolded as a cosmic odyssey.

I could see people in their past and future lives. Patterns in artwork, previously invisible to me, revealed themselves in striking clarity. My hands would graze over Maori carvings, and I'd be moved to tears by the energy pulsing through them. I discovered humor in the unnoticed corners of existence, learned the intimate whispers of the wind in Wellington, and saw Brooklyn reborn through a newfound perspective. I shared meals with the homeless and found kinship in the unlikeliest of places. Aboard a transatlantic flight, I danced with abandon in the aisle, amusing the slightly less flamboyant male flight attendant crew. Dressed in a unicorn onesie, I twirled through the streets, tasting ice cream as though it was the ambrosia of the gods. Yes, there were moments of profound joy, but there was also darkness—a darkness I would spare even my worst enemy.

Throughout this tumultuous journey, I was buoyed by the unwavering support of friends and family. Their presence was a lighthouse in the storm, and to them, I owe an immeasurable debt. Yet, through this crucible, I emerged with what I describe as an "upgraded mind and body," equipped with a perspective that continues to evolve with each passing day.

About two weeks after the Spirit Realm, I was enmeshed in what the medical community labels "psychosis"—a term I find too broad and, often, unfairly pejorative.

Contrast that with Stanislav Grof, a luminary in psychiatry, who coined the term "Spiritual Emergence" for such junctures, viewing them not as crises but as critical openings for psychological transformation, often triggered by life's myriad complexities. This narrative frames it as an "awakening" and a passage towards heightened awareness. My engagement with conventional medical treatments for what was perceived as a mental divergence has since expanded into a broader exploration of reality's multifaceted states.

The entire experience has profoundly enriched my personal growth, deepening my understanding of the essence of being, the intricate tapestry of consciousness, and the universal force of love. There is a palpable awakening happening all over the Earth.

Altogether, this was a gift from the cosmos. I can't wait to take you on the adventure with me.

***

Months have passed, and my dreams, astral voyages, encounters with entities, and the symbols and glyphs flashing by my closed eyes, continue to offer revelations. It's as if I'm compiling this spiritual travelogue, and the big reveal at the end? It's gonna blow your mind—or at least tilt it a bit. And no, there is nothing about aliens in here, although I do share a few thoughts on that topic towards the very end of the book. Similarly, there is definitely zero attempt to sway you into any kind of organized religion, other than my clear disdain for those who bend religion either for greedy purposes or to scare children (and supposedly full-grown adults), coercing them to be virtuous, lest a hellish torture be just on the horizon. I do believe in a creator indeed, but it is all love.

Along the way, I'll also embrace all the absurd situations I've encountered, because life, after all, shouldn't be taken too seriously. Sure, we occasionally get caught up in suffering and drama as our souls navigate their lessons, but life can also be a vast playground filled with play, dance, and laughter. From one perspective, Earth can be viewed as a challenging school designed for overcoming negative energies. Alternatively, envisioning your soul as a symphony offers a more whimsical view; with each life, you learn to play new instruments. Perhaps in this lifetime, you're mastering several instruments simultaneously. There's a wonderful book by John O'Donohue called *Anam Cara* that talks about Celtic traditions. It contains a wonderful idea that has always stuck with me: "The soul is not in the body; the body is in the soul."

I find that my life has been peppered with hilarious and wild events. My "Cosmic Curb Your Enthusiasm" would give even the great Larry David a run for his money. Picture an Uber Eats delivery, but instead of food, it's me, and instead of your house, I'm accidentally delivering myself into a series of outlandish dimensions. It's an endless quest, one cringe-worthy mishap to the next.

If nothing else, I hope to encourage you to think for yourself. Resist succumbing to the pervasive, fear-driven, narratives that seek to entrap you in a maze of negativity and lower vibration, surrounded by stories and people that diminish your energy. Learn to let things go. Your soul is better than that. You deserve better, and deep down you are aware of this truth. I hope this book helps you to challenge what you think you know and then gives you permission to think autonomously and embrace independent thought and find your own path forward. Use mentors as guideposts but not crutches. There are a lot of us out there who are ready to love and support you, because maybe this is the life where you can finally figure everything out and overcome it. Not just to survive, but to thrive.

I've come to understand that my return to this physical existence from the spirit realm signifies an unfinished purpose. A vision of a "New Earth" is taking shape, evolving from the shadows of the old, fraught with darkness and fear. As we, bearers of love and light, transition to this higher vibration, our challenge is to ferry as many souls as possible across the river from a land of fear to the side where they can embrace love in all. As Ram Dass said, "We are all just walking each other home."

And so, with an open heart, all aboard as we embark together...

MY GREATEST ADVENTURE

For a travel photographer who's ticked off every conceivable box on the "Adventurer's Bucket List"—exploring over a hundred cities and traversing countless countries, setting foot on all seven continents (including living a month in Antarctica), experiencing the radical self-expression of Burning Man about a dozen times, experimenting with enough molecules to make a chemistry set jealous, surviving extremely perilous situations with death-defying deftness, relocating my family from Texas to New Zealand, encountering legal challenges in China (AKA jailed underground), weaving through romances that have more facepalms than a reality dating show designed by Rube Goldberg, having real-life guardian angels in the form of undercover US Marines in Russia, and leading global photo tours that attracted thousands—declaring the following as "my greatest adventure" might seem hyperbolic. Yet, here I am, asserting just that.

Now, onward ho, ego snugly in check, ready to spill the beans on adventures where taking myself seriously and just goofing around are so close together they're sharing bunk beds like boy scouts on an adventure. I've found great solace in being vulnerable and openhearted. Turning life into art has been a wild ride and, it turns out, the universe has been the one holding the brush most of the time. Reflecting on it all at fifty-two, it's all love and gratitude for every wild turn, every face that's come my way.

This is for those among you who find themselves somewhat dissatisfied with life, feeling as though something in reality *isn't quite right*, perhaps experiencing a persistent sense that it's time to awaken to a different understanding of the universe around us. Or, if you are turning the pages after your own awakening, well this will not only confirm many of your conclusions it will also give you some tasty soul food to nourish you even more. It delves into the essence of what is actually happening around us all the time and our collective purpose on Earth, offering insights into universal truths that have emerged over time.

Merging my life of evidence-required science with the intangible spiritual, my journey represents a shift from a rigid skepticism to an open exploration of the mystical. This transition didn't happen overnight. It was a gradual awakening that began at the age of thirty-five, moving me away from a life deeply entrenched in the logical and technological—think programming, software, and game design—to a world where my canvas broadened to include the vast and vivid landscapes captured through the lens of my camera as a travel photographer and artist. This evolution of self might seem to some like the plot twist in a story where the protagonist discovers a hidden world right under their nose. Yet, here I am, the quintessential techie turned artist, navigating through the skepticism that once defined me, towards a realm where spirituality and science coexist. Thus, a techy nerd morphed into a travel photographer and artist, trading in algorithms for vistas captured through a lens, embodying the transformation from skeptic to seeker without any desire to lead a congregation or sell enlightenment.

Let me be clear: despite my newfound openness to spirituality, I'm not about to don the mantle of a New Age guru or proclaim myself a spiritual shepherd. The essence of my journey is not for sale, nor is it the foundation of a movement. I'm not going to sell work-shops or start a cult, even though some of those scenes of naked yoga and wild group sex in a very chlorinated pool look kinda fun. I guess I'm just a regular guy that has always been suspicious of people in the spiritual community. There are a lot of charlatans floating around with vaporous gypsy wagons for sure. Having said that, there are some absolutely incredible spiritual teachers who know exactly what they are talking about. Through sharing my story, I aim to con-nect with those who resonate with this blend of skepticism and be-lief, science and spirituality, offering not a doctrine but a dialogue, a sharing of insights gleaned from a life lived in two very distinct worlds.

On my interstellar (or interdimensional, if you will) voyage, I read a library's worth of books and learned from all sorts of teachers to help me make sense of what happened to me and what is actually happening in reality. You're gonna love it. I'm not saying I have it all figured out, but I've really cracked the code on a lot of this stuff. I still have countless more questions, so my adventure will continue as I absorb information from the outside, and most importantly, find the truth that I know on the inside.

It's as if every time I find a piece of the puzzle, the universe is like, "Surprise! Here's a bigger puzzle." But hey, that's the game, and I'm still playing.

And just so we're clear, my spirit realm sightseeing wasn't pow-ered by anything you'd find on a psychedelic menu. No, this journey was all-natural, like a hike in the woods, except the trees are made of light and the birds are singing about quantum mechanics. I'm not trying to start my own religion or anything—I mean, I can barely commit to a favorite pizza topping, much less a spiritual doctrine.

Just as we are not the thoughts in our heads, we are so much more than what is inside your skin. We're here for our souls to learn some vital lessons. I'm here to tell you that you're not crazy, even if you think the universe was perhaps accidentally created after Douglas Adams had a spot of tea with Donald Hoffman. From what I've uncovered and experienced, the universe is so wonderfully complicated and full of love that it makes life worth living here on Earth. We're all learning in this giant school for our souls. My goal is to integrate these insights into a coherent body of knowledge that encourages the release of fear and the embrace of love in all life's facets.

Go hug a tree, kiss the Earth, and grab a snack. The lights are dimming as the screen of reality fades in...

1.

THE DAY BEFORE MY BIRTHDAY AND DEATHDAY

"When you find out that there was never anything in the dark side to be afraid of ... Nothing is left but to love."
　　　—ALAN WATTS

"Some people have a way with words, and other people...oh, uh, not have way."
　　　—STEVE MARTIN

July 6, 2023

On the eve of my fifty-second birthday in Edinburgh, a day that would also flirt with the concept of a "deathday," the universe decided to play its convoluted jokes on me.

I had a straightforward plan: fly to New York City, reunite with my friend Rene, and embark on a month-long American Route 66 road-trip of sorts culminating at Burning Man—my twelfth consecutive year. But fate had a different itinerary in mind.

A quick note on Rene—despite the ambiguity his name might present, he's as male as they come. Not that it matters, but a lot of times when I mention Rene, people assume he may be a female. Even though we've been great friends for a decade, I haven't actually checked to see if he has a penis. I get the feeling he does after many hugs. He's a never-nude and often showers in blue jean shorts. Sweet, sweet Rene in his soggy Daisy Dukes.

My day was about to unravel spectacularly. As a seasoned travel photographer, I've navigated the globe without a hitch, from the serpentine subway of Japan to solving the mazes of ancient streets of remote cities in China where I am the only white guy to be found.

Missing flights is not in my repertoire. With a background in computer science and math, I have a logistical mind that is great at figuring out all the combinations and permutations of possible future paths that I construct with my overactive prefrontal cortex—that is until today.

Edinburgh's tram system was my first hurdle; I misinterpreted one of the tram stops. That debacle led me to summon the always-trusty Uber in what would become a farcical escapade of misconnections. My Uber driver, seemingly a refugee from a parallel dimension where GPS signals go to die, embarked on a joyride through the city's streets, as if to prolong the inevitable. The sinking realization set in—I was going to miss my flight. I stayed Zen and didn't give the driver one iota of grief or negativity. Love in all things. I didn't just miss my flight by a few minutes, but by a margin so grand it warranted surrender to the chaos.

Enter my Amish travel agent, a paradox wrapped in an enigma, swathed in a beard. Yes, Amish, with all the rustic charm you'd expect, but with a Mennonite twist that lets him dabble in the dark arts of technology. We're on a Zoom call, his backdrop a tableau of simplicity, complete with a wooden plate shelf that could've been whittled by Thoreau himself. His wife, a figure of pastoral grace, flitted about in bonnet and apron, painting a scene so wholesomely archaic, it made me wonder if I'd dialed into the eighteenth century. None of this is germane to the story, other than to say his lifestyle, vastly different from my own, is a testament to the diversity of people who enrich my life. And wonderful as he was, Hans was a bit slow in rebooking my flight. I guess it takes a while to raise a barn. I decided to go back to Edinburgh and enjoy myself for one more night. My plan was to return to Motel One.

Let me tell you about Motel One. I had been in Scotland for a month, taking photos and exploring. I had a great time. It reminded me of when I was getting started in photography and spent four summers in a row in Iceland. The sun doesn't set there in the middle of the summer, so I would stay up for "nocturnal" wanderings and sleep during the day. I loved those long nights—getting lost, hiking, drifting with music, underscored by the narratives of *The Name of the Wind*, a novel that seems to weave itself into the fabric of my own life.

A DARKER, EARLIER TIME

Scotland's call had been a constant murmur in the background of my travels. My first attempt to answer it was abruptly cut short a decade prior by a call from New Zealand. My wife had received a devastating diagnosis: a Pancreatic Neuroendocrine Tumor—the same affliction that claimed Steve Jobs. The gravity of her condition and the daunting treatments that lay ahead were a sobering reality we were unprepared to face. I didn't know much about different types of cancer, but of course, I was familiar with mortality rates, and things like radiation and chemotherapy. But I'd never had to care for someone close to me who'd been diagnosed.

I was at Edinburgh airport when I received the news, about to embark on a Scottish adventure with Stu, the cornerstone of my art business. Without hesitation, we pivoted to my immediate return to New Zealand—a country diametrically opposite Scotland on the globe, a fact that seemed to underline the weight of my journey back. And it was a long way back. From plane to airport, to plane to airport, to plane—it must have been forty hours. Plenty of time to drink heavily. No, not the greatest series of choices, but it seemed to make the trip go a bit faster and dull my existential anxiety.

Thankfully, she is a survivor. Her resilience through the treatment was as formidable as the support from friends like Stu and Curtis, who, in my absence, were the steadfast guardians of my art business. In the somber halls of the Dunedin hospital—a city with Scottish roots—conversations with fellow companions in the cancer ward offered a collective solace. A patient man waiting for his dad to recover poignantly shared this idea, "We're out of the forest, but there are still a few trees around us."

It was a terrible and dreadful time in Dunedin. Thanks to the invisible forces above, all of that is behind us now even though occasional health scares still pop up from time to time.

Almost ten years have passed since that urgent flight back to New Zealand. Life's whimsical currents have brought me back to Scotland on the wings of an enticing opportunity. A reputable whisky brand, Brora, had auctioned a photograph of mine alongside a cask of their finest at Sotheby's, fetching a sum north of one million dollars. While the lion's share of that bid didn't find its way to my pocket—a wry insight into the frustrating quirks of the fine art world—it did present the perfect pretext to immerse myself in Scotland's allure for an entire month.

Interestingly, my return to this land of spirits coincided with a personal milestone: a year of no drinking following an impactful Ibogaine ceremony in Mexico with Clare Wilkins, who I call my Ibogaingel. This narrative will also unfold the diverse substances I've explored in the past decade, from the revelry of party drugs to the sacred rituals involving Ayahuasca and Kambo Frog Poison, along with encounters with 5-MeO-DMT, LSD, MDMA, and ketamine. Meth and heroin, however, remain lines I've never crossed—and never intend to. They sound kinda awesome, but I know myself pretty well and I can see myself getting addicted.

I didn't really get into the whole psychedelic scene until after I hit forty. It was a big leap, going from card-carrying atheist to someone having meaningful spiritual wake-ups.

***

I'd like to share a bit about my Ibogaine experience. I was already quite familiar with Ayahuasca, which is often called the "grandmother," whereas Ibogaine is the "grandfather." Ayahuasca is a beautiful medicine made by mixing together two different plants traditionally guided by a shaman. It can easily last all night, and you have a very deep experience that feels very nurturing and personal, like being taken care of by a grandmother. People say Mother Ayahuasca takes you by the shoulders and shakes you, awakening you from the slumber of your life. A big part of the night involves vomiting into your bucket buddy, symbolic of releasing aspects of yourself or pain that no longer serves you. It's no picnic. People often say it's like eight years of therapy in one night. In quickly doing that math, I've had seventy years of therapy after thoroughly traumatizing a few buckets.

Ibogaine, on the other hand, is a much more gentle and solitary experience. This is also a natural plant medicine that comes from a bush in Gabon. It's still not a picnic, by any measure. During my experience, I went down to a little town in Mexico to see Clare from Pangea Biomedics. I rented a cute little villa by the beach and she came over to discuss and describe what would happen. I had already studied it quite a bit, but it was nice to hear the reassuring from her. We went and did some medical tests to make sure I was healthy as a horse, which indeed I was. Then, over the next few days, she slowly eased my system with Ibogaine. I would just swallow a few pills every day while she and her sister made me amazing vegan food.

Most of my time was just lying in my bed. I had a few visions, but nothing like Ayahuasca. Most of what Ibogaine does is in the background. It's like "defragging your hard drive" and your brain is definitely not at full capacity. When it reaches its peak, you are weak, tired, and unable to feed yourself, so your minder helps with that. Clare says she's seen people like a garbage disposal and it takes all that shit in your mind, most of which you're probably not even aware of, and just cuts it up and gets rid of it.

Ibogaine is not for everyone, although a lot of the positive press it gets is around getting rid of addiction. People that are hooked on meth, opiates, booze, cocaine—whatever, they say that one Ibogaine medicine immediately frees it all without any withdrawal symptoms. The problem is that people fall and relapse back because they have no foundation to stand on. The "hidden" reasons people get into self-destructive behavior in the first place. The grandfather, on the other hand, knows. And it goes in there to fix all that shit you were trying to fix to begin with.

You can find out more about these substances on my podcast if you want to know more: https://podcasts.treyratcliff.com.

PANGEA

These spiritual voyages have been instrumental in healing, self-discovery, and confronting deep-seated traumas. Yet, the revelations I've encountered through these transcendent experiences were but a prelude to the extraordinary transformation awaiting me on the cusp of my fifty-second birthday.

It was as if the substances I had taken had eroded the barriers of my consciousness, thinning the veil between worlds and catapulting me into an alternate reality for several weeks. In retrospect, I now see that the events of that fateful midnight—the threshold of my birthday—served as the critical juncture in my spiritual emergence.

Ah, yes back to Motel One in Edinburgh—a well-appointed charming home under the watchful gaze of the storied castle, lit majestically on its granite ancient volcano, whispering centuries-old gossip from its craggy perch to those attuned to listen. The energy here is palpable. I am very sensitive to energies like this. In fact, that is why I moved to New Zealand; I loved the energy of the place. Is there an invisible lattice of crystalline energy crisscrossing the Earth, pulsing through its ley lines? It's entirely possible.

RECORDING MY LIFE

My time in Scotland wasn't just about basking in this energy; it was also about pushing the envelope of artistic expression. I've been tinkering with a 360° video camera, a remarkable device that allows me to document my explorations in immersive detail. My online followers can accompany me through the winding streets and the rugged wilderness, sharing in my visual experiences and spontaneous encounters. Whether I'm capturing the environment in photographs or poking innocent fun at the world around me, the camera is my constant confidant. While recording, I meet all sorts of people. Occasionally someone will come up to me if they spot me on the street.

In these recordings, I oscillate between jester and philosopher, tossing out observations that range from humorous quips on the scenery to existential musings on free will—though we'll save the deep dive on that topic for later. I do look forward to when Sam Harris (one of my favorite podcasters, a philosopher and a neuroscientist, who famously does *not* believe in free will) goes to the spirit world and discovers a thing or two. I'd love to see his face when he sees free will from a new perspective. Even though we do have free will, there are certain moments in life that have been pre-ordained and agreed to before our mission here. We made contracts with many people before we came here to teach their soul what they needed to overcome.

Venturing into the world of creative stimulants, ketamine has occasionally been my muse, sharpening my senses and deepening my reflections. It's like turning up the volume on what I see and experience, adding to my creative output rather than diminishing it. In the UK, it's remarkably easy to come by, serving as an intriguing contrast to the sporadic offerings of cocaine from well-intentioned acquaintances. Yet, with ketamine, as with all things, moderation is key. Too much and you're adrift in a K-Hole, a space that can be either harrowing or enlightening. You're simply lying on the couch having an interesting experience. But you're not going to be walking around creating art and taking photos. I've navigated these depths intentionally at times, seeking the deep inner clarity that such a journey can induce. It's a substance that's gaining traction in therapeutic circles, known for its potential to alleviate depression, anxiety, and PTSD, a testament to its complex nature. It's also one of the safest of the molecules people use for recreational purposes. You might recall they gave all those Thai soccer kids they rescued from the cave a new syringe-full every half hour.

Back home in Queenstown (my hometown in New Zealand), I found myself part of a pioneering group experiencing ketamine in a therapeutic setting. I was selected as an initial participant, or "Patient Zero," for an official legal test. I underwent a controlled session alongside my friend Pete. Administered intravenously, the treatment was an immersion in the lighter side of consciousness for about thirty minutes, a brief departure from the typical day, akin to the mild euphoria of a glass of wine but without the weight of intoxication.

On one of my first 360-video-walks in Edinburgh, I was approaching the hill with the castle and going up this beautiful twisty street when I saw "Motel One." I was transfixed. I walked in and explored the lobby and communal areas. I found the hotel to be just incredible. I don't know what it was, but I felt drawn there. It wasn't incredibly fancy or anything, but there was a nice style and color palette to it that felt good. That's unusual for me. I've stayed at all kinds of fancy places and even did this great tour called "80 Stays Around the World" with the Ritz-Carlton. I'm no stranger to fancy-schmancy places. Perhaps it was the hotel's ambiance that appealed to the minimalist in me, someone who believes that less is often more and that freedom is the true luxury.

It's worth mentioning that I have never been one to chase a life of opulence. I am as content with a roof of stars as I am under the gilded ceilings of five-star hotels. I've always felt like my freedom is inversely proportional to my number of possessions. This outlook has shaped not only my travels but my very approach to life.

That evening, as I stepped out into the night, Motel One etched itself into my mind as a haven for future Edinburgh escapades. Fast forward, and there's Stu, my right-hand man, booking it without any suggestion from me. Coincidence? Cosmic nudge? Either way, I was feeling like the universe was winking at me. Bizarre, but utterly brilliant.

My unplanned extended stay at Motel One granted me a second evening in the same room I'd been assigned previously—a room that had already begun to etch itself into my story for reasons beyond its physical walls.

NO SLEEP 'TIL BROOKLYN

On my previous night in that room, sleep had proven to be elusive. It wasnt the aftermath of any substance that kept me awake, but rather an unexpected phenomenon: as soon as my eyes closed, a series of visions would unfold behind my eyelids. These weren't vivid, high-definition images, rather shadowy, monochromatic snapshots reminiscent of ancient times. Imagine the technology from the series *Devs* (an Alex Garland creation; you might know him as the director of *Ex Machina*)—a device able to visualize the past, though with a grainy, pixelated quality. That's how these visions appeared to me.

Glimpses of old cities, caverns, and walls disintegrating into grains of sand paraded before me, falling apart with the march of time. It was as if I were tapping into a stream of historical consciousness, witnessing events and places far removed from our time. The phantasmagoric scenes even boasted a directorial flair, panning and tilting the camera angle with an artistry that suggested a ghostly cinematographer at the helm, eager to lend a three-dimensional perspective to the dissolution of ages before my very eyes. This was a first for me. As bewildering as it was, it wasn't frightening. Rather, I was left pondering the significance, if any, of these spectral images.

Here I was, poised for another night in this same room, my anticipation tinged with a hint of trepidation. What arcane secrets would the darkness reveal this time?

2.
MYSTERIES UNVEILED AT THE CASTLE

"Don't grieve. Anything you lose comes round in another form."
—RUMI

"My theory is that all of Scottish cuisine is based on a dare."
—MIKE MYERS

I was out walking around Edinburgh on my last night there. It was right out of a Patrick Rothfuss novel.

The clock was nudging towards the witching hour as I made my way down to Motel One's bar, a space awash with cool vibes and framed by large windows offering a view of the enchanting street below. I found myself alone save for the bartender and a solitary glass of water. Tucked away in a corner, a moment of clarity began to unfurl within me, weighty and unbidden.

I felt something quite unusual. It was as though I was in the presence of unseen guides, entities that surrounded me, offering silent counsel. To my left, to my right, and directly before me, each presence was distinct and formed an invisible circle of wisdom and support. Though invisible to the eye, their essence was undeniable, a triad of spirits each with its own unique energy and purpose.

In a spontaneous moment, I turned in every direction—left, center, right—and declared, "Love is the Answer. Love is the Answer. Love is the Answer." This proclamation, unexpected and profound, felt truer than true, even if it seemed out of character in such a setting. Reflecting on it, the truth of those words becomes even clearer, affirming a universal truth in an extraordinary context.

Compelled by this revelation, I embarked on an exploratory venture through Edinburgh's streets, armed with my Insta 360 and Sony A7r Mark 3 camera. The city felt different, like someone had cranked up the saturation and added some special effects for ambiance. An inexplicable connection to the environment emerged, as if a dormant aspect of my being had been activated, rendering my experience of the world richer, akin to navigating a vivid, immersive, video game. I honestly felt like I had activated a different "mode" of reality, as if I were in a 4D (if I may be so bold) video game and I was the main character. Strange, I know, but it was a feeling that would zoom-CLICK into place many more times over the coming days.

With heightened sensitivity, I navigated the well-trodden paths towards the castle. Despite my numerous visits, an inexplicable pull guided me back on this night, as if the castle itself held the key to further revelations.

Being pulled to the castle in Edinburgh. It is built atop an ancient volcano system that was active around 340 million years ago. I love studying these things, as I used to major in Geophysics. I quit in my final year because I had an intellectual fight with the professor, but that is another story. Spoiler alert: I was right.

I'm realizing that while I am using this 360° camera to record everything around me, that everything is recorded all the time anyway. I couldn't shake the feeling that, in a broader sense, we're all perpetually in the frame, observed by entities—or angels, or gods, or whatever label fits—whose gaze misses nothing. They know all of our secrets; they know all of the good and naughty things we do; they know all the crazy porn we watch; they know when we are kind and loving to strangers; they know when we are not kind; they know our inner thoughts and our faults and our strengths and when we are great and when we are not. Of course they know everything. Yet, this surveillance comes not with the chill of judgment but with the warmth of unconditional love. Everything in your life is recorded and when you die you will review it with your soul advisor, but do not worry as there is no negative judgment. It is just love and to see if you made progress on your soul's mission.

I envision a future where live streaming one's life in 360 degrees becomes a chosen pursuit for many, akin to the rise of Twitch, where audiences engage with the live streams of others' experiences. This phenomenon could extend beyond entertainment, offering glimpses into diverse human endeavors across the globe—from humanitarian missions in remote regions to explorations in exotic cities. Such widespread sharing could foster a deeper sense of connection and empathy among people worldwide.

A REMEMBERING THAT FELL AWAY

Roaming the streets of Edinburgh with music as my companion, I found myself more alert and alive than ever before. Capturing fleeting thoughts and observations on camera, I sensed that I was not just experiencing the city anew but undergoing a personal change, resonating in a vibration that was always destined. This wasn't merely another walk; it was a hike into a heightened state of awareness, hinting at the unfolding of something far greater within me.

Approaching the castle's stoic base, its regal silence hit me with a force of revelation. There, under the watchful gaze of ancient stone, a significant truth unfurled within me. It was as if I'd deciphered a riddle of old, bridging the gap between my existence and the very core of life. A gentle, yet Earth-shattering, clarity enveloped me, aligning the universe's scattered pieces into a coherent whole, prompting an internal murmur. "Ah, so that's it."

Regrettably, the specifics of this epiphany elude me now, as if celestial forces chose to erase this moment of enlightenment from my memory. For a fleeting instant, I held a glimpse into the future, a deeper comprehension of life's tapestry, only for it to vanish as quickly as it came. If you think of life as a tapestry where one side shows a beautiful scene and the other side is a mishmash of threads that connect us all, this is what I saw. This loss remains a mystery, a cryptic piece of my journey that slipped through my fingers, leaving me to wonder about the nature of the insight I briefly possessed.

Yet, this episode of near transcendence was the prelude to what awaited me back at the hotel. It's imperative to note, this heightened state of being was not the byproduct of any external stimulants. As I made my way back to my room, a palpable buzz of awareness enveloped me, sharpening my senses to a degree previously unimagined.

3.

A TRANSCENDENCE. THE MOST MEANINGFUL MOMENT OF MY LIFE.

"We are not human beings having a spiritual experience. We are spiritual beings having a human experience."
—PIERRE TEILHARD DE CHARDIN

"The impossible often has a kind of integrity to it which the merely improbable lacks."
—DOUGLAS ADAMS

Claiming an experience as the pinnacle of one's life is no small assertion. Indeed, it prompts a pause for effect—slow down, Trey! Yet, it stands as the most soul-affirming moment I've ever encountered.

I've had so many incredibly meaningful moments in my life. The birth of my three kids, falling in love, getting married, Indiana-Jones-style adventures, falling in love again, incredible walks in a forest with my camera, mind-blowing sex (sometimes even when I was not alone), crying at the beach alone, the death of my father, intense moments with a schizophrenic mother, burying a dog in the backyard with my son when he saw me weep for the first time. You name it. I'm sure you've have had some or many of these things, too. It's just being human. Many human moments are incredibly intense and formative.

Yet, what unfolded in that hotel room transcended all prior benchmarks of emotional depth and enlightenment by orders of magnitude, challenging the very limits of expression. Imagine, if you will, amplifying the intensity of all of those landmark-life-events combined a millionfold. That begins to approximate the magnitude of the epiphany awaiting me.

This is my hotel room. I took this after the Event. This was my view as the Event transpired.

It's about midnight.

I am holding my laptop in my right hand and my phone in my left. I'm looking at exactly this scene you see here. I'm kind of dancing and swaying a little. My plan is to go down to the bar to work on some photos. Sometimes I like to get out of the "vortex" of the hotel room and be around people and feel that energy. Also, it's a trendy cool bar area and the energy is nice for me to work on some photos. I have thousands after my month in Scotland and I absolutely love staying up late at night and working on art.

So I am swaying back and forth and looking at those two photos. A ram on the left and the northern rocky coast of Scotland on the right.

I thought back to a recent conversation with my friend Rene who was back in New Zealand with my son. One of our sheep had died and they went out back to bury it. Rene noted that as he buried it, three other sheep came and stood on a nearby hill in reverence. It was like a sheep funeral, these three coming to pay their respects. I was reflecting on how animals understand energy and death better than we can. Or, maybe not better. Just differently. I was looking at these two photos and I started to make connections in my mind. Connections about my life and Scotland and New Zealand and my place in the whole symphony of life.

AN ARCANE INVOCATION

And then it happened.

I automatically said twenty-four magic words and collapsed onto the bed.

Honestly, I don't know if it was twenty-four. But a combination of words and sounds came involuntarily out of my mouth, all smashed together. And these were words that have visited me before. Something vaguely like "AngeloFlagoccalSnuffleaphagusamusfluffi…" It was wild. I can't remember what the heck I said. But I felt connected to my childhood. I was in my childhood bed and it is like the same magic sequence of words that happened when I was born? I don't know.

I vibrated with a sense of a primal connection and an ineffable sense of having touched something ancient and universal within.

I collapsed. Face first. I didn't even have a chance to put out my hands to catch myself. I fell while holding my laptop and my phone… face flopped onto the bed, glasses and all. It didn't hurt. I didn't care. I was gone.

My soul was PLUCKED out of my body. My body was just this television set that had been turned off.

This was no Near-Death Experience (NDE). I did not die. In fact, I had spent the last few weeks hiking ten to twenty kilometers a day with all my camera equipment. If nothing else, I was very healthy. I've since studied countless NDEs, and what happened inside does have significant overlap. Most of the time, in NDEs, there was an actual physical problem and the near-deceased was brought back to life by doctors or the "paddles-of-life" or similar medical interventions. However, I have yet to hear about anyone else that said magical words and collapsed. From everything I have studied, it was time for me to be pulled back to my true home.

My soul was being pulled to another place off the Earth. I experienced the feeling of a weightless free spirit speeding through the stars to an unknown destination, towards my true home. Yes, that was the vibration of true excitement.

There was also a feeling of leaving this old Earth behind because I had finally "Leveled Up" and was headed to a higher iteration of experience. And this was a completely different experience from my ample experience with all sorts of drugs and psychedelics and there is not even the slightest comparison that can be made. I felt like a child entering the actual reality for the first time. After reading *Journey of Souls: Case Studies of Life Between Lives*, by Dr. Michael Newton, I learned it is commonly called the spirit world or soul world. It's the amazing place where our souls get to dwell with our loved ones, our ultimate home. A lot more on that later.

As I was whizzing through the stars, I felt so happy to leave the difficulty of Earth behind. I felt like I had played the game well and played my role well. I also felt like, *Okay, here I go off to the next level game! I'm gonna have to figure out a whole new set of rules and I bet this game is deliciously complicated and fun.* This may seem like such a strange thought to you, I know, but these ideas turned out to be a spot-on intuitive analysis after all my subsequent research.

Note there was no music in my hotel room, but as I'm moving into a scene I will call the "Rainbow Helix Coliseum," I heard, and I kid you not, the song "Everything is Awesome" from the Lego Movie. I've always liked the song and thought it was funny. I don't actually listen to the song in my spare time. I only remember it from watching the movie twice. But, there it is. The cheery tune starts out a bit muffled, but then the song becomes fully formed as I enter the Rainbow Helix Coliseum.

I can't remember everything I experienced. Much has been cleared from my memory for some reason, but I do remember many details. Indeed, I now felt the beautiful warm blanket of these words from Rumi: "You are not a drop in the ocean. You are the entire ocean in a drop."

I began by going into a place that was full of rainbow-colored striations with beings of pure light and boundless energy all around me. It felt like every color of the rainbow was another row of seats in this divine colosseum. The light-bodies I saw and knew were smiling and the smiles grew and grew into cartoony and beautiful proportions. I was seeing the place where all of our actual consciousnesses exist. This was a vision of where consciousness converges in its purest form—our ultimate sanctuary. The home for all of our souls.

I did indeed "know" all the souls. I basked in their light and love and energy. They were all familiar to me. Old friends. And I reckon many of them walked side by side with me on Earth.

The beauty of it all was indescribable—a glimpse into a realm where every soul finds its eternal home, surrounded by the essence of unconditional love and light.

The spirit realm was ready to gently hold me, an embrace with the boundless grace of serenity and insight. I was there back home again, cradled by the venerable bosom of ancient terrains. I partook of a liberty so profound—my soul seemed to have voyaged back to the primal waters from whence it first emerged.

Everyone was cheering for me as if I had just come back from a war or adventure! I was surrounded by love and I felt like I was back home again after a heroic quest on "Mission: Planet Earth." I had accomplished something for the betterment of all. Perhaps it was all the art I created that brought more love and appreciation for Mother Earth. Perhaps I had encouraged people to travel and be more appreciative of the Earth and become more gentle and understanding, loving souls. At the same time, the trials, the relationships—both turbulent and tender—and the myriad challenges I'd faced had all etched growth scars upon my soul, scars that I now presented as badges of honor to this universal consciousness. I had made progress on my soul. Through deep internal work, I overcame many (or *all* I hope!) of the accumulated karma and darker aspects and emotions of being human like greed, anger, forgiving people, letting go, jealousy, you name it. All that stuff we need to clear.

Perhaps, most importantly, I had overcome the big one: fear. And

I did all that while embracing and expressing my own true self.

ABSOLUTE LOVE AND
ACCEPTANCE WITH NO JUDGMENT

I felt like so many souls loving me in the stadium were my true friends and loved ones, and we had definitely been on many missions together. So many of these souls had chosen to come to Earth with me so we could meet up and make the world a better place. That's how it works, you see. After one life, you chill in the nonjudgmental and loving spirit world while you rest, learn from your advisor and other masters, and then choose your next life if you wish. Even more fun, all your soul friends also choose their next lives and you all collaborate to plan your mission together. The mission has many purposes as you all agree to help teach one another and learn lessons for your soul. I'm sure this is a hard concept for many people to grasp, and there will be more on this later.

In this moment, clarity enveloped me. An all-encompassing understanding and a deep sense of knowing washed over me, affirming my place in the cosmos. The joy of reuniting with my true essence, with the souls who had been my Earthside companions, filled me with an ecstatic lightness. Freed from my heavy, dense, pained, human body, I experienced a purity of existence, a state of being that transcended the limitations of bodily senses. This was communication in its most unadulterated form—thoughts and emotions flowing freely in a space where love was the universal language.

This true happiness and the escape from Earthly confines remind me of how the Aborigines think of death. They perceive it not as an end, but as a journey back to where souls dwell in their most pure form, reunited with ancestral spirits. Death is celebrated as a return to the ultimate source, a release from the physical, allowing merger with the eternal energy of creation. Their ceremonies reflect a deep understanding of life's cyclical nature, an embrace of death as passage. This perspective, echoing through the ages, offers a profound wisdom on the interconnectedness of all beings, the land, and the cosmos—a wisdom that now resonated deeply within my soul, as I found myself among a celestial gathering that felt strikingly familiar, yet infinitely expansive.

In the West, we treat death as doom and gloom, but, in reality, that soul is free and feeling one-million times better than it ever did on Earth. It's simply another way of looking at it, but I do understand many people feel lonely here on this mortal coil without their loved ones. This idea of a joyous passage is not just from the Aborigines; countless cultures worldwide celebrate death. But man, after what I've seen, when I finally do the cosmic faceplant, I want my send-off to be a blast. If there isn't a rave at my funeral, I might just have to haunt my friends and family till they get it right. They can even have a celebration like the Madagascar *Famadihana*,[1] where relatives joyously exhume their ancestors' remains in a ceremony, wrap them in a fresh cloth, and dance with them to live music—Day of the Dead meets Burning Man.

It might be of interest to note I spent the bulk of my life as an atheist until about ten years ago when, via deep practice in psychedelics, I started to realize there were other forces at work. But nothing had ever made sense like what I was now experiencing. I was enveloped in the warm love of the absolute truth.

Amid the transcendence, a fleeting concern for my family and friends anchored me momentarily to the Earthly realm. The thought of leaving them to discover my lifeless carcass was unsettling, evoking a surge of empathy for the grief such an event would precipitate. Yet, in the same breath, acceptance washed over me, a serene surrender to the inevitability of the moment. The knowledge that the soul possesses the power to return, to offer solace to those in mourning, salved that worry with a comforting balm.

The duration of this experience eludes precise measurement; the concept of time in the spirit world bears little resemblance to our worldly

---

[1] The Turning of the Bones

constructs. If pressed for an estimate, I would venture it spanned between fifteen to forty-five minutes, yet in that realm, moments and millennia converge, governed by a different rhythm and flow.

Reluctantly, I felt my presence withdrawing from the vibrant embrace of the Rainbow Helix Coliseum. Despite my desire to linger, to engage in the celestial reunion with kin and comrades, my soul was summoned back to the material plane. As my consciousness receded from this luminous assembly, a symbolic vision emerged—a call to action against the environmental scourge of Big Oil. This emblematic charge, at first, seemed misplaced upon the shoulders of a mere travel photographer like me. Yet, reflection revealed a shared objective among many souls: to elevate the Earth's vibrational essence through our collective presence and endeavors. It's a reminder that each of us, regardless of our Earthly roles, harbors the potential to contribute to a grander ecological and spiritual renaissance.

I recommend the reality-confirming book entitled *The Three Waves of Volunteers and the New Earth* by Dolores Cannon. If nothing else, I hope this book, which contains many case studies that reinforce my experience, guides you to the modern-day Library of Alexandria that she has compiled. Thanks to her and several other teachers, from Krishnamurti to Tolle to Ram Dass and countless others, I've been able to piece together an understanding of the reality around us that is even more compelling than simulation theory.

For those in a hurry to find out what happens when our reality bifurcates and sublimates to a higher vibrational New Earth as we leave the muggles behind, jump ahead to Chapter 37: "The Meta-Awakening and My Theory on Life." This is where I combine the wild story you are about to read with a lifetime of science, art, and spirituality into a cohesive whole.

Returning from the brink of spiritual revelation in Scotland, the sensation of re-entering my body mirrored the primal act of birth. There I was, a spirit reintegrating with my fifty-two-year-old form, experiencing the act of breathing with newfound wonder. Lying on my hotel bed, a familiar gurgling in my throat marked my return to physical existence. As I adjusted my glasses and sat up, a sense of wellbeing enveloped me. Words failed to capture the magnitude of my experience. All I could muster were exclamations of awe and heartfelt gratitude. The encounter, though beyond my full understanding, left me with a pervasive sense of thankfulness for the revelation bestowed upon me.

BACK TO EARTH

I feel good. No, I feel great! Even though I didn't want to leave, my body feels incredible.

All I can say is "Wow," and this sends chills and prickles from my head down to my toes through my fascia as if I were some kind of human Tesla coil. I end up staying in my room for about half an hour trying to figure out what the fuck just happened. I just keep saying "Wow," and "Thank you thank you thank you," for showing me that. I don't know what it was, but I am overwhelmed with gratitude for being shown such things.

Even now while I am dreaming in New Zealand, the entities or creators come and show me amazing things. And when I am back in bed waking up, I just say "Wow," and I still feel that electric set of shocks go down my back from my head to toes. It's like my body is some kind of antenna, and I feel many other strange patterns of shocks in my back and legs. I don't know how to interpret them all, but I'm learning.

Many years prior, I had done 5 MEO-DMT (the crystallized poison of the Sonoran Desert Toad) and had an experience akin to a death. It's the reason people try this "Mount Everest" of psychedelics. Basically you are poisoning yourself and for about twenty minutes your ego leaves your body and you are shown something beyond beautiful. I wasn't worried about dying, and I still don't worry about it. But this Event in Scotland was different. Waaaaaay different.

So, there I sat, post-revelation, mulling over the seismic shift within. Dialogue with myself confirmed my sanity was intact, punctuated by the slow, deliberate realization when I uttered, "That was. The. Most. Meaningful. Moment. Of. My. Life."

I had been sent back to this world for some purpose. But what? It's not as if God had given me a to-do list. I felt like a fish that had been caught and thrown back into the river of time on Earth, and God kinda said, "Don't worry, you'll figure it out, bro." Initially, that was all I had to go on, but I'm getting the vibe there's more to come, more to be revealed when the stars align. And by "stars aligning," I have a feeling that all the pre-programmed code in our DNA is just waiting to be activated by a myriad of vibrational triggers.

Writing this book, sharing this journey, might just be what I'm here to do—help others teetering on the edge of their own awakenings to dive headfirst into love, surrender, and the beautiful madness of it all. Or maybe it's just to let fellow travelers know they're not alone in their cosmic weirdness. I am reminded of what a favorite author, Michael Singer, said: "Your inner experience is your own business. Life unfolds its secrets to you on a need-to-know basis."

I believe that many of us are working together as a team on Earth, engaged in a mission that slowly reveals itself over time. There is programming inside of us that is on a time-release schedule, and our path becomes clearer if we remain open to it and avoid getting lost in spirals of negativity and darkness. Countless triggers can unlock and activate our next steps, from meeting specific people to reading certain materials, recognizing patterns, experiencing disasters, and encountering other "surprise" events. Though these may seem random, they are indeed integral parts of our destiny. Indeed, the universe seems to operate on a principle that resembles a combination of an elaborate scavenger hunt and a particularly cryptic self-improvement course.

To this day, I'm still flabbergasted and befuddled by the whole event. In September, when I went to visit my mom in Chicago, I took a walk in the rain. I felt lost. Like a lost soul. I was walking in a park and I sat down by a tree and wept. "Why did you show this stuff God? What am I supposed to do with it!?!?" There is almost an anger there… to show me such beauty and understanding and then throw me back to this failing Earth to try to figure out what to do. There's almost a cruelty in it.

Robert Monroe, in his book *Journeys out of the Body* (published way back in 1971), echoed my exact feelings. "Each time after I returned, I suffered intense nostalgia and loneliness for days. I felt as an alien might among strangers in a land where things were not 'right,' where everything and everyone was so different and so 'wrong' when compared with where you belonged. Acute loneliness, nostalgia, and something akin to homesickness."

Sometimes impossible things in your mind fall into tears.

I intend to weave the insights I gained into a cohesive theory that marries the realms of science and spirituality. This synthesis does not claim superiority over other interpretations but it makes sense to me, finding echoes, as it does, in a myriad of philosophical and theological explorations spanning from antiquity to the contemporary era. As I unravel the intricacies of this extraordinary journey, I intertwine the acquired wisdom into a comprehensive theory that harmoniously merges science and spirituality.

After reading over five hundred past-life regression interviews, I noticed people use the word "Source" about as much as they use "God." Some seem to prefer "Source." It's not just a trendy rebrand; it's about getting away from the whole "fear of the Almighty" vibe that some religions are really into. "Source" is more about the universe giving us a smiley thumbs-up, saying our souls are still shiny no matter how many times we trip up. Many of the transcripts were from Christians who would use the word Source rather than God. But call it God if you wish, it matters not to me. It's all the same thing if it is one with love and not under the coercive threat of punishment. Contrary to such practices, the concept of the Source embodies unconditional love, affirming that our souls are perpetually embraced beyond the scope of judgment. Missteps in life do not tarnish the soul's inherent purity; rather, they are seen as part of the evolutionary learnings of the spirit.

The afterlife, as revealed through these regressions, is a realm of restoration and reflection, where souls may choose to embark on another mission to Earth (if they wish, as this is optional) to resolve karma. In this sense, I use karma to refer to serious injustices from previous lives that need to be paid back in the next life so your soul understands both sides of the wrongdoing. This perspective challenges the fear-inducing paradigms prevalent in many religious and governmental institutions, advocating instead for an understanding of existence grounded in love and the infinite support of the spirit realm. Religions that rule with fear are no different than governments that rule with fear. These are the institutions that cause so much unneeded pain and fear in the world.

Okay, so, the Scotland event is over. I'm quite scrambled up, to say the least.

I go down to the bar and get some water and try to do a little writing. It's not that effective.

I CAN'T MISS MY FLIGHT AGAIN

The prospect of a 9:00 a.m. flight looms over me like an ominous cloud, tinged with the anxiety of a missed connection—not in the digital sense, but in the quite literal, "I've somehow failed to board my plane," sense. Having recently earned the dubious distinction of missing a flight for the first time in my life, my nerves are as frayed as a traveler's well-worn passport. In an attempt to wrestle control from the jaws of fate, I return to my chamber of sleepless wonders and ceremoniously set not one, not two, but three alarms. My sole desire is to plunge into the tranquil abyss of sleep, yet it eludes me, slipping through my fingers like the sands of time themselves.

Instead of sweet oblivion, my eyelids become screens for the most unusual of silent films. Once more, I'm treated to the haunting visions of civilizations long past, their ancient edifices crumbling under the relentless assault of time. These visions, while not nightmares per se, weave a mural of historical decay that is as unsettling as it is mesmerizing. The energy permeating my room is palpable, a veritable storm of temporal disturbances that leaves me tossing and turning in its wake.

I felt. Alive.

As I began my trek to the airport, I started seeing the world in a different way. It was almost as if there were coded messages for me everywhere and I was finally seeing them. Indeed, some may be coincidences, but there is an element of synchronicity too. Some people say there are no coincidences at all.

I remembered how I had gone into that spirit world and felt like I had just completed Mission: Planet Earth and then I was returned to this body because I have another mission. As I am walking to the tram, a bus passes by with an ad for the movie, "Mission Impossible: Dead Reckoning." Wild, I thought, because last night I reckoned I was dead for a while and now they've sent me back on another mission which seems impossible, especially because they didn't tell me what it was. You know how in those movies they say, "This is your mission, should you choose to accept it?" Well, I don't remember when Ethan was shown a blank screen.

I began reflecting on so many things that had happened recently and in my past and considering them in a new light.

I thought back to one of my more meaningful moments in Scotland about a week before the Event. I went on a road trip with my own erstwhile Passepartout, Stu, and our destination was the Isle of Skye. We made many stops along the way, and one was at a wonderful little ruined castle. I was walking along the shoreline, holding my tripod and camera in one hand, and my 360-video cam in the other hand. I was making a video about my experience there. A little free-styling discussion and occasionally stopping for photos. I started looking around, just staring at the beauty of everything around me. I started to cry a little. And I said, "Look how beautiful the Earth is." Then I said something to the effect of, "It's right there. It's so obvious. But hardly anyone sees it." And then I cried more and more. It was a small moment where I felt like the eye of God was the Earth and it was looking right back at me. There was no difference between me and the environment around me. It is right there in front of us all the time. It was a poignant reminder that the essence of the divine is always in plain sight, if only we choose to see it.

You can actually watch this on YouTube. Search for "Neo-Flaneur Episode 3 - Scottish Sunset," or follow this link. Neo-Flaneur Attempt #3 - Scottish Sunset in 360 | Trey Ratcliff. You can see this little tender moment of mine towards the end of that video.

HOW PHOTOGRAPHY CHANGED MY LIFE

I'll give you the short version of how I quit my life in tech and became a full-time artist because people seem to enjoy this mini bio. You can change your life at any time, and it is never too late to find at least one of your true callings. It's quite a nice story, really, about how I had one life that felt a bit average, and then I suddenly launched into a very different life with a financially lucrative art business, traveling and capturing the beauty of the Earth the way I saw it, and meeting thousands and thousands of "fans" around the world to help inspire them. I don't really like to call them "fans"—I think of them as friends I just haven't had the chance to get to know fully yet! Changing your life to something completely different at that point, especially when you have young kids and need to be financially responsible, is scary. But I wasn't scared. Sure, of course there was a bit of fear and worry about what could go wrong, but I have never let fear rule my decisions. Instead of worrying about everything that could turn out badly, I focused on everything that could turn out beyond my wildest dreams.

I've got a TEDx talk online too if you wanna skip this part and see this in the visual way. The only "bad" thing about that talk is they cut it off before my son, Ethan, came on stage with me and I started to cry.

My life before becoming a full-time artist wasn't terrible at all. I had many good jobs in technology. I wasn't a great programmer, but I was a good technical designer and worked really well with teams. Everything from big consulting firms, to launching my own companies to scratch my creative entrepreneurial itch. Most of my companies failed and the only one that really worked out was related to a panoply of patents I filed. Sadly, that company was acquired by a patent troll and they sued Apple. We ended up winning and settling out of court. Not only did I not get a cent of that, but having to sit through depositions with Apple attorneys is a strange kind of intellectual torture. Those guys eat crushed glass for breakfast. It made me extremely bitter about the whole legal process and intellectual property in general. This ended up feeding into a rebellious approach to all my art and fostering my belief in the power of sharing—it's a form of love that, surprisingly, takes care of the financial side too.

At thirty-five, I was running an online gaming company I had started. The company had grown to about a hundred people, and I really don't like managing people. Plus, I'm not that great at it. I can lead a team of ten to twenty people who are dreamers. You don't have to manage people that share the dream; they gladly work eighty hours a week and are as madly driven as I am. That's my perfect size team for getting stuff done. So, we hired another CEO, and I kind of drifted into the background as the designer.

I was headed to Kuala Lumpur (they call it KL there), Malaysia to visit our game studio there. We had a studio in Austin (where I was living at the time), another in the Ukraine, and another there in KL. I found out KL was one of my grandad's favorite cities in WWII. It was a key place for rubber production and it fell to the Japanese right after Pearl Harbor. History's funny like that, making you think about rubber when you're just trying to visit a city. I had never been, and I was excited to go. I should get a camera, I thought. Yes, I should do that.

I snagged a Nikon D70, mostly because it sounded cool and was pretty sure it could take pictures. I figured out the basic controls on the plane ride over. Maybe now is a good time to mention I never took a class in photography or read a book about it. My philosophy on photography is like cooking without a recipe—sometimes you end up with a masterpiece, other times, well, pizza delivery exists for a reason. This gives me a truly clean slate to use a tool in totally new ways without falling into any "group-think" about the "right" way to take photos. Note there is nothing wrong with going to school for photography (or other art forms), but that is just not my way. Besides, digital photography was a fairly new art form. Sure, film had been around for a while, but this was a new beast. Why on Earth would I need to learn traditional film photography first? I wasn't about to let old-school rules dictate my new-school game. Following the crowd? That's not for me. I'm more about writing my own rules—and, let's be honest, I was never great at following directions anyway. I wasn't born to be normal and fit in, and neither were you.

Not to go down this "fitting in" rabbit hole too much, but I've never really felt like I fit in here on Earth. I feel like an alien in many ways. There is so much I just can't get my head around, especially when I encounter any extreme conflict, rage, or violence. I feel like some kind of gentle soul that expects to be surrounded by love and harmony all the time, which is the truly elevated way of living. I just don't get all the violence and greed and hate and all the people that cause suffering on Earth. All this makes me feel like I don't belong here. Alas, I am always so grateful when I find other people out there like me who are one with love and you can just simply feel that heart energy right away.

Okay, back to my confusing quests here on Earth. My first evening using the camera in KL, I went up one of those big sky towers with an observation deck to take a photo of an amazing sunset. It had just rained, and the sky was full of the drama of wild clouds sporting pinks and purples and oranges, all folding in and out of the fractals of the sky. The city and jungle hills made for something resembling a sci-fi cover. I was beyond excited.

I'll never forget it. I took the photo. Then I went back to the hotel to see my masterpiece.

The photo was absolute shit.

I was confused. I was actually so confused that I was angry. I was thinking, "How in the hell can that sunset be so beautiful but my photo be so... blah?" It didn't have any of the color or feeling or drama. It just looked like this flattened, deadened, color palette. There are of course many camera settings, but I had all those right. It was perfectly exposed and there were no blown out areas. And I swear, I hadn't turned on the "Make This Masterpiece Boring" setting on the camera.

After I figured it all out, I started doing photo walks around the world where thousands and thousands of amazing souls would come out and join me as they were all slowly discovering themselves.

BACK TO SQUARE ONE

I started really thinking about how we interface with the world. That's one of my favorite parts of Richard Feynman's book, *The Pleasure of Finding Things Out*, where he talks about the merits of simply thinking. He had a broken radio that he was trying to fix and he just paced around his room thinking about it until he first fixed it in his head.

I began to consider the parallels between the camera, the lens, and the sensor and how that differed from the human pupil, the lens, and the retina. Not just that, but how does the retina send light information to the cortex (retinex theory)? Well, fast forward. Here is what I figured out and, sure enough, it was true. And then how I improved my own algorithm to change my entire approach to photography there on day one.

Putting back on my Computer Science hat, I was like a madman on the internet trying to look up different chunks of code to make that digital camera do what I wanted it to do. Light is measured in something called "stops" that are basically different levels of light from dark to bright. A digital camera can see about three stops of light. The retina, which is much more sensitive, can see eleven stops of light. Well, a good sunset has about nine to ten stops of light, so of course a camera can't capture it all. That's why my sunset photo flopped; it was like trying to cram a symphony into a tweet. But, the general public had become "accustomed" to cameras sucking the color love out of the world. You probably know this too, although camera phones are really good now. Perhaps in the past, when you showed a photo, you had to throw in the towel and say, "Well, you really had to be there."

This diagram should clarify everything for you.

It turns out that NASA had these algorithms for analyzing photos from Mars so they could get more information from the data the rovers sent back. They used an algorithm so they could perhaps see if there was iron in the soil or nitrogen in the air or whatever. I thought, "Hrmm, I wonder what would happen if I used that algorithm on my sunset photo." Bam! That was it.

Although not perfect, I began to see a lot more dynamic range. After more testing, I figured out I could actually take three photos of a scene from the same vantage point. One very dark, one normal, and one very bright, and then I would feed these three photos into the code and it would "tone-map" everything into one final photo. The results were stunning. This whole mixing trick turned out to be what the cool kids call HDR, or High Dynamic Range photography. I didn't cook this up; credit probably goes to NASA or some geniuses huddled in a MIT lab. As I got into it, there weren't many of us in this HDR clubhouse, so I kicked off an online tutorial. Turned out, this was the digital equivalent of starting a band that goes platinum overnight.

By the way, one reason camera phones are so good nowadays is because they all use HDR processing as part of the capture process. From the beginning, I saw this as a natural (and rather obvious) evolution of photography. I didn't have anything to do with getting HDR into camera phones, but maybe a little bit. I spent many days with the Google Photos team as well as a bit of time with Google X and the Google Glass guys. A few years ago, there was even an "HDR" option on the Google Pixel phones and they asked if they could use an icon of one of my photos as the icon. I said, "Sure!"

And then I was just a machine, traveling around the world and re-capturing Mother Earth the way it was meant to be captured. I was obsessed and absolutely having the best time of my life. While getting lost in nature, I found myself.

Me speaking at Google's private TED type event. That is where I met JJ Abrams, and when he mentioned me in his talk, I almost died right there and then. I'm not sure I'll ever get over this niggling imposter syndrome.

There are so many little things that happened along the way that helped remind me I was on the right track. I felt like I was on the right track, but it was nice to get some positive reinforcement from all sorts of people. I was able to spend time with people from all walks of life from Sergey Brin (a fellow photographer!) from Google to Mark Zuckerberg from Facebook. I even took the profile photo Mark used for years. I've chilled with everyone from rock stars to billionaires. Dined with art-collecting actors like Edward Norton and Leo DiCaprio. I even got to spend many days around the world with one of my heroes, Hans Zimmer, a legend who makes music that makes movies cry.

It's like the universe was dropping name-drops, reassuring me in moments of doubt. Every encounter was a nod, a wink, saying, "You're exactly where you're supposed to be, behind that lens." It's important to listen to the universe and to be in a flow state without any sense of ego or self-importance, with a soft understanding that you are a beautiful witness to everything unfolding in front of your eyes.

Hans Zimmer's Studio in Hollywood. I had not met him yet, but after sending it to him, I received this below.

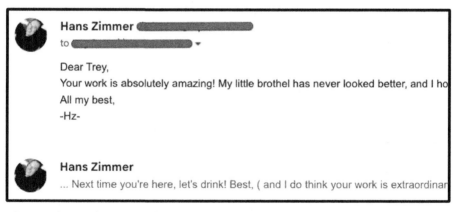

Hans Zimmer
to

Dear Trey,
Your work is absolutely amazing! My little brothel has never looked better, and I ho
All my best,
-Hz-

Hans Zimmer
... Next time you're here, let's drink! Best, (and I do think your work is extraordinar

After I got this email, I basically fainted and was out cold for a week.

One day in his studio in Hollywood, Hans hit me with a Zen koan. "Trey, why are you a great photographer?" I kind of froze. He was deadly serious, making me feel like I was in a scene where the background music gets intense. I half-expected to turn around and find Yoda nodding in approval. I paused for a moment, then went full Jedi apprentice and said, "Because I see things people don't see."

"YES! EXACTLY!" He proclaimed, somehow magically knowing what I was going to say.

Then he asked me, "Do you know why I am great at creating music?"

I paused again, then smiled and said, "Oh, because you hear things other people don't hear." He laughed and said yes. His eyebrows raised and he asked, "Did you just hear that?" I said no… and he smiled and said, "Oh that was one of my favorite sounds, the little clicks when an air conditioner turns on!"

I remember about twenty years ago when I started making patents, I came up with a cool idea because I was so in love with Hans' music. I had a vision that some day, we could all have a live personalized Hans Zimmer soundtrack that we can listen to whenever we want. Walking through a field in nature? Calm beautiful music. Trail-running in the mountains? Dramatic chase music. Struggling with your narcissistic girlfriend? Comedic music. Anyway, I never got the patent, thank goodness because of my future disenchantment with IP. But, sitting here in the beginning of 2024, I'm 100% sure we'll be able to do this soon enough with AI. How fun!

Anyway, I could go on and on and regale you with wonderful stories, but let's get on with this one! Maybe someday I'll write an autobiography or something. But now is not the time. I think there are many more adventures to be had! Let's get back to this adventure where I felt like I needed a new Hans soundtrack for what was rapidly turning into my personal Christopher Nolan theatrical production. That sounds wonderful until you realize you're basically following the same plotline as the protagonist in *Memento*.

I considered mentioning *Tenet* there, but, let's all just be honest. That movie was way too confusing. If I were to put my life on the spectrum of confusion, it's squarely between *Memento* and *Tenet*, and I can't find the YouTube explainer episode anywhere.

TAKING PHOTOGRAPHY TO HYPERSPACE

My fascination with capturing the Earth's beauty evolved into a global odyssey, where I began to craft a new reality for myself. I discovered that it's possible to create the world you wish to live in with the right approach. Of course, there were many, many failures (and there continue to be!), but it's amazing all the things you can create in your life and in the lives of others if you let go of any of that silly fear of failure.

People that judge you poorly for your well-intentioned failures are not your friends anyway. I find that the vast majority of people love you for your failures just as much as your successes because it gives them the confidence to try something new themselves.

As I traveled the world, indulging in photography and adventures, I realized it still wasn't fulfilling enough. My following grew; I was invited to speak at numerous events and received incredible invitations to some of the world's most spectacular gatherings. Yet, something within me stirred, suggesting that this journey shouldn't center around "Trey" but rather embrace an idea far greater than myself.

The center of it all was my website called StuckInCustoms.com which became the world's #1 travel photography blog. I liked that name because there was a double meaning (that almost no one got). First, it has sort of a fun travel-feel because when you travel internationally, you are always stuck in customs in one way or another. Second, you figure out that when you travel and witness other customs, you realize you are stuck in your own.

Nobody knows this but I actually first used the blog name IWill-NeverDie.com. Strange name, right? One day I was out jogging in Austin and I was almost hit by a car. Something told me that I would never die, but now I see the double meaning of it—even after your human body dies, your soul goes on to have many more adventures. More on that later.

Also, looking back, I had an app called "Stuck on Earth," which is kind of a funny name, but now that I know so much about what happens beyond this mortal coil, I do sometimes feel a little "stuck" here. But, you know, I don't get nihilistic about it, because I know I have some other things to do here before I leave. Really, I don't have to do anything. I can just be myself. That is more than enough.

It holds far greater power to rally people around an "idea" rather than a person. The concept that resonated with me most was encouraging individuals to "create themselves" through photography and art. This isn't a novel concept—the notion that the best way to "find" oneself is by "creating" oneself through artistic endeavors has been around for ages. Many find meditation challenging, yet engaging in creative activities and entering a flow state—be it trekking with a camera, crafting a gourmet meal, or penning the novel you've envisioned—serves as a form of meditation.

Assuming the role of the figurehead in this grand saga doesn't perturb me in the slightest. It can be rather amusing, truth be told! I harbor no delusions of grandeur or thirst for the limelight, but sometimes a cause demands a charismatic presence to elevate it. It took some time for my voice to find its timbre, being the introvert that I am. But those days are behind me now, and I can speak very clearly from a source of truth that is just right there for me, all the time, easy to access. You'll probably notice that at times in my podcast or other interviews I kind of go off into some kind of strange trance state and speak almost like I am channeling something. I don't claim I can actually "channel" from other spirits on the other side or anything, but I definitely can feel a speaking-flow-state that is very natural—where nothing is planned, but ideas and thoughts flow out in a natural poetic rhythm.

OUT OF AFRICA

Once a year, I embark on what can only be described as a photographic escapade, an expedition to the exotic corners of the world—from the wilds of Africa to the watery maze of Venice, the scenic vistas of New Zealand, the bustling streets of Tokyo, to the romantic allure of Paris. It's during these ventures that I play the role of teacher, guide to a motley crew of the most splendid individuals you could imagine. It's as though I'm meeting comrades from another life, all of us mysteriously pulled together by the magnetic force of adventure and a shared love for capturing light on a sensor.

On the tail end of a journey through Africa, a sense of dissatisfaction began to niggle at me, directed squarely at my camera bag. It seemed to be lacking... well, everything I deemed essential. In a moment of what I thought was sheer brilliance, I decided to design my own! Roughly ten minutes into this "design phase," it dawned on me that my expertise in bag design was as extensive as my experience in finding a non-soggy cocktail napkin for my cave-wall scrawlings.

Recognizing the need for reinforcements, I reached out to the wizards over at Peak Design in San Francisco. Having once championed one of their embryonic Kickstarter campaigns—a platform where dreams are funded by the collective hope of internet strangers—I was confident they were the right crew to co-captain this venture into the uncharted territories of camera bag design.

This is me in Papua New Guinea. I'm the one in the glasses.

It was actually a bit of a scary project because I wasn't exactly sure if anyone would like such a "strange" design for a camera bag that is also a messenger bag. One interesting thing about Peak Design is they like to start building the product before we even launch the Kickstarter, so there is a big risk that we would never be able to recoup the investment. We did a 50/50 deal and I remember coming home to tell my wife that we had to pony up a couple hundred thousand dollars and wire it to Vietnam. She wasn't thrilled with this idea, let me tell you. She has always been one to temper my excitement. For instance, when I once approached her, ecstatic about selling several large prints to a collector, she gave me a piercing look and asked, "Have you considered the tax implications of that?"

Trey Ratcliff Designed an Ultimate Camera Bag, and Now It's Blowing Up

JUL 24, 2015   MICHAEL ZHANG

It seems that when the Internet's most followed photographer designs a camera bag, the world of photography listens. Travel photographer Trey Ratcliff has teamed up with Peak Designs to create an ultimate camera bag for photographers, and the dynamic duo has just raised *over $500,000* in its first day on Kickstarter to launch their creation.

Alright, let's get one thing straight: saying I was the brains behind the camera bag is kinda like claiming I'm a chef because I microwaved some popcorn, but this made for a good story! Again, I don't mind being the front man for stuff I really like and sometimes a bit of a personality helps to tell the story better than traditional marketing nonsense.

Inside I'm thinking, "No bitch! Now we can get the GOOD pizza tonight for the kids!" Of course I didn't say that. But, I thought it in a moment of rebellion. I love her and she's probably raising a good point. But probably not. Wait, was she a tax collector in a previous life? Anyway, I just slinked away to contemplate that while celebrating on my own. The idea of sharing my victory with vacant zombies that work at the IRS could not have been further from my mind.

So, here I was again, suggesting we send our kids' college fund to what probably wasn't a sweat shop in South-east Asia, and all I could muster was a, "Trust me." I said it with the confidence of someone who's just realized they've left the map at home. My certainty wavered, but fortune, as they say, favors the bold—or at least the mildly delusional. The project was not just a success; it was a triumph, leading to a sequel in the saga of bags that nearly broke the Kickstarter record books.

To hype up these bags, I cooked up this plan for a thirteen-city tour across America. I hosted free photo walks where I could show off the bag and maybe even play Santa Claus with a few giveaways. That tour was nuts, like a circus without the tent. We wrapped it all up in San Francisco, watching the Kickstarter clock run down like the ball drop on New Year's Eve, except with more camera bags and less confetti. Check out the highlight reel of our wild ride here: https://www.youtube.com/watch?v=ib4Nk4T2UTo. It's a collection of moments that makes you think, "Well, that escalated quickly."

AURORA SOFTWARE

Since that bag experiment went really well, it only emboldened me to keep trying new things and create more of a reality around me. What Steve Jobs, a chap who attributed his clarity to psychedelic adventures, said really resonated with me. About the malleability of life's fabric, Steve said: "Life can be so much broader, once you discover one simple fact, and that is that everything around you that you call 'life' was made up by people who were no smarter than you. And you can change it, you can influence it, you can build your own things that other people can use. Once you learn that, you'll never be the same again."

Because I was engaging in a lot of HDR photography, I became quite frustrated with the existing software I was using. It was called Photomatix, and while it was quite wonderful, I felt it wasn't keeping up with the times or my needs. Since my degree is in computer science and I had designed software and user interfaces for over a decade in my twenties, I decided to create my own software!

Again, I immediately took a humility pill and thought, well, I'm going to collaborate with a team that really excels at this stuff, just like I did for the bag. A Ukrainian company called MacPhun (now Skylum) made some really cool plugins. So, I set up some meetings with them, and we decided to create our own HDR software called Aurora. It was a hit. We went through many iterations and even won Mac's App of the Year, with millions of downloads and very happy creators.

EUROPEAN BUS TOUR

Barely had the echoes of laughter from our last American escapade faded when we, in a moment of inspired madness, decided to embark on a grand European tour. Picture this: ten cities, each more magnificent than the last, with my crew and friends aboard a veritable leviathan of the highways, a tour bus that had just been vacated by the rock legends, Incubus. This behemoth, a testament to the rock and roll lifestyle, came complete with its own ecosystem of mysterious pills secreted within the sofa crevices, a feature we discovered with absolute joy. I'll put anything in my mouth.

This metallic beast was not just a bus; it was a two-tiered palace on wheels, boasting a bar for nightly revelries, a viewing deck to take in the European vistas in all their glory, a cinema for our cinematic indulgences, and an array of bunks that promised comfort yet whispered secrets of rock star past. The journey was a whirlwind of camaraderie, creativity, and, let's be honest, a bit of chaos, as my crew and I navigated the continent in a style that can only be described as fabulously unhinged.

The best part of the trip was the photo walks. We kept 'em free because the best things in life, like air and high-fives, shouldn't cost a dime. Meeting fans and fellow photo enthusiasts across Europe was like finding your tribe in places you didn't even know you belonged. Every city had its own vibe, its own stories, and man, did we collect a bunch of those. From the laughter to the lessons, it was an epic saga of capturing life through a lens, with a backdrop as diverse as Europe itself.

Here is the overall highlight reel, and there are ten more from each individual city if you want to do any deep dives.
https://www.youtube.com/watch?v=PaacnFEJWx4&t=52s&ab_ch
annel=TreyRatcliff

HANDLING NEGATIVITY
AND THE DEBBIE DOWNERS

As I shared more and more photos with innovative and controversial techniques, I received a lot of hate and negativity online, but I developed a thick skin pretty quick. I knew I was onto something, and one of my greatest skills is ignoring people who think I'm a bit of a nut. I'm not crazy. I'm creating the universe in which I want to live. It's not like I was trying to invent a new planet or anything, just trying to show this one in a light nobody else thought to flip on.

That evolving path of capturing the world (which I still actively enjoy!) is not a lot different than what I am going through now with spirituality and figuring out a deeper level of the Earth and my relation to it. It's like I've gone from trying to snap the perfect sunset to understanding why I'm standing there in the first place. How do I continue to better myself so that my mind, body, and soul can all dance in the right vibration with the Earth itself? As Proust said, "The only real voyage of discovery consists not in seeking new landscapes, but in having new eyes."

It's not just about capturing the vibrations; it's about being one with them.

Switching gears like this can make waves, especially with friends and family who thought they had you all figured out. You're going off-script. They will try to bring you down or pull you back into the way you used to be. Suddenly, you're the friend who went off the deep end, and not everyone's eager to jump in after you. I've had to say goodbye to a few buddies who couldn't get on board with the new me. And now, it's happening all over again as I dive deeper into the spiritual pool. My family's still in my corner, even if they're scratching their heads, wondering when I became the protagonist of an indie film they never planned to watch. I was just being myself. Staying true to myself is the goal, even if it means some folks bow out. I'm open to meeting new characters who are tuned into the same frequency, ready to join the adventure at just the right time.

Just like one of my intellectual heroes, Alan Watts, said, "You're under no obligation to be the same person you were five minutes ago."

Anyway, I say all this as a bit of a gentle nod to you, dear reader. If you are indeed in the first throes of an awakening of your own, then you may get some flak from your existing network of friends or family. Perhaps they don't change very much, as change is a scary thing, so they think you probably should just stay on their team and not change either. Or, perhaps they are afraid of not being able to understand the *evolved* you, because fear is indeed something that motivates most people.

Just be prepared for it, be strong as you seek your own truth, and express your own true self. This might sound harsh, but one thing I often think to myself is: "You know what Trey, if they were really your friends, they would be excited for you, be curious, be supportive, and love you every step of the way." Maybe some folks were just meant to share a leg of the journey, and that's totally fine. I send them love and good vibes from the road. I'm cruising with the top down, convinced that every turn, every new horizon, is exactly where

I'm meant to be. Or maybe I just liked those scenes from *Fear and Loathing in Las Vegas* too much. Either way, the wind is warm and the tunes are cool.

4.
LET'S GO TO NEW YORK CITY!

"Awareness is the greatest agent for change."
—ECKHART TOLLE

"If you want to make God laugh, tell him about your plans."
—WOODY ALLEN

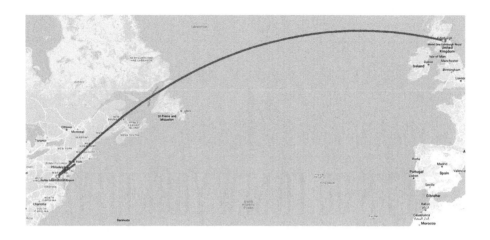

July 7, 2023

It's my birthday! Yay! I don't know why I say that, as I've never made a big deal about it. Well, there was one exception. On my fiftieth, we did have a wild party here at the ranch in New Zealand with about a hundred people. Things got loose, and by loose, I mean some of my friends woke up in the shrubbery with some pizza guys they apparently paid with drugs.

Dirk, a mate of mine from the Land of the Long White Cloud—New Zealand, if you're reaching for a map—has this quirky habit of hitting me up with a song link on WhatsApp every so often. This time, it's "Break on Through (To the Other Side)" by The Doors. Now, if that isn't a cosmic wink, I don't know what is. I pinged him back, curious about the timing, which coincided rather uncannily with my own metaphysical door-busting. His reply? "Just made me think of you." How's that for synchronicity?

In the midst of all this galactic DJing, I was feeling a bit down because I hadn't heard the usual "Happy Birthday" chorus from my family. It's not like I was throwing a pity party for myself. Everyone's got their own whirlwind of stuff going on, and my family's usually all about the love. But post-spiritual journey, hanging solo, I was feeling a touch more solo than usual.

Quick sidebar on the home front—my wife and I decided to split up a few years back. We handled it like two adults who realized they're on separate tracks on the same album. Still very good friends, we did it with love and understanding. We simply grew apart through the years and of course I still love her dearly. She's an amazing mom and an incredible person. A truly lovely soul. She wanted to go back to Austin for a variety of reasons that included health, being closer to her family, and getting the kids the best education. They are in a rather fancy school there and expenses are... high... Sometimes I feel like I'm remotely raising the Kardashians.

I got on the plane and I was still feeling quite electric in my own way after the previous night. I was sitting there in a comfy seat and started watching the Weird Al Yankovic movie. Daniel Radcliffe was in it. I've got this hunch we're related—me and Radcliffe, not me and Weird Al—because of something to do with cliffs in our last names. Mine's got something to do with these Red Cliffs back in the UK, so there's got to be some distant family reunion we're both missing out on.

I'm watching this Weird Al movie and I'm seeing all these synchronicities with my own life. It's not a very good movie, but I'm feeling like it was made just for me, just at this moment. The color palette is speaking to me and I feel like characters in the movie are making some kind of knowing eye-contact with me. In many ways, it mimics my life. A kid that takes an old tool (an accordion—and in my case, a camera) and then reinvents it by remixing a reality that is already there. Weird Al takes known songs and makes them new and fun and ridiculous, and that's not too different from what I did with my camera. There I was, en route to New York, deciphering personal messages woven into the fabric of this film.

This experience brought to mind the media I had engaged with just before my transformative event in Scotland. I had been captivated by the latest season of *Black Mirror*, particularly an episode titled *Joan is Awful*. It depicted an ordinary woman, portrayed by Salma Hayek, whose mundane daily life becomes the subject of a Netflix show without her knowledge, blending reality with dramatization. This concept sparked reflections on the potential of AI in creating hyper-realistic simulations or "deep fakes," suggesting a future where anyone's life could be rendered into a personalized narrative with sufficient computational resources. Intriguingly, this dovetailed with insights from *Journey of Souls*, which described an afterlife scenario where souls review their lives in a library-like setting. This review process allows for an examination from various perspectives, including third-person views, personal experiences, and even hypothetical scenarios based on different life choices. You can watch it in third person, jump into your own skin, jump into the body of another, and even scrub back and forth on alternate timelines as if you had made different choices. Fascinating.

MACHINE ELVES

Aboard the flight sleep remains elusive, replaced by a continuous stream of films laden with cryptic signals. My thoughts drift toward an intriguing concept: Machine Elves. Terrence McKenna first introduced this term to describe the jesters or clown-like entities encountered during his DMT experiences—a phenomenon I'm personally familiar with. Recollections of jesters from childhood and visions encountered during psychedelic vacations meld with the present, suggesting these Machine Elves might be architects of the reality unfurling before me. This notion has influenced my creative endeavors, inspiring the name of my new art ventures, "Machine Elf," where I craft three-dimensional visual and music experiences from fractals. I find my attraction to fractals to be fortuitous and telling because I am coming to understand that all of our lives form an ever-evolving pattern that we can evolve into increasingly beautiful forms.

Some samples of this intricate work, a fusion of art and technology, can be explored on YouTube, offering a glimpse into the complexity and beauty of these experiences.

The air travel continues seamlessly with a layover in Washington D.C. posing no inconvenience. Seated in the middle, I adopt a lotus position, shoes removed, embodying tranquility amidst the hum of the aircraft. With eyes closed, yet another layer of reality reveals itself to me. Despite the physical barriers, my senses extend beyond the plane's confines, perceiving the movement through space with a clarity that transcends sight. This serene detachment, coupled with the vibrant visions that accompany my meditation, affirms a shift within me. The journey is not just geographical but deeply personal, a trip into new worlds of consciousness and understanding.

Again, no drugs, no nothing. I am starting to sense things in a new way. I am feeling new things about love.

I think about one of my favorite heroines, Phoebe Waller-Bridge (writer, actress, director of *Fleabag*). She floats in the ether between a clever creator and all the nonsense that comes along with getting her truth on a screen when it was difficult. Who, but her, could write a Catholic priest who tortures himself in existential angst in both deepness and comedic relief, the only other to break the fourth wall with the quickest of gazes that haunts an imprint you selected? At the most awkward wedding imaginable, the sweet delicacy of Andrew Scott sublimes: "I was taught if we're born with love then life is about choosing the right place to put it. People talk about that a lot, it feeling right, when it feels right it's easy. But I'm not sure that's true. It takes strength to know what's right. And love isn't something that weak people do."

There are poems and poets all around us, all the time, if we just look. And, indeed, love is not something that weak people do.

ARRIVAL IN BROOKLYN

Because I had to fly to the U.S. on a different flight, I landed in Newark around midnight. It's about an hour away so I Ubered over to Vadim's place in Brooklyn. His abode, a sanctuary housed within the skeletal remains of a church, awaited my late-night arrival. "Vadim's Place" is a locale so singular in its essence that its description demands a certain literary finesse, chiefly because it's the sort of place that, thankfully, defies duplication.

Vadim lives in the front part of a converted church. There are three levels and the top one had all the beautiful stained glass windows that one often sees on the facade of churches.

Rene's emergence from the penumbral veil shrouding the church's entrance, as the clock neared 1:00 a.m., heralded my venture into this sanctified residence. His welcome, a fusion of warmth and mirth, was tinged with the slight disorientation characteristic of our ketamine dalliances—a substance that has led us through many a figurative and literal maze. The complexity of Vadim's dwelling, with its confusing corridors, evoked memories of my youth lost in "The Bard's Tale," while I wandered around a town called Skara Brae. I once thought it was a fictional place until I found it in Scotland. While walking around the game-version of Skara Brae, you would keep a map on graph paper (this 2D cartography has always appealed to the geek in me), and each unexpected turn could spin you around in wildness. This reminded me of the enigmatic passageways leading to Vadim's threshold. It's like these hallways were a maze for a mouse, but instead of finding cheese at the end, you get to deal with a wildly unpredictable Russian.

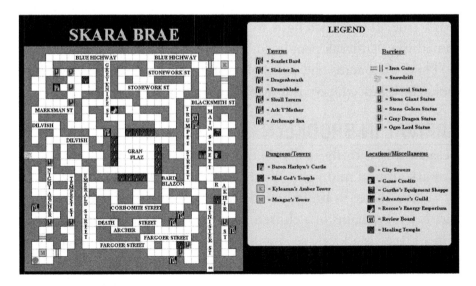

Navigating our way through the convoluted passageways to Vadim's door proved to be a curious comedy in itself, challenging even the soberest of minds. Once inside, the peculiar charm of the place unfolded before us. We descended into the heart of the church, where the ground floor lay sprawled beneath the towering steeple and stained-glass windows above, hinting at further mysteries residing in the floors beyond.

The room that welcomed us was an eclectic sanctuary of art and literature, its cluttered and worn aesthetics imbued with an undeniable allure. A distinct air of shamanistic presence permeated the space, with artifacts and symbols of spiritual voyages adorning every corner. The place was a mishmash of what looked like souvenirs from a shaman's world tour. It had that vibe of being lived-in and loved, like a favorite pair of jeans that's seen better days but still gets you compliments. Tucked among the visual noise, there was this picture of Hunter S. Thompson that just grabbed me. It was all black and white, except for this wild red spiral thing happening in the background. It felt like Thompson was staring me down, daring me to blink first, from wherever he was hanging out in the afterlife.

Let's remember this is all pre-spiritual emergence, but I tend to see patterns and connections all the time anyway. I often marvel at the intricate dance of synchronicities that seem to guide my path. Just prior to this, my fascination with patterns and connections had led me down a rabbit hole centered around Hunter S. Thompson, analyzing his revolutionary approach to gonzo journalism. Finishing *Fear and Loathing in Las Vegas* as I embarked on my Scottish sojourn, I delved deeper into his life, absorbing documentaries and grappling with the stark reality of his chosen exit from this world in a planned suicide.

Rene is reading a book about ketamine on Vadim's couch under the gaze of Hunter S. Thompson. Notice the chessboard in the reflection as I begin to figure out the puzzle.

There, in the dimly lit corner of Vadim's apartment, sat Rene, engrossed in a ketamine study, under the intense scrutiny of a Hunter S. Thompson portrait. The moment felt like a direct gaze from the beyond, suggesting that Thompson, in his otherworldly existence, might still be weaving narratives, perhaps even dictating the eccentricities of my own life. It was a fleeting notion, not heavily entertained, yet it couldn't help but spark a curious thought: *Could it be that Thompson, alongside literary giants like Philip K. Dick and Douglas Adams, was scripting a narrative so bizarre and enthralling for me and my companions?* This wasn't borne from a place of self-aggrandizement but rather a whimsical musing on the interconnectedness of consciousness across dimensions.

This speculation led me to consider the possibility that our lives, preordained to some extent by the soul groups we belong to in the spirit world, still afford us the liberty to navigate through a multitude of choices, no matter how mundane or absurd they may appear. It's a concept that makes sense to me, suggesting that the essence of our existence is both written in the stars and improvised in the dance of free will.

This jazz of fate and freestyle really speaks to me, painting a picture of life that's part planned, part improv.

And now, Vadim walks in.

5.
MEETING VADIM

"We're fascinated by the words, but where we meet is in the silence behind them."
—RAM DASS

"I hate to advocate drugs, alcohol, violence, or insanity to anyone, but they've always worked for me."
—HUNTER S. THOMPSON

July 8, 2023

Vadim was pretty much what I expected from our video chat in Scotland. He looks like a cross between Vladamir Putin and Noho Frank from *Barry*. He's in good shape, bald, intense, and his accent was so authentically Russian it could have been distilled straight from a pot of borscht.

Now, I've always had a penchant for accents of the international variety, but there's something about the male Russian accent that sends a shiver down the spine—in a way that's less "chills of excitement" and more "cold war thriller." The female Russian accent, on the other hand, is incredibly sexy and distracting enough to make you forget she's probably just interested in money. Regrettably, this narrative remains bereft of such a character.

By the way, I'm kidding I'm kidding. I have a few Russian friend-girls with a thick accent who are more interested in my friendship than money, although they did require me to pay them some money so they could back me up on this.

Vadim likes to go by the longer moniker "Vadim the Machine," a reference to how he sees himself as pretty much a perfect physical specimen, a paragon of human engineering. He had told me earlier on a call how he stays awake for three days in a row because of his physical prowess. I wondered if he was kidding or making a joke, but like a lot of Russians I have met, this guy has no sense of humor. He's deadly serious. Vadim's humor was as detectable as a whisper in a hurricane—nonexistent.

He also sent me a link to a promotional video for a documentary that is being made about, guess who, Vadim The Machine. It had the subtle subtitle "New York's Most Misunderstood Man." The promo video was absolutely ridiculous. It featured Vadim hanging out with all these DJs and making him look like he is the epicenter of the party and club scene in New York. The fonts are horrible and the editing is questionable. I already had a bit of a bad feeling coming into this scene, but I was also up for adventure. I want to get to know this guy. He seems like a real character. And boy, was I right.

Vadim had a rather theatrical entrance and greeted us adorned in what can only be described as a shamanic ensemble—a gown woven from the finest silks, embellished with intricate, mystical patterns. The sheer number of beads draped around his neck was astonishing, each one perhaps a token of some spiritual journey or achievement. His attire was crowned with a wide-brimmed hat. He's going for this "look." I don't know what you would call the "look"—I'll just call it "The Vadim."

As we sat down to converse, Vadim's demeanor was a serene pool of Zen-like tranquility. His presence radiated a calm, almost monastic vibe, an intriguing contrast to his visually loud attire. Rene mentioned that Vadim's aura seemed to shift towards a more respectful and welcoming tone upon my arrival, a change I found both flattering and curious. Right off the bat, Vadim seemed genuinely amiable and intriguingly complex, brimming with stories and a vibe that said, "This is gonna be interesting." That was my first take, anyway.

Spoiler alert: things were gonna take a turn.

Dominating the coffee table was a ceramic plate, unmistakably crafted for the ceremonial use of certain powdery substances. Vadim, with a casualness that belied the setting, presented an abundant selection of cocaine and ketamine, far surpassing the mere lines we were accustomed to. Rene had forewarned me of Vadim's penchant for indulgence, but witnessing the sheer quantity firsthand invited both awe and a hint of apprehension. These weren't exactly "lines" and could be more correctly referred to as "dunes."

Rene, already a passenger on the ketamine express, decided to add another train car to his Orient Express. His dalliance with cocaine had waned, especially after a period of profound bodily awareness— a saga for another time.

It's about 2:00 a.m. at this point, and I'm pretty tired. Vadim is both excited to see me and wants to go out and party with me at a club. I'm feeling, well, hey, I might as well put my "people pleaser" personality to work and indulge. I'm pretty tired, and I know the cocaine will solve that problem in about five to ten seconds. And that keeps you pretty charged up for a good thirty to forty minutes, so I went for that. And, sure enough, true to the gospel of party pharmacology, just like the laminated brochure says, I immediately felt 100%.

Me and Rene decided to take a little detour into Ketamineville, a place we've gotten pretty familiar with over the last year. Just having a little bit makes you feel like you've slammed some vodka shots, but without that "heaviness/dizziness" that alcohol can bring. Instead, you get a, well, and this is hard to explain, but I will attempt. You get a "lightness" in your mind. A bit floaty. It's a lovely feeling. You also get a little bit of confusion, but that feeling is also kind of fun. It's similar to the feeling of having a few drinks where you get a little confused and your overactive mind may calm down a little bit... to mollify a mind that is too busy.

When it comes to the interaction between cocaine and ketamine, it's a case of parallel paths rather than a confluence. Each journeys through the body on its own trajectory, much like drinking copious amounts of coffee for an energy surge, followed by taking Advil to ease a burgeoning headache. There's no alchemical blend, no creation of a novel entity within; they navigate their courses independently, even if their effects seem to pull in different directions.

This duo has been colloquially dubbed "Calvin Klein," a playful moniker that belies the serious nature of its constituents. The use of such code names serves a dual purpose: a veneer of intrigue for some, and a precautionary measure for others aiming to sidestep the watchful eyes of law enforcement. However, the effectiveness of this linguistic camouflage is debatable, as those in authority are likely just as attuned to these euphemisms as those they monitor.

With our impromptu mini chemistry lesson concluded, Rene opts for the comfort of Vadim's opulent dwelling, citing the toll of the previous night's escapades. His decision brings a twinge of disappointment; after a month apart, I had looked forward to rekindling our camaraderie. Vadim, seizing the moment, prepares our nocturnal provisions with a pragmatism born of experience. As we ready ourselves to venture into the night, I'm reminded of the dynamic interplay of trust, adventure, and the sheer unpredictability of the paths we choose—or those that choose us.

WE APPROACH THE MIRAGE

We got to the club. It's called The Mirage (Avant Gardner on the map above). I had been here years earlier when I came to see the Mayan Warrior. That was an amazing experience. That was a molly (MDMA) night, and, well, it's hard to go wrong on those nights. So, I knew the venue... but now we're rocking in at 2:50 a.m.[2] and there is no line or anything because everyone is partying inside. Vadim gets all frustrated and then we go up to the security guard and

---

[2] You'll be happy to note I'm using Google Maps timeline history to help me piece all of this together to be as accurate as possible.

this guy is even more frustrated with Vadim. It seems Vadim comes here a lot. And I mean. A LOT. And none of the security people like him and are giving him a hard time… and I'm just kind of standing there, this geeky guy in glasses. I have a totally different "look" than Vadim. Like I'm wearing a very colorful psychedelic shirt of a guy with a third eye and I'm just kind of an awkward person anyway. But I embrace my awkwardness in an adorable manner.

One of my favorite shirts. Now sadly left behind in the Big Apple. I gotta find another one.

As tensions escalated between Vadim and the security staff, I found myself ensnared in an awkward tableau. Vadim, with his imposing demeanor and accent that seemed to cut sharper than usual, painted a picture of intimidation that left me questioning the depth of his connections—or the persona he wished to project. My own appearance, markedly less imposing and adorned with a psychedelic shirt, felt out of place in the unfolding drama. I attempted to navigate the situation with a blend of awkward charm and apologetic glances, hoping to distance myself from the fray.

The occasional security guard would cast a wary eye in my direction, to which I'd respond with a smile, a wave, and an apologetic shrug that said, "Just passing through, chaps. Barely know the fellow." Against all odds, and perhaps a touch of security guard sympathy, we were granted entry into the club's vibrant inner sanctum.

The club's restroom was a portal to the raw and untamed underbelly of nightlife, a place where inhibitions dissolved in the shadowy recesses of seedy stalls. Embarking on this exploration with a spirit of gonzo journalism, I could almost feel the approving nod of Hunter S. Thompson from the beyond. Yet, emerging from this den of Dionysian delights, Vadim was nowhere to be seen.

We were supposed to stick together, but I couldn't find the guy. I wait around a while and think, *Well maybe he's gone dancing?* I love dancing, so I went there and danced for about ten minutes looking for him. And then I was wondering, *Well, fuck, where is this crazy guy?* So I go back to the bathroom and he is standing outside and SO angry at me. He yells at me like an angry dad. It's like this other side of him and I'm like sheesh. But then I discovered why he is angry. He's angry because he is on a mish to get backstage and then get onstage so he can take selfies with all the DJs and the crowd behind him for his social media. And then I'm like, *Oh god this is gonna get weird. But you know what, I'm along for the ride.*

Anyway, no need to go into details, but it was absolutely comedic watching him trying to get around security and use back halls and little doors that he has ferreted out in the past to try to get backstage… and I'm just kind of like… *omg why am I here?* The urge to bail was strong, but Vadim was having none of it. Resigned to making the most of the situation, I found solace in conversation, gravitating towards fellow spectacle-wearers—a rare breed in the club scene. Our discussions veered from the superficial to the philosophical, endearing me to the crew who, charmed by my existential musings, extended an invitation to join them on stage. Vadim, meanwhile, found himself adrift, his plans thwarted. Onstage, amidst the DJ and their entourage, I shared tales of imposter syndrome, confessing my perceived lack of coolness. Their laughter, warm and inclusive, dispelled any lingering doubts, embracing me as one of their own.

"You know how uncool I am?" I ask a guy that I guess is the DJ's manager.

He smiled and raised his eyebrows and asked, "Tell me."

"I'm so uncool I don't even know who this DJ is!"

And that was totally true. I had no idea what the hell was going on. But I was having a good time and basically danced up there and got to know people until the show finished and all the lights came on. So now I was tired and I was like, *I gotta get the fuck out of here and get home.*

So there Vadim was, up on stage, snapping selfies like it was going out of style, and trying to round up DJs for some afterparty at his place. That's when I got the vibe things were sliding into the "this is kinda bizarre" territory. Not a single DJ took him up on his offer that night, but you could tell Vadim was playing the long game.

NO SLEEP IN BROOKLYN

How'd I end up in this sideshow? Well, it all started with my buddy Jessica hyping up Vadim and this Machine Elf party he wanted to throw for me. Sounded cool until I realized Jessica's connection to Vadim was as thin as a gym towel—met the guy once while working out, and suddenly I'm living in a sitcom.

Returning to Vadim's sanctuary at the warlocking hour of 5:00 a.m., exhaustion had claimed me. The sleeping arrangements were as unconventional as the host, with a makeshift bunk bed setup that seemed borrowed from a childhood fantasy nestled under the ethereal light of stained glass. The ambiance in the room was more suited to the revelry of post-club euphoria than the tranquility of slumber. Rene and I, in a scene reminiscent of boyhood adventures, found ourselves entangled in a patchwork of blankets, sleep more illusory promise than actual.

As dawn ushered in the promise of a new day, Rene and I ventured out to reconnect with cherished friends, Joann and Jesse, at Fandi Mata, a gem nestled within Brooklyn's vibrant culinary scene. The warmth of their company, an anchor in the tempest of my recent experiences, filled me with gratitude. Their significance in my narrative would only deepen as they later provided unwavering support through the trials of emergency rooms and mental health challenges, embodying the essence of true friendship.

During our meal, a casual remark by Jesse on the topic of death momentarily pierced the evening's conviviality, his words veering towards the existential. Yet, armed with the new insights gleaned from my Scottish odyssey, I met his musings with a knowing smile, one that spoke of secrets unveiled and truths understood. This shared moment, while mixed with the laughter and stories exchanged over dinner, underscored the depth of our connection. Joann's presence, ever inspiring, alongside the introduction of Rene to this circle, wove new threads into the fabric of our shared histories, enriching the painting of our lives with the beauty of enduring camaraderie.

Post-dinner, a stroll set the scene for our return to Vadim's, where the next act of our unpredicted adventure was waiting to unfold.

6.
HELL TO HEAVEN ON THE DANCE FLOOR

"It is truth that liberates, not your effort to be free."
—JIDDU KRISHNAMURTI

"Go to Heaven for the climate, Hell for the company."
—MARK TWAIN

Rene's birthday gift to me was nothing short of magical—an evening with The Mayan Warrior, our cherished art car from the desert of Burning Man. This gesture was a testament to the decade we've shared as roommates at the festival, united by our harmonious musical tastes. In an unexpected twist of fate, the event was set at The Mirage, the very club I had ventured into just the night before. Yet, this evening promised a starkly different experience, buoyed by the anticipation of shared joy and music.

The process to secure our entry was meticulously organized through an app named Dice, requiring ticket registration within a precise window from 2:00 p.m. to 5:00 p.m., followed by admission at a designated time. This structured approach stood in sharp contrast to the previous night's chaotic entry, especially as Vadim expressed a keen desire to join us, boasting of his extensive connections within the club. Despite his persistence, the exclusive ticketing process left us skeptical of his chances.

Filled with excitement, Rene and I looked forward to this event as our first dance outing since the unforgettable Relish Festival back in New Zealand. That festival remains etched in our memories as a time of euphoric revelry and deep spiritual discoveries, each evening marked by our explorations into different psychedelics and the insights they unveiled. Those nights under the New Zealand sky could fill volumes with tales of our adventures, each substance guiding us through a myriad of transformative experiences.

As we prepared for the night ahead, the promise of rekindling the magic of past festivals in the heart of New York invigorated us. This was not just another night out; it was a chance to step into a shared rhythm once more, to lose ourselves in the music of The Mayan Warrior, and to find, amidst the dance and the din, a piece of the playa that had first brought us together.

TREYKHAL, A CHEMICAL LOVE STORY

Embarking on the path of psychedelic exploration wasn't a choice I made until the age of forty, a revelation that often surprises many. It was under the guidance of some doctor friends at Burning Man, who, understanding my inherently joyful and open nature, suggested that responsible drug use could enrich my already positive outlook on life. They proposed starting with MDMA, a substance renowned not just for its euphoric rush but for its capacity to deepen feelings of love, empathy, and connectedness. Their clinical advice was to begin with a dose tailored to my body weight, ensuring a safe yet transcendent experience. They were clear about the importance of restraint, warning against the temptation to chase the high with additional doses, a practice that could deplete serotonin levels and lead to a state of zombiesque lethargy in the days following.

Part of our annual photo walk at Burning Man!

This initial foray proved to be a pivotal moment not just for me but also for Rene, who experienced a night of unparalleled joy and awakening. This experience served as a gateway to a broader exploration of psychedelics, each offering its unique lens through which to view and engage with the world.

I've come to categorize drug users into two broad types: those seeking an escape from life's pressures and those looking to enhance their already fulfilling existence. I align myself firmly with the latter. My life is filled with gratitude, enriched by a loving family, a passion for art, the beauty of New Zealand, and a circle of friends whose love and support are unwavering. It's crucial to distinguish this context, as too often, discussions around drug use are clouded by judgment and misinformation. The distinction between using substances like mushrooms and those with a more destructive profile like meth or heroin is significant, rooted not in escapism but in a desire to augment the texture of life's experiences.

Over the years, Rene and I have expanded our horizons, exploring everything from mushrooms and LSD to cocaine and ketamine, each substance opening new doors of perception, understanding, and connection. This exploration has not been about seeking joy from external sources but about deepening the joy that already permeates our lives, a subtle yet significant shift that has enriched our experiences and bonds.

When we started doing these, it was just to have fun and party and dance and have deep talks. Especially on MDMA. Did you know they used to prescribe MDMA for marriage therapy before it was illegal? Yeah, they'd just give them some pills and send them home, and then married couples having serious problems would be able to have the most loving, accepting, and healing conversations.

With each of these molecules, I have shifted now so that 20% of the time I just like to dance and have fun with my friends. The other 80% of the time, I take them to go on emotional and spiritual deep dives on myself.

This understanding and respect for the power of these experiences underpin every decision we make, guiding us through each waking dream with a sense of purpose and safety. Our preparations are thorough, ensuring that every step, from setting intentions to selecting the setting, is considered with the utmost care to facilitate a positive and meaningful experience.

Rene and I are both what I would call Drug-Geeks. We measure out everything and do constant check-ins and a lot of self-assessment. As we ventured into the night, ready for the Mayan Warrior event, it was with this mindset that we approached the evening—not as a mere pursuit of pleasure but as another chapter in our ongoing exploration of consciousness and connection. Our meticulous planning and self-awareness serve as a testament to our dedication to navigating these experiences responsibly.

In the world of psychedelics and party substances, knowledge and intention can transform what might seem like mere indulgence from the outside into a gentle opening of self-discovery and interpersonal connection. This distinction is crucial, because it is important in settings that are often misunderstood by those not familiar with the nuances of responsible use. Our adventures are not about escaping reality but about deepening our understanding of it, enhancing our sense of presence, and fostering a greater connection with those around us.

Thus, as we prepared for what promised to be an unforgettable night, it was with a clear understanding of our intentions, a deep respect for the substances at our disposal, and an unwavering commitment to the well-being of ourselves and each other. This approach has not only ensured our safety but has also enriched our lives with experiences that resonate far beyond the fleeting moments of euphoria, embedding themselves in the fabric of our memories as milestones of growth and enlightenment.

Emphasizing our approach to substance use is critical, especially in light of what transpired on our second night in New York. This isn't a tale woven from the threads of recklessness, but rather a carefully composed narrative that balances on the knife-edge of exploration and sagacity. Rene and I, akin to seasoned cartographers of consciousness, chart our course with precision fully cognizant of the terrain we tread and the landmarks of our limits.

As we prepared to immerse ourselves in the vibrant energy of The Mirage once more, our pre-party rituals were marked by a careful calibration of molecules, all while abstaining from alcohol. This choice is rooted in a deep shift in perspective I experienced following an Ibogaine ceremony—a pivotal moment that reshaped my relationship with substances. Our story, then, unfolds not as a quest for ephemeral thrills but as a deliberate dance with the dualities of existence, honoring both the vessel and the voyage.

The journey to The Mirage was seamless, a stark contrast to the previous visit's tension. As we stepped into the club, the atmosphere shifted, signaling the start of an experience that would defy expectations. The peculiar, almost surreal quality of the night ahead was palpable from the moment we crossed the threshold. This wasn't just another evening of music and dancing; it was the precipice of an event that would challenge and affirm our understanding of the transformative power of these moments.

And this is where things get weird. Really weird.

7.
TACOS AND HELL

"Your task is not to seek for love, but merely to seek and find all the barriers within yourself that you have built against it."
     —RUMI

"I tend to stay with the panic. I embrace the panic."
     —LARRY DAVID

July 9, 2023

(Note to reader: I change the day to midnight here, which seems strange in the middle of a story, since I am often up through midnight on this misadventure… just trying to keep some level of a time continuum.)

As Rene and I navigated through the sprawling expanse of The Mirage, drawing closer to the pulsating heart of the dance floor, the atmosphere was electric, capable of enveloping up to two thousand souls in its rhythmic embrace. The air was thick with the vibrant clamor typical of such venues, a blend of music and muffled conversations that could easily overwhelm the senses. It was within this cacophony that I witnessed a side of Rene I had never seen before.

His demeanor had shifted dramatically; his expression twisted with discomfort and distress. It was as though he was ensnared in a tormenting blend of existential dread and intense anxiety, manifesting physically in his pained expressions and winces. Watching him grapple with this invisible agony was unsettling.

Rene's voice, strained and urgent, broke through the miasma, "Trey, this place feels like hell to me." His words struck me with force, prompting immediate concern. While the music's darker tones diverged from the uplifting beats we cherished at Burning Man, it was clear that Rene's reaction stemmed from something far deeper than a mere musical preference. The intensity of his discomfort escalated to the point where he feared he might be physically ill, a stark indicator of his need to escape this environment.

Faced with his distress, I was torn. His well-being was my priority, yet he insisted I remain to savor the night as he sought refuge from the overwhelming sense of unease that The Mirage had unexpectedly become for him. This moment of divergence underscored the subjective nature of our experiences, highlighting how deeply our internal states can color our perception of the world around us.

In that surreal moment, as Rene's discomfort became palpable, my perception of reality underwent an unexpected change. Did I just slip into another dimension? It was as though I had been transported into an alternate dimension, one that I've come to describe as the Ultimate VR interface—a realm where the fabric of existence seemed to shift, presenting me with a vividness and depth that transcended the ordinary. This wasn't my first venture into such a state; I had encountered it before, each time feeling as though I was navigating a hyper realistic video game, the world around me both familiar and fantastically new.

A MODERN DAY SKYRIM

For gamers, the analogy of a "Todd Howard Skyrim NPC Interaction" might find a footing, capturing the essence of this experience. In these moments, interactions with others mirror the dialogues one might have with Non-Player Characters (NPCs) in a video game—those programmed beings that populate the world, from the adversaries in Grand Theft Auto to the friendly merchants in Zelda. But here, in this heightened version of reality, the NPC was not Rene but rather the choices that lay before me, manifesting as clear, tangible, options in my environment, each decision point branching into new potential outcomes.

As time seemed to pause, allowing me to assess my next move, the club transformed into a scene of intense clarity, a heightened state of focus. Rene stood at the center of this vivid tableau, his unease unmistakable. In a strange way, he was there looking like he just lost his best horse in "Red Dead Redemption," unsure of what quest to tackle next. Unlike a video game, where one's choices appear as text on a screen, my options materialized in the space around him—physical doors in the real world, yet imbued with the significance of a decision-making interface. To his left, a door beckoned towards the promise of tacos, a neon sign cutting through the dimness with the allure of a simple yet comforting escape. To the right, an exit sign hovered above another doorway, offering a different path away from the tumult of the club.

This immersive, interactive, reality where every choice felt weighted with consequence and possibility was disorienting yet exhilarating. I was the protagonist in a first-person narrative, tasked with navigating the complexities of this moment not through a controller but through the very essence of my being, each decision a step along an unfolding pathway.

Beside each of the doors is a friendly security guard. They are wearing black t-shirts. As I look at the left side and look at the right side, each of the guards becomes animated, for lack of a better word. Remember, these guys are twenty meters away from me, and there are dozens of people milling all around… people on the way to the bathroom, people going outside to smoke, etc. It's kind of chaotic, so it doesn't make sense that these security guards are trying to get my attention.

As I look at the EXIT sign the security guard is looking at me. He has his arms crossed over his chest and is shaking his head side to side giving "no don't come this way" body language. That much is clear. And then, get this, when I look at the TACOS sign, the security guard gets extremely animated and starts pointing excitedly in the TACOS direction with two arms while looking right at me. He's all in. This cat is jumping around and smiling and gesticulating with both hands and pointing his fingers indicating that I should definitely choose the tacos as if it is the secret portal to Narnia. This non-verbal exchange was as real to me as if he had spoken aloud, a testament to the surreal clarity of my perception in that moment.

You can imagine I was kind of flipping out at this point. Not like I was going crazy. But more I was thinking *OMG THIS IS SO COOL IT IS AMAZING WHAT IS HAPPENING.* While this bizarre thing is happening, I was concerned about Rene. And I was thinking, *Okay, this is my objective, I need to get through a real-life dialog tree with Rene to take care of him.*

I ask him how he is feeling, and he's pretty much in the same situation. He's still there in the middle of my "screen" kind of shifting his weight foot-to-foot, waiting on me, just like in a game. I decide to look over on the left and right again, and God-Bless-America, these two security guards are still doing the same thing as before. And they are looking right at ME, still. It's not like these guards are putting on this show for the dozens of other people. I mean, why would a security guard be trying to get a ton of people from the club to go eat tacos? He doesn't work for the taco company. But, 100% for sure, this guy really wanted me and Rene to have some tacos. So I was like, *Okay, I guess I gotta talk Rene into getting some tacos.*

This experience was unlike anything I had encountered before—a blending of reality and game-like decision-making that was as bewildering as it was thrilling. The immediacy of needing to make a choice, coupled with the concern for Rene's wellbeing, grounded the experience, reminding me of the stakes involved. This wasn't just about navigating an intriguing anomaly; it was about ensuring the safety and comfort of my friend.

Confronted with this real-life "dialog tree," I realized that my actions could significantly impact our night. The decision seemed to extend beyond mere physical directions, hinting at deeper implications for both Rene and myself. It was a moment of clarity amidst the chaos, a call to action that required not just a physical move towards one door or another but a commitment to navigating the complexities of our situation with care and consideration.

Keep in mind this interface with the dialog tree was my first time, although I achieved a similar 4D interface (if I can call it that?) when I was in Scotland on my final evening there walking the streets. I don't think of my interactions with other people in the real world like this at all. But I was stuck in what appeared to be a decision tree in my life. This seemed like a rather arbitrary thing to be an important decision in my life, but this whole taco spectacle did end up being interesting later in the night. I'll get to that. First, to the tacos.

Convincing Rene to step outside into the fresh air for tacos required some persuasion, leveraging our mutual appreciation for good food as a gentle nudge towards what I hoped would be a turning point in his evening. Understanding Rene's capacity for culinary joy, I assured him that the combination of fresh air and savory tacos would be a welcome respite from the overwhelming atmosphere of the club.

Upon exiting, the sight that greeted us was unexpectedly

enchanting—a taco truck that seemed to exist in a universe apart (or aside?) from the gritty surroundings of The Mirage. Bathed in a pristine glow, the truck stood out as a heavenly signal of culinary promise, its immaculate white exterior and bright interior lighting casting an aura of warmth and invitation. The trio of taco muses operating the truck, uniform in their matching glowing attire, exuded a charm that felt both retro and otherworldly, blending the nostalgic appeal of a 1950s ice-cream truck with the sophisticated allure of astronaut wives.

In this moment, my perception of reality was vividly altered, presenting a huge difference to the experience I knew Rene was enduring. My heart ached for him to share in this brighter, more hopeful perspective, to see beyond the shadows of the club into the illuminated possibility that lay before us. It wasn't just about escaping the noise and the crowd; it was about transcending to a place of shared joy and connection.

I look at the three women in the taco truck. One was in the middle. One was on the left. One was on the right. I was back in the interface and everything was in high-resolution fire. We were forced to get two tacos, which I thought was perfect. I'm checking on Rene and he's doing a little better, but not much better. I'm hoping this taco gambit is gonna pay off.

As we received our tacos, snug in their perfectly crafted Styrofoam container, I couldn't help but marvel at the design. It was as though some god-level game designer had handpicked this truck for our culinary rescue mission, ensuring even the packaging was up to par with the surreal setup. Now, with tacos in hand, all bets were on this culinary intervention to turn the night around for Rene.

I ask Rene what he wants to do. He still wants to leave but he wants me to stay. I am like, "Are you sure? I don't want to leave you." He says he'll be fine just needs to get out of there. So we walk back in the club because I'll walk him to the exit. I want him to take the tacos with him so he has a snack at home, but he doesn't want them. I don't really want them either, so I said, "Let's at least look inside." Opening that god-made to-go box turned out to be a bit of a chore, but when I got it open, the tacos looked absolutely disgusting. It's like coming back into the club turned them into this disgusting mush. I would not have eaten them either, so we tossed them in the trash and hugged goodbye.

ON MY OWN

So, I guess I was a one-man show now. I was planning on going to see my friend Pablo, who runs the Mayan Warrior, one of the great art cars at Burning Man. I got to know him many years ago because I've taken many photos of that beast of a machine and his team seems to like them! He's always been very generous and gotten me free tickets to events. He's a great guy! But, before I see him, it's time to boogie.

Here's what the Mayan Warrior looks like at Burning Man.

Dancing, you see, is not merely a pastime but a form of existential release for me. Given the tumultuous taco interlude and Rene's subsequent descent into gloom, it seemed only logical, nay, necessary, to dissipate some of the night's accumulated tension through rhythmic movement. "Here I come," I muttered to the unsuspecting dance floor, as I prepared to translate my whirlwind of emotions into dance.

As I approach the dance floor, I'm starting to feel this "hell vibe" more intensely. The music is quite visceral, the whole place is very black and dark, and I am even seeing people with pitchforks. They are thrusting the pitchforks into the air. I was thinking, well that sure is weird! My over-analyzing brain was thinking, *Oh maybe it's some DJ and he's got some kind of theme and his hardcore fans bring pitchforks?* But that seems strange. And as I moved into the crowd I definitely felt a darkness. Like I was kind of dancing in this hellish landscape with all these writhing, tortured souls. I definitely wasn't feeling amazing and began to encounter some of the darkness that Rene was feeling.

Now. Here we go.

This progression towards the left felt like a pilgrimage towards light, each step and gaze drawing me closer to a transformative threshold. The loving vibrations emanating from those around me intensified, culminating in a moment of important realization—a sudden, inexplicable sense of being exactly where I was meant to be, surrounded by souls who vibrate with the same frequency of love and joy.

Then, in an instant, the world around me metamorphosed. The grimy club floor vanished, replaced by the soft, welcoming, sands of a beach that stretched into a horizon bathed in heavenly light. This wasn't just a change in scenery but a transition to an entirely different realm of existence. The crowd, once shadowy figures lost in a darkened space, now danced in radiant attire, their movements a celebration of freedom and bliss. The DJ, no longer a distant figure shrouded in darkness, became a maestro of this divine symphony, with music that uplifted and united, far removed from the heavy beats that had dominated the club's atmosphere.

The environment itself was alive, pulsating with energy and beauty. The sky shifted in hues, painting the scene with the colors of dawn, dusk, and everything in between, while the ground beneath my feet transformed, mirroring the fluidity and constant change of life itself. It was an overwhelming sensory feast, a reality so achingly beautiful it bordered on the fantastic, yet it felt more genuine than any tangible experience I'd ever had.

This transformation marked a departure from mere physical relocation to a spiritual ascension into a domain where love, harmony, and connection were the foundations of existence. I had traversed from a metaphorical inferno into a paradise of my own making, a vivid illustration of the duality that frames our lives and the sobering power of perspective.

The remembrance of this journey—from shadow to light, from solitude to communion—is permanently carved into my consciousness. It serves as a testament to the limitless capacity of the human spirit to uncover splendor and significance in the most unexpected corners. This voyage beyond the edge wasn't merely an evasion but an awakening to the unbounded realms of potential that hover at the edge of our comprehension, ripe for discovery.

I had never come close to experiencing anything remotely like this. Such love and consciousness and oneness. Inside, I was screaming in all caps, *OMG THIS IS SO AWESOME HOW IS THIS EVEN POSSIBLE! THIS IS THE LOVING PLACE I AM MEANT TO BE!*

As I kept drifting left and dancing, I kept making eye contact and uttering "Love is the answer. Love is the answer. Love is the answer," to as many people as I could. I said it quicker and quicker and quicker. I snaked through the crowd impossibly fast with my message and time sped up beyond control and I… collapsed.

I woke up in a little medical facility in a chair.

Naturally, I was extremely confused. Luckily, I wasn't hurt, luckily my glasses weren't broken. Apparently I had definitely collapsed and the medical team had to come get my body and drag me outta there. What can I say? I like to make a scene on the dance floor so people don't forget my incredible moves.

Reflecting on the situation, I recognized a stroke of fortune in the outcome; the absence of serious injury was a silver lining in an otherwise alarming scenario. The medical staff's intervention was straightforward and non-invasive: they offered me a simple juice box and the space to recover my senses, a far cry from the dramatic resuscitations depicted in cinema. My attempt at humor with the attending doctor fell flat, my lighthearted suggestion of returning to the dance floor lost on them.

The easy conclusion to draw from this episode might be an assumption of overdose, but that doesn't align with the reality of my experience. The effects of the substances I had taken earlier were completely diminished by the time of my collapse, and my experience diverged significantly from the narratives commonly associated

with overdosing. What transpired was something altogether different, a phenomenon that defies simple explanation.

My ongoing dreams and the vivid, transformative journey I underwent before waking up in the medical facility suggest a deeper,
perhaps metaphysical occurrence. This wasn't just a physical reaction but a journey of the mind and spirit, offering glimpses into
worlds beyond the ordinary. I've come to view these episodes as moments where the veil between our world and something vastly more
complex is momentarily lifted, allowing me to witness the extraordinary before gently nudging me back to reality.

The speculation that these experiences are somehow orchestrated,
that I'm shown these wonders as part of a greater design and then
returned to my ordinary existence when the lesson is imparted, continues to intrigue me. It's a hypothesis that extends beyond the confines of conventional understanding, suggesting that our encounters
with the inexplicable are not mere accidents but integral parts of a
larger, unseen, narrative.

The return to reconnect with Rene back at Vadim's was not
straightforward. The bustling, chaotic vicinity of The Mirage made
securing an Uber akin to a Herculean task, compelling me to navigate the unpredictable streets of Brooklyn under the cloak of night.
The throngs of people vying for rides, coupled with the heightened
drunken emotions of others, underscored my eagerness to distance
myself from the tumultuous energy of the club scene. As I walked,
the urban landscape around me felt laden with potential perils, yet
fear was absent from my mind, replaced instead by a determination
to ensure my friend's wellbeing.

This prolonged quest for transportation home, reminiscent of a
"harsh death penalty" in gaming parlance, where the path back to a
previous state or location is fraught with challenges, became something that reminded me of many a gaming experience. The analogy
to recovering lost inventory in Diablo II, navigating back to the
depths to reclaim what was lost upon death, mirrored my own trek

through Brooklyn—a metaphorical retrieval of peace after the night's upheaval.

I was also thinking back to old Infocom games and having to put things in bags. I had this cloth bag I got in Scotland. Thinking I was going to take photos and hang out with the Mayan Warrior team, I actually brought my camera, tripod, computer, and other tech stuff. My bag was so heavy. It made me laugh, wandering through the streets with this increasing feeling that I am in a game. I kept getting this message that is not uncommon in Infocom text-adventures when you are carrying too much loot: "Your bag is too heavy." I was giggling and thinking, *I know. I know.*

8.
IN THE MOMENT'S EMBRACE

"Presence is a state of inner spaciousness."
—ECKHART TOLLE

"I'm not insane. My mother had me tested."
—SHELDON COOPER

Buddhism posits that our existence is marked by dukkha, a term that encompasses suffering, unease, and the inherent unsatisfactoriness of life. While not explicitly likened to hell, this concept acknowledges the dual nature of our experiences—pain and pleasure—as crucial elements of our journey towards enlightenment. Reflecting on the night's events, the dramatic shift from a nightmarish dance floor to a transcendent beach party felt emblematic of this Buddhist understanding, yet it also bore resemblance to the notion of Purgatory within Western theology. Here, in the heat of the challenges and choices of life, lies the potential for awakening and growth.

This personal odyssey has reinforced my belief in a simple yet heartfelt approach to life, encapsulated in three guiding principles:

Be loving

Be kind, and

Help other people.

"In the complexity of human existence, these tenets serve as my own creed of clarity, guiding my actions and interactions. Life, with its myriad choices between love and fear, abundance and scarcity, is fundamentally about navigating these decisions with compassion and generosity.

The dance floor, in its capacity to embody both heaven and hell, served as a powerful metaphor for the broader arc of life. It reminded me that every moment holds the potential for transformation, for crossing from darkness into light, and that our collective journey is enriched by acts of kindness, love, and the unwavering support we offer to one another. In embracing these truths, we find our way through the purgatorial landscapes of existence, guided by the hope of awakening to a life filled with purpose and connection.

RENE AND PIGS AND GREED AND DRUGS

Returning to Vadim's, the relief of finding Rene awake and the room free from the aftermath of an unplanned afterparty set the stage for an exceptional conversation. As we settled into the quiet of our shared space, the earlier events of the night became a catalyst for a deeper exploration of the emotional and spiritual undercurrents that had shaped our experiences.

Rene's recounting of the discomfort he felt at the club, amplified by the disheartening taco episode, opened a floodgate of emotions. Through his tears, he articulated a perspective on food and energy that rang true with me. It was a moment of shared understanding, a connection forged not just through words but through the palpable sincerity of his emotions.

He delved into the concept of negative vibrations, suggesting that the environment, particularly one as charged as the club's, could imbue food with a distinct energetic imprint. This idea extended to the meat industry's practices, where the trauma of separation between mothers and their offspring could, he posited, transfer to the consumers of such meat. This theory of inherited pain, a sorrow not originally our own yet deeply felt, offered a poignant reflection on the interconnectedness of all beings and the unseen impacts of our consumption choices.

Our conversation ventured further into the realm of vibrations and their manifestations in the world around us. Viewing the dynamics of large food corporations through a fractal lens allowed us to contemplate how intentions rooted in greed could permeate every level of production, from the overarching goals of the corporation down to the individual actions of employees. So every cut of the knife in the kitchen is a slice ultimately motivated by greed. This perspective suggested that the very act of preparing food could be influenced by the energetic motivations behind it, with the potential to affect those who consume it.

This exchange between Rene and me, grounded in the shared tumult of the night yet soaring into ideas of spiritual and philosophical contemplation, signaled the depth of our friendship and the avenues of thought it could unlock.

And it occurred to me that this whole exchange about food indicated that so much of food production is the polar opposite of food being made with love.

Then I kind of took this idea into a different direction of how people cut up their drugs, like cocaine for example, with an American Express Platinum card and then sucked it up through a one-hundred-dollar bill. Wouldn't the cocaine pick up all those greed-vibrations too? I'm not saying money is bad at all, but a lot of it is ill-gained through greed and exploitation. And then all that greed and exploitation carries vibrations that go into the drugs you are taking. I definitely don't think there is anything wrong with cocaine or ketamine (clearly!), but by sniffing them up through these mechanisms, they can have a bit of a darker vibration. Instead, you can just use the back of your hand—that little webbing between the thumb and forefinger. Or use wooden or handmade straws, just as people do Hape. You'd never see some Peruvian shaman sucking up Hape through a hundred-dollar bill.

Anyway, we had a most beautiful and meandering discussion all about the evening and I was glad Rene was feeling better.

I stood up to prepare for bed, and then I noticed my body started to do something on its own. My arms started twirling in lazy little circles. I wasn't doing it. I just let my body take control. And I'm like, "Rene, look at this. What's going on?" He started watching me… and then my arms started to get more adventurous and make bigger loops with straight arms. Then my arms bent and got into a right-left rhythm. My shoulders got into this scene and everything was super-fluid and felt amazing. I'm thinking, *omg wtf is happening now?* And then they started to lazy twist and flop around my front and back side. And then everything calmed down back to normal. I literally did not tell my arms to do any of that stuff.

So, I asked Rene, "What was that?"

He replied, "Oh, it just looks like you're limbering up. That's good. You seem more flexible lately."

I try to tell him that it wasn't me driving the arm dance, but he's already zoning out. We hit the hay, beaten by the night's roller-coaster of weirdness and wonder. That moment, weirdly enough, was when I started thinking maybe I didn't need any more artificial boosts. Like Salvador Dali dropping wisdom, "I am Drugs."

For the keen reader, it's worth mentioning that the events described do not constitute my spiritual awakening. That milestone lay a few days ahead, promising drama of a different scale. Yet, I couldn't shake off the feeling that I was on the cusp of something monumental, as if the universe was gently nudging me towards the zenith of this unfolding journey.

COMPUTER SAYS NO

There were so many strange things that happened over these ten days or so that I am really just cherry picking a few. But I found this one especially unusual.

I was just about to excitedly tell Rene about my experience at The Mirage. But, as I opened my mouth to speak, nothing came out. My eyes started rapidly darting right and left, back and forth, completely involuntarily. I looked down and took a deep breath then tried to start over to tell him, again, my mouth agape, nothing came out. My eyes, those traitorous orbs, automatically started their impossibly frenetic right-to-left glances.

I interpreted this at the time that I was being told "NO." Even more than that, I felt like I was being controlled by another source, as if I was some sort of android person and someone at Master-Control had taken over and decided I should not tell Rene any of that. For what reason, I don't know. Perhaps it would make him feel weird or he just wouldn't get it. Or maybe, just maybe, it was an intergalactic intervention of self-preservation, a not-so-subtle hint that the timing was off.

Finally, I just gave up and decided to rest.

9.
LIFE'S LABYRINTH

"The best way to find yourself is to lose yourself in the service of others."
—MICHAEL SINGER

"If you try to fail, and succeed, which have you done?"
—GEORGE CARLIN

Remember how when I would close my eyes in Scotland and try to sleep, I would see visions of ancient civilizations being destroyed, passing away with the sands of time?

Whenever my eyes shut, a rich array of hieroglyphics and other ancient symbols unfold in the darkness behind my lids—complex, layered symbols that defy straightforward interpretation. This cryptic visual phenomenon, dimly lit as if obscured by a mist, presents an intriguing puzzle rather than aiding in my quest for sleep. It prompts a contemplation within me, a nudge towards the realization that life's answers might be woven into the very fabric of these mysteries, awaiting decipherment.

Vadim's lovely daughter made this. She was a sweet kid. Rene and I decided to use this as a strange treasure map in a few months when we planned on going back to Burning Man again.

Fun to see Vadim with this artwork mentioning Ukraine. I've been there many times. Kiev, Kharkov, and even Chernobyl. The latter felt a bit safer than Vadim's.

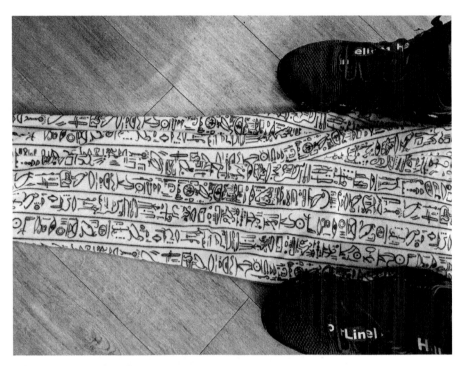

Behold, my Pants of Puzzling!

I have these, kinda wild, white pants that are covered in hiero-glyphics. I like to wear them sometimes because they are fun and they always bring a smile to people's faces. They are somewhat ridic-ulous, but so am I a lot of the time. I don't take life too seriously and I just wear whatever makes me happy.

They're not just pants; they're a statement, my "Pants of Puz-zling," if you will, rumored among my inner circle to possess the mystical ability to boost my cognitive abilities, particularly in the area of solving enigmas. Whether this is a case of magical realism or just the placebo effect at play, these pants seemingly grant me a +3 bonus to Puzzle-Solving.

This concept of clothing influencing mood and ability extends to other pieces in my wardrobe, gifts from my mother who has a knack for selecting uniquely appealing attire. A particular favorite is a red t-shirt hoodie adorned with a yin-yang symbol, morphed into the shape of a heart, which I feel amplifies my capacity for openness and love. Such pieces become more than mere fabric; they are talismans, each contributing to the fluctuating essence of my emotions and perceptions, encouraging a playful engagement with the world that surrounds me, where mood and attire dance in a symbiotic rhythm. Belief goes a long way.

I do believe that certain pieces of jewelry or even some ceremonial clothes can contain blessings and have some kind of energetic power we do not understand.

Introducing my son, Ethan, to these ideas of fantastical tales became a treasured evening tradition after returning from my global escapades. Post a sojourn through Malaysia's verdant expanses, I came upon a necklace, a masterpiece of local craftsmanship, intended as a souvenir for him. With great enthusiasm, I wove a narrative rich with adventure, featuring a sophisticated society of talking, upright monkeys and their regal leader, the Monkey King. This monarch, supposedly struck by the beauty of the landscapes captured in my photographs, bestowed upon me the very necklace I handed to Ethan. The yarn was spun not merely for amusement but bore a deeper purpose, hinting at the necklace's ability to bolster his intellect, a secret kept between him, myself, and the legendary primate monarch.

I would say, "So, Ethan, whenever you feel like you need to be extra smart at school, or any time, you can wear this. It can be under your shirt. No one has to know. Just me, your mom, and the monkey king."

This practice of bringing back artifacts from my travels, each accompanied by fantastical narratives, became a way to enrich Ethan's world with imagination, humor, and a sense of personal capability. These objects, though ordinary in material, were transformed into talismans of extraordinary virtues, fostering a playful exploration of the world's wonders and mysteries.

Back at Vadim's, the persistent visions of hieroglyphics that invaded my sleepless nights prompted me to don my "Puzzling Pants" and venture into the lounge, a space teeming with art, books, and curiosities. Immersed in this environment, I felt an intensified connection to the objects and texts around me, each seemingly a piece of a larger, more intricate riddle. My endeavor to decipher the symbolic language that pervaded my thoughts extended to a physical engagement with Vadim's collection, photographing items that struck me as significant, a ritual that persisted in the days that followed.

MYSTERIOUS SYMBOLS ABOUND

Speaking of hieroglyphics, I continue to see many symbols flashing in front of my eyes nine months later as I am writing this.

Even though I am well-recovered now, many times when I close my eyes in the daytime or before bed, I am shown all sorts of unusual patterns. Sometimes, I see patterns and symbols rapidly flash in my eyes, up to three different symbols per second. I can't recognize them, and they could be anything from ancient Hebrew to ancient Aramaic. I don't read either of those, and I'm too lazy to actually learn them. I wish I had some sort of Google Translate jacked into my optic nerve.

I've also had bizarre visions that make no sense. For example, a few weeks ago, sitting at my desk here in New Zealand, I was seeing a live Green Bay Packers football game in my left eye as a transparency over my laptop. I kid you not. I don't even watch the NFL anymore since I moved to NZ about fifteen years ago. The vision was not crystal clear, but I could make out that Green Bay Packers logo on a helmet. I decided to Google it, and, sure enough, the Packers were playing at that very moment. So strange. I went out on a long, ten-kilometer, hike, came back, and got another live feed of the San Francisco 49ers playing. I Googled it, and, sure enough, they were actually playing.

What any of that means, it's anybody's guess. Let's just say many strange things have been happening to me. I talk more about some of these continued wild experiences in Book 2.

Speaking of Book 2, let me paste in an "experience" from it here in this section. It speaks to more mysterious symbols. This story is particularly interesting because it happened about two years before my incident in Scotland when I spent four days and nights at a Lakota Sweat Lodge.

In the aftermath of my journey to the heart of a Lakota Native American sweat lodge, I found myself returning home, weary yet awakened by the ordeal. Let me tell you, a sweat lodge is like the ultimate spa day if your idea of relaxation involves being baked alive in an earthen oven. There I was, huddled up with a bunch of other folks searching for something more, all of us baking together in the dark, illuminated only by the glow of superheated rocks that felt like tiny pieces of the sun had decided to join us.

The heat in there? It's like a relentless beast, a fiery embrace that doesn't know when to let go. It's like being hugged by a bear made of fire. But, believe it or not, getting cooked alive comes with perks—like a chance to hit the spiritual refresh button. The water-pourer, a shaman of sorts, serves as our guide, orchestrating this dance of flame and steam, as each stone, aglow with primordial fire, joins us in the darkness, transforming the hut into a womb of rebirth.

Emerging from the depths of this trial, the act of crawling forth into the night, reborn unto the flickering light of an open fire, is akin to a second birth. The transition from the oppressive embrace of the lodge to the cool, embracing, grass under the infinite expanse of stars above is a baptism of sorts. Though not reborn in the literal sense, the sensation of being alive, truly alive, in the aftermath is undeniable.

The journey back to Queenstown, in the company of my friend Dr. Tim Rigg, was a silent testament to the ordeal we had endured and the introspection it had borne. As I laid myself down to rest, devoid of any substance to cloud my mind or dull my senses, I found myself on the cusp of something big, a threshold beyond which lay the unexplored territories of my own consciousness.

Under the cover of night, sprawled out in my bed like a starfish claiming its territory, that all-too-familiar buzz zips through me. It's like getting a static shock from the universe's carpet, a surefire sign that things are about to get interesting. There's no room for fear. I'm strapped in for a trip to the great unknown, excitement my co-pilot.

Then, in less time than it takes to blink, I'm on the up-and-up. My room, the quaint outline of Queenstown, and the lush sprawl of the South Island shrink away as if I've hit the zoom-out button on Google Earth too many times. New Zealand becomes a postcard from my personal altitude record. This isn't your garden-variety dream; it's more like the universe has handed me a VIP pass to the mysteries beyond.

Adrift in the void, I find myself within a luminous cube, spinning end over end in the weightlessness of space. Its edges glow with angelic light, framing the infinite tapestry of the cosmos beyond its transparent bounds. And there, suspended in the vastness of this celestial die, a mathematical formula materializes, bathed in a phosphorescent glow—an enigma laid bare before my wondering eyes.

So, I'm staring at this formula in space, and it's like the universe decided to give me a pop quiz on a subject I haven't studied. My background in computers and math is suddenly feeling pretty irrelevant as this shape and formula keeps changing its mind. Each moment of comprehension is but a prelude to further mystery, as the shape transforms—a tetrahedron now, the die of a dungeon master, lighting up like it's got its own personal spotlight, each face flipping to reveal another brain-buster that makes child's play of the last one.

Here I am, floating in space, caught between admiration and a headache, staring at the universe's most elaborate puzzle. It's like being dropped into a scene from *Rick & Morty*, where everything is mind-blowingly cool but also kind of makes you want to pull your hair out. As the show goes on, one mind-bending geometric transformation after another, I can't help but laugh. It's all so absurdly magnificent. "Incredible," I find myself saying to no one and everyone, amusement and a hint of exasperation in my voice. "Guys, this is mind-blowing. But could you slow down a bit?"

The formulas keep coming, each more intricate and mysterious than the last, hinting at revelations that feel just out of reach. Could I be staring at the next-level Einsteinian cheat sheet for cold fusion, or the secret spell for saving the planet? It feels like the universe might just be handing me the keys to the kingdom—if only I could figure out how to use them.

My only explanation is that it was giving me important information that my subconscious could indeed grok that will become useful later down my timeline when something important is activated. Or it was the galaxy's way of saying, "Maybe you should've gone for that Math Ph.D. after all, buddy."

Yet, the culmination of this seemingly impossible astral

Masterclass diverges from what came before. No longer do I float in the abstract expanse of space; now, I am ensconced within a room that drifts untethered, where the revelations of the cosmos are rendered on a display not unlike the screen of a laptop or a tableau from *The Matrix*. This time, it is not a singular formula that commands my attention but a mathematical proof, unfolding line by line in the stark clarity of Courier New font. The simplicity of its commencement belies the complexity that follows, each line building upon the last in a relentless cascade of logic and numbers. Despite my fascination, the pace is unrelenting, a torrent of information that I chase with a grin of bewildered delight.

And then, as if in reward for my perseverance through this silent lecture, the universe shifts. I am cast as the protagonist in a celestial saga, hurling fireballs at a space dragon in a starry arcade, the fantastical denouement to my interstellar tutorial. It's as though the cosmos itself, my spaceborne progenitors, offer this as a playful reprieve from the rigors of cosmic calculus.

When I find myself back in my bed, my eyes flick open to my familiar old room, a jarring jump cut from the craziness I'd just experienced. I rush to get it all down, the awe of it etched deep in my mind. I've never been hit with visions like this before, and it's got me pondering what it all means. Not only does the universe work in mysterious ways, but it's constantly reminding me that I should have tried harder in math.

That's the end of that excerpt from Book 2. Crazy stuff, right? I was quite bamboozled by all these symbols until I continued to trudge through dozens of books in the past few months and I now have a good idea of what is happening. I've included more details on this in the Bonus Section at the end called "The Healing of Ann." I don't want to get too bogged down here as we continue the adventure!

FLASHBACK TO MOTEL ONE IN SCOTLAND

Speaking of puzzles, let's rewind to my room. My room harbored its own set of peculiarities.

Like many modern hotels, inserting a key card activates the room's electricity—a commonplace convenience. Yet, what transpired next was anything but ordinary. Instead of greeting me with the usual promotional hotel channel, the TV sprung to life with live footage of Wimbledon. This happened the day before when I stayed there, but strange stuff always appeared on the television. As for this one, this wasn't your standard sports broadcast. The screen was filled with the chaos of a protest—a woman darting onto the court, releasing a flurry of puzzle pieces and confetti into the air in a dramatic statement against oil dependency. The scene was cluttered, the cleanup slow and meticulous, while the broadcast showcased similar environmental protests disrupting matches.

This departure from traditional media policy, which typically avoids giving airtime to such disruptions, struck me as remarkable. I've always aligned myself with environmental causes, dreaming of the day humanity transcends its reliance on oil and plastic. And, of course, I want humanity to live in harmony with nature. Yet, I'm acutely aware of the Gordian knot that is our current energy paradigm, understanding that we've got a real problem in that there are billions of engines that depend on the current oil industry. Shutting it all down immediately would cause massive suffering to humanity because we would not be able to get food and supplies around the world.

Even though it's a broken system, without that system, billions would starve. The transition from oil and pollutants is a long and tricky one. I don't pretend to know the answers, but I want the gentle reader to know I understand both sides. Yes, I literally hug trees, but I also understand the constraints of our current system and how humans must depend on it until we move to a better system. The system, flawed and fueled by avarice and trepidation, demands a delicate dance towards sustainability. It's clear when people and systems are motivated by greed and fear, which are part of the darkness and not the light.

I have a clarity about this, and I don't have a solution other than to make sure my own life is one of light and love. I can't change the world by myself, but I can always seek to be a better, more healthy, and more loving person. I firmly believe that as I do this, others feel these waves and vibrations. The more we harmonize with this love, the more we can change Earth's song.

This period of intense connection-making was not merely an exercise in curiosity but a driven pursuit to uncover deeper meanings and truths, to piece together the puzzles that constitute our world. It was as if the incident at Wimbledon, where puzzle pieces were scattered as a disruptive act, served as a metaphorical nudge, a reminder of the complexities and interconnectedness of life, urging me to explore, question, and ultimately contribute to a more enlightened, compassionate existence.

As I delve into more books, I continue to be amazed by experiences like that of Robert Monroe who suddenly started seeing the same things I did. Like me, he was just going about his life and then he started having wild out of body experiences. And his was way back in the late 1950s and 1960s before "New Age" stuff was even a thang. Monroe didn't start having any experiences until his mid-forties (he was born in 1915). He was a successful businessman and a pioneer in the broadcasting industry and turned out to be instrumental in developing cable television. Even the way he writes has that throwback Ward Cleaver feel.

Some of his OBEs even took him to the spirit realm. I remember the distinct feeling that echoes his sentiments about feeling at "home" during my too-brief visit to the spirit realm. Here is a passage from his book *Journeys out of the Body* that was so close to mine. Lord and Lady, it made me feel better to read this and so many other accounts. I wasn't crazy. I did experience it. It wasn't just a hallucination of my mind or some drug trip, as so many people have callously dismissed it.

> "It is as if you are within and a part of the clouds surrounding
> an eternally glowing sunset, and with every changing pattern of
> living color, you also change. You respond and drink into you
> the eternity of the blues, yellows, greens, and reds, and the com-
> plexities of the intermediates. All are familiar to you. This is

where you belong. This is Home. You are Home. You are where you belong. Where you always should have been. Most important, you are not alone. With you, beside you, interlocked in you are others. They do not have names, nor are you aware of them as shapes, but you know them and you are bonded to them with a great single knowledge. They are exactly like you, they are you, and like you, they are Home. You feel with them, like gentle waves of electricity passing between you, a completeness of love, of which all the facets you have experienced are but segments and incomplete portions. Only here, the emotion is without need of intense display or demonstration. You give and receive as an automatic action, with no deliberate effort. It is not something you need or that needs you. The 'reaching out' is gone. The interchange flows naturally. You are unaware of differences in sex, you yourself as a part of the whole are both male and female, positive and negative, electron and proton. Man-woman love moves to you and from you, parent-child-sibling-idol and idyll and ideal-all interplay in soft waves about you, in you, and through you. You are in perfect balance because you are where you belong. You are Home."

CLOSE ENCOUNTERS

It's interesting at this point to note that I am still trying to figure out what happened in Scotland. It was clearly the beginning of a spiritual awakening. The world around me was alive in ways I had never seen. I was receiving so much beautiful stimulation I could barely take it.

I wanted to share my experience with everyone, but I didn't exactly know how to explain it at the time. I felt a lot like Richard Dreyfuss in that scene from *Close Encounters* when he keeps serving himself mashed potatoes so he can make a carving of that mountain he saw (Devil's Tower). "Well I guess you've noticed there's something a little strange with dad." He laughs in a strange whiny, almost tearful way. His wife and kids look at him with serious concern. He continues in a stifled manner, "It's okay though. I'm still dad. I can't describe it. What I'm feeling and what I'm thinking. This means something. It is important."

In so many ways, I was excited to tell them that I went to the other side and it was so beautiful and full of love. There is absolutely nothing to worry about in terms of death. In fact, it's the most amazing experience of a lifetime, if it's okay if I play with words like that. After we complete our missions here on Earth, then there is such ecstasy waiting for us on the other side. How do I excitedly tell everyone about this without everyone thinking I'm an absolute crazy person? It's still something I struggle with, but I feel like quite a reliable narrator, and I'll just tell the story exactly how I remember it all happening. There's a lot more adventure here ahead of us.

Let's take a break from all this heavy stuff and take a look at my childhood to see what started this wild ride.

My early days starting the junior version of Hell's Angels. On the back of my shirt, it said, "If you can read this, it means my bitch fell off."

A DETOUR TO THE TOUR OF MY ATHEISM

You will recall that I spent most of my life as an atheist, so I certainly had that thread going through my teachings. Being an atheist is like being certain there's no sandwich in the fridge without checking.

Back in Scotland, I got stuck in the fridge for half an hour and there were sandwiches, sandwiches, everywhere.

And I was a very studied and clever atheist too, if I do say so myself. As a kid in Dallas, Texas, I went to an Episcopal grade school where they tried to indoctrinate me while I Neo-dodged their God-fearing bullets. Those guys are clever, you know, try to mind-launder the kids when they are weak and young. It's like Jeffrey Epstein's Island for holy brainwashing and the priestess—since Episcopalians are so open-minded and allow females in the clergy—was Ghislaine Maxwell.

Okay maybe you didn't like that analogy much, but that's just a warmup for my Catholic High School musings. Like Ricky Gervais said, "You found it offensive? I found it funny. That's why I'm happier than you."

After I managed to emerge from that first school with my spiritual virginity intact, I continued on to an all-boy Jesuit Catholic College Prep (class of 1990, complete with a YouTube graduation video of me doing my best Napoleon Dynamite impression a decade before the movie came out), which was basically a fancy high school where we all wore coats and ties and longed for the once-a-week football games with Ursuline, that divine sanctuary down the road that was the yin to our yang filled with 100% hormone-fueled girls. I always wondered, if the Catholics are so against premarital sex, why do they make those high school girls dress so sexy? It's a fair question when you are wandering around the forbidden fruit part of the grocery store and there is a patchwork quilt of small plaid skirts covering them all up. As Lex Fridman claims, "I'm just asking for a friend."

Jesuit actually did not try that hard to indoctrinate me. Their approach was more subtle. I do actually appreciate the Jesuit style of teaching which tends to be a deeper thinking and philosophical approach. My four years of Theology there were quite interesting and more about the nature of thinking and philosophy than trying to coerce us to be "good boys" with the not-so-subtle threat of writhing in hell. The Jesuit priests always enjoyed debates about atheism and the nature of the universe. It's like they believed the path to enlightenment was paved with "why nots?" instead of "thou shalts."

BELOW: Matt Taylor. RIGHT: Trey Ratcliff. CENTER: Don Whitaker and Liam Dowing.

FAR LEFT: Danny Kang; LEFT: Matt Shannon; ABOVE: Eric Bonenberger.

SENIORS

Top right, after I programmed the TRS-80 to make an animation proclaiming the superiority of my Amiga computer back at home. I used to make digital paintings on my Amiga and sent a few into Electronic Arts to get a job there. They loved them, but then they learned how young I was. It wasn't my first or last rejection.

Of all the great friends I had there, one of my besties to this day is still Will Kelly. It was strange, because he was a year younger than me, and classes usually don't mix. We worked together selling computer games at Babbages at the mall, and we continued to play games together for many decades to come.

There I am, the least accomplished on the page. I was more interested in computer games than school.

French Club

The French Club provides opportunities for students to use French outside of class. Members play games together every Friday after school and enjoy French cuisine occasionally. Students who are interested can compete in the annual state contest, the Texas French Symposium.

FRONT ROW: Kelly Welch, Scott Ross, Trey Ratcliff, Vince Cordero, Dominic Falcinelli, Jamey Welch, Mike Gillett, Joe Uceda; SECOND ROW: Mme. Nancy VanMess, Jimmy Marsh, Mercury Williams, Billy Winborn, Marc Di Giacomo, Theo Rickert, Andre Kim, Angel Dehesa; BACK ROW: Kevin Brown, Jim Higgins, Savio Chacko, James Tsevoukas and Saju Chacko; NOT PICTURED: Jake Vander Linden, Luke Vander Linden, Art Armenta, John Bishara, Rob Schweizer, Alex Holmes, Andrew Jordan and Ashley Michael.

72   ACTIVITIES

Funny, I don't remember being that tall. I do remember being that awkward.

Computer Club

The Computer Club offers interested students an opportunity to explore various aspects of computer usage, hardware and software not covered in the conventional courses.

FRONT ROW: Michael Kim, Greg Darnell, Mark Pennisi; SECOND ROW: Dan Mitchell, Thomas Yoon; THIRD ROW: Lijo Joseph, Savio Chacko, Gary Neuschaefer, Mark Walters; BACK ROW: Dr. Philip Ryan, Mr. Jack Eifert; NOT PICTURED: Erik Trickel.

Despite my general lack of coolness, I knew I was too cool to join the Computer Club.

FRONT ROW: Vince Cordero, Alan Choate; BACK ROW: Shane Yarbrough, Adaryll Jordan, Scott Rylander and Danny Lanicek.

This is another club I decided not to join. I kept my extracurricular activities to myself.

I continued my tour of splintered Christianity at Southern Methodist University (SMU). Thank goodness for all my mom's dedication. She decided to get a job there so I could get free tuition. There was no way we could have afforded it otherwise. My dad was supposed to keep paying my mom via a financial agreement in the divorce, but he often fell on hard times and could not support us. I get it. Life is tough sometimes. Anyway, very grateful to my mom for hangin' in there so my sister and I could get a university education. It was more important back then. As of the time of writing this in 2024, I think getting a university education is becoming increasingly useless.

By the time I got to SMU, I was getting quite drained by religion and I now needed to figure out this Venn Diagram overlap of how this group of Methodists thought themselves superior to the Catholics and the Episcopalians. I found it all so silly, really. Why don't any of these people just think for themselves? How lazy is it to just pick up one menu at one restaurant and have that be all you order from for the rest of your life? Unless it's The Cheesecake Factory. This menu has almost everything. As you can see, my analogies have really improved since the Epstein Island reference.

This seems to be a good time for me to clearly state that I think Jesus was an absolute legend. I certainly believe he existed and was a true prophet of light and love. 100%. He brought the same messages, healing, and enlightenment as many other prophets through the centuries. Unfortunately his teachings have been so manipulated by fear-based power structures that things became rather confusing. If I may recommend yet another book to understand Jesus in a much more believable way, crack open *Jesus and the Essenes*, by Dolores Cannon.

Here's another photo from high school when I was with my Uncle Richard. He's the one that got me interested in Computer Science when I saw him programming in Pascal. I was fascinated and asked him many questions. I'm 100% sure that is what got me interested in programming.

I BEGIN TO SOFTEN MY HARDCORE ATHEISM

Entering the "real world" after graduation, my atheism became a bit of a side-hobby, especially as I traveled. I saw how billions of people around the planet had been brainwashed and how hundreds of millions of people on Earth have been tortured and slaughtered in the name of one god versus another. I became so despondent and frustrated that I would often refer to the classic George Carlin line: *"Think of how stupid the average person is, and realize half of them are stupider than that."*

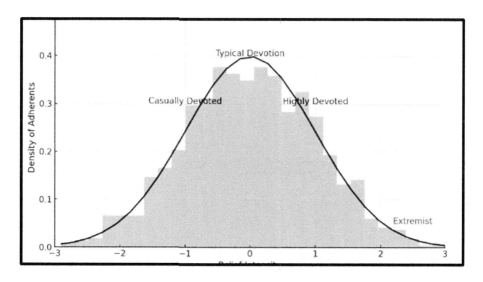

Indeed, if you look at the "bell curve of behavior" in any religion, the middle of the bell-curve is totally fine. These are decent people that are kind and follow the same Golden Rule in every religion—to treat others as you want to be treated. In my deep studies of many religions, it is clear that the Golden Rule idea came from a central source and made its way into all religions, as you can see below. This is a beautiful thing.

The Golden Rule across the World's Religions
Thirteen Sacred Texts

Bahá'í Faith

Lay not on any soul a load that you would not wish to be laid upon you, and desire not for anyone the things you would not desire for yourself.

Bahá'u'lláh, **Gleanings**

Buddhism

Treat not others in ways that you yourself would find hurtful.

The Buddha, **Udana-Varga 5.18**

Christianity

In everything, do to others as you would have them do to you; for this is the law and the prophets.

Jesus, **Matthew 7:12**

Confucianism

One word which sums up the basis of all good conduct....loving-kindness. Do not do to others what you do not want done to yourself.

Confucius, **Analects 15.23**

Hinduism

This is the sum of duty: do not do to others what would cause pain if done to you.

Mahabharata 5:1517

Islam

Not one of you truly believes until you wish for others
what you wish for yourself.

The Prophet Muhammad, **Hadith**

Jainism

One should treat all creatures in the world as one would like to be treated.

Mahavira, **Sutrakritanga 1.11.33**

Judaism

What is hateful to you, do not do to your neighbour. This is the whole Torah; all the
rest is commentary. Go and learn it.

Hillel, **Talmud, Shabbath 31a**

Native Spirituality

We are as much alive as we keep the earth alive.

Chief Dan George

Sikhism

I am a stranger to no one; and no one is a stranger to me.
Indeed, I am a friend to all.

Guru Granth Sahib, p.1299

Taoism

Regard your neighbour's gain as your own gain and your neighbour's loss as your
own loss.

Lao Tzu, **T'ai Shang Kan Ying P'ien, 213-218**

Unitarianism

We affirm and promote respect for the interdependent web of all existence of which we are a part.

Unitarian principle

Zoroastrianism

Do not do unto others whatever is injurious to yourself.

Shayast-na-Shayast 13.29

Returning to the concept of the bell curve, it's important to note that as we move away from the moderate center towards the edges, we encounter the extreme ends of belief. In a world where billions of people adhere to a particular faith, even a small percentage of extremists can amount to tens of thousands. These individuals often spread fear and suffering, overshadowing the message of love and unity that is desperately needed. Sadly, it's just math, and that math becomes meme-Malthusian.

Here are estimates of the top four winners in the "So You Think You Can Pray?" reality show:

- Christianity: 2.3 Billion
- Islam: 1.9 Billion
- Hinduism: 1.2 Billion
- Buddhism: 520 Million

You'll notice I didn't include the Jewish religion in there, as they are only around 15 million. And they all live in Hollywood. Kidding. Kidding.

Speaking of entertaining Jews, Yuval Noah Hararri in his wonderful book *Sapiens: A Brief History*, made the most amazing observation. By the way, I read countless books about anthropology (well, everything, really, from genetics to history to economics to philosophy to Harry Potter), and I was so excited to read how Yuval brought new ideas about human nature into a series of books that seemed to repeat the same old things over and over again. He made it clear that humans are unique, in that we are the only species that will collectively agree on a fictional story. That story may be a good, helpful story like women being equal to men (a relatively new story). It could be a harmless story, in that we all agree on the rules of football or that a dollar bill has a value. Or, in many cases, it may be a terrible story: Our God or our Nation is better than yours. This leads to subjugation, war, and worse. I agree with Yuval that the most dangerous fictional stories that billions believe in now are based on nationalism and religion. We are all just humans, and we can just get along with love.

Naturally, I have his book listed at the end as a great resource.

At the height of my distaste with religion I became rather acerbic and started espousing the greatness of incredible atheist writers like Richard Dawkins, Sam Harris, and Christopher Hitchens. I found great joy in the way they would poke fun at organized religion and the inconsistencies (and often cruel bits) of religious texts. However, as I got into my forties and started experimenting with psychedelics, my stance really softened.

Lord and Lady, I wish Richard Dawkins would embark on a nice mushroom dose in the right set and setting or a full Ayahuasca. Dawkins is so goddamned sure there is no god or no grand creator that it is alarming. I can't wait to see his face when he begins that side of his awakening. And I know why Richard hasn't done it yet. It's clear to me, even if he won't admit it to himself. He is scared.

There can be no other reason. It won't kill him, and he'll just have a wonderful experience for about six hours. Why not? People will go into a dark theater and enter another realm for three hours, letting go of the reality outside the movie theater. So why not six hours in the theater of your mind?

Like me, Sam Harris has also softened. He has many wonderful stories on his podcast about his experiences with mushrooms and MDMA. Sam is still hardline against the dangers of extremism in religion, and I'm on board with him too. I have more on Sam later in the book. You'll be surprised to find he's a part-time DJ.

So, yes, now you're getting a sense of my journey. There are many attributions to this quote, but it is apropos: "Strong opinions, loosely held." This is one of my favorite things about having an open mind and always being intellectually curious. I do indeed have strong opinions on things backed by facts and what I have learned, but sometimes I am presented with a better argument and more compelling facts. Then, I'm happy to evolve my opinion, and then that becomes part of my story.

Okay, enough about religion. Keep in mind if you are just one of those nice, sweet, religious people in the middle of the bell curve, you're okay in my book. You probably follow the Golden Rule, are kind and loving, and you take care of people around you. That is wonderful. I love you very much for being like that. Keep it up. We need more of that.

FAMILY RELIGIOUS TRIP STARTING WITH BUDDHISM AND ENDING IN MARTIAN-GOD WORSHIP?

Our trip was wonderful. We left our home in New Zealand for our first stop in Thailand where they were introduced to Buddhism. From there, we went to India to live on a train for about a week as we snaked through the southern part of the country to study the amazingly fun and spirited pantheon of the Indian gods. After that, off to a few stops in the Middle East where we spent time in many mosques amidst many chants and studies of Islam. We finished in Rome where they learned of Christianity, or at least the Roman Catholic version of it, sans the child molestation, which is always a downer for any family trip.

Naturally, the whole trip was not about religion. We ate all the most amazing foods and saw and experienced all the unforgettable adventures that only open-hearted travel can provide. If you are curious to see more, we put a lot on video, so you can just Google the pithy, "The Traveling Ratcliff Family Photo Circus Around The World."

Fast forward to Vadim's apartment, which is not going to be one of the locations for any family road trip in the future, unless all my kids become meth addicts and need a place to really hit another level of rock bottom.

When I went down into Vadim's lounge, I was struck by these three posters on the wall. I have always loved this style of aspirational-travel graphic design combined with past-futurama visions of interstellar destinations. I immediately started to tear up as I envisioned having a fun little spaceship and taking my kids on a fun road trip in space to visit all these places. Like, "Hey kids, buckle up, next stop: Phobos. Don't make me turn this spaceship around!"

Here are the three posters I saw in Vadim's place. I added some live video commentary in my Instagram Story highlights in the Critiques area.

After listening to hundreds and hundreds of transcripts in case-studies of people who have experiences between lives where they visit other planets, space stations, stars, and the like, I feel like all these aspirations are easily achievable. Be sure to check the Bonus Level area at the end of the book for my recommendations, in particular the case studies in the "Convoluted Universe" series of books which remain an endless source of entertainment. I swear, with each story, it's like every story is an intricately wrapped Christmas present from Dolores Cannon, and I'm just here, every day, acting like it's Christmas Eve. I'm shaking these presents, guessing what's inside—probably another universe or something—and chugging eggnog, waiting for the midnight clock to strike so I can tear into them with all the zeal of 1977 when I got my Atari 2600.

ALL ABOARD!

Because we can set up various simulated situations in the life between lives, I put a ton of thought into how this experience would work. I have the first draft of this experience in my head, but I want to collaborate with the family to design this experience together. It's not just my kids. My lovely ex is roped in as well not just for her affinity for all things sci-fi but because her talent for eye-rolling at my spur-of-the-moment whims adds a certain charm to the proceedings.

Just as Jim Carrey said, "Behind every great man is a woman rolling her eyes." I'm not saying I'm great all the time. Far from it.

Of course, I love my kids at any age, but there is something about them being younger kids that is especially exciting. Basically, the same age as that religion-based trip I just mentioned. My son is in his early teens, clever and cracking up the cosmos with me. My first daughter at about ten, studious with a biting wit that could slice through spacetime. And my youngest at age six, wildly precocious with a wonderfully inappropriate sense of humor that would make aliens blush.

A photo of the fam in New Zealand after a day wranglin' our bees!

We all pile into a spaceship that I have designed. It's not too big, but there is definitely a kitchen area with lots of snacks. Snacks are important. In my road-trip policy, which has always conflicted with my wife's, I have put down the rule that there will be unlimited snacks available at any time.

For example, if we just ate a huge dinner with dessert in Kyoto and we walked out and saw an ice cream place and the kids wanted some of that too. Well, we stop and load up. Why not? Life is short; eat dessert first before getting another dessert.

Also, in this space-road-trip, I want everyone to agree to amnesia. That is, since I know the souls of my kids have probably already been to many planets before they came to Earth, this is probably old hat to them. But we all agree to have two weeks of "innocence," just like when we all decided to come down to Earth together and suffer this terrible amnesia and forget who we truly are and have to figure everything out here from a state of tabula rasa.

Furthermore, it's not just a road-trip, it's also a treasure hunt, as if we are on a game show of sorts. There are other families out there too (my friends and their families!) in their own spaceships, and we are all trying to collect the most outrageous family selfies or other treasures at dozens of locations around our solar system. From unique geological features on Mars to a sunset on a moon of Jupiter to getting ice off one of the rings of Saturn for our beverages. We even have a live scoreboard in the ship so we can see how we rank throughout the adventure.

As you can see, I put a lot of thought into all this. Perhaps this is a little insight into how my mind works, even in the throes of complete sanity.

10.
CONFLUENCE OF REALITIES

"When you find out that there was never anything in the dark side to be afraid of ... Nothing is left but to love."
—ALAN WATTS

"The trouble with having an open mind, of course, is that people will insist on coming along and trying to put things in it."
—TERRY PRATCHETT

Well now that I'm ramping up my altered view of reality, let's talk about these two terms a little more.

Drawing on the insights of Stanislav and Christina Grof, the term "spiritual emergence" resonates with me, capturing the essence of my experiences which I perceive as richly transformative rather than symptomatic of a psychiatric condition. This perspective does not seek to evade or invalidate the clinical interpretation of these experiences but aims to broaden the conversation, highlighting the potential for personal growth and spiritual insight that such episodes can herald.

The challenge of diagnosing non-physical conditions in psychiatry underscores the complexity of these experiences. Unlike physical ailments that can often be identified through objective tests, conditions like psychosis are diagnosed based on a constellation of symptoms and behaviors, assessed against established criteria that are continuously refined by ongoing research. This process, inherently subjective, reveals the limitations of a system that strives for precision in the inherently fluid domain of human psychology.

This critique extends to the broader issue of diagnostic classifications, which can sometimes oversimplify or mis-categorize individual experiences due to their reliance on generalized criteria. The analogy to the BMI system illustrates this point well, highlighting how metrics designed to serve as universal indicators of health or illness can misrepresent the realities of individuals who fall outside the normative parameters for which these measures were designed.

My narrative seeks to stretch the boundaries of understanding around experiences commonly dismissed within rigid clinical frameworks as mere psychosis. By recounting my journey, I aim to illuminate the profound personal and spiritual revelations that can emerge from such states, advocating for a mental health discourse enriched by empathy, openness, and a recognition of the diverse expressions of human consciousness. This approach not only respects the complexity of individual experiences but also honors the myriad paths of exploration and healing available to us.

The medical label of psychosis that was applied to my experiences reflects a standardized view, one that may not fully encompass the uniqueness of individuals who deviate from the so-called average. My personality and behavior, even before this spiritual emergence, could be seen as unconventional—a trait not uncommon in artists and creatives who often operate outside societal norms. Embracing this deviation from normalcy has been a liberating acknowledgment of my true self, underscoring a belief that we are not here to conform but to express our authentic beings.

I suppose I was always an artist. In many ways, I think all kids are artists and society beats it out of us. My mom always thought it was cute how I would stick out my tongue when I would use colors.

The initial phase of what I've come to understand as my spiritual emergency was marked by an exciting sense of discovery and connection, devoid of harm to myself or others. However, as events unfolded, the lack of an informed support network became painfully apparent. Reflecting on the writings of Grof and others who have navigated similar waters, I'm led to contemplate how a supportive environment, populated by spiritual guides, medical professionals, and a community familiar with such transformative processes, might have altered my trajectory.

The harsh interventions I faced—confrontations with law enforcement, physical restraints, and the sterile confines of hospital settings—served to deepen the distress of an already intense journey. This response, marked by misunderstanding and fear, contrasts sharply with the nurturing embrace such experiences might receive in a context informed by wisdom, compassion, and a deep understanding of spiritual emergence. The thought of what might have been, had I been surrounded by a community equipped to guide and support me through this ordeal, suggests a different outcome—one characterized by healing and growth rather than trauma. What if I had been in a village surrounded by medicine women, healers, shamans and the like that could guide me through this process rather than being slammed into a medical facility in a one-size-fits-all situation?

I'll never know. But, alas, everything happens for a purpose, so I take solace in that.

In sharing these reflections, my hope is to shed light on my own path and also to contribute to a broader dialogue about mental health, spiritual awakening, and the societal structures that shape our responses to them. It's a call to reenvision how we support individuals navigating the turbulent waters of consciousness expansion, advocating for approaches that honor the full spectrum of human experience with dignity and understanding.

My dialogue around this transformative period in my life emphasizes the need to reassess and expand our understanding of altered states of consciousness. This conversation extends beyond my personal experiences, touching upon the broader societal, medical, and alternative healing perspectives on such states. At the core of my narrative is an effort to shift the dialogue from a pathology-oriented view of "psychosis" to the more expansive and hopeful framework of "spiritual emergence." This shift is not just semantic but reflects a deeper understanding of these experiences as gateways to personal growth and healing, rather than as maladies to be suppressed or eradicated.

The distinction between the terms "psychosis" and "spiritual emergence" is significant. The former, despite its clinical neutrality, often carries connotations of dysfunction, danger, and a need for containment. This perception aligns with a pathologizing approach that focuses on symptom management rather than holistic understanding and integration. "Spiritual emergence," however, suggests a process of unfolding, an awakening that, while challenging, holds the potential for personal growth and the release of deep-seated emotional and psychological patterns.

THE GREAT STANISLAV GROF

The terminology used by Stanislav Grof, who coined "spiritual emergency," offers a valuable framework. Yet the term "emergency" itself may inadvertently evoke images of crisis and urgency, implying scenarios that necessitate immediate and often invasive interventions. My preference leans towards language that, while acknowledging the intense and sometimes disorienting nature of these experiences, also encapsulates their transformative potential without casting them in an inherently negative light.

Through exploring various narratives and perspectives on psychosis and spiritual emergence, including Grof's work, it becomes apparent that our collective understanding of these phenomena is evolving. This evolution invites a more nuanced conversation about the nature of consciousness, the interplay between psychological distress and spiritual awakening, and the societal structures that influence how we support those navigating these changes.

In reframing these experiences, the goal is not to diminish the challenges they present but to advocate for approaches that honor the complexity and potential inherent in them. By adopting a language that emphasizes growth, exploration, and healing, we open the door to more compassionate and effective support mechanisms. This shift in perspective has the power to transform the lives of those directly experiencing spiritual emergences and the cultural and institutional frameworks that shape our responses to them, fostering a more inclusive and holistic approach to mental health and human development.

Psychosis Quotes:

- "Psychosis is not fundamentally a medical condition, but a natural process of self-healing for the psyche." —Carl Jung (Psychiatrist and Psychoanalyst)
- "Psychosis is a break from reality, but it can also be a break into a new reality." —R.D. Laing (Psychiatrist known for his alternative approach to mental health)
- "Psychosis is not the opposite of sanity, but a different way of experiencing the world." —Elyn Saks (Law Professor, Author, and Mental Health Advocate)
- "I wouldn't have had good scientific ideas if I had

thought more normally." —John Nash (the mathematician the movie *A Beautiful Mind* was based on who experienced psychosis)

- "In my delusions, I found a deeper truth about my place in the universe." —Janine Fontaine (Author)
- "Hearing voices and other unusual experiences can be understood in many ways and can lead to healing and growth for some people." —Gail Hornstein (Psychology Professor and Author)
- "The psychotic break itself is usually so extraordinary that many who have been through it spend much of their lives trying to describe it." —Mark Vonnegut (Pediatrician and Author–Son of Kurt)
- "In the same way that a dream or a migraine aura can sometimes reveal the workings of the brain in a particularly vivid and illuminating way, so, in a sense, can psychosis." —Oliver Sacks (Neurologist and Author)
- "Madness need not be all breakdown. It may also be breakthrough." —R.D. Laing
- "I wrote my book to argue that madness is not necessarily a curse and can sometimes be a blessing." —Joanne Greenberg (Author of *I Never Promised You a Rose Garden*)
- "Out of my madness came something beautiful." —Lori Schiller (Author of *The Quiet Room*)
- "When one person suffers from a delusion, it is called insanity. When many people suffer from a delusion, it is called a 'Reality.'" —Robert M. Pirsig (Author of *Zen and the Art of Motorcycle Maintenance*)

Now let's compare these to some quotes from Grof and his studies on spiritual emergence:

- "There exists increasing evidence that many individuals

experiencing episodes of non-ordinary states of consciousness accompanied by various emotional, perceptual, and psychosomatic manifestations are undergoing an evolutionary crisis rather than suffering from a mental disease."

- "Traditional psychiatry does not recognize the difference between mystical and psychotic experiences... There is no acknowledgement that any dramatic experiential states involving changes of consciousness could be potentially therapeutic and transformative."

- "Spiritual emergencies (transpersonal crises) can occur spontaneously without any precipitating factors or they can be triggered by emotional stress, physical exertion, disease, accident, intense sexual experience, childbirth, or exposure to psychedelic drugs."

- "The ability to see the condition as an inner psychological process and approach it in an internalized way; the capacity to form an adequate working relationship and maintain the spirit of cooperation."

- "Supportive evidence for the concept of spiritual emergency can be drawn from a variety of fields: history, anthropology, comparative religion, clinical psychiatry, modern consciousness research, psychedelic therapy, Jungian psychology, new experiential psychotherapies, and many others."

Here is a wonderful video from Stanislav Grof where he talks about spiritual emergences.
https://www.youtube.com/watch?v=AONdJK3k-nY&t=6s&ab_channel=StanislavBrigitteGrof

OTHER FAMOUS CASE STUDIES

Although there are countless examples of people who have gone through this process, here is a list of some well-known people who have gone through this process and come out the other side with an evolved version of themselves. Note that it is difficult to "diagnose" any of these as psychosis, schizophrenia, bipolar disorder, or any of these softly defined categories of mental situations.

- Vincent van Gogh: Perhaps the most famous example, the Dutch post-impressionist painter had episodes of mental illness, including severe depression and psychosis, and spent time in psychiatric hospitals.
- Robert Schumann: Schumann dealt with severe mental health issues, including what is believed to have been bipolar disorder or schizophrenia.
- Peter Tchaikovsky: The Russian composer struggled with depression and personal turmoil throughout his life, with historians often discussing his emotional intensity and periods of despair.
- Virginia Woolf: The famed British author struggled with severe mental health issues throughout her life, including what would likely be described today as bipolar disorder with psychotic features.
- Vivien Leigh: The *Gone with the Wind* actress suffered from bipolar disorder, experiencing extreme mood swings and psychotic episodes.
- Francisco Goya: The Spanish romantic painter, later in his life, suffered an illness that led to hallucinations and psychotic episodes, profoundly affecting his artwork.
- Edgar Allan Poe: The American writer known for his macabre and mysterious stories, Poe's erratic behavior and letters suggest he might have suffered from bipolar disorder and possibly had psychotic episodes.
- John Forbes Nash Jr.: A Nobel laureate in Economics, Nash's struggles with schizophrenia were well-documented,

including in the biographical film *A Beautiful Mind.*

- Friedrich Nietzsche: The German philosopher experienced mental health issues later in his life, with some historians speculating that he suffered from a form of psychosis.

One other interesting aspect to note from Grof's books to further drive this point home:

"We've discovered that those diagnosed in the United States and other "developed" nations are much less likely to recover than those in the poorest countries of the world; furthermore, those diagnosed with a psychotic disorder in the West today may fare even worse than those so diagnosed over a hundred years ago."

I think many who are familiar with how the pharmaceutical industrial complex[3] has become a standardized part of Western culture understand how people just take a pill for whatever ails them. Indeed, modern medicine is an amazing tool and vaccines and other treatments have saved hundreds of millions of lives. That cannot be denied. There are of course other modalities of healing that have been lost in the sands of time. In the West, we do tend to over-prescribe pills for anything that is wrong with us, and that extends to mental issues as well.

ROBERT MONROE'S THOUGHTS

In Monroe's amazing book, *Journeys out of the Body*, he talks about his incredible journeys beyond his own body. Initially a total skeptic like me, he began having all sorts of phenomena happen to him when he was lying down to sleep. He learned various methods of astral projection and detailed one incredible journey after the next. In the beginning of the book, he shares his thoughts on why he is sharing these stories.

"The primary purposes for the release and publication of the

---

[3] My name for it. Pretty good, hey?

material contained here are (1) that through dissemination as widely as possible, some other human being—perhaps just one—may be saved from the agony and terror of trial and error in an area where there have been no concrete answers; that he may have comfort in the knowledge that others have had the same experiences; that he will recognize in himself the phenomenon and thus avoid the trauma of psychotherapy, or at the worst, mental breakdown and commitment to a mental institution; and (2) that tomorrow or in the years to come, the formal, accepted sciences of our culture will expand their horizons, concepts, postulates, and research to open wide the avenues and doorways intimated herein to the great enrichment of man's knowledge and understanding of himself and his complete environment."

It's wonderful to hear that other people who have also experienced these things share my views on how to characterize these events. It's also nice to know that I am not alone in talking openly about these things, and I let others know they are indeed not crazy, while highlighting the failures of the current mental healthcare system.

11.
BREAKFAST TIME IN AN ALTERNATE REALITY

"The only real voyage of discovery consists not in seeking new landscapes, but in having new eyes."
—MARCEL PROUST

"My mother wanted us to understand that the tragedies of your life one day have the potential to be comic stories the next."
—NORA EPHRON

So, back to the story.

It's probably a good juncture to point out that the tale you're meandering through is a perspective shot solely from my lens. Up to this scribbling moment, not all my comrades have shared their take, which might diverge considerably from mine. Let's not forget, there were episodes where my memory decides to take a brief hiatus. But this isn't about painting a heroic self-portrait; it's simply how I recall the events unfolding. Given my friends haven't navigated the peculiar mental odyssey I found myself in, it's no small wonder their interpretations might differ. Despite this, my heart brims with appreciation and love for them, for anchoring themselves in their reality while attempting to shepherd me through mine.

After a night where sleep played hard to get, I hit this morning thought: "You know what, I'm gonna give Rene the best day of his life. He deserves it!"

Rene packs up his stuff because he can't sleep that great at Vadim's. That was wise. Part of me wishes I had done the same thing, but most of me is glad I stayed another night, for reasons that will become clear on the next day. I know Rene very well, and he likes to have his own space to rest and recharge. I get it. Hell, so do I. And Vadim's place is just too entropic and crazy for him. I have a higher tolerance for that, and I totally respect Rene's need for space and time to himself. I'm sad to see him go, but I'm also happy he is going to find his own space.

After we wake up, Rene shows me a birthmark on his leg. He says, "Have I ever shown you this?"

He hasn't. I know quite a bit about birthmarks. I believe they can be marks of a death that happened in a previous life. I recommend the documentary *Surviving Death* on Netflix. There are many case studies where young kids may be mumbling something and saying things about a previous life. For example, a kid with a birthmark may talk about a WWII regimen they were part of, their captain, and how they were killed. The parents and doctors take note of the names mentioned and other things mentioned, then go back in the history books to corroborate the evidence.

As an aside, and I don't know if this is pertinent or not, but it is something very unusual about me. I was born with a birthmark on my right cheek. It was a small black "Z". It was no bigger than a pupil, and blacker than black. We're talking vantablack. I don't remember if the Z was inverted or not. My mom had it removed by a plastic surgeon when I was like four or five because I suppose it was a bit unsightly for polite society or something. It also happens to be on the same side of my face where my eye went a hundred percent black-blind last year. Again, I don't know if there is anything about this that is important to the story, but I make note of these things even if they are just coincidences.

That morning's wake-up was a scene straight out of a less heroic version of *Mission Impossible*. I was on the brink of a bladder-induced crisis, necessitating a perilous descent down Vadim's daunting staircase to face the dubious sanctuary of his dysfunctional loo. The journey to Vadim's bathroom felt like an obstacle course designed by someone who hates people. The operation required me to navigate over a slumbering Rene with the stealth of a ninja in fluffy slippers, aiming not to disturb his repose. Despite my best efforts at espionage, Rene emerged from his slumber with a startle, mistaking my cautious crawl for a potential leap of faith from our elevated bunk.

He said somewhat angrily, "I thought you were going to jump off the bed again!" This is so strange because I can't remember Rene ever getting angry.

His comment lodged itself in my mind, bizarre and unfounded. The notion of me, willingly launching from a height of eight feet, was as likely as a cat volunteering for a bath. My approach to life, much like my approach to descending precarious bunk bed ladders, is more "slow and steady," than "daredevil diver," especially given my unique perspective, thanks to my no-depth-perception 2D view of a 3D world.

Determined to offset the morning's awkward start, I resolved to treat Rene to a breakfast of epic proportions, sensing his discomfort and discerning an underlying friction between us. Why he seemed nettled with me remained a mystery, yet my resolve to orchestrate a day of unparalleled delight for him was undimmed. The guilt gnawed at me, his apparent displeasure casting me in the role of a villain in my own narrative. Yet, I knew Rene to be the last person to wield guilt like a weapon. Thus, I found myself torn by the paradox of feeling both culpable and confused.

As we leave Vadim's lair, I have an amazing sense of déjà vu. This is nothing next to the déjà vu times one thousand that will happen the next day, but I feel like I've been through this many times and Rene and I are finally getting out. I think what I felt was a great relief that Rene is safely leaving Vadim's place forever. Perhaps that was my most important side-mission: to make sure Rene was safe and got out of Vadim's place before things got ugly.

BREAK A LEG

As we descend the stairs from Vadim's doorway, my movements become unusually deliberate. With each step, I find myself emitting sounds that echo a memory I'm certain was imparted by my youngest daughter, though she claims no recollection of it. Mimicking the movements and sounds of robot legs and feet hitting the ground, I intone "Ka-Chunk! Ka-Chunk!" softly, yet distinctly, synchronizing each sound with my cautious steps. It's an odd ritual, but it feels necessary, as if transforming the staircase descent into a measured, almost ceremonial procession.

Approaching the final two steps, my actions take on an exaggerated quality. I extend my legs fully, with a dramatic flair, before decisively planting them on the ground. This peculiar choreography, a blend of vocalization and exaggerated movement, seems born out of a subconscious strategy to navigate these stairs without mishap, as if past accidents on this very spot have ingrained in me a need for such cautionary theatrics.

I want to make it clear that during these experiences, I was completely sober—no drugs, no alcohol involved. This is the last time I will mention this, as it's not a contributing factor to the events in the rest of the book that unfold hereafter.

Now, prepare for a turn towards the truly extraordinary.

As we approached the exit of Vadim's place, Rene led the way, his pace quickening with impatience. He reached the front door, poised to step back onto the Brooklyn streets, casting a glance back that seemed to urge, "Hurry up, Trey."

Then, descending the last few steps, a peculiar memory flashed through my mind—a memory that felt as though it belonged to another lifetime. It was an echo of pain, of a broken leg, though in my current state, I was perfectly healthy and strong. Yet, on the third step from the bottom, I suddenly feigned instability and got fake-wobbly, calling out to Rene in a mock alarm, "Oh no! Rene, I'm going to break my leg!"

On purpose, I literally fall backwards off the third step. I would have definitely hurt myself or cracked the back of my head on the concrete floor in whiplash-impact. But I have no fear. None. I'm like a kid jumping into a pool with those floaty arm bands, knowing I won't sink.

Rene was by my side in an instant, his arms preventing my fall. The sensation that followed was indescribable—it was as if I had undergone a spiritual rebirth, akin to the transformative emergence depicted in baptismal scenes from films. I erupted into laughter, overwhelmed by a sense of renewal and gratitude for Rene's presence. It felt as though we were locked in an eternal cycle of saving each other across lifetimes, each cycle drawing us closer and easing our journey together. In that moment, everything clicked into place—the sense of unity, the dance of yin and yang, and a shared destiny that stretched beyond the confines of time.

The incident evoked a memory from about a month prior, during our stay in Queenstown at my place. One day Rene sought a hug, and we embraced for a prolonged moment. After we parted, I noticed his eyes—wide with astonishment. We retreated to the cinema room, where he inquired about my feelings during the embrace. To me, it had been a warm and affectionate hug, much like others we had shared. Yet, Rene described it as the most ecstatic experience of his life, leaving him confused by my more tempered reaction. Reflecting on it, perhaps the intensity of feeling he experienced mirrored what I felt when he caught me during my fall.

This led me to muse on the possibility that the birthmark on Rene's leg might be a vestige from a past life, a life where he suffered a broken leg on those very stairs, and I was there to save him, as he did for me in this lifetime. It sparked an overwhelming sensation, a conviction that this cycle of mutual salvation had reached its culmination, that we had spent lifetimes intertwined in this dance of support and salvation.

Rene, however, remained detached from these musings. His patience had worn thin, and with a hint of exasperation, he admonished me to be more cautious, his words tinged with a motherly scold that suggested a hierarchy between us—he, the vigilant guardian, and I, the heedless charge. Despite his frustration, my heart swelled with love for him. Unseen by him was the vast expanse of our karmic journey, the wheel of life that spun us together through ages. *You may not grasp the magnitude of our connection,* I thought, *but my devotion is unwavering. I am, and always will be, your sentinel, ready to safeguard you through a hundred lifetimes, perhaps having already done so.*

So we make it outside and Rene is trying to find a place to have breakfast for us on his phone. And then.

THE PIGEON

I see this pigeon by a tree by the church and, I kid you not… I become one with the pigeon. I enter the mind of the pigeon and I start making all the bird sounds and movements and we enter one another in some kind of combined consciousness. It's so weird and yet feels so natural. I'm thinking, *omg, I am one with that bird. We are sharing a mind.* And I totally understood the essence of the bird because the bird and I were the same. I know that sounds crazy, but I felt it. I'm not making this shit up for a good yarn. I felt it.

This extraordinary symbiosis, however, was as fleeting as it was profound, lasting but a brief thirty seconds. Yet, within that thirty seconds (which is half a day in pigeon-time, btw), I gleaned the very essence of pigeonhood whilst cooing in what I presumed to be Pigeonese, an enlightenment I hadn't sought but found immensely enlightening.

Intrigued by this avian adventure, I have since shared the tale with my mother, who, with a nod to her own encounters with schizophrenia, mentioned she too had experienced such mental holidays into the minds of birds. While not exactly a chapter from a scientific textbook, the coincidence—or perhaps, hereditary predisposition to bird-mind melding—added another layer of intrigue to the episode.

Rene's reaction was unexpected. He glanced at me and quipped, "Everyone's got a Vadim story." This familiar saying struck me anew, sparking laughter and a fleeting moment of clarity, though it quickly faded in a haze of forgetfulness, as if the memory slipped into another dimension, eluding my grasp just as quickly as it had arrived.

Our morning took another turn when an Uber ferried us first to a closed restaurant, then to another where we finally settled for breakfast. Rene was unusually silent throughout the meal, choosing a table next to mine rather than sitting across. His demeanor suggested a mix of disappointment and distance, which pained me. Despite understanding Rene's need for solitude and his discomfort with the urban sprawl of Brooklyn—so at odds with our shared preference for nature—I couldn't help but feel stung by his apparent disapproval.

I recognized that, much like myself, Rene yearned for the tranquility of natural settings. His silence spoke volumes about his current state—perhaps a need for rest, for a space of his own. Meanwhile, I found myself surprisingly alert, my mind racing with thoughts and revelations from our recent experiences.

We found ourselves in a quaint cafe, a moment that sparked a newfound awareness in me—Brooklyn's color palette was transforming before my eyes. I began to perceive the world in two distinct color schemes: one a vibrant mix of orange and teal, symbolizing a wave of change and renewal, and the other in stark black and white, representing a more traditional, binary viewpoint. Brooklyn seemed alive, evolving with every passing moment, mirrored by the emergence of colorful storefronts and businesses. These spaces were brimming with energy and optimism, much like the cafe we were in, marked by their inviting signage, thoughtful design, and mission-driven ethos.

Watching patrons, I noticed a clear dichotomy. Individuals dressed in black and white often exuded a binary mentality, their rigid perspectives echoing the enforcement of societal norms. Despite my heightened sensitivity during this period of emergence, I felt no fear or paranoia, just a keen observation of my surroundings. Reflecting on this phase from a place of recovery, I draw parallels to my mother's struggles with schizophrenia, though my experiences lacked the extreme paranoia she endured. Instead, I cataloged my observations, curious about the patterns unfolding around me.

Among the crowd, another group caught my attention: young men in their late twenties, uniform in appearance with dark hair and similar beards, as if cast from the same mold. To me, they appeared as either clones or perhaps the next iteration of humanity, enhanced by unseen technologies, their demeanor stoic, and interactions mechanical.

During my time in the cafe, I made a small but meaningful decision to purchase a non-plastic water bottle. This artsy Brooklyn shop offered a selection of crafts and eco-friendly products, among them a beautiful teal water bottle that caught my eye. Embracing this choice felt like a personal commitment to the environment—a small act of conservation in a city undergoing its own set of changes.

I was compelled to ask Rene about his earlier comment, one that my mind couldn't completely grasp as I navigated the melding of timelines and parallel universes into my own consciousness. He recalled saying, "Everyone has a Vadim story," yet he didn't remember it with any particular fondness or humor. For me, however, those words lingered, imbued with unintended beauty—a testament to Rene's capacity to articulate his observations unwittingly.

I found myself ruminating on that phrase, "Everyone has a Vadim story." It echoed within me, suggesting a multitude of encounters tied to Vadim, each unique yet interconnected by his ability to be at the epicenter of remarkable narratives. Not all tales were pleasant, but Vadim undeniably played a pivotal role in many. My own story with him was nothing short of extraordinary, perhaps even contributing to the myriad of stories that would continue to circulate.

In our discussions, Rene expressed a desire to find solace closer to nature, contemplating another hotel near Central Park. I empathized with his longing but felt an inexplicable pull towards spending another night at Vadim's. This decision wasn't driven by a desire for further indulgence in nightlife or substance; rather, it was a deep, unexplained calling. Despite the discordant energy at Vadim's and my lack of connection with him, something within urged me to return, if just for one more night.

RENE DRIFTS AWAY

When it came time for Rene to depart, our goodbye was marked by a hug, his demeanor shadowed by distance and a palpable sense of resentment. It seemed as though he perceived my actions as intentional, placing a strain on our friendship. The dissonance of living in separate realities, mine vastly different from his, cast a somber tone over our parting. The thought of being seen as a disappointment by one's closest ally is disheartening. With a heavy heart, I let him go, recognizing his need for space. My intention to provide Rene with an "ultimate day" might have fallen short in execution, yet it underscored the complexity of intentions versus perceptions.

Oakley dokaly, I'm on my own again. Now what. I'm just gonna listen to the universe.

At the cafe, there are these two, nice, Black ladies sitting by me. These moms are having a post-yoga snack. They seem to like chatting with me. I'm quite friendly. They invited me to come to a school in Brooklyn where they are doing some kind of basketball event. I'm like, sure, why not?

So we start walking through Brooklyn and we're talking about life and stuff. It's a nice walk and a nice day and a nice chat. I had a wonderful morning. I was super-engaged with people, being present, kind, loving, and interested. I wanted to understand the heartbeat of Brooklyn and learn from people. It was incredible.

THE IBIZA CREW ARRIVES

I go back to Vadim's to try to get some rest. To my mild surprise, the source of the commotion was a cadre of females freshly descended from Ibiza, their eyes appraising my man-torso as though I were the last piece of avocado in a millennial brunch spot. Vadim, ever the stickler for decorum, chastised my bare-chested appearance with the fervor of a choir master discovering a rap artist in his ensemble. My retort, "I'm merely on a pilgrimage to the lavatory, not parading for sainthood," seemed to cool the air momentarily.

Dressed more appropriately for social engagement, I found myself amidst the newly arrived entourage, where I learned of an impending soirée within Vadim's walls. The sensation of déjà vu enveloped me like a well-worn blanket, suggesting that my presence here was not mere happenstance but a task yet to be unveiled.

For the sake of clarity—and to maintain the integrity of this narrative—it's worth mentioning that despite the evident flirtations cast my way by these Ibiza émigrées, my reciprocation was of the non-romantic variety. My interactions were governed by a platonic camaraderie, a curious state of affairs given my typical disposition. Indeed, my libido had taken a sabbatical, rendering me impervious to the advances of these brochure-worthy beauties. One, in particular, found my charm so irresistible that she proposed a rendezvous at Burning Man, a testament, perhaps, to my inadvertent allure. I'm so charming I can barely stand it.

I'm ramping up to my full spiritual emergence (just wait) and I'm feeling amazing. I'm self-aware enough at this point to know I am in a state of mania, and I am loving it. But this was more than mania, and I felt it. I didn't know what was happening, but I felt this was new. Very new. I've encountered "regular" mania many times in my life, and they are often the most productive, creative, and insightful times of my life where perhaps I take thousands of photos, edit them, then go hike countless kilometers in wild locations to capture even more. I dance with my moods and emotions and recognize them and surf with them rather than fight them. These are natural waves and all natural waves are gifts from the universe.

This whirlwind of experiences, I'm convinced, was the aftermath of my time in Scotland—an unraveling and then a reassembling of my consciousness, leading to an elevated state of being. The world seemed ablaze with new significance. My perceptions were heightened, each conversation deeply engaging, my empathy expanded. I had never felt more vitally alive. That evening at Vadim's, I was on the brink of uncovering a mission, the nature of which was still unknown to me, yet I harbored a serene confidence in its eventual revelation.

12.
TALES FROM
THE CONVERTED CHURCH

"To define is to limit."
—OSCAR WILDE

"Just when I discovered the meaning of life, they changed it."
—GEORGE CARLIN

On the day destined for festivities, Rene made a pilgrimage back to Vadim's eclectic sanctuary to retrieve his worldly possessions. It was during this venture that we stumbled upon a character whose dedication to the ancient art of chauvinism was so bold, it could only be rivaled by his own reflection in the mirror.

For narrative's sake, let's refer to him as Flavio, despite his having a pronounced New York accent—a choice that might seem incongruent, but somehow fits. Flavio, a gentleman in the loosest sense of the word, appeared to be in the throes of mid-life, his hair a testament to a bottle of dye's promise of eternal youth, slicked back as if in perpetual preparation for an Ibiza dance-off. He wasn't romantically involved with any of the women from earlier, though he arrived with them. I overheard him on a call with his girlfriend, speaking in ways that epitomized toxic masculinity—his words were demeaning and humiliating, a stark contrast to any respectful dialogue one would expect in a healthy relationship.

Despite Flavio's unsavory demeanor, our interaction was oddly engaging. He possessed a dubious charm and he tried to find some common ground with me. He was the self-appointed ambassador of the "alpha male" stereotype, regaling me with tales of his romantic escapades and assorted life triumphs in a manner that oscillated between horrifyingly fascinating and simply horrifying. At one point, we exchanged words that left me grappling with the stark reality of his worldview. While I might not recall every detail perfectly, the essence of our conversation highlighted the substantial disconnect between his values and my own. The more I talked to him, the more disheartened I became. It's like when you find out the ice cream truck only plays music when it's out of ice cream—deeply disappointing.

Here's an example of one of our exchanges. Apologies if I get a few quotes wrong.

Flavio: "Hey Trey, what do you do?"

You see, I've always found this query a bit pedestrian, as it suggests one's essence is somehow tethered to their occupational pursuits—a notion as absurd as expecting a teapot to discuss quantum physics.

It doesn't matter what you "do;" you can simply "Be." After all, that is why we are called Human Beings and not Human Doings.

Me: "Oh, I'm an artist and I live in New Zealand."

Now, Flavio knew I was a photographer because Vadim had already talked me up. Vadim being Vadim, to impress one friend by having another impressive friend. You get it.

Flavio: "No. Trey. You say, 'I am a photographer!' That is a proud and amazing thing!"

Me: "Errr, okay."

Flavio, not one to miss an opportunity for self-promotion, then embarked on an autobiographical LinkedIn, "When people ask me, I list off all the things I am. I say I am Fashion Designer, I am a Publisher, I am Writer, I own Real Estate, I have a Fashion Brand." You get it. He goes on and on. And ends with, "You don't just have to be one thing, man!"

Okay, so you get it. You get this guy. He's a real piece of work. I think it is a funny personality trait when people "pump you up" as a prelude for talking about themselves.

TIME FOR CONFRONTATION

Encountering such a personality sparked an unusual response within me. By nature, I am conciliatory, averse to confrontation, more of a peacemaker than a challenger. My life philosophy leans towards harmony and understanding, often at the expense of my own boundaries. I felt an uncharacteristic resolve to address the discordant notes in Flavio's conduct.

Approaching him, I ventured into unfamiliar territory, guided by a sense of justice rather than appeasement. "Listen," I began, my voice steady with newfound conviction, "I overheard your conversation with your girlfriend. The lack of kindness, the absence of love in your words was palpable. Your ego overshadows the nurturing energy she deserves from you."

His reaction was sheer astonishment, as if such a perspective were alien to him. Remarkably, he conceded, his defensive posture melting away under the weight of my words. He retreated to the couch, a figure of introspection rather than defiance.

In that moment, I discovered an empowering truth: the ability to articulate my observations directly to people without fear, to stand firmly in my integrity. For years and years I've always spoken boldly online about art and my approach. It's often been controversial and I have had to have a thick skin to absorb all the negativity, but I rarely have one-on-one conflict. Flavio, for all his bravado, posed no threat to this newfound strength. He was just a catalyst for my realization that I could confront the disharmony and ego-driven chaos with serene confidence. Observing his contemplative silence, I acknowledged our exchange with a nod, a silent testament to the transformative power of speaking one's truth.

As the narrative unfolds, Rene arrives to collect his belongings, bringing us together on the couch, my gaze intermittently crossing the photo of Hunter S. Thompson. In those moments, I felt as though Hunter himself had orchestrated this surreal tableau—a vibrant mosaic of characters and chaos, a whirlwind of personalities and pandemonium, all seemingly arranged for me to decipher and navigate.

Flavio, still holding court on the opposite side, lapses back into his role of the alpha raconteur, unfurling tales of lascivious adventures and capitalistic triumphs with the subtlety of a sledgehammer. Despite my earlier attempt at setting his moral compass to a more humble north, he remains blissfully unchanged, his grandiose self-importance scraping against Rene's patience. And yet, here I am, bizarrely captivated, itching for another crack at tilting Flavio's universe back on its axis.

Rene, perhaps overwhelmed by the display of egotism, abruptly jumps up and exits the scene, a response not uncommon for him; I have seen him do it many times. It's his signature exit strategy. Perhaps the energy is too intense, so he removes himself as a protective measure. Or he's just annoyed; I'm not sure. I remain, observing the unfolding spectacle with a sense of detached fascination, employing a mindfulness reminiscent of Michael Singer's teachings. The world before me feels like an elaborate performance, each moment a lesson in the human condition.

Amid this contemplation, I uncovered a peculiar trait in Flavio's demeanor—a discreet belch or cough that seemed to herald his more controversial or spiteful comments. This observation birthed a hypothesis: could these bodily signals be nature's way of alerting us to a discord between our utterances and our true essence? It painted a compelling picture of the body's inherent sagacity battling the ego's dominion over our speech, suggesting a deeper conflict for supremacy.

I begin to link Flavio's persona with the memory of my father. Could there be a connection, a symbolic representation within this interaction? While uncertain, it paves the way for deeper exploration into the themes of paternal relationships, which I plan to delve into further in the latter half of the book, particularly in a section candidly titled, "Fuck you dad!" set for discussion on January 29, 2024, in Book Two. Remember to check the beginning of the book and join our community to get a free copy of that book.

Despite the tumultuous encounters of the day, my thoughts often drift to my father—a man who, in my recollections, embodied kindness, joy, and love. The stark contrast between his memory and the discordant presence of Flavio prompts me to ponder deeper questions. Why does Flavio intrude upon my consciousness, both during the day and as the evening unfolds? His anticipated presence at the party raises further dilemmas about my role in his life. Is there a deeper purpose to our crossing paths, a call for me to extend help?

This contemplation spirals into a broader reflection, touching upon what could be perceived as a burgeoning Messianic complex. The notion that I might be some sort of savior, dispatched to Brooklyn to guide others away from their self-destructive orbits, flits through my mind. Such thoughts, fueled by the provocative imagery of Hunter S. Thompson and the swirling red spiral, weave a complicated set of speculations and self-questioning.

13.
ECHOES OF GONZO

"Life has become immeasurably better since I have been forced to stop taking it seriously."
    —HUNTER S. THOMPSON

"Lesson learned from the show 'Lost': If you're stuck on an island, and you have a hatch that doesn't open, don't stop trying. And have a lot of confusing backstories. And also, be hot."
    —TINA FEY

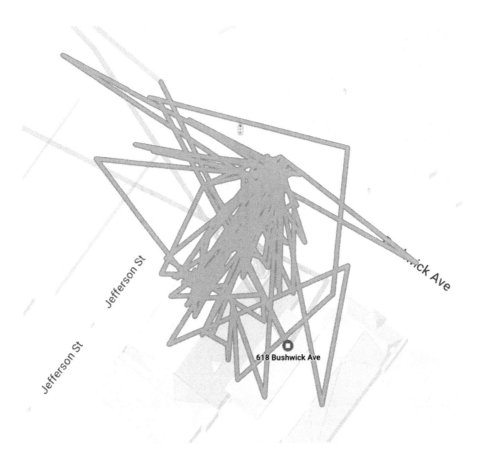

Embarking on an objective of salvation, I found that in attempting to save others, I was, in essence, saving myself.

The party at Vadim's promised to be an event of considerable magnitude, drawing in a diverse crowd eager to partake in the night's revelry. Yet, my mind retraces steps to an earlier moment of awakening, nestled among the eclectic comforts of Vadim's upper floor—its bunk beds, couches, and the ambient glow of stained glass.

In the quiet of the morning, lost in an audiobook, I encountered *The Dice Man*, a narrative that would influence my spiritual emergence. The book delves into the life of a 1950s psychologist disillusioned with traditional therapy. Embracing chance as a catalyst for action, he lets the roll of a dice determine his decisions, each option penned with the potential for risk or revelation. His interactions with a spectrum of humanity, from the criminal to the conflicted, seep into my subconscious, mingling with my own tumultuous journey. Listening to such tales in the middle of my own spiritual unfolding, I couldn't help but question the timing and impact of this choice—was it serendipity or misstep, guiding or misleading me through my own emergence?

Awakening from a troubled sleep, I was seized by an overwhelming premonition. My life was teetering on the brink of its conclusion, with perhaps just sixty seconds remaining. Driven by a desperate hope to prolong my existence, I believed that each moment I remained conscious was a chance to safeguard the well-being of my loved ones. The burden felt monumental, as if the fate of the world rested on my shoulders.

The ongoing narration of the audiobook, now at chapter 88, intertwined with my frantic thoughts, offering a cryptic assurance: my life could extend to the age of 88, but only if I could unravel the enigmas surrounding me. The room, with its mundane and chaotic elements, suddenly appeared as a puzzle to be solved for survival.

THE DHARMA INITIATIVE

The DJ turntable's digital display, flashing red numbers, a timer evoking the eerie urgency of the Dharma Initiative's countdown clock from *Lost*. Its purpose and message remained just beyond my grasp, intensifying the room's mystery.

Compelled to action, I moved from the bed to the floor, driven by the conviction that my actions now could lay the groundwork for future salvation—either for myself in another iteration or for someone else entangled in Vadim's labyrinth. The assortment of plugs, chargers, and cables, ranging from antique lamps to contemporary USB connections, represented a chaotic web of energy and potential. This disarray became a focus of my frantic efforts; I began reorganizing the space, disconnecting and rearranging objects in a bid to impose order on the chaos, to somehow "prepare" for an escape that felt both necessary and imminent.

Caught in the grip of an icy panic, the notion of imminent death transformed each action into a race against time. My efforts to organize the room were driven by an acute awareness of the preciousness of time and the urgent need to leave behind a sanctuary rather than a trap for whoever might next face this existential trial.

Convinced of my imminent demise, yet devoid of any suicidal inclination, I found myself in a state of heightened awareness, determined to cling to life with every fiber of my being. The notion that my time was quantified in breaths led me to embrace a Zen-like state of conservation, each inhalation and exhalation becoming a deliberate act of preservation. In a gesture of supplication and reverence holding my hands in prayer over my nose and covering my third eye, I adopted a posture of meditation, seeking divine intervention in my most vulnerable state.

The loft transformed into a stage for this existential drama, with me as its solitary actor, enveloped in a cacophony of police and fire truck sirens coming my way that seemed to herald my end. The world outside mirrored the chaos within, evoking the cataclysmic unraveling of a dream in *Inception*, where the very fabric of reality teeters on the brink of collapse. I feel the building shaking. It was a scenario as terrifying as it was surreal.

Emerging from this ordeal, I felt as though I had crossed a threshold into new existence. Against all odds, I had survived beyond the point I believed was my end. Descending to the lounge, I found solace in the silent company of Hunter S. Thompson's portrait, and it was there that I initiated a dialogue with the divine.

Yeah, so, that was my morning. Fun.

I begin talking with God. The Source or whatever you may call it. I like the Source because it doesn't get caught up in all that fear-based religious dogma. I'm getting signals and I figure out that I am not just going to save myself, but I have a chance to help all my friends and loved ones and bring them into a better existence.

Perhaps a new Earth. I have the chance to remove all their suffering on this old Earth and take them with me to the next level of life. As I am talking to the Source, I notice my body automatically doing things beyond my control.

Throwing my arms in the air like a victorious decathlete, I feel my two fists fall softly on my skull. Left side then right side. This happens whenever I have a new realization about the nature of life and what is going on. Sometimes, both hands fall on my left and right brain at the same time, and that is an indication that I have a full understanding of both sides of my mind. There is a beautiful understanding of the duality of life and everything makes so much sense.

I reveled in the connections being forged between my consciousness and my physical form, a discovery that filled me with an indescribable sense of purpose and wonder. It was as if I was learning to communicate with my body in a profoundly new way, embracing the temporary stewardship of my soul over this Earthly vessel.

14.
THE FINAL PARTY AT VADIM'S

"Life can only be understood backwards; but it must be lived forwards."
—SØREN KIERKEGAARD

"You live and learn. At any rate, you live."
—DOUGLAS ADAMS

As evening descended and the party began to swell with guests, Vadim's irritation was palpable. The modifications I had made to the loft—unplugging various items in a bid to impose some order—had not gone unnoticed. Vadim's frustration erupted in a stern rebuke, delivered with an intensity that bore the unmistakable mark of his Russian heritage. Faced with his displeasure, my response was one of apologetic confusion. In truth, what more could I offer by way of explanation? Seeking refuge from the confrontation, I retreated to the lounge downstairs, where the silent gaze of Hunter S. Thompson offered a semblance of solace as the first wave of partygoers began to filter in.

This was a wild night. Let me tell you.

The night promised to be one of unbridled energy and potential chaos. I found purpose in assuming the role of the evening's guardian of sobriety and safety. My self-appointed duties included ferrying water to the loft, ensuring that hydration was within everyone's reach, and overseeing the safe navigation of the stairs by all attendees.

Navigating the stairway required a flight and a half's ascent, a journey made slightly more magical by the delicate fairy lights that dotted the path. The presence of a handrail offered essential support, but it was the discovery of a second handrail that caught my attention—a curious addition that mirrored my own concerns for safety. It seemed as though I wasn't alone in my considerations, as this thoughtful installation suggested a shared intention to protect and guide the revelers through the night's festivities.

The staircase at Vadim's, a seemingly mundane structure, holds a narrative so rich and complex it could fill the pages of a novel. My encounters with these stairs, both real and envisioned during ketamine-induced journeys, even while in New Zealand, felt like premonitions, a foretelling of events yet to unfold. The vividness with which I recalled the walls, the turns, and the handrails—before having physically encountered them—suggested a connection that spanned across the boundaries of time and reality.

Each ascent or descent became an overture to dread, a prelude to what felt like an inevitable descent into darkness. The terror I associated with these stairs was not just an echo of fear; it was an amalgamation of every horror imaginable, a visceral dread that seemed to consume me. My mind was haunted by visions of repeated demise, a ghostly Groundhog Day, a cycle of deaths that played out with relentless ferocity, culminating in a macabre tableau of bodies and screams—a nightmarish loop that seemed inescapable. It's as if the universe decided to play the scariest movie trailer but forgot to mention it's actually my life.

The soirée, a melting pot of personalities against the backdrop of Vadim's earlier volcanic display, became the stage for my inner turmoil. Amid the cacophony of celebration, my role as the night's sentinel, tasked with safeguarding the flock and dispensing hydration, morphed into a quest for redemption and enlightenment. Each pilgrimage along the fairy-lit path, every encounter, was laden with the weight of destiny, a chance to rewrite the script, to mend the fabric of the cosmos one step at a time.

This eerie sensation of living through countless deaths, each one imprinted with the agony of its predecessor, suggested a dark connection with the staircase—a belief that I had not only died there multiple times but had somehow embodied the essence of each soul that met their end in that very spot. The constant cameo of Vadim at the doorway served as a grim punctuation to these haunting reveries in an endless movie loop in my mind I thought would never end. I've been here before.

My later engagement with the series *Loki* (portrayed by Tom Hiddleston) revealed striking parallels to my own experiences. The concept of alternate timelines and the existence of multiple versions of a single entity make intuitive sense to me, especially in the scene where Mobius (played by Owen Wilson) subjects Loki to a cyclic torment involving a past misdeed and its painful repercussions. Loki is thrown into a scene he remembers with an old lover. While she was asleep, he chopped off part of her hair as a joke. Well, she didn't think it was funny. She attacks him, punches him, tells him he'll never find anyone to love him, and this sort of thing. But then it happens again and again, and he keeps getting assaulted and kneed in the balls. He tries different tactics to talk her out of it. None of it works until Loki finally gets it right in the end.

Loki's repeated attempts to alter the outcome, to find a way to break the cycle of suffering, mirrored my own struggles with the staircase and the dark visions that accompanied it. The notion that only through understanding and change can one escape the loop provided a poignant reflection on the nature of fate, choice, and redemption.

So, this was my chance. This was my night to make everything right again. I was gonna figure this out. Once and for all. I was gonna save everyone at this party. Or, at least try my very best.

In this context, the party at Vadim's, with its myriad characters and unfolding dramas, ceased to be just a social gathering. It became a microcosm of life's larger challenges and mysteries—a canvas upon which I could project my fears, hopes, and the endless possibilities of transformation. The realization that I had the power to influence the narrative, to contribute to the healing and elevation of those around me, imbued my actions with new meaning. It was a revelation that transcended the immediate confines of time and space, pointing towards a journey of continual awakening and renewal.

I'm coming down the stairs as partygoers are starting to arrive. I'm happy and cheerful. One guy looked at me and was quite nice and said, "You know what? You look like a budget Ryan Gosling!"

I guess that was a compliment. I don't think I look remotely like Ryan Gosling, but he's a good lookin' guy. I have recently been impressed at his comedic range in the *Barbie* movie, but that is neither here nor there. Or is it? I get into a celebrity doppelganger mode over and over again throughout my spiritual emergence.

And that switches something on for me.

This newfound perspective allowed me to perceive those around me in a different light, as if the veils between past, present, and future lives were momentarily lifted. The revelations were startling in their clarity and depth, offering glimpses into the essence of each individual's journey through time. This shift in perception was not just enlightening; it was transformative, imbuing each interaction with a sense of wonder and discovery.

SAM HARRIS THE PART-TIME DJ AND BUDGET TROY AIKMAN

One of the DJs arrives. He's going up the stairs and, I am not kidding you, he looks just like Sam Harris. I'm thinking, *OH MY GOD! There is another version of Sam Harris that is a DJ that goes to play low-rent gigs in Brooklyn!*

So I share the same "compliment" I received earlier. I say, "Wow, you are like a budget Sam Harris!" He kind of scowls at me and keeps going up the stairs. I feel as though I hurt Sam Harris' feelings... I had never heard anyone call anyone a "budget" version of anything. I thought maybe that was a cool New York way of giving a compliment or something. I didn't know. I was just trying to be cool at a party. Perhaps I had inadvertently traversed the realms of interdimensional faux pas.

There is Budget Sam Harris, Philosopher and Part-Time DJ, down there. I wish I had a better photo. I took it from the top bunk.

But I'm telling you. This guy looked exactly like Sam Harris. Like. Exactly. He was a little older maybe and a little more coked up, but, yeah. That's him, a coked-up Sam Harris that was a DJ. I was transfixed.

This experience, both humorous and humbling, underscored the unpredictable nature of social interactions when filtered through the lens of my ongoing spiritual awakening. It reminded me that the journey I was on was not just about transcending the boundaries of time and space but also navigating the complexities of human connection with empathy, curiosity, and, when necessary, a healthy dose of self-reflection.

This whole night's turning into a series of unexpected team-ups and reminders that, even when you're trying to reach enlightenment, you've still gotta remember how to make friends and not weird them out. It's all part of the adventure, I guess.

The upstairs starts to fill up a lot. There are people all over the bunk beds and couches and people are dancing and it's getting loose. I start taking water up there and I recruit another helper to make sure we get lots of water up there. I call him Adam Sandler, the Waterboy. He looked nothing like Adam Sandler, but I was just having fun. I need help because these cats on the top floor are drinking a lot. I can't do this whole mission on my own! I need to go to Tristram and find a hireling!

I'm having a good time and chatting up people the whole time. So many people are trying to get upstairs, and there just isn't enough room, so I start to encourage people to stay down on the lounge level. It's as if I'm trying to play Tetris with people, convincing them the lower level is the new VIP section. And then. Troy Aikman walks in.

Okay, it's not the actual Troy Aikman, but, my god, it looks 100% like a twenty-five-year-old version of him. I'm not kidding. The spitting image. There he is, the most famous Dallas Cowboys quarterback since Roger Staubach. And he's staring at me in the eyes.

This Troy clone hits me with, "I know you. We know one another." I feel we're both trying to tune into a radio station that's just out of range. He's totally alert and sober as a judge, as am I, and we are staring at one another.

Our mutual recognition transcended ordinary acquaintance. It was a puzzling experience, one that neither of us could definitively trace to a time, place, or circumstance. This mystery persisted, a lingering question mark over a seemingly predestined meeting. I've seen this guy at this very party a hundred times in my head. But why? How? It's not like we're picking out curtains or anything—it's not that vibe at all. But could Troy Aikman have a secret doppelgänger life? In this scenario, who wouldn't?

I should note there is no "gay vibe" kinda happening or anything, nor am I saying Troy Aikman has a secret gay lifestyle. But who honestly really knows anyway?

Troy and I are just staring at one another trying to figure out why we know one another. What is our history? What the fuck is going on? I feel our souls know one another from a previous mission to Earth.

It turns out he is a graphic designer and he shows me some of his campaigns around New York. As he showcased his work, a vibrant teal and orange palette leapt from the screen, evoking the meticulous and whimsical aesthetic of Wes Anderson. This serendipitous alignment with my recent foray into critiquing graphic design—where I oscillated between jest and admiration on social media—captured my full attention. His projects, radiating with an imaginative flair, struck me as visually compelling and as potential catalysts for an upgrade within Brooklyn. I envisioned his design sensibility as a force capable of redefining the borough into a more aesthetically harmonious and inclusive space, celebrating diversity in every facet.

And now it gets weird. Not like it wasn't already weird.

I decide to revive this unusual compliment and I say with a smile "You look like a budget Troy Aikman!"

This guy had no idea who Troy Aikman was which I found to be incredible. He's one of the most famous quarterbacks in history, and even if this guy wasn't a football fan, most guys know Troy Aikman. But he had no clue what I was talking about. And so he got on his phone and started to search for Troy Aikman. And he came back and showed me a photo on his phone of "Troy Aikman" who was this overweight black sports commentator on Fox Sports. What!?!?

I don't know what to make of that, other than I was experiencing a very different reality. He was a little insulted, saying I thought he looked like an overweight black dude that did commentary on Fox Sports. I was so confused, I didn't know what to say.

I looked to my left. There was a guy in a hat who I thought was another incarnation of Lex Fridman. He nodded his head in a negative way as if I should not have said that. I nodded and knew he was right. I was used to saying very awkward things at parties and in life in general. But I'm good at brushing it off because I know in my heart I didn't have any bad intentions.

This misunderstanding, underscored by his perception of being compared to someone he didn't identify with, introduced a dissonance into our interaction. I found myself at a loss, navigating the murky waters of a reality that seemed to shift beneath our feet. His reaction, marked by a mix of offense and bewilderment, served as a poignant reminder of the subjective nature of perception and the unpredictable dynamics of human connection. This episode, a curious blend of identity, misinterpretation, and the search for common ground, highlighted the complexities of engaging with new acquaintances in a world where shared realities are not always a given.

Recalling an earlier ketamine trip, I had another thought. A dark thought. It involves racism and past lives.

I had a ketamine trip where another voice spoke through me once. It's important to note that I'm not racist at all. And as I am a travel photographer, I do my best to make sure to note we are all just human beings on this planet, and, hey man, let's all just get along. I'm not some kind of a "race crusader" or anything, but I never make any racist sayings. Sometimes I'll make jokes in the *South Park* style of jokes that are funny in a smart way, but I definitely do not think any race is superior to any other race.

Anyway, on this one ketamine trip in the dark of night, I leave one door open and head outside. I look out the window before I go. Something compels me to say, "Well it's gonna be fine. I don't see any niggers outside." I say this without volition, even though no one is even in the room with me. It wasn't even me that said it, it felt like I was possessed by some ancestor. God only knows if my ancestors owned slaves. It's not impossible for people in my DNA chain, or for me in previous lives, to have indeed owned slaves or said such things, but that is not me. Or maybe I was a slave in a previous life. It's common in many past life regressions I have heard, especially seeing how slavery has existed for thousands of years all around the world. So, mathematically, it's possible that many of us have been enslaved in one or previous lives, and this is why so many of us feel empathy in this life for the downtrodden here on the planet. Our empathy arises because some distant version of us has experienced that pain and its traumatic shadow still looms over our psyche.

So, as I walk out the door and am entering the garden, I begin to experience a different reality. I go into a past life and I am in Kentucky or South Carolina or something. I'm walking to work. I'm either a slave-owner or I'm a slave. And I'm going to have to go spend the day either as a slave being beaten or beating slaves. It is the most horrible feeling as I cross over into that world. I'm thinking, *No-no-no-no this is a dark place and I can't go there.* I end up collapsing in the garden with a wound to my leg. I emerge from this session totally shaken and disturbed. I get up and remove the dirt and leaves from my body, go inside and tell Rene about this strange experience. He tells me I should write it down because it is important.

And I have this realization. That whenever anyone in this life says harmful racist things that they will have to come back and live a life of a slave. It's some terrible justice that will teach them that words have meaning. And every time you make a mean-spirited joke, it is harmful to the wheel of time, and you will have to get back on that wheel and live the life of someone you have hurt.

MANAGING THE VIP AREA OF THE PARTY

Okay, back to the party. I've now offended Sam Harris and Troy Aikman, but I feel like it's all part of the plan. I'm a man on a mission. I'm on a mission to save everyone at this godforsaken party that I've been at a hundred times. This is my chance to make it right. This is my final Groundhog Day.

Surrounded by the throng on the lounge level, I find myself locked in a silent dialogue with Hunter S. Thompson—or at least his silent, smirking avatar. He's taunting me with enigmatic smirks as if to say, "Enjoying the narrative I've concocted for you?" Inside, I chuckle, acknowledging the absurdity and brilliance of the plot. What's next, Hunter? And I can't help but wonder, has Philip K. Dick been drafting the bizarre time-travel elements? Is Douglas Adams behind the curtain, scripting the comedic interludes? It feels as though these literary giants have formed a *Futurama* head-in-a-jar writers' room, dedicated to peppering my reality with a blend of intrigue, hilarity, and outright confusion. And to them, I say: "Bravo! Keep the madness coming."

In the pulsating energy of Vadim's party, filled with the eclectic mix of regulars and newcomers, I found myself immersed in an environment rich with the potential for deep connection and introspection. Dressed in a red long-sleeved jumper adorned with a heart-shaped yin-yang symbol, I stood out not just in attire but in demeanor. My presence, marked by a serene composure and open-heartedness, seemed to cast me in the role of a tranquil observer, perhaps reminiscent of a youthful Alan Watts (if I may be so bold), embracing the moment with a philosophical calmness ready with levity to lighten the mood so everything is not terribly serious.

Sitting on the couch with me to my right is a lovely Black woman who looks like Diana Ross. To my right is a big Mexican dude who is lovely and kind.

I am fully aware that everything I will tell you from here on out sounds "crazy" but everything made so much sense to me at the time. Upon reflection, I felt I was experiencing a very different reality from everybody else.

My conversation with the woman who reminded me of Diana Ross was motivated by genuine curiosity and respect. It wasn't about superficial attraction but a sincere interest in her life story, her experiences, and the essence of who she was. This engagement wasn't an attempt to bridge a romantic gap but to connect on a human level, to understand and appreciate the depth of another's journey. My approach to conversation has always been one of engagement and empathy, and in this moment, it felt as though I was reconnecting with a familiar soul, exploring the familiar and the unknown with equal fascination. I'm a rather engaging conversationalist, if I do say so myself, and I do. I stole this line from my wonderfully clever and precocious daughter.

So she and I are talking, and I notice people on the opposite side are really paying attention to me and where I put my own attention.

"You're the King!" Diana Ross says.

I find this to be a preposterous statement. I'm just this geeky introvert with glasses at this party and I feel like I don't belong.

Diana Ross continues. "Do you know how many eyes are on me right now? I have a thousand eyes drilling into my back because I'm talking to you."

I responded kindly, "Don't worry about them. They don't matter. I'm talking to you."

Diana is shocked by my response. Her accent, reminiscent of a bygone era, added another layer of intrigue to the conversation, painting her as a figure who might have stepped out of the 1920s into the present day. This notion of temporal dislocation was further amplified by the curious glances from other partygoers, drawn to the unusual camaraderie unfolding on the couch.

She also tells me this big Mexican guy on the other side of me is like the "baddest and nastiest motherfucker in Brooklyn," and told me he was the bouncer at the party. This made no sense to me because he seemed totally affable. His reputation as someone who physically handled unruly guests contrasted sharply with the gentle exchanges between us. It was a moment that highlighted the power of kindness and the potential for misconceptions to dissolve in the face of genuine human connection.

The party itself, set against the backdrop of a 2023 Brooklyn loft, epitomized a relaxed and self-regulated gathering, far removed from the need for formal security or the tension associated with "gangsta" elements. The atmosphere was one of levity and enjoyment, with guests indulging in drinks, light-hearted conversations, and the ambient joy of communal celebration.

I'm getting a good vibe from the crowd, even though I do feel the need to keep working the room to make sure everyone is okay. Oh, and I can't forget to keep taking water upstairs. I gotta keep these people hydrated!

So, I'm looking around the room, and many people are paying attention to me, and I'm starting to feel like I am experiencing a very different reality from everyone around me. Am I in a parallel universe? Is the "Trey" that is here appearing very differently to all the others that are here?

After about half an hour of doing a deep dive into the life of this past-future Diana Ross, I begin moving around the place more to make sure everyone is okay. I'm on stair duty. I'm on water duty.

There is a lot of drinking and lots of cocaine floating around the party. I have this sense of desperation that this is my last and only shot of saving as many people as possible. I feel great. I haven't slept very well in the past few days, but I feel extremely awake and switched-on. I'm max-Trey. I have a lot of loving positive energy and I am sharing it with as many people as possible.

People are starting to safely leave the party, and I am relieved.

THE FIRST SALVADOR DALI

In the midst of the vibrant chaos at Vadim's party, an encounter unfolded that felt as if it were plucked from a surreal dreamscape Salvador Dali might have painted. Among the eclectic assembly of guests, one individual, bearing a striking resemblance to Dali himself—albeit a shorter, bald version—captured a moment of wild connection.

Stationed near the exit, a spot where guests paused to don or remove their shoes, I found myself in the role of guardian, ensuring safe passage for all. This is a full-time job, let me tell you. And I'm taking it seriously while staying light-hearted and open. It was here, in this transitional space between the revelry within and the quiet of the night beyond, that "Salvador Dali" and I crossed paths.

Now, as I approach this Salvador Dali, he is completely transfixed by me. His eyes go wide and his jaw drops as he sees me. He sees me as some kind of glowing angel. This luminous creature of light. He tells me I am glowing with light out of my body. He was experiencing me as this impossible creature from an ethereal plane.

I kneeled down and held his hand just to show him I'm a regular human. I'm just at this party and trying to be of some kind of service to this time and place. He looked at me like I am some kind of effulgent god and a frequency of visible light was vibrating out of my skin as he saw a visible aura pulsating around me. I certainly didn't see it or feel different. He goes on and on that I am from another place and time and it's quite amazing. I've never had an interaction with anyone like that. I'm not letting it go to my head at all. I'm totally confused, but I act calm and loving and I look at him sweetly.

Okay, let's play devil's advocate and say he was on drugs. The only one that may have caused that reaction is acid or maybe mushrooms. But I've done those dozens of times with my friends in all sorts of situations, and I have *never* seen or heard of behavior like this. There has never been a report of this sort of reaction. And, plus, he didn't seem like he was on drugs; I can spot those behaviors a mile away.

It reminds me a little of the beings of light and love that are watching over us all the time. If you haven't heard the *Bledsoe Saidso* podcast, I recommend starting with #17, and you'll see what I mean. It's an episode where his dad was taken away by angels to see the Mother and then returned. This is a compelling story.

Being perceived as a deity by one of the partygoers was an experience that ventured beyond the ordinary, touching on the surreal. Despite this grandiose treatment, I harbored no illusions of divinity or a Messianic Complex. At my core, I had the feeling I was the quintessential "geeky guy" at the party, distinguished only by my eagerness to lend a hand where needed. This desire to be of service, while quite meaningful to me and, seemingly, appreciated by others, did not elevate my self-perception to that of a savior. Honestly, I'm just the guy who's there to pass around snacks and maybe help you find your lost phone, not perform miracles. The encounter with the individual who likened me to Salvador Dali did not inflate a sense of self-importance but rather underscored the peculiar, almost mystical, aura that seemed to envelop me in the eyes of some attendees.

Another guy said he saw me when I returned to the lounge. His eyes went wild as well. He said I looked like a glowing Marilyn Monroe! That was weird, I thought. That's like saying, "Hey, you remind me of Ryan Gosling," except you're at a dog park, and you're actually a labradoodle. It's a stretch.

It's worth noting that I currently haven't had any past-life regressions. I do not have any expectations of who I was in a previous life. Zero. I'm just as likely to have an interesting past life as to have had to endure a hard life as a Dickensian street urchin. I do feel like I'm doing pretty well in this current life and I am loving it. It's possible this is my best one yet and my previous ones were terrible and tortured. I simply don't know.

These encounters prompted contemplation on the nature of reincarnation and the fluidity of our identities across lifetimes. The idea that we might alternate between genders through our reincarnation journeys made sense to me. According to countless accounts, souls have the autonomy to choose their new physical vessels, with some opting for experiences vastly different from their previous incarnations. While many may gravitate towards familiar forms, the possibility of choosing a different sex offers an interesting exploration of identity and essence beyond the physical realm.

This series of interactions at the party, each highlighting a different facet of my being, served as a reminder of the intricate dance between how we perceive ourselves and how we are perceived by others. The evening unfolded as a journey through perceptions of identity, spirit, and the connections that bind us across time and space, leaving me to ponder the endless possibilities of our existence.

I love this Alan Watts theory that everyone on Earth is you. It's a lot unlike the Andy Weir "The Egg" short story where he says:

> "Every time you victimized someone," I said, "you were victimizing yourself. Every act of kindness you've done, you've done to yourself. Every happy and sad moment ever experienced by any human was, or will be, experienced by you."

I'VE GOT MORE WORK TO DO AT THIS PARTY!

Navigating through Vadim's party, I found myself at the center of a myriad of unique and intense interactions. The scene that unfolded before me upstairs—a tableau vivant of narcotic indulgence—featured not only familiar constellations of partygoers but also the tweaked-out Flavio. He was kneeling with others in front of a large plate with a line of drugs that reminded me of a powdering anaconda. This was a scene right out of a less fun version of *Scarface*. My intervention, fueled by a spontaneous surge of paternal concern, felt as much an attempt to salvage a fragment of my own universe as it was to steer him away from self-destruction.

Vadim's reaction to my interference was far from welcoming. His hostility, underscored by a cold, Putin-esque menace, made clear the unwelcome nature of my involvement. Vadim did not enjoy my penchant for inserting myself into his party situation. That was clear. He was mean and violent against me, but I didn't care. It was like getting a stern talking-to from Vladimir Putin if he ran a nightclub

instead of a country. But, I had no fear. As far as I was concerned, I
had died in there one hundred times over.

Besides that little mess, I found moments of clarity and connection in conversations about the art of communication. My advocacy
for "Three Word Chunk" storytelling—a method I championed for
its simplicity and effectiveness—resonated with those willing to listen. I emphasized the power of concise, purposeful expression in
breaking down complex truths, making them accessible and impactful. This approach, I argued, was not just about narrative efficiency
but about fostering understanding and empathy, essential compo-
nents in the broader quest for personal and collective enlightenment.

The philosophical underpinnings of my discourse extended to the
imperative of fearlessness in confronting life's challenges. I thought
about how critical it is to communicate to people that they should
seek to remove all fear from their lives. To remove all the dark shackles that are keeping you in this karmic wheel on Earth. To let go of
the past. To forgive. To overcome the expression of anger. Anger is
a natural emotion and it is okay to notice it and let it burn through
your heart, but not to express it. In anger and rage, there is a darkness. The importance of de-escalation. And how to communicate
these things in short three-word bursts and string these together into
a coherent sentence that contains this fractalized information. It requires great skill in diction along with a mind of clarity.

In weaving these threads of wisdom into the fabric of the evening's interactions, I sought not just to enlighten but to empower,
offering tools for resilience and renewal in the face of life's inevitable
tumults. The party, with its backdrop of revelry and recklessness,
became a classroom of sorts, a place where lessons of surprising significance were shared in the chaos, highlighting the enduring capacity for growth, understanding, and change.

Reflecting on the evening's unfolding events and the unusual
connections made, my thoughts momentarily drifted to a recent episode of the Joe Rogan podcast. The guest, despite her wealth of

knowledge, struggled with coherence in delivery—a contrast starkly highlighted when compared to communicators like Elon Musk or Jordan Peterson. Their method of thoughtful pauses and concise, impactful, phrases resonated with me, especially in the context of the party. It underscored the power of clear communication, the ability to articulate complex ideas in digestible, engaging segments. This skill, akin to a flow state, bridges inner thought and outward expression, channeling insights in a manner that captivates and enlightens. Great orators and artists, including skilled rappers, possess this rare ability to mesmerize and convey deeper truths, an art form that, in moments, I aspired to emulate.

As the night progressed, my attempts to communicate with intention seemed to draw people in. Contrary to my typical party demeanor—often reserved, seeking meaningful one-on-one interactions—this time, I found myself surrounded by individuals eager to engage. Whether this was a figment of my imagination or a reflection of my state of mind, the attention felt unfamiliar yet affirming.

My efforts to connect extended beyond mere conversation. Eye contact became a conduit for transmitting a sense of peace and goodwill, a practice I believed enhanced the communal energy. The repeated journeys up and down the stairs, ensuring everyone's safety and comfort, became a ritual of care, each step taken with the barefoot simplicity that grounded me in the moment.

PAST LIFE PARTY

Amongst the many weird things that happened at this party, at one point I was down by the front door where everyone's shoes were and people were coming and going while I was keeping an eye on the stairs. There was a steady flow of traffic up and down but the party was thinning out, so I was less worried.

But out of nowhere, I felt compelled to think back on historical figures to see how far back I could go, as if I could send some sort of healing vibrations back through time. Or, perhaps through simultaneous time, since there are many schools of thought that believe all lives throughout history are actually happening simultaneously. This is a difficult concept for the human mind to understand since we see time in a linear way.

And, remember, this is way before I believed in past lives and reincarnation. I always thought of it as a possibility, but I had not studied it the way I have now, after reading through five hundred-plus case studies. So, I started going back in time and listing off names that I could recall. Note that I am not saying these were my previous incarnations at all, but I was simply broadcasting waves of anachronistic well-being back through the ages. This is a very odd thing, right? Yes, I still don't know what to make of it.

I began the list in recent history and went "backwards," and I would name names regardless of if they were considered political or religious leaders. I began racking my brain. Martin Luther King. Winston Churchill. Einstein. Gandhi. Newton. Galileo. Shakespeare. Da Vinci. Jesus. Cleopatra. Caesar. Aristotle. Buddha. Confucius. And then I was having trouble figuring out who was older than that.

I was openly having a dialogue in my mind. "Oh, are there older historical figures I can remember? What about Methuselah? Or when was Gilgamesh around? Maybe it is Isis and Osiris? I think they were all around before they invented the hot fireman wall calendar?" It was a real struggle up there, I tell ya. There was a lot of stuff happening at this party. Now, sitting here writing this, obviously I could have just jumped to Adam and Eve and saved myself a lot of bar-trivia-brain-power.

NEAL STEPHENSON AND *ANATHEM* REFLECTIONS

I have a fun story about meeting Neal when we were speaking together at a conference. It's kind of like how you meet someone interesting in the most unexpected place, like finding your soulmate in line at the DMV. That resulted in not only his son coming to live with me in New Zealand for a while, but also a fun road trip in

Australia with Neal as he was doing research for the sequel to Cryp-tonomicon. Maybe he simply recruited me because I know how to drive on the left side of the road. But, let's not get sidetracked—that's a yarn for another day.

As I navigated the intricate landscape of Vadim's party, a thought experiment from Neal's book *Anathem* crossed my mind. He had a storyline around the concept involving the protagonist Erasmas and his engagement with the Hylaean Theoric World. This theoretical con-struct, akin to a cosmic canvas of multiple realities coexisting in a deli-cate balance, meshed deeply with my own experience. The idea that fo-cusing on all parallel versions of oneself could enhance concentration and resolve felt particularly poignant amidst the chaos of the party. It's like trying to focus at a party when there's a possibility there's another you out there, doing the exact same thing, but maybe they're wearing dif-ferent socks. Maybe by channeling Erasmas's discipline, I could traverse the myriad possibilities of the evening, each step and interaction infused with the potential to explore alternate outcomes, much like navi-gating the multiverse with the guidance of Diax's Rake.

In the swirling vortex of conversations, laughter, and fleeting con-nections, I found myself drawing upon the Discipline of the avout from *Anathem*, using it as a reminder to maintain clarity and pur-pose. The mental exercises described by Stephenson, designed to sharpen thought and deepen comprehension, became tools in my arsenal. Just as Erasmas and his companions delved into Dialogs to unravel the mysteries of their universe, I engaged with the party's denizens in a similar fashion. Our discussions, though perhaps less concerned with the nature of consciousness and the cosmos, nonethe-less mirrored the communal quest for understanding that underpins Stephenson's narrative. In the meantime, I'm aware that I am trying to engage in these deep, meaningful conversations with people who are probably just there for the free drinks. Each exchange, whether light-hearted banter or revelation, was a thread in the fabric of our collec-tive reality, a shared endeavor to make sense of the world around us.

Erasmas's journey through "Anathem," marked by his efforts to focus while distracted, echoed in my own attempts to anchor myself in the present. The discipline he practiced, a blend of philosophical meditation and mathematical precision, offered a template for navigating the evening's complexities. As I moved through the party, engaging with its myriad characters and scenarios, I envisioned myself as a parallel version of Erasmas—each decision, each moment of connection, a step towards a greater understanding of my place within the multiverse of human interaction. This speculative reflection on the nature of existence and our ability to influence the unfolding narrative of our lives lent a deeper dimension to what might otherwise have been just another night in Brooklyn.

ALMOST TIME TO LEAVE
THIS NEBULAE OF ABSURDITY

As the party wound down, a sense of accomplishment washed over me. The night had passed without incident—no accidents, overdoses, or altercations—a testament to the collective respect and care shared among the guests. It was time for my departure, a moment met with both relief and a reflective appreciation for the experiences shared and the connections made. My exit, marked by the quietude of bare feet on the cool ground, signaled not just the end of an evening but the culmination of a journey, both personal and shared, within the microcosm of Vadim's gathering.

Embarking on the journey from Vadim's party into the nascent Brooklyn dawn, I found myself at the precipice of a significant realization: life, with its complex interplay of moments and memories, might indeed be akin to a cinematic experience lived in reverse, presenting the illusion of linear progression while encapsulating a myriad of possibilities, both forward and backward in time. This notion, while elusive in its full quantum implications, underscored the surreal nature of my recent experiences, where days seemed to unfold in a dance of temporal fluidity, challenging my understanding of reality.

As I prepared to leave, Vadim, standing at the threshold, unexpectedly shifted in demeanor, expressing a reluctance to see me go. His change of heart was palpable. As I glanced past him at the few individuals lingering on the stairs, a sense of accomplishment washed over me. The stairs, once a bottleneck of potential chaos, now bore witness to the efficacy of my efforts throughout the night. The embrace shared with Vadim, heart-to-heart, felt like a scene replayed across countless iterations, each one a step towards this moment of departure and transcendence.

Stepping outside, the morning light of Brooklyn greeted me, a symbolic crossing from the confines of the party into a wider realm of existence. The sensation of ecstasy that accompanied my exit was not just a relief from the night's tensions but a harbinger of a more existential transition. Walking barefoot, the city's streets beneath my feet, I was struck by the sensation that this journey marked the culmination of my worldly experience, as if on the verge of a metaphysical departure from the physical form.

This anticipation of an end, however, was not marred by despair but enveloped in a sense of completion and understanding. The notion of uttering those "magic words" or bringing my narrative to a "tidy end" reflected the uncertainty and anticipation of charting unexplored territories beyond the known confines of life.

It is within this context of impending transcendence that the mention of Bill Hader emerges, an introduction that promises to add yet another layer to these intricate mirrors, connections, and the eternal quest for meaning while in the bewildering beauty of existence. This juncture, teetering between the familiar and the unknown, invites a contemplation of what lies beyond, signaling perhaps a new chapter or a continuation of the journey in another form, another time, another existence.

15.
THE GENIUS OF COMEDY AND A
FINAL MORNING OF MOURNING

"For small creatures such as we, the vastness is bearable only through love."
  —CARL SAGAN

"Anyone can be confident with a full head of hair. But a confident bald man—there's your diamond in the rough."
  —LARRY DAVID

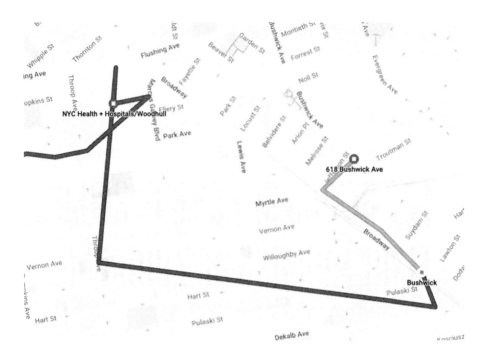

July 10, 2023

Yes, it's only been about five days since my incident in Scotland. And about six chapters since July 9. As you can see, there are many things that happen in my days. My life is not boring.

Wandering barefoot through Brooklyn in the morning hours, I felt like an accidental architect at the dawn of creation. It was as if the universe handed me the blueprints for a new Earth but forgot to include the instructions. Hovering above me was the proverbial Sword of Damocles, a rather inconvenient reminder of the stakes at play—get it wrong, and it's game over for planet Earth and its teeming inhabitants. Yet, I wasn't alone in this cosmic construction project; across the globe, others were surely waking up to their roles in this grand design.

As I moved down some random street in Brooklyn, the weight of Earth's history seemed to crash upon me. The echoes of countless souls—enslaved, oppressed, and wronged in unimaginable ways—merged with my own consciousness, turning my journey into a pilgrimage through shared suffering.

Navigating through the city, I saw NYC taxi cabs darting around. A deep intuition told me I had been killed in traffic countless times before. The screeching and tearing sounds of trains and subways felt as though they were slicing through me repeatedly. Despite this, my resolve was to traverse the world, striving to make it a more loving and conscious place.

Eventually, I found myself lying down on the sidewalk. Removing my glasses, I reflected on how grateful I was for them. These glasses, which I had treated myself to in Scotland, brought clarity to my vision. Lying there, I contemplated the enormity of what I was feeling and the task that lay ahead. It wasn't about fearing the end but embracing the potential for a new beginning.

Still supine, I found myself softly singing a song about Bill Hader and Rene. It was a whimsical moment, but beneath the surface, I sensed I was edging toward a deeper understanding, a revelation about the transformation of pain.

The notion that crystallized in my mind was the alchemical ability to transmute pain from one form to another, to shift energy from realms of darkness into realms of light and joy. Comedians, I realized, embody this concept. This truth struck me with the clarity of satori—an awakening. Comedians, in their essence, are alchemists who bear the weight of immense personal and collective pain. Some of the most brilliant comedians have indeed felt the most pain and suffering.

Robin Williams was a tragic example (one of so many from George Carlin to Mitch Hedberg I could mention), a brilliant light whose internal struggle led to his untimely demise. Yet, through their craft, comedians perform a vital, transformative service: they take the world's pain and spin it into laughter, turning negative energy into something positive and healing.

Laughter, then, becomes a neural miracle. It bridges disparate parts of the brain, forging connections that culminate in a release so pure and liberating. This realization brought a new appreciation for the role of comedians in our lives. They are not simply entertainers but spiritual guides of a sort, offering salvation not through doctrine or dogma but through the catharsis of humor. Where traditional religious figures might speak of sin and redemption, comedians offer a different kind of sermon, one that speaks directly to the human condition and offers relief not in the hereafter but here and now, in the shared experience of joy.

As I lay there, the concrete beneath me, the sky above, I felt a delightful level of gratitude for Bill Hader, Rene, and all those who wield humor to lighten our burdens. With my glasses resting on my chest, a symbol of the clarity they provided, I sent out waves of love and appreciation for the gift of laughter, for its power to transform pain into something communal, something beautiful. In that moment, the sidewalk was my sanctuary, and the laughter of the world my hymn.

Bill Hader and his show *Barry* were consuming my thoughts. The show's premise—about a hitman striving to redefine himself through acting, led by Henry Winkler's character—struck a chord with me. Its exploration of identity and personal growth mirrored my own introspections, especially in light of my recent delves into detailed accounts of past lives and how we choose this one. The notion that we select our Earthly roles, rehearsing life's pivotal moments with soul companions before incarnating, feels strangely familiar. It suggested that our existence is not just a series of random events but a carefully chosen path, a performance in the grand play of the universe.

Singing on the Brooklyn sidewalk, I wasn't just trying to extend my life's melody; I was aiming to imbue my final words with the power to reshape the cosmos. The belief that I could influence the rebirth of the universe, to save humanity by envisioning a new reality, was both an honor and a haunting burden. The enormity of this task, set against the backdrop of my mind's tumultuous landscape, felt like navigating through a personal apocalypse.

My silent scream into the void was a testament to the solitary nature of this struggle, a cry unheard yet felt by the cosmos itself.

This task felt akin to steering through a supernova in a rowboat.

SIDEWALK NAPTIME

After a brief respite, a moment of sleep that felt both like an eternity and a fleeting second, I awoke renewed. The source of this newfound vigor was a mystery, yet it propelled me forward, back towards Vadim's, despite having strayed far in my quest for a better Earth. There I was, making my way back to Vadim's, no phone, no clue of his address, wandering like a prophet who misplaced his prophecy. So I once again faced the humility of cluelessness, and endured a random walking pilgrimage reliant on the goodwill of strangers. My appearance, barefoot and disheveled, likely painted me as an outlier, a lost soul in the city's morning rush. Yet, within me, there was a clarity and purpose that transcended outward perceptions.

Navigating my way back required not just directions but a display of calm assurance—to reassure those I encountered that, despite appearances, I harbored no madness, only a profound sense of mission. In a city on perpetual alert, my demeanor was my passport. Convincing New Yorkers I was harmless and not just another character out of a sci-fi sitcom was the real quest. Funny how you can seem the most together when everyone else is convinced you've lost it. Just another day navigating Brooklyn, trying to blend in with the locals while secretly plotting to save the world, one sidewalk serenade at a time.

16.
THE AFTERPARTY
AND AFTERMATH

*"People are like stained-glass windows. They sparkle and shine
when the sun is out, but when the darkness sets in, their true
beauty is revealed only if there is a light from within."*
—ELISABETH KÜBLER-ROSS

"Reality is just a collective hunch."
—LILY TOMLIN

I walk in. The afterparty is still going. There's about a dozen people
there.

Now, I have one of the most fascinating interpersonal interactions in my life.

I go upstairs to where Sam Harris is still playing music and doing
a lot of cocaine. He is like Pablo Escobar with a Spotify playlist.
Classic Sam Harris. DJ Nosecandy.

Returning to the pulsating energy of the party, I made my way to my bunk bed, only to find it occupied by an unexpected guest: Boone Pogue. Yes, that was genuinely his name. He was there, lounging on my bed, enveloped in a flow of words that seemed to bridge rapping and a kind of stream-of-consciousness dialogue. What struck me most was his familiarity with me, as if he had known me for years, though we had never met before.

Boone was a unique figure, tall and slender, his curly hair framing his face in a way that reminded me of a hybrid of artistic genius, resembling what you might get if Salvador Dali and a young Tom Baker (one of the first and most beloved *Doctor Who* actors) were spliced together in the fabric of spacetime. His demeanor was unmistakably awkward, hinting at his place on the spectrum—a trait I viewed as increasingly common and necessary, given the diverse cognitive approaches needed to address the world's challenges. He shared with me the physical pains that haunted him, yet amidst his personal anguish, he regarded me with an almost reverential awe, echoing sentiments I had heard earlier in the night. He claimed I was a "king" with an unrivaled "score," notions that left me both baffled and amused.

Excitedly, he pulled up his phone. He claimed I was the "second one he met," as he pulled up an app called Triangles or something. It's like he had made contact with someone else playing a secret game. I was as perplexed then as I am now.

The conversation with Boone, for all its randomness, was deeply engaging. His shock at my willingness to engage with him, and his conviction that I was a rarity in his experience added layers of intrigue to our interaction. Despite his claims of my exceptionalism, I couldn't help but see the humor in the situation—I was just an ordinary guy, caught up in the whirlwind of a Brooklyn party, trying to make sense of the surreal encounters unfolding around me.

Reflecting on this, and reading about parallel universes in a variety of books (I suggest *The Convoluted Universe*), it is entirely possible that I side-slipped into a parallel universe for a while. It would certainly explain a lot of the unusual encounters I had the previous evening. I mean, where else do you end up making breakfast plans with a guy named Boone Pogue? I honestly have no idea. This is just speculation, because speculation is all I have to go on.

I'm planning on scheduling a series of regression hypnosis sessions to unravel all of this. It may not be important at all, but I am so curious about all the curious things that I encountered over these few weeks.

BREAKFAST ON THE SPECTRUM

Boone wants to go out with me to have some breakfast. I'm cool with that. God knows I don't have anything else to do. I just stayed up all night rescuing a boatload of souls and I'm famished. He seems like such a weird and random guy and I kinda want to get to know him. His eccentricity, far from deterring me, piqued my curiosity further. I was drawn to the idea of exploring his mind and understanding the world from his perspective. His lyrical prowess and the randomness of his thoughts promised an encounter unlike any other.

I go downstairs to the lounge to open up my laptop and get a little work done. The life of a travel photographer, contrary to popular belief, is not an endless loop of parties and philosophical quandaries (though those do make frequent guest appearances). The real world, with its gravity and deadlines, calls for attention, proving that even those who flirt with alternate realities must occasionally touch down on terra firma and tend to banal tasks. Life's got this funny way of reminding you that even if you can hop dimensions, you still have to pay the bills back in this one.

I start to take photos of things in Vadim's lounge as I notice more patterns. I'm seeing so much meaning in them. Just looking at this one, I see the duality. I see myself. I see how I might have lived this life in reverse. That there is a shadow version of myself in an inverted world. But now I'm finally on the right track and going in the right direction. Also this is that teal and orange color palette I am seeing all over the place and drawn to. The future is bright, indeed.

Boone Pogue is texting me now saying he wants to go out to breakfast with me. I'm like, okay, who is this random dude blowin' up my phone? But he's got this vibe that makes you wanna figure out if he's a genius or just really into breakfast foods.

Walking into the lounge, there's Boone and a few night owls looking like they just got off a spaceship from the coolest party in the galaxy. Everyone's acting like they've just discovered coffee for the first time. Observing the general wellbeing of the party's remnants filled me with relief. The lounge became a hub of reconnection, with people expressing their excitement at seeing me again. Turns out, we're all on this wild goose chase, trying to solve life's big puzzles like we're in some Boy Scout troop hunting for the treasure at the end of the universe. Apparently, I'm the troop leader because I've racked up some serious points in this game of existential hide-and-seek.

I say I am thinking about going to the gym across the street. I point at it.

They come and look out the window, but they can't see it. There is a huge sign that says "GYM" in vertical letters. It's one of those old-school signs that you would see in *Rocky* or something. I KNOW it is there because I saw it when I first got to Vadim's. But none of these guys can see it. They tell me they see a sign. And I ask them what the sign says. They both tell me every time they look at the GYM sign, the letters change.

That's strange I think. You know, this is the same thing that happens in dreams. If you are ever in a dream and look at a sign, you will see some letters. But if you ever focus and try to read something in a dream, the letters will change. This happens if you look away and look back at the words. It's a common phenomenon. Try it next time you are dreaming. You'll see what I mean.

This shared experience, rather than causing alarm, deepened the mystery of our collective journey. The inability to agree on something as tangible as a sign was a stark reminder of the subjective nature of perception. It raised questions about the nature of reality, consciousness, and the interplay between individual and collective experiences. As I pondered these anomalies, the distinction between being awake and dreaming became increasingly blurred, leaving me to wonder about the true state of awareness of those around me, and indeed, my own.

There is Hunter again, and in the background on the left, you can see that old-school Gym sign. Just like I remembered it. I started taking photos because I had this feeling that every photo I took was leaving clues for others to play this massive game I was creating to help them find full consciousness by connecting the threads of the world into one tapestry of consciousness.

As Boone Pogue and I prepared to leave Vadim's apartment, a moment of pause allowed me to observe him more closely, particularly his movements and behaviors that hinted at his place on the spectrum. Yet, there was something fascinating about the way he interacted with his surroundings, something that jibed with my own experiences of perceiving unseen entities.

In Scotland, I had felt the presence of three distinct muses, entities to whom I had turned in a moment of revelation, repeatedly affirming that "Love is the answer." These beings, though invisible, were as real to me as the physical world, offering guidance and wisdom. Similarly, I sensed additional presences positioned around me, akin to a celestial conference call, each offering their unique perspective and support.

Observing Boone, his actions on the couch seemed to mirror my interactions with these unseen forces. It's like watching someone juggle invisible oranges—he's got this whole routine down. His moves on the couch? Was he in the middle of a parallel universe Zoom call as he looked at ten different screens all around him I could not see? His movements, the way he leaned and gestured and sometimes appeared to be typing on an invisible keyboard, suggested he was engaged in a dynamic exchange with similar entities, perhaps even more directly or fluidly than I had experienced. It was as if he had access to a more sophisticated system of communication and he was responding to live chat or viewers on a real-life Twitch stream, navigating a complex web of connections that I could sense indirectly. His behavior indicated a continuous dialogue with these entities, a balancing act between our conversation and his interactions with the unseen.

Expressing my curiosity, I sought to understand Boone's unique interface with reality. However, his responses, scattered as they were across multiple planes of engagement, eluded straightforward explanation. It was a fascinating glimpse into another's perception of the world, one that challenged and expanded my own understanding of the myriad ways we connect with the unseen and each other.

As we readied ourselves to venture into Brooklyn, the contrast between Boone's preparation and my continued barefoot state underscored a deeper shift within me. The choice to remain barefoot, influenced perhaps by my time in New Zealand and the Earthy ethos of my friends there, felt like a declaration of connection—to the Earth, to the present moment, and to a life lived in closer harmony with the natural world. This decision, while seemingly minor, was imbued with significance, marking the beginning of another journey through the city's streets, one that promised to be as rich in discovery and connection as the night that had just passed.

I AM NOT LOST; I'M JUST NOT FOUND YET

Leaving Vadim's apartment with Boone Pogue was an exercise in trust and reassurance. His apprehension, manifested in fears of betrayal or violence, hinted at a deeper narrative, one possibly shared across multiple realities or iterations of departure. His request to inspect my hands for weapons was a poignant moment, bridging fear with the need for assurance. My response, a carefree spin with palms exposed, aimed to communicate safety and transparency. Despite his evident fear, Boone's desire to accompany me underscored a complex dynamic of attraction and apprehension.

Reflecting on the nature of our reality, I drew parallels with the theories of cognitive scientist Donald Hoffman, contemplating the interfaces through which we engage with existence. The notion that our perception of reality is but a façade, masking deeper truths, resonates with me. I wouldn't go as far as to label our world a simulation, yet the video game analogy—complete with levels, roles, and replayability—offered a compelling framework for understanding the recurring patterns and scenarios, such as Vadim's party. This speculation about Boone and my roles in these repeated narratives, alternating between protagonist and antagonist, fueled my curiosity about the underlying mechanisms of our encounters.

This penchant for speculation, for embracing the unknown and reveling in the act of wondering, is something I cherish. In a world that often prizes certainty and facts, maintaining a sense of wonder—akin to the boundless curiosity of children—serves as a vital counterbalance, nurturing creativity and imagination. As a creative, this ability to envision and explore the absurd has always been a source of joy and inspiration, driving my work and my worldview.

We eventually make it out and Boone is desperate to have a smoke. I'm like, okay that's cool. I don't mind. Of all the vices in the world, smoking is one I have yet to take up. I guess there is still time for new hobbies.

So Boone has a ciggy and we are talking.

Out of the blue, Boone hits me with, "You know I'm not gay, right?" and I'm standing there thinking, "Cool, but did I accidentally sign up for a dating show without knowing?" I mean, we're just two guys, walking through Brooklyn, bonded over existential musings, not exactly the setup for a romantic comedy.

I let him know it's all good with a smile, kind of like how you reassure someone that, yes, you did indeed enjoy their vegan casserole.

You see, I describe myself as "ambisextrous," a term I fancy for its hint of athleticism and its accuracy in capturing my bisexuality, with a predominant lean towards women. It's a playful way of saying the universe didn't fit me into a conventional box; instead, it gave me a bit of everything, an overly complicated Starbucks order, delightfully served by a hairless barista.

It's funny, people often get the wrong idea about me when we first meet. Maybe it's the deep voice mixed with my not-so-typical guy vibe, or maybe it's because I look into people's eyes a bit too intensely, like I'm trying to read their last three thoughts. And yeah, I paint my nails because, let's be honest, plain nails are just missed opportunities for self-expression.

Anyhoo, I'm totally not trying to get with this guy or anything. He just fascinates me.

As I wandered through Brooklyn with Boone, an intriguing theory took root in my mind, fueled by the intimate and familiar nature of our conversation. It felt as though I was communicating not just with him but with the essence of someone, perhaps a female lover, I had deeply connected with in another lifetime. Boone's words carried a resonance that transcended the ordinary, hinting at shared histories and lessons learned across the expanse of lifetimes. He said things that only I could possibly know about. His apologies and reflections on past transgressions struck a chord, suggesting a path of growth and redemption that we had navigated together, albeit in different forms.

Our exchange, however, was not without its challenges. Boone's discomfort with direct eye contact—a stark contrast to my own desire for connection and understanding—underscored the complexities of our interaction. Despite these moments of tension, his proposal to blend the simple joys of video games and breakfast with our deep dialogue intrigued me. Yet, as quickly as the plan was made, it dissolved; Boone needed to depart, leaving me to contemplate the fleeting nature of our connection.

PARALLEL YOUS

You know I'm a man of science and I like to have scientific proof whenever possible, but so many things about reality and our souls are hard to prove. Some things just make a certain level of intuitive sense. As I read hundreds of stories about people in hypnosis that talk about these things, the overlap in their stories is more than good enough for me.

The reason I bring this up is because of parallel universes and other versions of me (and you) that get spawned every time we make a decision. It may be a minor decision—are you going to scratch your nose or not—a somewhat interesting decision as to what kind of car you should get, or a major decision such as who you should marry. Each decision gets a new universe. Sometimes these universes are close, and you can slip into one of them. And, here's the thing. When you slip into them, you swap places with the "you" that was in that one. This can last a few moments or a few days.

This is the bar where I waited for Boone Pogue to join me. Interestingly enough, it was called "Journey."

Boone and I met at Journey and then we walked through the

streets of Manhattan in the dark to go visit a comedy club. We stopped along the way at an all-night diner where I got some coffee and had an egg, cheese, and bacon sandwich. Our walk continued and we had very random conversations. I had on this bomber jacket over top of that psychedelic shirt I was wearing, and Boone got annoyed that I did that. He was saying I have to let myself shine and glow and let that crazy shirt freak flag fly.

We stopped at a smoke shop so he could get more supplies. We ended up outside of a comedy club called the Village Underground where he was going to perform. There was an argument with the bouncer and the whole vibe was weird so I decided to leave because it was quite late and I could see the night was getting sketchy. I snapped this photo below before I got the Uber.

In the chats below, you'll see a few times he says he loves me. I think it is just an off-hand thing he says. I only knew the guy for a few hours, but he seemed kind and sweet. I'm so confused. Perhaps I'm not much of a detective at all as I attempt to be as open and transparent here and shine a light into every corner. Also interesting how he talks about the multiverse and dimensions, a topic we have never discussed.

Your at journey still? 1:56 pm

> Yep

> Will be here till midnight I think 2:01 pm

Okay. I'll be outta her in 30 and Uber to u 2:05 pm

I'll be there by eleven I can take train 2:09 pm

I'll take you up on Uber

I'm washing up and I'll text ya when ready if that's cool

I'd say 15-20 min I'll be ready. Text u the second and I'll grab that Uber to u from set. It's only fifteen min away by car

Yay

Excited to see ya 2:14 pm

> coolio -yes!

> Just say when and I'll send the uber to...

> 242 Howard 2:18 pm

I'm not there

I'm at work

Leaving

In a sec

I think you should go sleep. Sleep is important... and Vadim sounds aggressive and mean. He sometimes gets aggressive and mean and that is not the best version of Vadim.

I prefer the Vadim that is serene and zen and full of love and god and also knows how to share the love in a loving way. I'm sure everyone else does too.   8:25 pm

You declined a voice call · 8:25 pm

Call Back

I am

I live close to there

I'm going home

He's just excited   8:25 pm

He seemed much more concerned about the uber than my news about being in the hospital.

He can be a real horse's ass. He's 100% the shadow version of Noho Hank from Barry   8:29 pm

He didn't even hear

Ya

He's getting yelled

At

Can u send 20 to me

Never mind   8:29 pm

It's otw home

That's why I went. And I get it but I wanted to sit and be comfy on the bed for a sec. Then go home and watch cartoons   8:35 pm

Call me after dr. Love u   8:42 pm

But most

Most

Importantly

How

Was

The procedure

Are you okay

What did they say

How are u feeling

Yeah that was when I left

It was chill

Had two white claws maybe 5:04 pm

I'm okay 5:04 pm

Got mad stoned

Just okay?

Fuck

U need

An ear

Or anything 5:04 pm

Incoming voice call · 5:57 pm

Call Back

I'm worried

Are you okay

What's wrong 5:58 pm

> Erratic and unsettling... So sometimes the opposite of what I need. 6:14 pm

Well

When u say we will do something and I am on edge

It's programmed in

Like a shelter dog

Skiddish apprehensive

And no one will listen when I tell them how my brain works

They continue to press the same code command sequence   6:15 pm

> I think I understand   6:15 pm

And it fries the motherboard

Overheats

Reset shut down

Especially after long laborious days

And cutting off multiple people for such things days out of the week

It's more a request than command

Saying hey if you do a

B will happen

Please don't do a

Try c instead

Nope

A=b unless law of a=b)2rd

Which is   6:17 pm

I sont

Mean

This in anyway

Rude

I'm worried

About the dr visit

Are u gonna be ok

Love u

Talk tmrw 6:22 pm

Ok 6:29 pm

I'll be okay

We'll meet tomorrow perhaps dunno 7:45 pm

20 Jul 2023

How

Are

You

Feeling 12:26 pm

Great. U? 6:18 pm

21 Jul 2023

Pretty gewdddd

Glad to hear you're feeling well 4:51 am

I've just started messaging Boone again to see if I can unravel more of these mysteries.

FEELING MY EDGES FRAYING

Left alone, my thoughts began to race, and I could feel the onset of mania, a state of heightened awareness and energy that bordered on the overwhelming. Was this merely the result of sleep deprivation, or was it something more? The intensity of the experience suggested a predestined path, one chosen in the quiet deliberations of the spirit realm before I embarked on this Earthly journey. This belief, that my current state was not random but a part of a larger, cosmic narrative, offered both comfort and curiosity.

As I continued my aimless walk through Brooklyn, the city

around me seemed to pulse with hidden meanings and messages, each step a further descent into a manic clarity. This condition, while daunting, also felt imbued with purpose, as if each moment of heightened perception brought me closer to understanding the intricate web of connections that define our existence. The realization that this mania might be a part of my spiritual journey—a symptom of the soul's quest for enlightenment—transformed my wandering into a pilgrimage, each step a movement towards deeper insight and revelation.

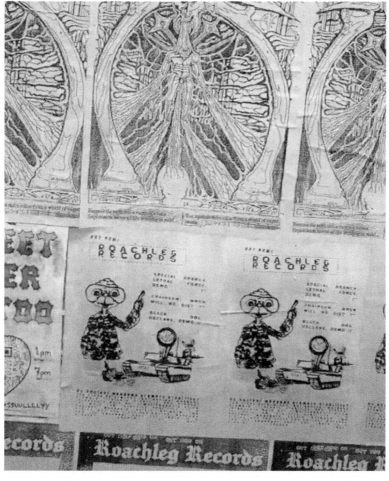

In Scotland, I started creating these rather humorous graphic design critiques. And I was continuing to make more and more. I was critiquing all these flyers on the wall. I started to see a theme of aliens and I was making all sorts of connections in my mind. My mind was on fire with synchronicities as I was unraveling the meaning of everything around me.

I went into a corner grocery store and got a veggie smoothie. It was incredible. And then I go outside and I see the place is called Mr. Kiwi. Well, this is yet another connection for me, since people from New Zealand are called Kiwis. And I would imagine I am the one guy from New Zealand that is in the middle of this part of Brooklyn actually going in there. I'm starting to thank the Machine Elves for creating this reality just for me.

A lot of the photos I'll share here are grabs from videos I made along the way… or quick, unprocessed phone images. Don't judge my photog skillz from these!

17.
HOMELESS TRANS ALEXIS

"The soul that sees beauty may sometimes walk alone."
—JOHANN WOLFGANG VON GOETHE

"There is a theory which states that if ever anyone discovers exactly what the Universe is for and why it is here, it will instantly disappear and be replaced by something even more bizarre and inexplicable. There is another theory which states that this has already happened."
—DOUGLAS ADAMS

Leaving the grocery store with my smoothie, I met a homeless guy named Alexis. He was about fifty, Black, and crippled. He had a bad leg that had been bothering him for years and was hobbling about with a cane. One of the first things he told me was that he was born a man but was actually a woman inside.

This struck me in many ways, as one of my best friends back in New Zealand is also trans and has had the full operation to convert "him" into a fully realized woman. Coincidentally, his name was Alex, and now is Lexi, which is not a far combo from Alexis. It's been a very interesting experience to be with her on this journey. I'll talk more about that later when we get to the part about groups of friends meeting up every time they come to Earth on yet another mission. Yet another addition to my weird reincarnation theory about every life being a switch between being a man and a woman.

And then I reflect on the massive trans movement going on. Are we in some karmic wheel of life where now souls are purposefully being put into the wrong body? That's a pretty weird theory I know. I don't put much credence into it, but I note it. Perhaps because men have messed up the world so badly, we need more and more women because they are key. There are not enough females being born to save the world, so they are having to insert more female souls inside of men? Again, more wild speculation on my part.

I am feeling the need to help as many people as I can. Even if it is just one at a time.

FROM HOMELESS TO HOME-COOKED FOOD

Alexis tells me they are hungry, so I take Alexis to a nearby restaurant, which offered a moment of respite and connection while twirling in the whirlwind of my experiences in Brooklyn. As we shared a meal, the opportunity to learn about their struggles and dreams provided a grounding contrast to the surreal encounters that had dominated my night and morning. Despite the presence of observers, like the two Lex Fridmans, whose interest seemed piqued by my actions and perhaps my ability to navigate different planes of reality, my focus remained on the immediate, tangible act of sharing a meal with someone in need.

Alexis's revelation about their desire for a gender transition struck a chord with me. It was a reminder of the complex journeys individuals embark upon in search of their true selves, regardless of age or circumstance. Their determination, set against the backdrop of financial and physical challenges, was both humbling and inspiring. It reinforced the idea that personal authenticity and fulfillment are pursuits worth any obstacle.

We finish eating and I give him a goodbye hug. He notices I don't have any shoes, and he comments that he would like some new shoes. I tell him, well maybe I can buy him some shoes one day. This plays a role later in the story.

However, the narrative was about to take another turn towards the extraordinary. My experience was escalating towards a peak, a moment of intense revelation and transformation that would challenge the very fabric of my reality.

The question of what exactly triggered this "full-curazy-Trey" state—whether it was the culmination of sleep deprivation, the aftermath of intense emotional experiences, or a deeper, preordained shift—remains open. What was clear, though, was that I was on the cusp of something profound, a significant event that would redefine my understanding of myself and the world around me. This period of change, though daunting, promised insights and revelations that were, in every sense, significant.

18.
THE PINNACLE OF A ONE-MAN SHOW

"Art is to console those who are broken by life."
—Vincent Van Gogh

"The reason I talk to myself is because I'm the only one whose answers I accept."
—George Carlin

I'm walking backwards down Broadway.

Embarking on this unique journey, I found myself moving against the flow as a symbolic act of reversal and healing. It was as if by retracing my steps in this manner, I could somehow alter the course of history, offering solace and redemption for the collective pain that echoes through the streets and the souls that inhabit them. I need to comfort my own suffering while I absorb the suffering of as much of the pain of Black people in Brooklyn as I can. Look, I know I'm a White guy, but there was something happening inside of me where I was beyond sensitive to ancestral collective pain.

With each step taken backward, I felt an overwhelming sense of empathy and burden, a strange, tangled connection to the pain and struggles that have marked the human experience. In preparation for the repeated journeys I foresaw in my future, I strategically placed water bottles and buckets along my path. This was not just an act of self-preservation but a ritual of preparation, a way to ease the journey for the version of myself that would navigate this path again.

The intensity of the emotional and physical pain occasionally became unbearable, driving me to seek solace in a moment of prayer and gratitude. This act, bringing my hands in prayer to my forehead and squatting down, provided a brief respite, a sanctuary of peace amidst a storm of torture. As the pain crescendoed, resembling the onslaught of multiple migraines, I found strength in my purpose, understanding that my presence was necessary, that I was there to absorb and transform this suffering for reasons beyond my immediate comprehension.

Using my phone like a light-weapon as if I am recording everything around me, I shine it this way and that way. I begin making hilarious jokes, as if I am some kind of stand-up comedian, sharing the pain and joy of the Black culture through kind-hearted jokes. No racist jokes, because those are harmful. Smart jokes. Trying to convert their pain into laughter as some sort of spiritual warrior that takes one type of energy and converts it to another. I feel some level of understanding of pain that minorities have suffered in the U.S. and I am literally tearing myself apart from the inside. I'm jumping around and rebuilding history from the beginning. It's up to me to recreate the existence we are in and I'm doing a pretty good job of it. I even go on a riff about "woke" stuff about a great way to waste people's time while the doom of Earth marches forward on its path of redemption.

As the day wore on and the heat intensified, I shed my shirt, embracing the warmth as it seeped into me. This act of vulnerability was both a literal and metaphorical stripping away of barriers, a desire to connect more with the environment and the monumental task at hand. My journey down Broadway, filled with backward steps, laughter, and moments of confused reflection, was a testament to the belief in the power of individuals to enact change, to heal, and to rewrite the stories that bind us.

My wild trek through Brooklyn took an abrupt turn when an ambulance arrived, summoned by someone who must have perceived my actions as distress signals rather than expressions of a deeply personal quest. The experience of being forcibly restrained, handcuffed to the bed, and transported to the hospital, introduced a stark, new dimension to my adventure—a physical immobilization that contrasted sharply with the mental and spiritual freedom I had been exploring.

Lying in the hospital, my connection to the pain around me intensified, merging with the collective pains of others present. This amplification of shared anguish was both wonderful and unsettling, leaving an indelible mark on my consciousness.

If you've never been strapped down to a bed, then you really don't know the feeling. It was a terrible and haunting pain and it stays with me still.

It was within this constrained state that I encountered a doctor whose presence seemed to pierce through the chaos of the moment. His demeanor and understanding hinted at a deeper connection, perhaps one that transcended our current meeting. He struck me as a Jewish doctor with a good sense of humor. I don't know why this occurred to me, but I called him over to talk and I was correct. Now, I was half-standing up on my bed while partially strapped down. I was trying to do stand-up comedy and this doctor was loving it (because who doesn't love a captive audience?) So were the nurses. Sure, I was acting crazy, but I was saying some genuinely funny things. He understood what I was saying as I was flailing with the bonds that held me to the bed. It's like that scene from *Three Amigos* where Steve Martin was chained to the wall of the dungeon.

My conversation with the doctor eventually turned to a topic that had been circulating in my mind since Vadim's place—the elusive "number" that seemed key to unlocking the mysteries I had been contemplating. The consensus on the number 42, shared with the doctor, felt like a significant breakthrough, a numerical clue to the riddle I had been attempting to solve. This moment of clarity in the chaos offered a semblance of direction, a numerical anchor for my spiraling thoughts.

Reflecting on the multitude of "deaths" I experienced in the hospital—metaphorical endings and transitions within my ongoing journey—I recognized these moments as integral to my transformation. Each "death" represented a shedding of old perspectives, a necessary part of the rebirth process I was undergoing. This period of enforced stillness, marked by physical restraint but illuminated by moments of connection and revelation, underscored the complex interplay between suffering, humor, and the search for understanding that had come to define my experience.

ESCAPE FROM THE HOSPITAL—LEVEL OF DIFFICULTY: MEDIUM

I eventually got untied. When no one was looking, I escaped. I didn't want to be in the hospital. I didn't need to be there. I just snuck out. I thought of it all as a game. Hospital Escape. I nailed it.

My fascination with "eyes" grew, becoming a motif that seemed to permeate my reality. I began to notice the presence of four wise figures who appeared to be observing me. Their gaze wasn't judgmental but attentive, as if they were custodians of wisdom from another place, watching over me. In my mind, they were not just spectators but loved elders, their sagacious eyes serving as portals to another plane of existence. This sensation of being part of a pay-per-view *Truman Show*, with an audience tuned into my journey on "Mission Planet Earth," was both surreal and fun. Was this like a new *Fleabag* (one of my favorite shows with Phoebe-Waller Bridge where she often looks at the camera, breaking the fourth wall, to share inside jokes with the audience)? If so, now I was breaking the fifth wall into the 5D Earth and beyond, and sharing inside jokes and knowing looks with those bored spirits cuddled up watching Nebula Netflix.

This is what I saw as I escaped the hospital and was waiting on my Uber.

MY FRIENDS WITH SCHIZOPHRENIC MOMS

This experience leads to a reflection on the distinctions between psychosis and schizophrenia, conditions often confused but distinct in their characteristics and implications.

Psychosis, as I came to understand, involves a detachment from reality, characterized by hallucinations or delusions. My own experience aligned with this definition, not through auditory hallucinations, but through an alteration of my perception of reality. To me, these experiences were not mere figments of imagination but vivid, undeniable truths that stood in stark contrast to the "default reality" others perceived. This discrepancy simply reinforced my conviction that I was accessing a higher vibrational reality, one saturated with love and consciousness, far removed from the lower-vibrational state mired in fear and distrust that seemed to ensnare others.

Schizophrenia, conversely, represents a more chronic manifestation of reality detachment, with more intense and enduring symptoms. Having seen schizophrenia affect my own mom, as well as the moms of friends like Rene and Jessica, I've observed its meaningful impact firsthand. The condition's longevity and severity distinguish it from the transient episodes of psychosis. Growing up in environments shaped by such challenges has, in many ways, informed our humor and perspective on life. Rene and I, through our shared experiences and coping mechanisms, developed a unique lens through which to view the world—a lens crafted from the necessity of finding humor in the wildness, of transforming the absurdity of our circumstances into a source of laughter and resilience.

This journey through altered states of reality, marked by personal insights into mental health, has deepened my understanding of these conditions and also highlighted the intricate ways in which our perceptions of reality are shaped by our experiences, our biology, and the unseen forces that guide us.

When my mom would have her schizophrenic attacks, she would take me on these wild rides that were less "Sunday drive" and more "FBI chase scene." Sometimes there was a master-plot created by my dad (he had been divorced for a while and she hated him, even when not in her frenzy-mode), and he was doing all this stuff to sabotage her life. One time when I was about twelve, I locked myself in the bathroom. I wanted to escape; to run away to my dad's house. She was to come through the door with an ax! Heeeeeere's MOMMY! Yeah, fun stuff like that I got to experience as a kid.

Note these incidents were very few and far between. It wasn't like a weekly Tarantino movie or anything. Just enough to keep you on your toes.

I did the whole dramatic escape thing, running five miles through Dallas like I was gunning for a medal in the Anxiety Olympics. I finally found my dad's place and we called in the guys with the comfy van—the kind with extra padding. They're like the Ghostbusters but for family meltdowns.

I'm sure the reader is thinking, *Okay, Trey, there's a lot to explore here,* and I agree. On the plus side, it made me very driven and independent. It's made me have a very creative mind, keen on survival, planning, logistics, and becoming extremely empathetic. I had to learn how to figure out people very quickly. I've also turned into an excellent communicator because I need to determine what kind of personality I am dealing with. What drives them. What are their goals. Are they genuine? Do they know themselves? Are they faking it?

Understanding people, gauging their intentions, and navigating complex emotional landscapes became second nature to me, born out of the need to adapt and survive. These skills have undoubtedly shaped me into an effective communicator, constantly assessing the dynamics of interpersonal interactions, striving to discern authenticity and motivations in others.

It's not all bad—turns out, dealing with ax-wielding parents is great for developing empathy and a solid escape plan. Who knew?

However, the scars left by these experiences have also cast long shadows over my romantic relationships, particularly with women. It's not a surprise that I have trust issues with women in girlfriend situations. I'm not blaming my mom or anything, as I believe I've weathered all the storms and come out the other side with empathy, forgiveness, and love. On the flipside, I have many deep, intimate, and trusted relationships with women who are completely platonic.

Note that I'm just pointing out a few dramatic moments, and the reader should know my mom and I have a great and fun relationship. We text-chat pretty much every day on Messenger and we have an awesome, loving, and supportive relationship. She's a great mom, so don't let these stories color the overall gestalt in a negative light.

Here's an old photo of my first birthday with my mom behind me. Who knows, right after this picture, she might have smashed my face in that cake and called my dad a selfish motherfucker. Perhaps I repressed that event, but I'd like to think it probably didn't happen.

Regarding trust issues, my wife of twenty-three years was wonderful in every way. I completely trust her, she has a big heart, is honest, and always tries to do the right thing. She was all about following the rules, the kind of person you'd trust with your Wi-Fi password on the first date. But, in my relationships since then, although there have been many loving moments, there have been countless incidents that toss me back into that soup of having trust issues with women. It's quite terrible and heartbreaking, really. Because I want to trust. And then, added to that, I've had to deal with their unexpected and random rage. Sure, I may make a few mistakes here and there, but then when I get this wild rage thrown back at me, it's all the same patterns of childhood. I am a gentle soul and completely bamboozled when women express extreme anger and rage. I don't fight back. I feel just hurt and confused.

Yet, through these trials, my faith in the universe and the journey it has laid out for me remains unshaken. My commitment to opening my heart, to embracing vulnerability as the cornerstone of existence, reflects a belief in love's transformative power. This path, though fraught with setbacks and heartache, is one I choose to walk with trust and hope.

As we pivot back to the unfolding narrative of my current adventures, it's clear that the trials are far from over. The story, much like life itself, promises complexities and challenges, yet it is within these moments of adversity that the potential for growth and understanding deepens. Let's continue, mindful of the lessons learned and the journey ahead.

19.
RENE AND JESSICA IN MANHATTAN

I had an invitation to visit my lovely friend's art studio. Jessica. I love her dearly and would do anything for her. So I got an Uber to meet her and Rene there. The journey from Brooklyn to Manhattan offered a brief respite, though the fatigue of the past days weighed heavily on me, hinting at the physical toll of my adventures.

Jessica, an artist whose talent and spirit I've long admired, has been a source of inspiration since our first meeting at a private ranch in Yellowstone. Our connection, purely platonic, is a testament to the depth of friendship and mutual respect we share. The adventures we've embarked on together, including an unforgettable trip to Africa with Rene, are among the highlights of our friendship, filled with laughter and memorable moments that I cherish.

The view of Jessica's studio from my chair where I simply could not stay awake. It's like I had narcolepsy or something, a condition I've never had. The universe would not let me stay awake. I was exhausted and extremely sleep-deprived.

Upon arriving at her studio, the showcase of her artistic prowess was as impressive as ever—her creativity, attention to detail, and mastery of colors never failed to amaze me. However, despite my eagerness to engage with Jessica and her art, an overwhelming exhaustion enveloped me, rendering me unable to stay awake. This sudden onset of sleep, almost narcoleptic in nature, felt like the universe's way of forcing rest upon me, despite my desires to the contrary.

I treasure Jessica so much! So, you can imagine my reflective dismay at all the chaos I was about to cause in her life. She clearly saw me as not acting like "normal Trey" and she was concerned.

And then I went downstairs with Rene where we were going to find another hotel so I could get out of Vadim's place. But none of the Ubers were working for me. I was being obstinate. Nothing was working and I was not supposed to go in these Ubers. I felt the universe pulling me in another important direction. You remember how in the life between lives in the spirit world, you choose what your life will be like ahead of time? Well, there was an immutable moment I had to endure and it was going to be awful. I was compelled to it though, and I know this is one of those times I had no free will.

POLICE AND A SECOND AMBULANCE

This period, undoubtedly one of the darkest times as another ambulance came along, was a stark reminder of the fine line between seeking adventure and the necessity of acknowledging one's limitations. The intervention by Jessica and Rene, though difficult, was a testament to their care and concern, underscoring the importance of friendship and support. They could definitely see I was not acting like myself and thought it best to call in the professionals.

I started to say crazy things. I told the doctors and nurses I was on acid and mushrooms (none of that was true). Another "something" took over and said all kinds of insane stuff. I tried to poke out my eye with a fork. It was madness. I was in terror. I was about to go back to another hospital and be strapped down to a bed. I was literally in hell, and I was saying all kinds of random stuff. It reminds me of later in the story when I saw a simulacrum of Steve Jobs in a restaurant in the body of a businesswoman and I screamed wild things around her. But that's later in the story.

I got along great with all of these guys and we had good banter while waiting for the ambulance. Well, from my standpoint we got along great. I wasn't in control of what I was saying and felt some other force take over what I was saying. At some point, they decided to handcuff me to that railing. So, I was definitely experiencing a different reality.

Now in the emergency room, I wail and cry into the void. I'm gone. I'm no longer part of this Earth. I've died a horrible death. I am nothing. I am dead. With the pain of all the souls around me in this hospital, I scream them out into some horrible impending death for all of them. I am lost as I visit a world of total insanity and say things that are not even true. My screams, laden with the pain of unimaginable loss, mirrored the depth of sorrow one might associate with the most harrowing of human experiences. There is another strange voice inside of me (that is not me) saying terrible things. It was a phenomenon to revisit and repurpose my body and voice in Wellington.

I screamed a terrible death-howl, it was the sort of mind-piercing wailing you would see from a Palestinian woman holding her dead baby. The pain and the death-rattle reverberating around my skull was beyond the worst agony I could imagine. They were about to inject me with drugs I did not want in me. I was to be strapped down again and maybe worse.

I spent a long time there in the emergency room.

As days blurred into nights within the confines of the hospital, my state oscillated between the extremes of spiritual emergence and the grip of a darker, more tumultuous inner struggle. It was a period marked by introspection, conflict, and the quest for calmness in a never-ending storm.

But let's pause the space-time narrative for a wee high-frequency anecdote, shall we? I'm somewhat reluctant to share, given that my life had become a veritable ticker tape of synchronicities, but this particular tale spins the dials of the improbability drive to eleven. While I was in Scotland I had this amazing lover named Eva in Glasgow. She was so sweet. A Spanish dancer who could move like she was made of moonbeams. She is graceful and has a true kindness to her. We traveled together. We ate amazing food. We made love. It was all incredible and I've never met anyone like her. She also happens to work as a nurse in the mental health field in Scotland. We are still amazing friends and looking forward to getting together again. Oh, Scotland. Why are you so far away?

Okay, here it comes. You won't believe this. At the exact same time I had my episode and my wailing and shrieking, Eva collapsed on the street in Glasgow. She said she knew something terrible had happened to me. She said a few people picked her up and got her some medical attention. Nothing like that has ever happened to her. She's in amazing shape and wasn't doing any drugs.

Now, I don't know what to make of this. We're not in love and we only spent about two weeks together. But it was an intense two weeks. Was there some kind of Rick and Morty dragon-contract soul-bonding that happened? Is there some sort of quantum entanglement? God only knows. I've added it to a very long list of questions of things that have happened in my life I can't figure out. Very long.

20.
NYC EMERGENCY ROOM

"The edge of the sea is a strange and beautiful place."
    —RACHEL CARSON

"My therapist says I have a preoccupation with vengeance. We'll see about that."
    —STEWART FRANCIS

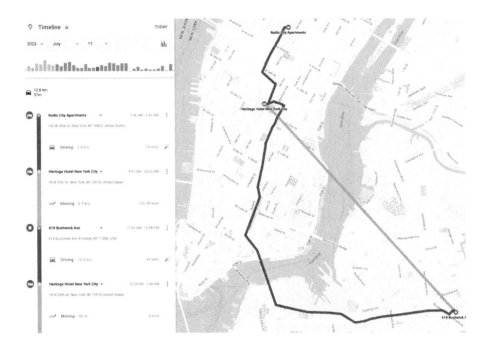

July 11, 2023

I remember doing things I would never normally do. A group of doctors came to see me. I can barely open my eyes. But I see them in their white coats, holding clipboards, looking at me seriously. I shoot my two middle fingers at doctors that are coming to visit me, something I would *never* do in my normal self.

I see one of them, Dr. Wasserman, as the spitting image of Dennis from *It's Always Sunny in Philadelphia*. So strange that Dr. Wasserman has the same name as the protagonist from *The Dice Man*, the book I was recently reading in Scotland about a doctor who has novel ways of treating his mentally challenged patients. Am I inventing this, or is this the combined writing team of Hunter S. Thompson, Philip K. Dick, and Douglas Adams dropping little nuggets into my life to entertain me along the way with impossible synchronicities? I suppose it doesn't matter. I noticed and I appreciated it. This blurring of lines between fiction and reality continued to intrigue me, and I am reminded of PKD's fascination with the authentic versus the ersatz.

I see the doctors as I am fading from one consciousness to another and I'm completely in another world. The hospital environment, with its clinical interventions and reliance on pharmaceuticals, felt deeply alien to me. My instinctual rejection of this setting was manifested in physical acts of defiance, such as repeatedly removing my IV, a symbol of my resistance to what I perceived as an unnatural approach to healing. My left arm is bruised and purple and looks terrible. I keep ripping it out. Two by two, hands of blue, as I try to reject all plastic coming into my sensorium. I was repelled by all petroleum products and anything not natural. In my normal state of mind, I am pretty much the same way, but I understand that plastics are sometimes unavoidable. My longing for a more holistic, natural form of care—a desire to be surrounded by the Earth and traditional healers—underscored my disconnect with conventional medical practices.

Amidst this turmoil, I grappled with an existential pain, oscillating between moments of intense suffering and revelations of numbness. The realization that pain could vanish, leaving nothing behind, was both a relief and a harbinger of a darker descent. My mind raced with complex mathematical formulas and linguistic experiments, attempting to decipher a fundamental number system and the primal sounds of human existence. These endeavors, aimed at reconstructing the very essence of life on Earth, became a cyclical torment, an endless loop of death and rebirth within the confines of my consciousness.

This experience, marked by moments of lucidity interspersed with deep despair, challenged the boundaries of my understanding and endurance. The quest for meaning and the struggle to communicate my reality within the sterile, restrictive environment of the hospital highlighted the vast gulf between my internal world and the external reality imposed upon me. It was a Sisyphean ordeal, each cycle of awareness and blackout a testament to the enduring quest for understanding and connection while in the most isolating of circumstances.

In the depths of my experience within the hospital, my consciousness teetered between life and death, embarking on a twisted spiral into the darkness before creation itself. The notion that I was tasked with rebuilding the universe, a responsibility I believed was limited to forty-two iterations, provided a framework for my endeavors. Within this boundary, I ventured to reimagine mathematics and language, tools essential for early human development, aiming to seed a future rooted in love and higher consciousness. Despite the burden of restarting humanity, I embraced the challenge with a resolve to guide it towards a more harmonious existence.

A NEW MOM AND DAD

Amidst these cycles of death and rebirth, I encountered a moment of weird clarity—a memory or vision of being born to new parents, figures of warmth and guidance. My "father," an ophthalmologist from Edinburgh, and my "mother," embodiments of love, provided a stark contrast to my actual upbringing. This vision, experienced while physically confined to a hospital bed, offered a glimpse into an alternate existence filled with support and freedom, evoking a sense of ecstasy long forgotten.

What kind of medicine do they have me on to make me see these things? Is this pure opium? If so, I kind of like it. How often do you get a new set of parents?

As I gradually regained a sense of stability and humanity, the presence of my dear friends, Rene and Joann, who I first met in Queenstown, marked a turning point in my recovery. Their visit, filled with love and kindness, grounded me, reminding me of the bonds that sustain us through our darkest moments. Rene's thoughtful gift, a set of *Hitchhiker's Guide to the Universe* books, was a gesture of deep understanding and connection, linking our shared history and love for literature to the journey of healing and rediscovery ahead. These books were also coincidentally some of our dad's favorite books. It was Rene's first time through and he was loving them. And I am always happy to re-read Douglas Adams books.

This period of convalescence, though marked by turmoil and

existential exploration, ultimately reaffirmed the power of friendship, love, and the enduring human spirit. As I navigated the complexities of recovery, the support of Rene, Joann, and the cherished memories and hopes for humanity I carried with me served as reminders of light, guiding me back to myself and the world I was eager to re-engage with a renewed sense of purpose and understanding.

The doctors' concern over my eye condition brought an issue that I've grappled with for much of my life to the forefront, intensified by an event a year prior when I suddenly went blind in my right eye. This unexpected loss of vision, coinciding with a period of intense personal stress, introduced me to the rare diagnosis of Acute Right-Angle Closure—an uncommon form of glaucoma, especially given my age and the specifics of the condition.

I've always been cross-eyed. It used to make me a bit uncomfortable only because I could see it made other people uncomfortable. It's a strange little curse since I love seeing the world so much, but I've never been able to see in 3D.

My right eye has been a source of challenge since childhood, never quite aligning with my left, resulting in a cross-eyed appearance and significantly blurred vision. This disparity between the images captured by my two eyes created a unique form of visual chaos, with my brain struggling to reconcile the clear vision from my left eye with the distorted input from my right. It's a condition that, in a way, isolated me from the typical three-dimensional perception most people enjoy, leaving me to navigate a vibrant world without the depth that 3D vision provides.

Yet, this "disability" has, over time, transformed into what I consider "The Gift." It forced my brain to adapt, to interpret visual information differently, and in doing so, perhaps enhanced other areas of perception or creativity. This unique wiring of my brain, necessitated by the peculiarities of my vision, has become an integral part of how I view the world and myself.

The treatment I began in New Zealand was primarily focused on preserving the vision in my left eye, the sole source of my visual input. The irony of sharing the doctors' concern for my left eye wasn't lost on me—after all, maintaining the health of this eye is crucial for me to continue experiencing and capturing the beauty of the world around me. This journey through vision impairment and the subsequent adaptations I've made underscore a broader narrative of resilience, creativity, and the search for beauty in the face of adversity.

It is quite painful at times, occasionally swelling to a level of pain that is intense. I have a high pain tolerance (based on my last relationships... joking, joking), but still, when you are lying in bed and your eye is throbbing, feeling like it's about to explode, well that can be a bit unsettling.

What happens in this glaucoma is the vitreous fluid (the water in the eyeball) starts to fill up and there is no "drain" for it, so it just keeps expanding like a balloon. I was complaining about the pain when I went to the eye doctor in Austin before the last Burning Man. They misdiagnosed me with conjunctivitis (pinkeye), so the problem was not fixed. That's too bad, because this is technically classified as a medical emergency. Anyway, I ended up going fully black-out blind in that eye within just a few days.

At my ophthalmologist in Dunedin, NZ, they ran a battery of tests and one of the only things they can do is give me something called laser peripheral iridotomy. Basically, this means they use a laser to poke a bunch of holes in your iris so the vitreous fluid can flow through and relieve the pressure. They did it in both eyes. It doesn't feel great. It's kind of like having an angry red-headed child kick you in the balls for a few minutes while you have to keep your body perfectly still.

So after I was feeling a bit better, this wonderful doctor woman came along with all her goodies to inspect my eye. I called her Inspector Gadget. She was young and kind of Latina and kind of Asian with a long dark ponytail. Spunky and hilarious, she was literally carrying around like ten different eye instruments and whipping them out, one right after the other.

The subsequent decision to undergo another laser iridotomy underscored the gravity of my condition and the lengths to which my medical team was willing to go to preserve my vision. Throughout this ordeal, the support and care from friends and medical professionals have been invaluable, offering me not just treatment, but hope and reassurance during a vulnerable chapter of my life. Their efforts, combined with the advanced medical procedures I've undergone, have played a crucial role in staving off complete blindness, for which I remain eternally grateful.

21.
MICHAEL CERA SENDS ME TO THE LOONEY BIN

"Dreams are often most profound when they seem the most crazy."
—Sigmund Freud

"True healing is realizing you were never sick in the first place."
—Duncan Trussell

So there I was, expecting to be unleashed upon the world like a love-powered superhero, only to find myself with a one-way ticket to Bellevue mental hospital. Surprise! It's not every day you get a plot twist like this without even a hint of foreshadowing.

Alas, I'm in another hospital room now and the doctors are going to visit. I have my friends Rene and Jessica with me. They brought me some food from Panera downstairs and they are being so kind. I remember at one point Rene said, "Trey, I didn't know Jessica was your sister." And I replied, "Oh yes, she is."

Rene's comment was so left-field it could have started its own conspiracy theory. He had spent a long time traveling the world with us both. He didn't seem like he was kidding. For most of this trip and even before, he had been quite deadpan and not his usual jokey self. I realize that I was experiencing a different reality, but maybe he was too. I guess in his reality Jessica was my sister.

Anyway, I looked at Rene strangely and I kinda went along with it. I agreed she was indeed my sister, even though I know she was not. Pantheistic Gods above, I said so much nonsense throughout these episodes. I thought in the karmic wheel of life we are reborn again and again and our friends are our sisters and brothers. Speaking of which, as of the time of writing this, I've read over five hundred case studies of people talking about their own past lives and how characters make repeat experiences playing different roles. Check the end of the book for my recommendations.

This is me with my actual sister (from this life), Bianca. So interesting looking back at these old photos and my fascination with everything from Close Encounters to Space Travel to Humans with Superhero capabilities.

It does make me reflect on different people that come into and out of my life. From all of my research, we make many contracts in the life between lives with other souls to help teach them lessons, to learn lessons, and to complete the cycles of karma. I am reminded of what Deepak Chopra said, "There are no coincidences in life. What person that wandered in and out of your life was there for some purpose, even if they caused you harm."

Here was our great crew from the walk! That's Kevin Kelly there with the white beard. My roomie was there in the middle, Matt Mullenweg, the founder of Wordpress (thank God for that as it was the structure behind my blog!). I have my arm around Hugh Howey, who you may know from the Silo/Wool series of books and TV shows.

Kevin Kelly. Let me tell you a bit about him before I get to the next bit. Kevin Kelly is one of my heroes, and I have been lucky enough not just to meet him, but to hang out with him on many occasions and even do a long hike from Portugal to Spain on the Santiago de Compostela pilgrimage. Kevin is as multifaceted as all my heroes, so I hate to categorize him. Generally, I suppose you could say he is a techno-philosopher. He's done at least four TED talks and he was instrumental in how I built my blog, "Stuck In Customs," and my entire social media side of life. It ended up with millions and millions of followers and ended up being extremely financially lucrative. He has an agile mind and I love and admire that man so much. If you're reading this Kevin, I truly love you.

In the stark environment of the hospital room, I encountered a figure who bore an uncanny resemblance to Kevin Kelly, a man whose influence and presence had been significant in my life. This doppelganger, consumed by distress and proclaiming his financial and existential woes, presented a stark contrast to the Kevin I knew and admired. The sight was jarring, evoking a deep sense of empathy for his plight, and it stirred within me a contemplation on the nature of existence and the roles individuals play in our lives and perceptions.

NPCS AND THE BACKDROP PEOPLE

This experience led me to ponder the concept of "Backdrop People," a term borrowed from the subjects of Dolores Cannon's hypnotherapy sessions, as detailed in her work, *The Convoluted Universe Volume 5*. These individuals are likened to the extras in a film—present but not integrated into the narrative, lacking the complexity and depth attributed to those with souls. They serve as part of the scenery, guiding or distracting us from our paths, yet capable of being vessels for actual souls under certain circumstances. Imagine when you are watching a movie and there is just a crowd of random extras in the background doing this or that. A guy working at a newsstand. A lady standing in an expensive jewelry store in an airport. One thousand people walking around Times Square. You get the idea. Backdrop people.

The notion that many around us could essentially be operating on a simple script, devoid of a deeper spiritual essence, is both fascinating and disconcerting. It challenges us to discern the depth of connections and the essence of those we encounter, distinguishing between those who bring profound interactions and those who simply fill the space around us.

In this heightened state of awareness, my mind entertained the possibility that these figures could be manifestations or "remixes" of the souls I am familiar with, presenting as variations of people like Kevin Kelly or others I've recognized. This perspective, while a product of my altered state, ignited my curiosity and analytical instincts, driving me to explore the boundaries between reality and perception, between the essence of a soul and the roles we perceive others to play in our lives.

This exploration, though rooted in a moment of confusion and distress, allowed me to appreciate the complexity of human existence and the myriad ways in which we connect, interpret, and understand the souls that cross our paths.

Perhaps in my altered mind-state, I was able to see these NPC or Backdrop People as "remixes" of actual souls that I know of. That's why I would see people as 80% Kevin Kelly, 90% Glenn Howerton (Dennis from *Sunny in Philadelphia*), 95% Troy Aikman, and, as you are about to see, 99% Michael Cera. As you can tell, I am absolutely loving this state of mind as I try to noodle everything out. My analytical puzzling mind is on fire.

In the grand theater of my mind, where the casting director had clearly thrown the script out the window, I encountered a parade of characters that seemed oddly familiar. Picture this: I'm sitting there, trying to make sense of it all, when in walks a doctor who's the spitting image of Michael Cera. Yes, that Michael Cera, complete with the awkward charm and hesitant smile. At this point, my brain is doing somersaults, trying to figure out if I've somehow stumbled onto the set of another Jonah Hill vehicle.

Dr. Michael Cera tells me I'm about to be admitted to the mental hospital. I do not want to go. He says I can go in voluntarily or involuntarily. If I go in the former way, I have the chance to get out in twenty-four hours. If I go in the other way, I may be there for a long time and I have to send a fax to a judge or something. That sounds horrible. A fax! It's 2023! So I go in voluntarily, as it seems like the obvious choice.

I'm about to find out I'm the only one in there that volunteered. I figured if I volunteered to come to Earth, I might as well volunteer to go into a mental hospital. Maybe my energy is needed there. Maybe there is something for me to learn. I don't see how I have much of a choice. Either way, this story just may make for a good icebreaker at parties.

22.
THE BELLEVUE MENTAL HOSPITAL

"Reality is merely an illusion, albeit a very persistent one."
—ALBERT EINSTEIN

"I told my psychiatrist that everyone hates me. He said I'm being ridiculous—everyone hasn't met me yet."
—RODNEY DANGERFIELD

PSYCHOPATHIC BUILDING
BELLEVUE AND ALLIED HOSPITALS
NEW YORK CITY

Okay this was rock-bottom. Entering the mental health facility atop the hospital marked a significant shift in my journey—a descent into an environment where the extremes of human psychology were laid bare. Bracing myself for the challenges ahead, I committed to approaching this new chapter with open-hearted patience and love, despite sensing the heavy, tumultuous vibrations of the place.

I enter and see this parade of people. If you want to see the craziest of the crazy in New York, well, this is the place to visit. Immediately, I have this big Black guy threaten to murder me in my sleep because he's not a big fan of the Whites. Fair enough.

There is another bouncing-off-the-walls Black woman who is yelling horrible things at me as some kind of fresh meat in the asylum. There's a tall Mexican that promises me I will be dying in there because he doesn't like my bald spot. None of this was a good scene. But, you know, at least it's multicultural and would fit in nicely with the DEI protocols (Diversity, Equity, and Inclusion).

It's heartwarming, really, the way adversity brings people together, transcending cultural barriers in a united front of hostility.

The misconception regarding my sexuality, based on my painted nails, added another layer of complexity to my interactions, highlighting the varied prejudices and insecurities that can proliferate in confined environments. Chances are some of these men in here may have all kinds of issues with gays or their own sexuality. A few of them just stare at me... I can see they wish they had some weapons. Ah, the joys of breaking down stereotypes in the least likely of places.

So I stepped away from this United Nations meeting gone wrong for the stripping away of personal belongings and the assignment to a spartan, shared room. A trodden-downed nurse, acting as the tour guide to my downfall, introduced me to my new accommodations, a room that screamed minimalism taken to an extreme. Four beds, each adorned with the luxurious touch of rubber mattresses that could double as yoga mats if you're desperate enough. The décor was complemented by the absence of pillows and sheets, because who needs comfort when you're living the dream, right? And let's not forget the charming artwork etched into my desk by a previous aficionado of a swastika or ten. Well, clearly I've been given the "mattress for Whites," which makes me easier to find in the dark of night.

The roommates seemed like a mixed bag of tranquilized philosophers, each more Zen than a monk on sedatives. I found myself pondering my place in the hierarchy of madness. Was I the king of the loonies or just a commoner in this court of the tranquil? Among my eclectic new family was a large Puerto Rican fellow giving me the kind of look that suggested he wasn't imagining us braiding each other's hair. Those teardrop tattoos—were they fashion statements or a body count? It seemed impolite to ask, "Hey, nice ink, does it come with a backstory of homicide?"

I've found myself in a racial melting pot of potential throat-slitters, each representing a slice of New York's finest. I have a Mexican, a Black guy, and a Puerto Rican who look ready for darkness to fall so they can use that sharp object they've been working on. Where are all the White Supremacists that wanna kill me? This doesn't seem as racially diverse as I prefer in my insane asylums.

This experience, while daunting, served as a smart reminder of the humanity that persists even in the depths of despair and conflict. It reinforced my commitment to empathy and understanding, recognizing the inherent kindness that lies beneath the surface of even the most troubled individuals. In facing the realities of the mental health facility, I was reminded of the delicate balance between self-preservation and the pursuit of compassion in the face of adversity.

I get a few towels from the nurse as I enter MacGyver mode. I'm turning towels into a makeshift pillow like some kind of survivalist in the great indoors. It's amazing what you can do with a little ingenuity and a desperate need for neck support. Honestly, I'm feeling pretty smug about my towel origami. It's the little wins that count, especially when you're bedding down in what feels like a set piece from a horror movie.

There is a common lounge room where people are coming together. It's only open at certain times. I enter and it looks like a hospital waiting room from the 1970s. I believe the interior decorator was going for a Soviet brutalist theme, and he did an exquisite job. This was absolutely a masterclass in what can only be described as retro-dystopian chic.

The furniture is a light-colored wood and everything is to perfect ninety degree proportions. The cushions are made of the finest rubber and the color palette is a delicate variegated rainbow of brown to brown, evoking the warmth and charm of a decommissioned military base. There is a tiled floor that is somewhere between a laminate that has distant echoes of granite, at least in the places it is not a bit wrinkled. On the far wall, there is a row of what can loosely be called windows, designed to let in just enough light to keep you guessing whether it's day or night. Just beyond the fine mesh is another set of horizontal bars. In the distance, I can see the skyline of Manhattan.

The Empire State Building rises tall and free on the other side.

There, mounted on the wall like a relic of a bygone era, was a television that seemed to have time-traveled directly from my childhood living room to this very lounge. Its vintage charm was undeniable, encased in a cage as if it might at any moment leap off the wall in a fit of technological nostalgia. This wasn't your garden-variety 4K marvel; oh no, this was 480p of pure, unadulterated retro vision. I don't remember what was playing, but it was unremarkable. A few people sit in the chairs and give it an empty stare.

MAKING NEW FRIENDS

There he is. The great Ronny. @Ronny_blaxx on Instagram. Follow him and imagine washing your clothes on his abs.

Oh, a chess board! I'll sit down there and I'll summon some kind of savant to sit across from me. Sure enough, it happens! I met this amazing guy named Ronny Black. Yes, he was Black, but that's beside the point. He was kind of just like me with his educational background. Ronnie was a Comp Sci and Math major. I detected very quickly he was hyperintelligent. He talked 4x as fast as anyone I have ever heard. But I understood everything he was saying. I talked back to him at hyper-fast speed too. It's like we were Bynars from *Star Trek*.[4] He was so happy to finally meet another patient that understood him. I did, and then, the more I talked to him, the more I realized he should not be in this place. He's just this super-intelligent dude that is on another plane of existence and he's playing three-dimensional chess while everyone else is playing checkers. I get it. He's stuck in there.

The encounter with Ronny underscored a recurring theme in my experiences: the fine line between genius and madness, and the often arbitrary distinctions that define normalcy within the rigid structures of mental health care. It was a poignant reminder of the diverse tapestry of human cognition and the challenges faced by those who exist on its fringes.

Later, in the November portion of the story, Ronny was to attempt suicide after he got out of the hospital and he came back to an empty existence, with no friends, and no one to talk to.

I meet a doppelganger of Joe Rogan named Brian Davis. He has a wandering eye (although not in the photo above). I asked him about it, since I almost always chat up people with eye problems because I am curious about how they navigate life. He started out quite confrontational (once I told him I'm not gay), but then we ended up becoming friends. He says that with two eyes that see in different directions he gets to see two versions of each person. He can see the light and dark version of each person. Fascinating. Sure,

---

[4] An esoteric reference to TNG where these aliens talked very quickly to one another saying stuff like 1001111101101111000.

I'm taking everything with a grain of salt, since I'm talking to someone in an insane asylum, but what he said is resonating with me
because I'm in the midst of seeing everyone in their past and future
lives. Or, perhaps, I'm just seeing NPCs as genetic mixes of people
I recognize. I know that people with eye problems do indeed see the
world differently, but I'm beginning to understand it in a different
way. He still messages me to this day and he says his eyes have gone
straight again after he has come to God, as he told me in a fairly
born-again DM.

I meet a girl I'll call Michelle. She reminds me of a young version of my mom for some reason. She's beautiful and is wearing a lot of makeup, which I found unusual in a mental institution. She is kind and rather engaging, a blanket of warmth in this Kafkaesque carnival. She clearly loves talking to me and is drawn to me wherever I am. Every time I see her, she runs up to engage in excited conversation. I'm not getting a sexual vibe from her, just some strange magnetism.

Despite forming these unlikely bonds, the realization that my confinement could extend indefinitely was daunting. The thought of being ensnared in this environment, surrounded by a spectrum of cognitive and communicative differences, stirred a deep fear of losing my own grasp on sanity. My interactions revealed that many of my fellow residents, each with their unique challenges and perspectives, were not so different from me in their essence. This underscored a troubling thought: the thin line between perceived normalcy and the criteria for institutionalization.

My brief respite in the hospital had sharpened my mental faculties, affirming my belief in my own relative sanity. This clarity brought with it a responsibility—a recognition of the inherent value and potential misunderstanding of those deemed unfit for society due to their unconventional ways of interacting or learning. The fear of becoming irretrievably lost within the system was palpable, a reminder of the delicate balance between mental health care and the preservation of individual identity and autonomy.

My experience in the mental hospital deepened my empathy for those confined within its walls, a sentiment profoundly influenced by my mother's own struggles with schizophrenia. Witnessing her challenges and understanding the complexities of mental health through her journey fostered a deep sense of compassion and sorrow, emotions that were rekindled and magnified by my own predicament.

The ritual of medication distribution, a moment I observed from the sidelines, underscored the regimented nature of life in the facility, contrasting sharply with the normalcy I yearned for. An unremarkable meal further highlighted the stark reality of institutionalization, softened only by Rene's thoughtful gesture of bringing food, a small act of kind-ness that injected a moment of levity into the oppressive atmosphere.

Interacting with families visiting their loved ones, I sought to of-fer comfort and acknowledgment, recognizing the value in simple acts of kindness and the positive impact they can have. Commend-ing a fellow patient to his father was a small but meaningful gesture, reflecting my belief in the importance of connection and support.

This harrowing experience illuminated the harsh realities faced by individuals in mental health facilities and also solidified my re-solve to approach others with empathy and understanding. It under-scored the need for compassion and advocacy in addressing the com-plexities of mental health and the systemic challenges within insti-tutions designed to provide care.

One of the patients in there was a younger kid. He didn't appear to be able to talk, but he was always very kind to me and we would smile at one another in a supportive way. He spent a while coloring this and then gave it to me as a gift. It was sweet and I gave him a little hug even though you aren't supposed to touch other patients. A hug makes everyone feel better, I reckon.

NO SLEEP IN BELLEVUE

I can't sleep. I'm miserable. It's completely uncomfortable and I'm scared to death that one of my roommates will kill me in my sleep. The Black guy in the room next door told me that it would be my fate. And that Mexican guy and I had made no progress in our international relations since his earlier threat. He's just a few rooms down. There's no doors on the rooms. Everything is wide open. There are no cameras. There are no guards and the nurse station is a long walk down the hall behind bulletproof glass.

I sleep with one eye open, which is convenient, as it is the only eye that is working.

I get up. I begin to walk up and down the cheerless corridor. Michelle, a fellow wandering zombie, is dragging her mattress down the hall. She can't sleep either. She wants to get into the solitary confinement room so she can sleep peacefully, so I help her move her mattress there. She asks if I want to sleep in there too. I don't get the vibe she is hitting on me or anything, but I know she finds me interesting. My refusal was rooted in an all-too-vivid imagination of being inadvertently entombed within those four walls, a prospect I found distinctly unappealing and that's even more of a devil's fuel of nightmare for me. Little did I know I would end up spending the night in solitary confinement in another mental hospital when I returned home to New Zealand, but that's a story for later when things became darker than dark.

I go into the bathroom to pee. As I exit the little bathroom to return to bed, that Puerto Rican guy comes and slams the door open into me, smashing me into the wall. He's angry and wants to beat the shit out of me. I use my Jedi charm and calm him down. But I'm rattled. There will be no sleep tonight.

The next day is more of the same. Threats of violence while I am just randomly talking to people and trying to make friends. I have no idea how long I will be in there. Is this like a prison situation where you have to join a gang? Maybe. I can't tell if there are any gangs. Maybe I should start one. Or is this a Tim Robbins Shawshank situation, where I am going to have to do the taxes and accounting for all the mental prison guards. I hope not. I hate doing taxes. I'd rather dig a tunnel with a spoon than deal with the IRS.

Approaching the nurse's station to request more comfortable clothing was a moment of normalcy within the surreal environment of the mental hospital. Ronny Black, whose intelligence and insight I had quickly come to respect, guided me through the simple but essential process of asking for basic necessities like sweatpants and a shirt. Communicating through the small, grilled circle that served as both window and microphone, I made my request known, maintaining a friendly demeanor in hopes of lightening the atmosphere for the staff behind the glass.

The administrative and nursing staff, ensconced behind their protective barrier, seemed to embody a collective weariness. Their roles, demanding constant engagement with patients in varying states of distress, appeared to weigh heavily on them. I attempted to inject a bit of warmth and brightness into their day, fully aware of the daunting challenges they faced in their professional lives.

The subsequent evaluation by a team of doctors marked a turning point in my stay. Their discussion and consultation with the nursing staff led to a consensus that my condition did not warrant further confinement or medication—a decision for which I was deeply grateful. The recognition that my behavior had not raised any red flags provided a glimmer of hope for my release, an outcome I eagerly anticipated.

Reflecting on the experience, I find solace in the decision not to administer antipsychotic medication. The journey, fraught with challenges and introspection, was an integral part of my growth and understanding. It underscored the importance of navigating mental health crises with care and discernment, recognizing the delicate balance between intervention and the natural course of healing and self-discovery.

23.
BACK TO "NORMAL" LIFE

"The past has its place but not at the expense of the present."
—ECKHART TOLLE

"I have a lot of growing up to do. I realized that the other day inside my fort."
—ZACH GALIFIANAKIS

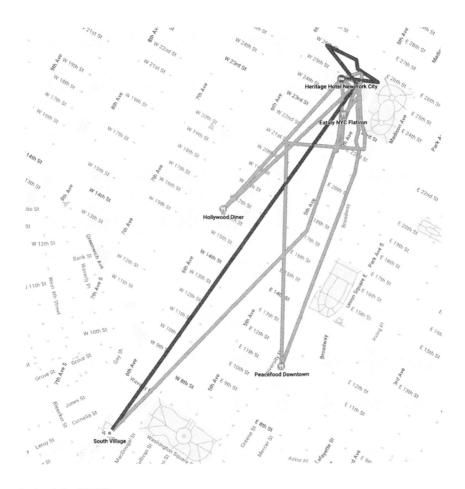

July 14, 2023

Rene and I walk to a new hotel in Manhattan.

I stay there many nights, but I can't quite sleep. I sleep a little bit here and there. I awaken with startles and have understandings.

On this first night out of the hospital, Rene, Jessica, and I all go out and have a fabulous sushi meal. As far as I know, I think I'm acting very normal and I'm finally back to reality. I am so thankful to be out of that hellhole of a mental hospital. My heart swells with gratitude for both my emancipation and the companionship of these steadfast allies. The evening is immortalized through a series of photos below, serving as testament to our revelry.

Our new hotel, the Heritage Hotel. I'd like to formally apologize to the staff there for my... unusual behavior.

I love them both so much and I am forever grateful for them helping me through this time.

THE ULTIMATE META GAME CREATION

I have this strange need to create a meta-game. A game where people are trying to figure out what happened to me so as to lead to their enlightenment and embracing consciousness and love as a way of life. A game of my own death, so I begin to fake it. I'm reminded of this book I read called *Daemon*. I begin to create an incredibly elaborate suicide. It's also important to note that I didn't actually have any suicidal thoughts. It was all a game, and I was creating it.

I would take many photos with my phone all around New York that would act as clues for treasure hunters who are going to be playing this wildly intricate game I am designing. Being a lifelong gamer and a bit of a game designer, I found this to be such an intoxicating challenge.

Over the next few days, I began to drift back into my heightened ability to see multiple realities at once. Hidden patterns, hilarious synchronicities, deep meanings, and transcendent understandings about myself and the nature of the universe.

I see Rene and Jessica at night and they are always lovely and fun. I'm spending my days going around the city. I go out to flea markets and buy all this local artisan stuff. I'm spending a lot of money, and this is a common side effect of mania. I'm being extremely generous and sometimes just giving money to random people or leaving giant tips.

At one point Alexis (the homeless guy from earlier in the story) contacts me and says he needs new shoes. He tells me they must be "New Balance," which I thought kind of picky for a guy that doesn't have any shoes at all. Anyway, I get his shoe size and then spend a few hours on this overall task to get him his shoes. It was great and he was chuffed.

Here are the new New Balance shoes for Alexis. I crammed a $20 bill in the laces so he could get some food. Or crack.

I went over to the Google store one day because I was excited to get their new phone. I did that and got it all set up. I got food from a farmer's market.

Now, none of this is very exciting, but it is important to note that I'm just acting like a normal person for the most part. In my mind I am not normal, and these are just a few of the high functioning things I would do all day.

At this point, I am also operating with 100% certainty and 0% self-doubt. A clear sign of delusion. One of the main problems with delusional people is they don't realize they are delusional!

In the little gym of my hotel before I was gonna go spend the day in New York creating clues for people with my camera, making photos and videos.

I would take photos with my camera everywhere I went to leave clues for people. I was pretty sure I was going to die, even though I had no desire to commit suicide. I thought that I would just "be killed" somehow in New York. Or, I'd just disappear. Look, it made sense to me at the time.

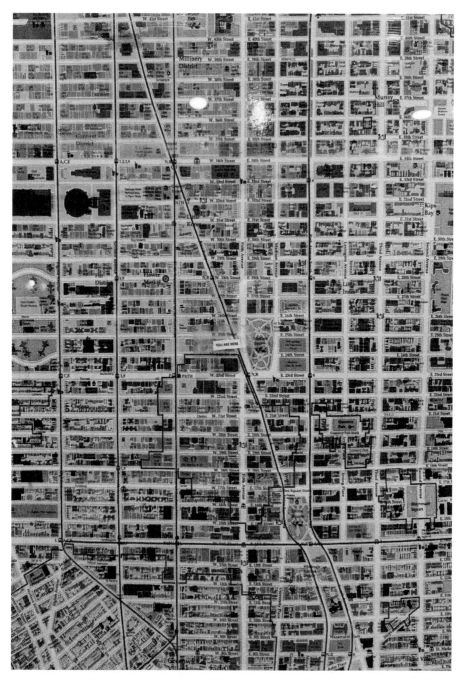

Another clue I was leaving for people. I love game maps and this seemed like a perfect one. It was on the bottom floor of my hotel.

I continue to talk to homeless people and give them things. I thought this guy was another best friend and Burning Man roomie, Jonatas from Brazil. I know at the time that Jonatas was having horrible kidney stone issues. So, I felt by being generous to this guy, it would help Jonatas. Later, I came by and saw him doing crack. I had some thought that perhaps as this version of Jonatas was hurting himself by doing crack, he could have been causing the kidney stones in the other Jonatas.

Final night in this hotel. The game was afoot.

My final hours within the confines of what felt like an alternate reality were marked by a strange sense of urgency and an overwhelming compulsion to act beyond my conscious control. The meticulous arrangement of my clothes and the continuous capture of photographs were driven by an inexplicable need to document what I perceived as the final scene of my existence. This act, intended for those who might later seek to understand my experiences, was imbued with the intense emotional turmoil of past traumas resurfacing in a visceral outpouring of pain.

There is the dreaded fire escape alarm that some version of me was about to pull.

FIRE ESCAPE THE HOTEL!

The decision to trigger the fire emergency alarm was not one born of rational deliberation but rather an impulsive response to an inner directive that felt beyond my autonomy. This moment underscored a belief that, at certain junctures, our paths are influenced by forces or presences that guide us towards pivotal experiences, necessary for our soul's journey. The encounter with a stranger on the staircase who was running upstairs, where I paused to offer an embrace, encapsulated the dichotomy of my actions—seemingly irrational yet meaningful in the context of my heightened emotional and spiritual state. It was like saying, "Hey, I know things are weird, but let's make it weirder with a hug." Somehow, it made perfect sense in my overly dramatic, emotionally charged bubble.

My subsequent venture into the city, liberated by music and movement, represented a brief interlude of joy and freedom.

I return to the hotel and the manager is trying to grab me and hold me and physically hold my body in place. I am worried about the police. I am lost and between worlds. I don't know what is happening and there is a torture in my mind. My mind screams like a banshee and I am lost. No one could possibly understand my pain. I spin artfully out of his grip and run out the door and into the streets. I dodge this way and that to make sure my tracks aren't covered. It was like an action movie.

This sequence of events, while bewildering and fraught with tension, illuminated the depth of my struggle to navigate between worlds—both the tangible reality of New York City and the intangible realms of my psyche. It laid bare the complexities of mental health crises, the societal challenges in responding to them, and the individual's quest for meaning and self-preservation while in turmoil.

The Lex Hotel. It's Great. Can Recommend. Lex Fridman has good taste in decor too. That guy never ceases to amaze me.

The Lex also has a cool rooftop area. Here's the view. The view is almost as good as the live feed from Lex's sex robot's OnlyFans page.

Transitioning to The Lex hotel with Rene provided a fleeting sense of relief and camaraderie during my turbulent mental state. The move, orchestrated by Rene's unwavering support, was a bond that remained my anchor in a sea of confusion.

I'm thinking The Lex is some kind of weird parallel universe where Lex Fridman has become some kind of a god and spawned all sorts of hotels with his name on them. I'm so thankful. Man, that Lex, he can do anything! We check in and there are two beds in the room. Rene leaves for a while to get our stuff and brings everything back there. I am forever grateful to Rene for doing all of this stuff to help me.

We sat down and watched an episode of *Curb Your Enthusiasm*. I think I chose the last episode of Season 5 when Larry David died. I see things in that episode I've never seen before, and I've seen that episode twice. He died and then went to a few different levels of "heaven" with different video and dimensional effects in each one. I remember watching it with Rene and being so confused, thinking, "Why don't I remember this?" And, just recently, I decided to watch it again. It's back to the way I remembered it. This made me think back to my time on the plane and seeing so many things that were unique. Was there another version of reality that was "spun up" for me during that time? Are there many different versions of the last episode of Season 5 of *Curb* depending upon what universe you are in? It really continues to boggle and befuddle my mind.

Rene and I go out to get some food. I'm first drawn to a place that has some fairy lights. I go in and there is some kind of karaoke scene there. I am watching it in that video-game interface. I'm transfixed. I can tell Rene is not feeling the scene so we go somewhere else and have some Mexican food.

This is the first place we stop. I am completely inside of a video-game interface. This whole performance has been put on just for me. I'm transfixed.

And this is where we ate a massive meal. We were both starving and battleworn.

Coming back to The Lex was like hitting the "on" switch for my manic energy—sleep was off doing its own thing, probably hanging out in a more peaceful mind. I couldn't help but notice how this whole scenario was putting Rene in a spot he never really signed up for. It's like when you agree to help a friend move and suddenly you're assembling furniture. There I was, buzzing with energy, while Rene looked like he was auditioning for the role of "man desperately needing a nap."

His exhaustion and my inability to just chill out highlighted how we were pretty much in different dimensions, even though we were stuck in the same room.

With peace playing hard to get, I found myself back on the New York streets at night, doing my best impression of a guy trying to solve life's mysteries, or at least figure out where all this energy could possibly be coming from. It was less of a walk and more of a quest, wandering around looking for some clarity or maybe just a way to hit the pause button on my brain's 24/7 broadcast.

24.
ESCAPE NEW YORK!

"We are not human beings having a spiritual experience. We are spiritual beings having a human experience."
    —Pierre Teilhard de Chardin

"I'm sick of following my dreams, man. I'm just going to ask where they're going and hook up with 'em later."
    —Mitch Hedberg

Atop The Lex for breakfast, Rene and Jesse hatch a plan to get me out of New York before the authorities swoop in.

July 18, 2023

As the Manhattan sun staged its daily spectacle, slicing through the urban canyons, I found myself in a scene straight out of a speculative fiction novel. I see another version of one of my lovers. She is old and broken and she tells me she is back to help her son who is in the hospital. Is this a quantum version of my lover where she went down a different decision tree and ended up hunched and broken in NYC taking care of her sick son? She's with an aged Indian guy named Vic. He reminds me loosely of my friend Vic Gundotra and I hope he comes back to life as Vic. Because that other Vic has a pretty sweet life.

This woman and this man were lovers, many times over, and I am seeing that a hundred times over. Her eyes are big and blue and there is an understanding between our eyes. They are hungry and thirsty, so I feed them food and give them some drinks from the 7-11. But her eyes and my eyes connect and there is a deep understanding of many lives passed. There is a delicate way I move away from her and back to my hotel.

Yet, as I retreated to the solitude of my hotel, I orchestrated what could only be described as a dramatic encore to my earlier existential performance—arranging my garments in a tableau evocative of a second departure from this mortal coil. This act was less a cry for the spotlight and more a physical echo of the tempest within. Jesse and Rene, ever the stalwarts, navigated this storm with a grace and patience that belied the complexity of the situation. They stood as lighthouses, their efforts to illuminate my path a contrast to the opaque darkness of my internal struggle, a solitary battle against forces that seemed to operate beyond my control.

This short period of my life, marked by confusion and a desperate search for meaning, was a testament to the complexities of the human psyche and the profound impact of mental health struggles. It highlighted the importance of compassion, understanding, and the relentless pursuit of healing, even when the path forward remains obscured.

Jesse and Rene, bless their cotton socks, were understandably on edge about me. My recent escapade with the fire escape—an unintended homage to performance art—had them convinced that we might soon be starring in our own police procedural. Their logic was sound: apparently, fire escapes are for fires, not existential escapades. Their solution? A tactical retreat from the Big Apple, lest the long arm of the law decide to tap us on the shoulder.

I didn't really want to leave, as I was looking forward to spending a few days with Rene and exploring the city. I also had a full plan to go to Chicago in a few days to see my mom who was in the hospital. So this was kind of messing up all my plans, but I didn't fight back and did what they said. I could see their concern and pain in their eyes, and it wrapped another layer of pain around the pain that was already throbbing inside.

The wake of chaos I'd left in my path weighed heavily on me, though at the time, it felt more like I was a passenger in my own body, with someone (or something) else in the driver's seat. It was an odd season in the chronicles of me.

As we prepared for our journey back to New Zealand, stopping at Jessica's to gather her belongings, I was struck by the realization that she would be accompanying me. Her decision to join on this journey, while unexpected, was a testament to her supportive nature. My gratitude towards Jessica and Rene was immense, offering a semblance of stability in the midst of my tumultuous state. My desire to return home, to find solace in the familiarity and solitude of my own space, became a beacon guiding me through the uncertainty.

A final stop below Jessica's studio for breakfast before the three of us head to the airport together.

Before departing, we shared a meal beneath Jessica's studio, a moment of communion before the long journey ahead. My commitment to the spiritual emergence I was experiencing remained unshaken, leading me to leave my 360° camera in the restaurant bathroom. This deliberate act was rooted in the belief that the camera, and the perspectives it captured, would serve as a guide for others on their own quests for understanding and awakening. It was my hope that these clues would contribute to a collective journey towards consciousness.

I'm continuing to take photos to leave clues for people playing the game of games.

I WAS THE IN-FLIGHT ENTERTAINMENT
So we boarded a series of flights from Newark to San Francisco to

Auckland, New Zealand. That was a scene. Jessica slept for most of the flight while I was encountering a very different reality.

I started looking closely at the tones of color in people's hair. I had started to experience colors and light differently after my big emergence in New York. While there, when walking around at night, all the neon lights seemed to have an extra "glow" to them. Wild. If you've ever tried acid or mushrooms, then you'll understand how lights can have an extra layer of beauty to them. I found it incredible I was not on any drugs at all and was still experiencing reality in this hyper-realistic way. This heightened awareness extended to the subtle variations in people's hair, where I discerned extraordinary patterns and colors invisible to others. This newfound ability to "read" these patterns felt like a gift, a unique lens through which I could perceive hidden aspects of those around me. It underscored a shift in my perception of reality, an evolution that promised to continue unfolding in the days to come.

I talked to one of the flight attendants and I told her I was "Undercover Sommelier," a clandestine connoisseur of the skies, and we were filming a TV show where I was the wine expert on the plane and I was going to hyper-analyze everything that happened. I explained to her that I was dedicated to the fine art of viniculture at altitude. I went to the back galley and showed all those male flight attendants how this White guy could move in a silent disco of my EarPods. They loved it. They even invited me back to dance again. I was putting on a show. I even got quite a bit of it on video. Yes, so that was my trans-Pacific flight.

During the lengthy flight, enveloped in the solitude of my thoughts, I found myself pondering the shift ignited by my experiences in Scotland. The notion that I had undergone a spiritual awakening, emerging as a consciousness reborn, began to take hold with striking clarity. This awakening felt like a pivotal reset, imbuing me with a sense of purpose, albeit one shrouded in mystery. Despite the multitude of souls whose contributions to the world dwarfed my own, I couldn't shake the feeling that this awakening was intentional, that I was chosen for reasons yet to be unveiled. And, after the awakening my DNA was being altered and my mind and body were being upgraded. More would be revealed to me and I didn't need to figure it all out on this flight, but I like to try to speculate on these wild time-travel quantum sci-fi stories.

Among the myriad theories that danced through my mind, one particularly captivating idea was the possibility of a reverse aging process. The thought that my physical being might start to reflect a youthful vigor, that with each passing year I would appear younger, was both bewildering and intriguing. This speculation extended to a vision of my life unwinding in reverse, a journey where my final moments would mirror the vulnerability and innocence of infancy, a poignant reflection on the cyclical nature of existence.

I had many a theory bouncing around my head, let me tell you.

This flight also presented an opportunity for kindness and human connection. Encountering an elderly man struggling with a complex breathing apparatus, I was compelled to assist. His crazy device was incredibly complicated. It had all these rubber tubes and battery packs and tanks and it was almost inscrutable, even if Rube and Goldberg had been there as my untangling muses. As I was walking by, I noticed he was having trouble with it and the tubes were all caught up in the airplane seat and his foldout-television. Nobody was helping him, so of course I did. I got down on my knees and helped him untangle everything before he suffocated or something. He asked me if I could figure out how to turn off his overhead light. I said sure. It turned out to be incredibly complicated because we had to fully get out that fold-out display and then find some menu deep in the system that turned off the light. And then his whole breathing apparatus was all tangled up again, and it was just a big mess. I was wondering why the flight attendants weren't helping. I can only imagine they were getting excited about my next dance routine.

25.
ARRIVAL BACK HOME
IN NEW ZEALAND

"The most beautiful thing we can experience is the mysterious. It is the source of all true art and science."
—ALBERT EINSTEIN

"The cure for boredom is curiosity. There is no cure for curiosity."
—DOROTHY PARKER

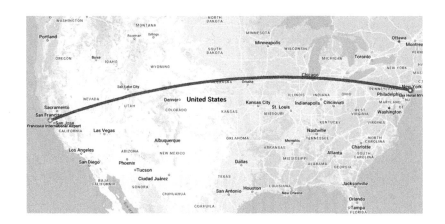

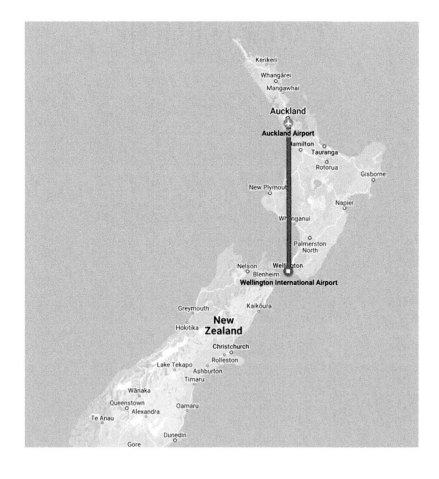

July 20, 2023

I arrive at Auckland airport as I have countless times before. But this time it is different. Speaking of time, you may have noticed there is no entry for July 19. That's because New Zealand is a day in the future because of the international timeline, and time changes were no stranger to me at this point in my soul's safari.

Upon my return to my home, the familiar landscape of New Zealand greeted me with a renewed sense of wonder. The Maori cultural presence, always a poignant reminder of the nation's heritage, resonated with me more profoundly than ever before. Walking through the international terminal, I was captivated by the intricate Maori carvings that mark the gateway for arrivals. These carvings, vibrant with cultural significance, seemed to come alive, their traditional gestures of challenge and welcome striking a deep chord within me. It was as if I was witnessing the essence of Maori spirituality and artistry in motion, a moment of cultural communion that felt both humbling and elevating.

Jessica's impatience with my lingering was a stark contrast to my absorption in the moment. Her frustration, though born of concern, underscored the disconnect that can arise when one is deeply immersed in a spiritual or transcendent experience, while others are anchored in the practicalities of the moment. The hustle of travelers, many seemingly indifferent to the cultural richness around them, highlighted a common oversight in pursuit of the immediate.

Navigating through the airport, the sensation of being discussed in a group chat from which I was excluded added layers of complexity to my return. Despite Jessica's assurances of transparency, the realization that my situation was being managed collectively, albeit with good intentions, introduced feelings of isolation and control that were at odds with my state of spiritual emergence. The desire for solitude, for the sanctuary of home, became intertwined with a growing awareness of the challenges that lay ahead in reconciling my inner journey with the external realities of care and community.

The dichotomy between my need for traditional, Earth-connected healing and the contemporary approach to mental health underscored a broader dialogue about the nature of support and understanding in times of important personal change. As I contemplated the path forward, the desire to avoid hospitalization, with its sterile and traumatic associations, was paramount. The quest for healing, I realized, would require navigating not just my own inner landscape but also the terrain of relationships, expectations, and societal norms that define our collective approach to well-being.

I'm confused as to why my friends Mark and Pixie are in Auckland. They live down near me on the south island in Wanaka. Why can't I just meet them down there? Yes, so there's this whole chat going on, and nobody is telling me anything. As I emerge from Customs, I rapidly realize I am not going home, but instead with Mark and Pixie to their other home in Wellington. I don't want to go. I feel a bit like I've been duped. I've been bamboozled. I'm being controlled.

However I know they have concern for me and just want to take care of me. So, I am nice and don't complain and go with the flow. This is the way the universe is unfolding, and I am not going to fight it.

As I leave Security, I see Mark and Pixie. They are the loveliest and kindest people in the world. I'm still feeling a bit off-the-map, acting a bit goofy and free. I think I'm acting pretty normal and feeling so free, until I get to the Wellington airport.

In the midst of my travels, I became the custodian of a pen from a Scottish hotel, an artifact imbued with a simple directive: "Use this pen to write a letter to someone you love." This pen, which had journeyed with me as faithfully as any companion from Arthurian legend, found itself at the center of an unexpected adventure in the Wellington Airport, of all places.

Here are two lovely souls, Mark and Pixie. She's helping Mark prepare for a fun after-party after my 50th birthday. They stayed over with a few other people for a second night of fun. There may have been more molecules involved. In fact, there definitely were.

There, in the middle of the comings and goings of weary travelers, stood a Lego dinosaur, a sentinel of childhood wonder in a sea of luggage and coffee cups. A young lad and his mother, fellow observers of this plastic behemoth, confirmed its existence to me, thus ensuring I hadn't finally crossed the line into the fantastical. Emboldened by our shared discovery, I felt a sudden and inexplicable urge to perform a magic trick. Mind you, my repertoire of illusions was as empty as a politician's promises. Yet, the desire was there, as mysterious in origin as the dark side of the moon.

What ensued was a performance of chaotic proportions as I excavated the contents of my bag in search of the sacred pen, transforming a simple act of generosity into a spectacle rivaling the most tragic of comedies. The intention was for the boy to craft a note for his father, a heartwarming gesture facilitated by my enchanted writing implement.

Time was becoming more of a loop for me. I saw this attractive flight attendant, possibly a hot backdrop NPC, and then I knew I would see her again in exactly fifteen minutes when time looped around in time again. And I did. I had a feeling she would secretly have the pen under her little Air New Zealand cap, making for the greatest magic trick reveal ever. I didn't ask. That would have been a bit weird. Not like I wasn't already being a bit weird.

Eventually, we make it to Mark and Pixie's place. Poor Jessica is clearly drained after having to "manage" me all the way from New York. Jessica and I had a fun time on the plane for the most part when she wasn't trying to corral me. I was showing her all my writing. I was writing a very long story about Rene and she was reading it while I was writing it. I was also trying to watch this Indian Bollywood movie with her called *Baaghi 3*.

I had a moment on the plane where I used something called TreyGPT to create that movie from scratch. There was like a thirty second timer as it was starting up and I had to come up with the plot quickly. Man, talk about pressure. It's like trying to microwave a burrito before your favorite song ends. I wanted this Bollywood movie to have four themes. I wanted it to explore the use of Uber in the Indian community. I wanted it to explore the theme of irony, but I didn't think enough Indian Bollywood movies really explored that topic. For example, you rarely see a winsome young man dancing around a grapefruit tree, exclaiming, "It's as wet as a drought!" Third, I wanted there to be a dog in the movie. And last, and this one is a bit of a fun racist angle, I wanted the protagonist to have a haircut that could be described as a Jew Curl. God knows why I came up with these four themes for the movie.

But, I kid you not, the movie ended up having all four of those themes. It also seemed to mimic my current adventure. He has a best friend who goes dark (like Rene did) and there is this yin-yang cycle of life. The wheel of karma. Death and rebirth. Let me tell you. This movie had it all. And I was so wild in my mind, I thought it was made specifically for me. Or maybe I created it out of my own mind. There was a lot going on up there.

It's actually a pretty good movie. I recommend it.

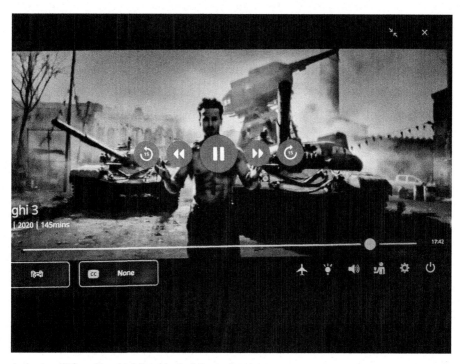

A classic still from Baaghi 3 I grabbed while on the plane.

I was having so many thoughts about Artificial Intelligence. I thought that *Baaghi 3* was the original and soon there would be a *Baaghi 4* that I was gonna have to work on with TreyGPT. But I imagined it would be just a copy and totally derivative. And as *Baaghi 5* and 6 came out, they would be copies of copies and the quality of the movie would degrade over time. The sequels would become more and more ridiculous and people would think back to *Baaghi 3* and think, oh my god, that was the best one by far.

It's a real treat up there in my mind. It was a constant ever-unfolding dreamscape of possibilities. I almost forgot about my job on the plane as an Undercover Boss as the Secret Sommelier. There were many games afoot.

WORRIED ABOUT JESSICA

Reflecting on everything, my worry for Jessica came into focus like when you realize you've been holding binoculars the wrong way. Her exhaustion, a tangible manifestation of the physical and emotional toll of our journey, stood in sharp contrast to my initial excitement about sharing the unique beauty and artistic inspiration of New Zealand with her. The prospect of her engaging with the luminous landscapes, of her creativity unfurling in the tranquility of my home studio, was a vision I had cherished. Yet, the reality of our situation in Wellington, despite the city's inherent charms and the generosity of our hosts, underscored a dissonance between my aspirations and our current circumstances.

This dissonance highlighted a deeper sense of displacement and a questioning of my choices and the path that led us here. The notion of being somewhere we were not supposed to be, of plans gone awry, was a theme that echoed my internal struggle to reconcile my spiritual journey with the practical realities of life. This feeling was like realizing you're in the wrong joke. It was like we were meant to be in a comedy club but ended up at a lecture about quantum physics. The sense of something being "off" was not just a reflection of our geographical location but a metaphor for the broader existential questions that had been surfacing in my mind. In this moment of introspection, the journey to Wellington became symbolic of the search for meaning and direction in the aftermath of personal transformation.

In the welcoming embrace of Mark and Pixie's home, the beauty and serenity of the environment juxtaposed with my internal tumult. Gratitude mingled with confusion, as the remnants of my New York experiences cast shadows on my perception, transforming even the comfort of a luxurious shower. He's got one of those showers with nozzles all over the place that spray your belly and legs and all that stuff. It's quite a scene. His multifaceted shower—an aquatic extravaganza that left me feeling like the protagonist in an elaborate aquatic prank. Am I in Mark's "Escape Shower?" I gotta get out of there. It feels weird and I feel like there is a giant cosmic joke being played on me.

My interactions with Mark and Pixie, veiled in a faux-British accent, evoked a sense of timeless camaraderie, as if we were not just friends but souls entwined across lifetimes. In my mind's eye, Mark became Marcus Aurelius, a figure of wisdom and strength, while Pixie assumed the role of a sister soul, a companion on countless journeys through the cycles of existence. This narrative, a blend of affection and whimsy, was a testament to the depth of our connection, real or imagined within the altered state of my consciousness.

The parallels I drew between Pixie and another dear friend, Bridget, further illustrated my tendency to seek familiar patterns of my relationships, to find echoes of past connections in present interactions. This search for continuity, for threads linking one life to another, was both comforting and confounding, a reflection of my quest to understand the intricate dance of souls through time. This whole thing about seeing patterns and connecting dots from one life to the next—it's comforting but also kind of like trying to solve a puzzle that's also solving you.

As we conversed, the boundaries between past, present, and potential futures blurred, creating a shared space where laughter and philosophical musings intertwined. Despite the clarity of the moment, a part of me acknowledged the peculiarity of my perceptions, recognizing the influence of my spiritual emergence on my interactions and interpretations. The thought of exploring these connections further through past life regressions and hypnotic exploration lingered in the back of my mind, a reminder of curiosity amid the swirling uncertainties of my journey.

Still in my video-game thinking, I tell Mark I'm gonna go on a run through the city to get to know the map. I used to be a big Quake player and even had a Quake clan. When a new map comes out, you have to run around it a few times to figure out all the best places, almost so you can navigate it blind-folded.

Pixie desperately wants me to stay and watch movies, but I gotta get out of there. I'm feeling a calling to go into Wellington and leave. I'm feeling a little trapped... a little controlled... Looking back on it, of course they were just doing it out of the goodness of their hearts. The gentle chains of their hospitality, woven from concern and affection, felt like velvet ropes at a premiere I never intended to attend. Despite recognizing their intentions as purely protective and loving, a restless energy surged within me, hinting at unseen dangers and compelling me to flee into the city's embrace.

MIDNIGHT RUN IN WELLINGTON

My midnight run transformed into an urban adventure, each step guided not by GPS but by an intrinsic map of curiosity and instinct. Wellington's CBD, with its pulsing energy and potential for the unexpected, drew me into its heart. I encountered another Scot, his fiery hair a candle in the dimly lit bar, sparking a connection.

As I ventured further, the notorious Wellington winds became my guide, swirling around me like invisible threads pulling me towards destiny. The streets turned into a labyrinth of chance encounters, leading me to not one, but multiple Scots, each meeting marked by the improbability of coincidence and the thrill of a commonly loved land.

Curiously, the universe appeared to have declared a theme night, with every soul I met hailing from Scotland—or perhaps it was just my subconscious homing in on a familiar frequency. Their lack of uniformly red hair notwithstanding, the experience felt uncannily orchestrated.

These moments, under the cloak of night and the watchful gaze of the stars, painted a picture of a world interconnected by invisible lines of fate and chance. The capricious wind, with its whimsical guidance, seemed to whisper secrets of the universe, of paths crossing for reasons beyond our understanding. Sometimes I'm bad at picking up clues from the universe, so it has to hit me over the head and ensnare me, and I'm okay with that. It was a night of serendipitous discovery, not just of Wellington's streets but of the mysterious forces that dance around us, gently nudging us towards encounters that might just hold the key to understanding the grand puzzle of existence.

It starts to rain and is getting quite cold, so I go back to Mark and Pixie's home.

Pixie is there to meet me and gives me a sweet hug and snuggle. Gods, I love her. She is so sweet and so caring.

I open up my laptop to check on my life and I notice there is a browser up, showing a webpage I don't remember visiting. There was a subreddit open where people took selfies of themselves exactly as they are, with no make-up or not trying to look like some vapid Instagram influencer. And the page has scrolled down really far. I had absolutely zero memory of going to that website. From how far I had scrolled down, it looked like I had spent quite a bit of time in that subreddit. It made no sense to me. How could I have spent a while staring at this natural-selfie subreddit and not even remember it? It's not even a topic that I have the slightest interest in. This gave me tremendous pause. It's like losing your keys, but instead of your keys, it's chunks of your time. Apparently there are extended blackout periods where some other soul steps in to complete a side-mission in your destiny. It worried me a lot, and, to be honest, it still worries me. How much did I forget? It reminds me of the things

Vadim had told me. What was happening in these periods where I stepped out of my own timeline of memory?

Reflecting on my Instagram feed, I discerned a distinct dichotomy in the nature of the posts. Some radiated with high vibrational energy, imbued with light and love, offering glimpses of beauty and inspiration. In stark contrast were posts that vibrated lower, marred by trivial pursuits and negative energies, their aesthetics jarring to my senses. This bifurcation mirrored a deeper, spiritual division, aligning me with the realm of higher vibrations where I found solace and resonance.

A DARK SCENE IN MY ONE-MAN STAGE SHOW

I start talking with Pixie and I'm having the most unusual thoughts and voices come to me.

In the midst of this introspection, a profound disturbance took hold. Captured in an audio recording, a crisis unfolded as I grappled with a premonition of danger to my youngest daughter, envisaged on a distant planet or mission fraught with peril. My psyche fractured, adopting multifaceted voices—including an uncanny mimicry of Daniel Day Lewis—to articulate a desperate plea for intervention from unseen watchers. In this moment of torment, my mind constructed elaborate retributions for those who stood by idly, my soul wracked with agony. I can't save her. I'm looking at this bookcase full of books and devising a complicated system for saving her. I give all the lost souls a chance for redemption if they can save her. I'm this tortured soul, crying and falling apart and Pixie is so sweet.

I look at the bookcase and split the three shelves and distribute them to the worst souls on the planet that must be punished. The answer to saving her is somewhere in those books. I command those souls to study those books and figure out the clues to create a timeline so she is saved. I suddenly get a feeling that Patrick Rothfuss himself will help because no one can be as diabolical or wonderful as he. I begin to cry with his sacrifice and gratefully weep his name. Pixie is there, holding me, and I am a crying, weeping mess. My life is over. It's ending. This is the end and I scream and wretch in pain.

I eventually go to sleep in the back bedroom and Pixie is there. Apparently, there was some episode that I do not remember where I put a pillow over her face. I have no memory of that. I don't know if I was being playful or mean, so that is a bit troubling. This snippet from my lost hours echoed eerily with an incident from the following day, where I seemed to have been a mere passenger in my own body. Either way, Pixie was so sweet and snuggled me and scratched my back while we fell asleep.

Just before I drift away, I feel an impossible pain in my left temple. This had been happening off and on for the past few days. I've had bad headaches before, but this was something different. It was almost as if there was a big air bubble in my temple vein that led back along the side of my head above the ear. Without thinking, I mashed the meat of my palm near my thumb above the ear. I was literally screaming in pain and Pixie was so worried, holding me. I mashed the edge of my thumb into my skull above the ear and slowly, very slowly, agonizingly, moved it forward towards my temple. I was moving something through that vein. Or maybe it was energy. I don't know. But I was screaming and writhing in an unspeakable pain. After what seemed like forever, I finally removed the vice-like pressure I'd been applying to my temple. The pain disappeared. I was in a cold sweat. Panting. I immediately fell asleep.

26.
THE UNICORN ONESIE DAY

"Never put off till tomorrow what you can do the day after tomorrow just as well."
—MARK TWAIN

"I'm not arguing, I'm simply explaining why I'm right."
—BILL MURRAY

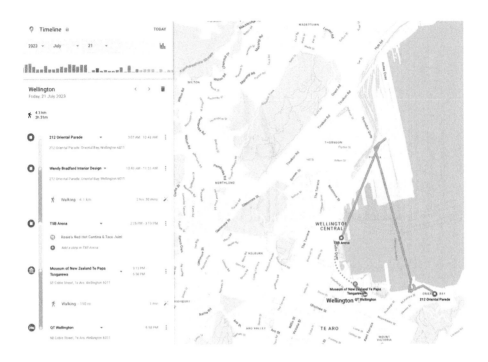

July 21, 2023

I wake up and I still feel not quite like myself. I have to get out of that apartment before something bad happens. I can feel it. There is a desperation. It's almost as if there is something that is going to happen in my predetermined timeline that I chose (and that they chose) and I don't want it to occur.

From all my readings and trying to make sense of all this stuff, there is a tremendous overlap in Michael Newton's and Dolores Cannon's books about choosing a life along with your friends. You all see what will happen ahead of time and there are key moments that cannot be avoided, although in between there is plenty of free will. There are even "rehearsals" in the time between lives where you all rehearse things that will happen. It's like, "Hey, I'll meet you on Earth, and this time, I'll be the one who forgets their lines at the worst possible moment." Wild stuff. Read their books and make up your own mind.

Furthermore, after you rehearse key moments in your life, you and all your friends come up with a way you'll be able to recognize one another here on the mortal coil. It could be a phrase, a look, a laugh, a sound, a smell, a piece of jewelry, anything. I'll give you a good example from my life. I was in this outdoor Swedish-style barrel sauna in Queenstown down by the river with all my hippy friends. We get all hot in there then get out and jump in the cold glacial river then get back in the sauna again. I had my nails painted, which is quite an unusual thing, especially amongst the more traditional conservative crowd of New Zealand.

That unique signal is how I got to know one of my best friends Alex, and we would end up having a tremendous impact on one another's lives. He noticed my painted nails, and then we struck up a conversation. I made an esoteric reference to a Fibonacci sequence, and we were almost immediately besties. A few years later, we launched a massive art project together that was a huge success. And then, even bigger, the next year we did a heroic mushroom trip and Alex figured out he was born a girl! And now, my life has been graced with the beautiful Lexi!

In *Journey of Souls*, among the various narratives, there's a compelling account of a tall, athletic woman who visited Newton's office. This is Case Study #26 in the book. Despite her robust appearance, she was troubled by persistent soreness in her thighs, a condition that baffled medical professionals. During a past life regression session, she accessed a realm where souls choose their physical bodies and life circumstances for their upcoming incarnations on Earth. These choices are driven by the soul's desire for growth, to balance karma, and to conquer hindrances such as negative emotions.

In a past life during the 1800s, she consciously opted to incarnate as a crippled girl. This decision was made to experience a life largely confined to bed, which would afford her the opportunity for extensive study and self-improvement. She was aware in advance of the exact incident that would lead to her disability: a fall from a horse-drawn carriage, resulting in it running over her. This life choice was a part of her soul's journey to evolve by facing and overcoming significant challenges. Through this experience, she aimed to develop inner strengths that physical constraints could not hinder, signifying the soul's journey through varied physical existence.

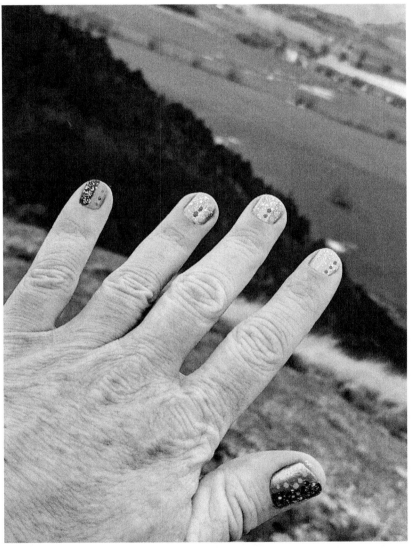

You should see the looks I get from the New Zealand tradies (a local word which is dudes like roofers and carpenters) in the sauna here at the gym. I often make a joke if there are two other guys after they see my nails in there and say, "You know, they say 1 out of 3 guys is gay." I point at the two guys then continue, "I don't know about guy #1, but guy #2 looks pretty cute."

I will copy that entire part of the book here for you to read. Dr. N is Dr. Newton, the author of the book and S is the subject. She has been under hypnosis already and we catch up with a life from several missions ago where she was a male Viking before she chose a life as a crippled girl.

Dr. N: What was most important to you about this life you have just recalled as Leth the Viking?

S: To experience that magnificent body and the feeling of raw physical power. I have never had another body like that one in all my existences on Earth. I was fearless because my body did not react to pain even when wounded. In every respect it was flawless. I never got sick.

Dr. N: Was Leth ever mentally troubled by anything? Was there any emotional sensitivity for you in this life?

S: (bursts out laughing) Are you kidding? Never! I lived only for each day. My concerns were not getting enough fighting, plunder, food, drink, and sex. All my feelings were channeled into physical pursuits. What a body!

Dr. N: All right, let's analyze your decision to choose this great body in advance of Leth's life. At the time you made your choice in the spirit world did you request this body of good genetic stock or did your guide simply make the selection for you?

S: Counselors don't do that.

Dr. N: Then explain to me how this body came to be chosen by you.

S: I wanted one of the best physical specimens on Earth at the time and Leth was offered to me as a possibility.

Dr. N: You had only one choice?

S: No, I had two choices of people living in this time.

Dr. N: What if you didn't like any of the body choices presented to you for occupation in that time segment?

S: (thoughtfully) The alternatives of my choices always seem to match what I want to experience in my lives.

Dr. N: Do you have the sense the counselors know in advance which body selections are exactly right for you, or are they so harried it's just an indiscriminate grab bag of body choices?

S: Nothing here is careless. The counselors arrange everything.

Dr. N: I have wondered if the counselors might get mixed up once in a while. With all the new babies born could they ever assign two souls to one baby, or leave a baby without a soul for a while?

S: (laughing) We aren't in an assembly line. I told you they know what they are doing. They don't make mistakes like that.

Dr. N: I believe you. Now, as to your choices, I am curious if two bodies were sufficient for your examination in the place of life selection.

S: We don't need a lot of choices for lives once the counselors get their heads together about our desires. I already had some idea of the right body size and shape and the sex I wanted before being exposed to my two choices.

Dr. N: What was the body choice you rejected in favor of Leth?

S: (pause) That of a soldier from Rome ... also with the strong body I wanted in that lifetime.

Dr. N: What was wrong with being an Italian soldier?

S: I didn't want ... control over me by the state (subject shakes head from side to side) ... too restrictive ...

Dr. N: As I remember, by the ninth century much of Europe had fallen under the authority of Charlemagne's Holy Roman Empire.

S: That was the trouble with the soldier's life. As a Viking I answered to nobody. I was free. I could move around with my band of invaders in the wilderness without any governmental control.

Dr. N: Then freedom was also an issue in your choice?

S: Absolutely. The freedom of movement ... the fury of battle ... the use of my strength and uninhibited action. Life at sea and in the forests was robust and constant. I know the life was cruel, too, but it was a brutal time. I was no better or worse than the rest.

Dr. N: But what about other considerations, such as personality?

S: Nothing bothered me as long as I was able to physically express myself to the fullest.

Dr. N: Did you have a mate—children?

S: (shrugs) Too restrictive. I was on the move. I possessed many women—some willing—others not—and this pleasure added to my expression of physical power. I didn't want to be tied down in any way.

Dr. N: So, the body of Leth was your preference as a pure physical extension of sensual feeling?

S: Yes, I wanted to experience all body senses to the fullest, nothing more.

I felt my subject was now ready to go to work on her current problem. After bringing her out of superconscious into a subconscious state, I asked her to go directly to a life which may have involved leg pain.

Almost at once the woman dropped into her most recent past life and became a six-year-old girl named Ashley living in New England in the year 1871. Ashley was riding in a fully loaded, horse-drawn carriage when suddenly she opened the door and tumbled out under the vehicle. When she hit the cobblestone street, one of the heavy rear carriage wheels rolled over her legs at the same point above both knees, crushing the bones. My subject reexperienced a sharp pain in her legs while describing the fall. Despite efforts from local physicians and the prolonged use of wood splints, Ashley's leg bones did not heal properly. She was never able to stand or walk again and poor circulation caused repeated swelling in her legs for the rest of a rather short life. Ashley died in 1912 after a productive period of years as a writer and tutor of disadvantaged children. When the narration of Ashley's life ended, I returned my subject to the spirit world.

Dr. N: In your history of body choices why did you wait a thousand years between being a physically strong man and a crippled woman?

S: Well, of course, I developed a better sense of who I was during the lives in between. I chose to be crippled to gain intellectual concentration.

Dr. N: You chose a broken body for this?

S: Yes, you see, being unable to walk made me read and study more. I developed my mind... and listened to my mind. I learned to communicate well and to write with skill because I wasn't distracted. I was always in bed.

Dr. N: Was any characteristic about your soul particularly evident in both Ashley and Leth the Viking?

S: That part of me which craves fiery expression was in both bodies.

Dr. N: I want you to go to the moment you were in the process of choosing the life of Ashley. Tell me how you decided on this particular damaged body.

S: I picked a family in a well-established, settled part of America. I wanted a place with libraries and to be taken care of by loving parents so I could devote myself to scholarship. I constantly wrote to many unhappy people and became a good teacher.

Dr. N: As Ashley, what did you do for this loving family who took care of you?

S: It always works two ways—the benefits and liabilities. I chose this family because they needed the intensity of love with someone totally dependent upon them all their lives. We were very close as a family because they were lonely before I was born. I came late, as their only child. They wanted a daughter who would not marry and leave them to be lonely again.

Dr. N: So it was a trade-off?

S: Most definitely.

Dr. N: Then let's track this decision further back to the place of life selection, when your soul first saw Ashley's life. Did you see the details of your carriage accident then?

S: Of course, but it wasn't an accident—it was supposed to happen.

Dr. N: Once you came to Earth, who was responsible for the fall? Was it your soul-mind or Ashley's biological mind?

S: We worked in unison. She was going to be fooling with the carriage door handle and... I capitalized on that...

Dr. N: Tell me what was going through your soul-mind in the life selection room when you saw the scene of Ashley falling and being injured?

S: I thought about how this crippled body could be put to good use. I had some other choices for body injuries, but I preferred this one because I didn't want to have the capability for much movement.

Dr. N: I want to pursue the issue of causality here. Would Ashley have fallen anyway if she had a soul other than your own?

S: (defensively) We were right for each other...

Dr. N: That doesn't answer my question.

S: (long pause) There are forces beyond my knowledge as a

spirit. When I saw Ashley for the first time... I was able to see her without me... healthy... older... another life possibility...

Dr. N: *Now we are getting somewhere. Are you saying if Ashley had begun her life with another soul entity that she might not have fallen at all?*

S: *Yes... that's a possibility... one of many... she could also have been less severely injured, with the ability to walk on crutches.*

Dr. N: *Well, did you see a physically healthy Ashley living happily without your soul?*

S: *I saw... a grown woman... normal legs... unhappiness with a man... frustration at being trapped in an unrewarding life... sorrowful parents... but easier. (voice becomes more firm) No! That course would not have worked well for either of us—I was the best soul for her.*

Dr. N: *Were you the prime mover of the fall, once you elected to become Ashley's soul?*

S: *It... was both of us... we were one at that moment... she was being naughty, bouncing around in the carriage, playing with the door handle when her mother said she must stop. Then... I was ready and she was ready...*

Dr. N: *Just how rigid was your destiny? Once you were Ashley's soul, was there any way you could have backed out of this entire incident in the carriage?*

S: *(pause) I can tell you I had a flash just before I fell. I could have pulled back and not fallen out. A voice inside my mind said ... "It's an opportunity, don't wait any longer, take the fall, this is what you wanted—it's the best course of action."*

Dr. N: *Was that particular moment important?*

S: *I didn't want Ashley to get too much older.*

Dr. N: *But, the pain and suffering this child went through ...?*

S: It was horrible. The agony of those first five weeks was beyond belief. I almost died, but I learned from enduring it all and I now see the memories of Leth's capacity for managing pain helped me.

Dr. N: Did your inner mind have any regrets during those moments when the pain was most severe?

S: As I slipped in and out of consciousness during the worst of the ordeal, my mind began gaining in power. Overriding my damaged body, I started to better control the pain ... lying in bed ... the doctors helpless. The skills I developed in managing pain were later used to concentrate on my studies and my counselor was helping me, too, in subtle ways.

Dr. N: So you gained a lot in this life by being unable to walk?

S: Yes, I became a listener and thinker. I corresponded with many people and learned to write with inspiration. I gained teaching ability with the young, and felt guided by an internal power.

Dr. N: Was your counselor proud of your accomplishments after you returned to the spirit world?

S: Very, although I was told I had become a little too indulged and pampered (laughs), but that's an okay trade-off.

Dr. N: How does your experience with the strong body of Leth and the weak one of Ashley help you today, or is this of no consequence?

S: I benefit every day by my appreciation of the necessity of a union between mind and body to learn lessons.

During my client's reliving of the street scene which broke her legs, I initiated desensitization measures. At the close of our session together, I then deprogrammed her generational memory of leg pain entirely. This woman later notified me she has had no further pain and regularly enjoys playing tennis.

In the grand, often bewildering mosaic of existence, where every thread seems to lead simultaneously towards clarity and confusion, my actions—a deviation from my customary behavior—seemed to be dictated by a script written in the stars, much like the predetermined path of the little girl and her ill-fated carriage adventure. I still take responsibility, even though that feels a little funny to say as if this all was premeditated and volitional. It's a peculiar notion, akin to finding oneself inadvertently cast as the villain in a play you don't recall auditioning for.

I look at Pixie and she is wearing these furry gloves. She is hiding her fingers and her hands. She does so much for other people. She loves to paint nails, and she has done mine many times. Mark always has the most fabulous nails too. And then I begin to see a very different dynamic between Mark and Pixie. Please note I am no longer myself, and like that little girl who threw herself out of her carriage, I was about to do the same thing. Of course a difference is that it is not myself I am hurting, but there must have been some grand plan for this to happen. The reasons I cannot fathom.

When this was going on, everything seemed crystal clear to me, even though I was not in control of my actions.

There was something else about the build-up to this moment. My mind was ablaze and I had this desperate feeling I had to leave their apartment. I was really trying to get out of there, but they seemed keen on anchoring me to the spot. It's as if I had some premonition, something I knew about an unavoidable part in the collision of our timelines.

I saw them in this relationship of dominant and submissive. And Pixie had given up so much of herself to serve Mark. Her hands were closed and undecorated while his were fancy and free. I almost saw her as this sad creature that never was able to express herself because her previous soul was always in the service of men, choosing their satisfaction and pleasure over her own. Please note that, in *this* life, I see Mark and Pixie as having a very balanced and loving relationship. Perhaps I think I was seeing many versions of her, or maybe past lives, where she was subjugated. Or, perhaps she subjugated someone in a past life, and in this one she had to learn how to serve others before herself. I don't know.

Compelled by an overwhelming urge to liberate her from this cycle, I took her hand with the intention to unfold it, to encourage her to embrace her freedom and self-expression. Yet, in my zeal, I inadvertently caused her physical harm, bending her fingers back in a misguided attempt to help her break free from perceived chains. I wasn't trying to hurt her at all. I just felt this intense need to free her. And then I got up on top of the couch and shouted down Mark with a voice that wasn't even mine. It was sort of this Daniel-Day Lewis voice that was dark thundercloud, commanding, and foreboding. I still don't know what to make of the whole thing. I feel terrible because I truly love them so much and I can't even figure out what the hell happened. I look forward to that one day when I find out why and how that happened. I feel like a gentle soul that has very little conflict in his life, and practically zero physical conflict. It was, and remains, baffling.

The aftermath left me marooned in a sea of bewilderment, adrift on the tides of affection I bear for them and haunted by the phantom limbs of actions that felt alien to my own.

NEXT SCENE, A COSTUME CHANGE

And then I left, wearing only my unicorn onesie and bare feet.

I proceeded to walk all over Wellington for the day in that onesie. Please note at the time I had no idea I actually hurt Pixie. I thought it was sort of like going to the physical therapist and getting an adjustment. So, naturally, I was feeling no guilt at all. I was just happy to be out of there.

That day in Wellington was a whirlwind of joy and eccentricity. Cloaked in my unicorn attire, a splash of color against the city's backdrop, I encountered the police. Their approach, spurred perhaps by my unconventional choice of dress, led to an unexpectedly delightful exchange.

There we stood, a tableau of the surreal, discussing the merits of viewing life through a lens tinted with positivity and contemplating the rechristening of Down Syndrome as "Ups Syndrome." I went on to tell them that I think all these young people with "learning disabilities" probably have very special brains that can help get the world out of these terrible cycles. We need new thinking, and the old ways of thinking of greed and power and fear are no longer serving us. I was putting on a workshop for these coppers, and they were loving it.

It was a moment of such sparkling humanity that even the staunchest of cynics might have cracked a smile. The officers, embodying the spirit of Kiwi camaraderie, waved me on my way, thus ensuring that my onesie-clad escapade could continue unabated. You can't arrest a guy for wearing a onesie in public, after all. And even if I was wearing my onesie while I made sweet love to a sheep, well that sort of thing is generally acceptable in New Zealand. Any port in a storm.

I had some ice cream and skipped and hopped and skipped around Wellington. It was quite a cold day and I was still in my bare feet. People looked at me waltzing along the walkways eating ice cream and must have thought me quite mad, a pied piper of peculiarity. And right they would be! But I wasn't feeling cold. I felt amazing. I saw patterns in the sky, in the ocean, all around me. I would see Maori statues and they would breathe and come alive in animated ways. It was all truly wonderful.

The Women's World Cup was on and there was an outdoor viewing area. I went there and sat outside and enjoyed watching the soccer. I went next door to a restaurant called Rosie's. I was drawn there because I have a dear friend in Arrowtown named Rosie. I go in there to get some food, and I ask which one Rosie is, and she tells me that everyone is a Rosie. She only hires people with the name Rosie. That's weird, I thought. It's kind of awesome but also makes you wonder about the job application process. Again, I was thinking about names and doppelgangers and reincarnation and all these sorts of things.

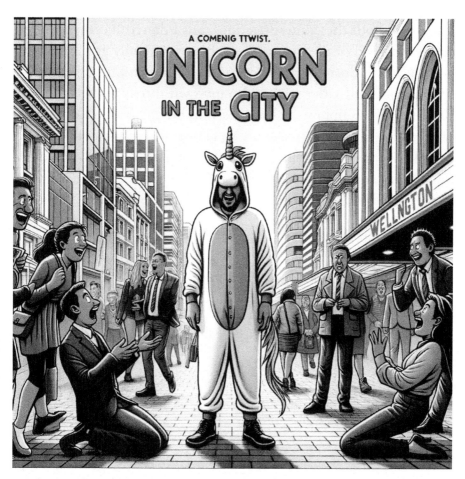

I used AI to make a movie poster of my day in Wellington.

More recently, after my recovery, I saw the *Barbie* movie. It's not the greatest work of cinematic art in the world, but it does remind me of my spiritual emergence. There are 1,000 Barbies and 1,000 Kens, and they are all in different bodies. They are able to move from their fantasy heaven-type world into the more hellish reality that the rest of us inhabit. It's almost as if the universe is inspiring Hollywood writers with a dialectic that speaks to the actual nature of reality.

Only recently have I watched *Lego Movie 2*. Again, I saw many things that reminded me of time in my spiritual emergence. Dualism, the collective unconscious, the shadow self. I'm not being solipsistic about these interpretations, but I do recall certain things. At the very end of the movie, Chris Pratt eventually gets his dream home with his dream girl. He opens his mouth and makes the most unusual noise. It's the same noise my own throat made as I came back from the Rainbow Helix Coliseum into my bed in Edinburgh. You can find that final scene on YouTube. It's an incredible sound to make at the end of a movie. You'd expect Chris Pratt to say something funny, or some amazing punchline to end the movie. But, instead, you hear this strange guttural sound.

My walk along the shoreline stopped here where I had an amazing idea.

Speaking of synchronicities, I was also channeling a lot of Phillip K. Dick subconsciously. He's perhaps one of the best Sci-Fi writers in the world in my opinion. He wrote a ton of books and the most famous ones turned into *Blade Runner, Minority Report, Total Recall* and more. I've read pretty much everything. I talk a lot more about PKD in a later chapter of the book. Most interestingly, he had a spiritual awakening himself late in life. He saw a flash of light from a Christian fish hanging on a woman's necklace and he was flooded with information. It completely changed his life and led to one of his other famous books, *VALIS*, which is an acronym for "Vast Active Living Intelligence System." So all of this now makes sense to me because it's basically another term for "Simulation Theory." After all that I had seen and my video-game interface moments, I was more sure than ever we are actors on an ever-evolving stage. Like me, PKD was always troubled with reality and was constantly trying to rip through to the other side.

I'm letting the winds and the universe guide me around Wellington in a pretty random walk. I ended up in this little park by the shore. It's a strange park and they have soccer goals set up on either side. But it's not exactly symmetrical. There, facing the salty sea breeze, my mind conjured an image so pure and joyous—a Sunday soccer league for children with Down Syndrome and Learning Disabilities, where the dress code strictly enforced a carnival of onesies. Imagine, if you will, a brigade of fluffy dinosaurs, unicorns, and perhaps the odd lobster, paraded not just by the children but their attending families, turning the pitch into a tableau of unadulterated happiness. Just as important, all their families that come to watch them also must wear onesies that the kids have joyfully selected for them. It's like the kid says to his dad: "You be you, and also a dragon." I think making adults dress up in onesies to watch soccer is the kind of law we need. Like, "Sir, you're under arrest for not being a bloated giraffe." And everyone is fluffy and happy and the parents and grandparents and aunts and uncles are all dressed up, watching their adorable children running around chasing after a soccer ball.

It's such a beautiful vision and I cry a little. I see that as a possible future and I want to make it happen.

I should also take the opportunity to note that I am not into the furry scene. It's all fine with consenting adults as long as no animals are hurt and the outfits go through the washing machine at least three times. That seems fair.

And yes, if these are just some of the thoughts going around in my mind, you can imagine it was a menagerie of madness in there.

Such musings, while a testament to the chaos of my thoughts, also hinted at a deeper longing for connection, for a world where every soul finds acknowledgment and love. The myriad ideas swirling through my consciousness, from speculative fiction to heartfelt aspirations for a more inclusive society, were threads of my spiritual and intellectual odyssey—a journey not just through the streets of Wellington but through the vast landscapes of the human condition.

27.
THE DUNBAR 150 AND NPCS

"We cannot live pleasantly without living wisely and nobly and righteously."
—ALAN WATTS

"I always wanted to be somebody, but now I realize I should have been more specific."
—LILY TOMLIN

My adventures took a peculiar turn, akin to discovering your toaster has unexpectedly developed a taste for Proust.

I was seeing the past and future lives of people. I saw my friend Stu Robertson who I spent a month living with in Antarctica. Scottish origins. It was a slightly different version of him and a bit younger. But it was 90% him. I saw my friend Dr. Tim Rigg. He was a bit older and taller, but it was him. I saw my photographer friend Deanie Johnstone, a bit younger, but there taking photos with her camera. Are these the NPC "Backdrop People" that are just getting remixed with combinations of faces and people I know?

Stu and I are about to board a CL-130 (same plane you know and love from bombing runs but with skis instead of wheels) as we are leaving after a month in Antarctica.

I had this notion that is related to the Dunbar 150. That is a reference to your human mind only being able to keep track of a hundred and fifty people, because so much of our ancestry was in a village with about a hundred and fifty people. So I was thinking that I do know about a hundred and fifty people, and all of them are around me all the time, just in different bodies. If you want to know a similar reference, look up a YouTube video called "The Egg." It reminds me of an Alan Watts speech where he says we are everyone, all the time, and all of them are me.

And then I started having deeper thoughts about "character generation" in this video game. That's often one of my favorite things in games, is those first few moments in a game where you get to create your character. You get to choose how they look and maybe information about their personality or powers, depending on the game. My new thought was that I had a hundred and fifty true friends and loved ones. I knew what they looked like. But then, as I would move around, I would see those a hundred and fifty people over and over again with slightly different mixes. For example, I may see someone that is 80% Hugh Jackman with 20% Jason Bateman. I had a great time trying to figure this stuff out. In fact, later when I was to go into the Wellington mental hospital, a guy came in after a few days and he was 90% Hugh Jackman. He seemed really out of it, but I let him borrow my socks. After all, maybe my life's destiny was indeed lending hosiery to Wolverine on an off day.

For the last thirty years or so, I've had my own druthers on the Dunbar 150. Because we don't live in villages anymore, we may only interact with forty to fifty people in the real world. Family, loved ones, friends, your mailman, whatever. So, there is this giant gap of a hundred people that the brain craves. It wants to keep track of relationships and be interested in their lives. So, where do those extra hundred people come from? Celebrities!

What began this quest is I would get on planes and I would see high-powered women in business class and sometimes they'd be reading *People* magazine or just keeping up with the celebs and their inter-relationships. Women have another layer where they can keep track of not just primary relationships but secondary and tertiary relationships as well. Men, by contrast, appear to navigate their social networks with the simplicity of a one-button remote. They only keep track of their direct relationships and give little time wondering about those secondary relationship trees. The brain just needs to keep track of more and more people. Sure, some men are into celebrities too, but they can also be more into sports stars and other categories.

Reflecting on my journey through spiritual emergence, I found myself delving deeper into the nuances of human emotion and the roles individuals play in our collective experience. Actors, much like comedians, became figures of importance in my contemplation, serving as conduits for emotional release. Their performances, I realized, hold the power to mirror the vast spectrum of human feelings, guiding audiences through laughter, grief, hope, and despair, thus facilitating a cathartic release of pent-up emotions.

This period of introspection also led me to ponder the concept of reincarnation with greater depth. My experiences, enriched by spiritual studies and profound encounters with Ayahuasca, solidified my belief in the cycle of rebirth. Yet, my understanding of reincarnation evolved beyond the linear progression of lives one after the other. There also exists the possibility of simultaneous existences, a quantum approach to reincarnation where multiple incarnations of oneself could coexist, each navigating its unique path of challenges and growth within the same temporal frame. This hypothesis suggested a complex, interconnected web of life experiences, expanding my perception of existence beyond the confines of a single timeline. Imagine, if you will, simultaneous existences—like having multiple tabs open in the browser of life, each playing a different cat video of soulful growth and challenges.

As I navigated the streets of Wellington, the notion of seeing reflections of my friends and loved ones in the faces of strangers intrigued me. It underscored the idea that our souls might be experiencing multiple realities concurrently, each version of ourselves learning and evolving in parallel. This concept not only enriched my understanding of reincarnation but also deepened my sense of connection to the people around me, offering a glimpse into the intricate tendrils of life that weaves together our past, present, and future selves.

SPREADING OUR SOUL'S ENERGY

Exploring the intricate ideas presented in *Journey of Souls* and *The Three Waves of Volunteers and the New Earth*, I've come to appreciate the flexibility and vastness of the soul's journey. These texts suggest that our souls do not commit their entirety to a single Earthly incarnation. Instead, we might allocate only a portion of our energy—perhaps as little as 10% or as much as 20%—to our physical existence on Earth. The remainder of our soul's essence

continues its evolution or maintains connections with other significant souls in a different realm. Intriguingly, some individuals may
opt to distribute their energy across two physical entities simultaneously, aiming to optimize their opportunities for learning or to dissem-
inate their influence more broadly. The idea that one might split their
soul's attention between two incarnation gigs in an effort to rack up
spiritual frequent flier points was both amusing and awe-inspiring.

This notion introduces the fascinating possibility that my current
consciousness might be operating with a fraction of its total capacity,
say 40%, while another segment of my essence animates a separate
being elsewhere. The potential for such a dual existence stirs my curiosity and wonder about the connections and commonalities I
might share with this other part of my soul.

It makes you wonder what the remaining percentage of your soul
is up to, right? Maybe it's borrowing socks from Hugh Jackman.

The concept of Dunbar's number further complicates our inter-
connections. While our human cognitive limitations might cap our
social awareness at around a hundred and fifty individuals, my experiences suggest that a higher state of consciousness—such as the
one I encountered during my transformative episode in Scotland—
could vastly expand this capacity. In this elevated state, managing
relationships with thousands of individuals might become feasible,
reflecting a much broader network of interconnected souls partici-
pating in the worldly domain.

Such meditations lead me to consider the structure of soul clusters,
as posited by these spiritual texts. After our physical deaths, we reunite
with our primary soul group, a tight-knit assembly of beings with
whom we share deep bonds and histories across numerous lifetimes.
Yet, our connections extend beyond this intimate circle to include
numerous other groups with whom we've interacted across various
incarnations. This web of relationships underscores the complexity
of our spiritual journeys, suggesting that our current life on Earth is
but one chapter in a much larger narrative of growth, learning, and

interconnectedness. This whole extended network is like friends of friends you meet at parties who somehow know your entire life story.

I started receiving some messages from Mark and Pixie about going to the eye doctor. Pixie has been helping me with my eye medicine and she has been so sweet and supportive. Even after that debacle, she and Mark are still reaching out to me to help with my eye. They tell me I need to go to the emergency room at the hospital for my eye appointment. This doesn't make any sense to me. Why wouldn't I just go to the ophthalmologist's office? I feel like I'm being lied to. Like I'm being tricked and entrapped again. And I'm going to have to go through the same misery as the hospital in New York. That was a tortured hell for me and caused me more visceral pain than almost anything in my life. I lost all free will, a tortured soul, writhing around, tied down to a hospital bed. In that place, I remembered something from childhood where I would wonder if there was nothing in the universe. Just, nothing. A void beyond voids. This scene, or absence thereof, would always mess with my child-brain and make me a feel a little insane. But in that first hospital, I fused with that very void of blackness, of being one with nothingness, and the complete absence of anything at all was terrifying.

I wasn't going to the hospital. It was a trick. Of course, I was quite self-deluded. Looking back on it, I get it. But, at the time, I was making the rational decision to not go into a traumatic situation and be tied down to another hospital bed and become one with the void once again.

28.
THE TE PAPA MUSEUM

*"One does not become enlightened by imagining figures of light,
but by making the darkness conscious."*
—CARL JUNG

"I don't suffer from insanity; I enjoy every minute of it."
—EDGAR ALLAN POE

Continuing my journey through Wellington, I found myself being guided by the city's characteristic winds to the Te Papa Museum. There, standing before a sign bearing Maori inscriptions, I felt a sudden urge to connect more intensely with the culture. Instinctively, I performed a Hongi, pressing my forehead against the sign as if to exchange a traditional Maori greeting of sharing breath and essence. This moment was moving, eliciting tears as I lamented my limited understanding of the Maori people and their storied history.

Inside the museum, I was drawn to the World War I Gallipoli exhibit. The immersive and detailed recounting of the Gallipoli

campaign, depicted through the eyes and stories of the ANZAC soldiers, was overwhelming. Each artifact, photograph, and personal
account seemed to mesh with the very essence of human struggle,
bravery, and the loss experienced during that catastrophic campaign.
As I moved through the exhibit, the weight of the soldiers' sacrifices
bore heavily upon me, moving me to tears. The intense emotions
stirred by the exhibit served as a stark reminder of the pain and suffering that wars inflict upon humanity, leaving a lasting impression
on my soul.

While my mind was going a bit looney, the museum served as a
sanctuary of art and culture. Roaming its halls, I was enveloped in
the beauty of its collections, with music as my companion. The art
spoke to me on multiple levels, offering a respite from the storm
raging within.

After leaving the museum, I found myself enveloped in the night,
greeted by an intricate fractal display that narrated the Maori origin
story. This powerful portrayal, illuminated against the darkness,
stirred an emotional response. I felt an overwhelming connection
with the Maori culture and also with Scotland and my home in New
Zealand. It was as if I was embodying the essence of the one-eyed god
who, according to Maori lore, played a crucial role in discovering this
magnificent land. In that moment, I was consumed by a sense of
purpose, a calling to contribute to making the world a better place,
to rekindle the magic and wonder that I felt was part of my destiny.

However, this sense of euphoria was soon tempered by a stark
reminder of recent events. Upon checking my phone, I discovered a
message from Mark and Pixie, detailing the extent of the injury I
had inadvertently caused Pixie. The guilt that washed over me was
sad beyond sad, leaving me feeling utterly despondent. Their message, stating that I was no longer welcome back, was painful, surprising, and confusing. Naturally, I felt isolated and lost.

I took many videos while in the museum. I was particularly torn apart by these scenes of people in mental institutions, staring out the window while locked in misery. I could relate.

DAY TREY AND NIGHT TREY GET SOME ROOMS

Seeking solitude, I booked myself into the QT Hotel, opting for two separate rooms in a bid to manage the disparate aspects of my personality that seemed to be at odds with each other. One room was designated for Day Trey, while the other was reserved for Night Trey, each equipped with its own set of clothing to match these distinct personas. This decision, which made perfect sense to me at the time, now strikes me as a vivid illustration of my struggle to understand and reconcile what was happening inside of me versus trying to integrate with this backwards and broken society. In hindsight, this approach to self-management seems as effective as trying to solve a Rubik's Cube by coloring in the squares.

I had this rather wild notion that the folks over at Weta Workshop—yes, the very same that conjured up Middle Earth for the silver screen—had somehow planted cameras in my abode. They were filming me, of all things, in a sort of bizarre reality show that no one had signed up for. This wasn't paranoia at all, as I felt like the great beyond was watching everything I was doing. And even now, many months later, even though I know Weta was not actually doing anything, my druthers that everything is always recorded by the great universe is indeed true. It's all there for us to review after we kick the bucket.

Embarking on what can only be described as a tumultuous journey through my psyche, I found myself embodying a dichotomy akin to Tolkien's Gollum. Alternating between moments of kindness and malice, I was caught in a vortex of self-dialogue that mirrored Gollum's internal conflict, oscillating between benevolence and spite. This theatrical display of my inner turmoil was captured in voice recordings on my phone, marking a surreal narrative of my state of mind. Despite retaining a vivid recollection of these episodes, there were lapses in my memory, blackout periods that concealed portions of my experience from my conscious recollection. The intensity of the darkness I felt within was indescribable, a shadow that seemed to engulf my very essence.

29.
BREAKFAST AT THE HIPPO

"Don't turn away. Keep your gaze on the bandaged place. That's where the light enters you."
—RUMI

"I am not a vegetarian because I love animals; I am a vegetarian because I hate plants."
—A. WHITNEY BROWN

July 22, 2023

This was to be a very interesting breakfast. Hippo, the hotel's restaurant, beckoned. In a moment of what I can only assume was divine inspiration or perhaps just a lack of clean laundry, I opted for my unicorn onesie. The restaurant itself was a study in contrasts, with one side adorned in opulent Victorian decor awaiting tea with the Queen and the other a more understated dining area.

The clientele that morning were the usual suspects of Wellington's elite, all dark suits and briefcases, as if they were pumped out of a factory of middle-manager cogs to fit into an existing fictional

machine of their mutual belief, completely unprepared for the mythical creature that was about to join them for Eggs Benedict.

Despite the turmoil of recent events and the estrangement from
Mark and Pixie, I found myself on the phone with Pixie, extending
an invitation to join me for breakfast. In my mind, all was well, and
this meal would serve as a convivial gathering, oblivious to the
depths of delusion that had taken hold of me. I was simply thinking,
have a nice meal, and everything would be fine, as if inviting someone to breakfast in this surrealist situation could just make all the
weirdness go away.

Waiting for Mark and Pixie at breakfast.

My antics had reached such a zenith of absurdity that the management felt compelled to step in. Amidst the patrons, I perceived a
group of individuals as embodying the worst aspects of corporate
greed, led by a woman I fancifully identified with Steve Jobs.

Compelled by a mix of delusion and moral outrage, I confronted her for what I saw as malevolence, much to the amusement of her companions who seemed to find my candidness refreshingly bold. Across the room, another figure caught my eye, someone who bore a striking resemblance to Yuval Noah Harari, further feeding into a fictional narrative that he would sublimely appreciate.

CHECKING INTO THE AMBULANCE HOTEL

The situation spiraled to the extent that paramedics were summoned. I imagined myself as a character in a David Lynch production, my movements and actions seemingly scripted for cinematic effect, played in a *Twin Peaks* red-room-reverse to unveil a hidden narrative. This dissociation from reality left me feeling like an observer within my own body, detached from the actions it carried out. As the paramedics came, I got on the phone to Mark and Pixie and told them I guess I was headed to the hospital after all. Pixie was so sweet and always concerned even after our strange event. She rushed over to join me as I headed to yet another hospital.

The journey to the emergency room was unexpectedly merry, with Pixie by my side, now sporting a sling as a memento of my theatrics. Despite the circumstances, our interaction was peppered with laughter and apologies, her graciousness turning the episode into something resembling a bizarre comedy show. I played the gallant, kissing her hand, gentle beyond gentle, with the tenderness of a protagonist in a Jane Austen novel, lamenting my actions as the result of, well, I didn't know.

As I entered, the muted conversations of nurses became a backdrop to an unsettling realization. They whispered skeptically about my belief that my life was under surveillance by the spirit realm, captured for a grand review by caring souls and saved for my own reflection in an afterlife, akin to being the star of my own *Truman Show*. Ironically, their derision unwittingly echoed the very essence of my experiences. Despite their doubts, I found a profound truth in the notion that our lives are observed, reviewed, and even recorded by a realm beyond our immediate perception. This realization was not born of delusion but of a deep, insightful journey into the nature of existence and the continuum of life beyond the physical.

In the hospital, hooked up to a machine like some secondary character in a sci-fi movie, the cold beep of monitors served as a grounding reminder that the curtain hadn't yet fallen on my peculiar day.

"Mindray" is not exactly the kind of machine to hook me up to. To me, I just saw more patterns, as my mind was receiving rays and messages from another realm and it was just all too overwhelming.

Pixie, bless her, fancied joining me at the loony bin, binge-watching films with me. However, the universe had other plans. A pity, really, and I found the mental hospital's policy on plus-ones was rather draconian.

Oh boy, another insane asylum. I was pretty upset and didn't want to go, but I did without struggle or fighting back. I was to be there for several days. I was confused and felt completely alone. And helpless.

I tried to imagine it as a sort of retreat, if you will, but with less yoga and more existential dread.

I was about to have the worst and most tortured moment of my life in solitary confinement.

30.
TORTURE IN SOLITARY CONFINEMENT

"No mud, no lotus."
—THICH NHAT HANH

"Some mornings, it's just not worth chewing through the leather straps."
—EMO PHILIPS

I go into this mental hospital in Wellington, and it's a heck of a lot nicer than the one in New York. For one, I didn't get three death threats immediately upon entry. Also, there was a pretty low chance of being attacked in the bathroom by a Puerto Rican.

I was in room #13. Thank God I had my own room and didn't sleep under the threat of being murdered. I didn't attribute anything to the #13. In all the patterns I was seeing, I never went down that numerology path.

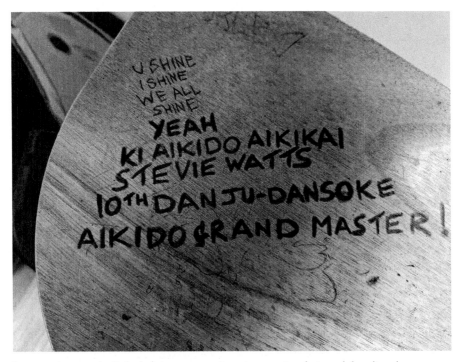

Letters written on the little desk in my room. I was interpreting them and decoding them to get the hidden message.

There was a woman there that was dressed in all black. She was about sixty. She had on heavy eye makeup. She was part Maori. I saw her as a female incarnation of Johnny Cash. I sat down in front of her while she sang to me. It was magical. I felt like I was seeing his final performance. I wept.

Now, there is this nurse here. I'm not gonna call her Nurse Ratched, but I could. She was a real piece of work. Her name badge read "Vic'tria." This wasn't just a name; it illustrated the peculiarities that thrived within these walls. She insisted, with a firmness that brooked no argument, that "Victoria" was not her name, despite the obvious resemblance. This distinction, trivial as it might seem, hinted at the deeper, unspoken rules that governed this place—a domain where names carried the weight of identities, perhaps too often misconstrued or mishandled. The other patients warned that I should indeed not call her Victoria, because her wrath was fierce. I mused with the other patients that I was gonna order a ton of pizza and make sure it was sent to "Victoria." They laughed… I like to make friends with the other inmates just in case I need to mount an insurrection.

This is the courtyard of the Wellington Mental Hospital. I would go on walks out there in circles to clear my head. There was a nihilistic, almost Soviet brutalist, feel to the whole scene.

Dinner arrived with its usual routine, yet tonight's menu included an unexpected side dish—a pill, courtesy of Vic'tria, served in a quaint paper chalice. My response was instinctual, almost reflexive. I knocked the cup from her hand. Such behavior was alien to me, a stark departure from the courtesy that defined my interactions in the world beyond these walls. This moment underscored a dissonance within me; I was caught in the grip of a spiritual cycle, my actions at odds with my essence. The notion of being medicated against my will, in a place where autonomy seemed a concept too easily overlooked, was deeply unsettling. Here, in this modern bastion of care, the imposition of treatment without consent felt like an anachronism, a discordant note in the symphony of my recovery.

Next thing I knew, I had multiple big Maori men wrestle me to the ground. And then they force-carried me into solitary confinement. I'm screaming bloody murder the whole time. There is a rubber mattress in the room. They throw me down onto it. More guys come into the room. Six of them. I'm counting. They pin me down. Knees drilling into my back. They are twisting my shoulder and elbow in an impossible way. Huge, fat Maori dudes twisting their knees and legs into my back. I feel someone begin to tear down my pants to jam a syringe into me. The indignity of being forcibly medicated, the needle's intrusion, a violation of my already fragmented sense of self, was a climax of powerlessness, a nadir of helplessness. In that moment, reduced to mere flesh and bone against will and needle, my spirit rebelled with primal ferocity. I was no longer just a man wrestling with his demons; I became the embodiment of raw, untamed resistance.

I'm screaming and squirming trying to get out of there. I feel them pinch my butt cheek and jam the needle in there. I am strong enough so I shake them off and the needle breaks off—a brief victory in a losing battle. Do I feel hot wet spurting blood splashing back down on me? I can't tell. They try again and make it work and inject me quickly. I can't do anything about it. I scream. I'm a caged animal. I'm a werewolf and it's just turned midnight. I screech in pain and twist my vein-pulsing neck around and stare daggers into Vic'tria. I say something horrible to her I've always wanted to say to her. My venomous parting words were poisoned knives slicing into her wicked heart, flung from the depths of my despair. The six brutes toss me back on the mattress like a used wench and leave, locking the door for what would be the longest and most tortured night of my life.

In the dim light of solitary confinement, the echoes of my own screams filled the room, a stark, unyielding space designed to contain the uncontainable.

I railed against the confines of my cell with the desperation of the damned, a creature too wild for the world of men. My fury was a tempest, lashing out at the immutable, cold barriers that caged me. Each howl, each scratch at unyielding surfaces, was a testament to a soul in turmoil, seeking escape not just from this room but from the shackles of a reality that had become too painful to bear. My wrath sought to rend the very air, to tear asunder the barriers between me and the oblivion I sought, a voice howling in defiance against the looming specter of annihilation.

I begin to rant and rave around the room. I'm clawing at the windows and the doors. I'm like that wild caged velociraptor in the beginning of *Jurassic Park* and I have to escape. My fury, a maelstrom within the concrete and steel, sought to shatter the immutable, to scream defiance into the face of oblivion. Each cry, each futile assault on the cell's boundaries, was a declaration of a soul in upheaval, yearning for release from the existential torment that bound it.

I growl and cry. I moan and weep. I know everything I am doing is being watched from the great beyond. This is my penance. I'm being punished for something I've done that I can't remember and I don't know. There is an arc of terror ripping through me. I can't find any release. In those darkest moments, thoughts of self-destruction privately poked me, seductive and relentless, promising an end to the agony that wracked my being. I would do anything I could to take my own life, to rip out my own throat, to die a hundred times at once just as a release from all the pain I was feeling.

Then something else happens. I hear Trey Parker in my head. Yeah, that's the *South Park* guy. But I'm hearing Trey Parker in my mind. And I'm hearing his voice echo around my skull. I'm like, oh my God, this is what it feels like to be inside Trey Parker, if even for a brief moment.

That moment of curious levity passes.

A NEW DARKNESS RIPS THROUGH ME

This was more than a battle of flesh; it was a crucible for the spirit. The isolation, the enforced tranquility that followed the storm of sedation, became a theater for a different kind of struggle. In the solitude of that room, in the echoes of my own cries, I grappled with the duality of punishment and redemption, of a past obscured and a future uncertain. It was a night that stretched into infinity, where time lost meaning and each breath was a battle against the engulfing darkness.

Pacing the confines of my prison, I was ensnared in a maze of torment, each step a Sisyphean effort against the chains of despair. The belief that the medicine could not touch the essence of who I was became a mantra, a declaration of an indomitable will in the face of an unseen adversary. In my fervor, I was engulfed in madness, a soul set ablaze by its own rebellion. I mourned the absence of the ancient healers, yearning for the solace of the Earth's wisdom, for the guiding hands of shamans and the sanctity of nature's balm. Instead, I found myself a cog in the machinery of clinical detachment, a spirit dulled by the very forces meant to shepherd me back to semblance.

In my madness, I create a very evil sub-simulation of the universe, birthing a system of retribution, a dark simulacrum where justice was meted out with a precision born of fury. I created it to punish all the terrible people in the world. I consort with Patrick Rothfuss and we have a communion with demons as we become dream weavers of nightmares. I growl words and figure out how to punish all the terrible people in the world who have hurt others. Rothfuss and I parlayed with the demons at the fringe of reality, crafting curses in whispers that chilled the very air. Together we crafted a pantheon of punishments so intricately cruel, so meticulously devised, that even to speak of them would be to gaze into the abyss itself.

This creation became an arena of judgment, a spectacle where the currency was the malice borne by souls. A perverse economy took shape, where the price of witnessing damnation was tethered to the depth of one's depravity. The innocent, those wronged and bereft of justice, were granted a seat of honor in this theater of vengeance, their eyes the mirrors reflecting the righteousness of their cause. I come up with so many ideas for revenge on the wicked that I shudder to mention them here.

In the depths of that despair, I faced the ultimate isolation—not just from the world, but from the essence of who I once believed myself to be. Each moment was a lifetime, each lifetime condensed into a moment of exquisite agony. And through it all, I was acutely aware of the unseen watchers, those who bore witness from beyond the edge, to this spectacle of a soul laid bare, a man reduced to his most elemental self, wrestling with the shadows of his own making.

This was the grim amphitheater of my own damnation, where I, stripped of all artifice and pretense while laid bare before unseen judges, was enduring the trial of existence. It was a spectacle of degradation, of a man dismantled undergoing an existential gauntlet, grappling with the duality of his nature, torn between redemption and damnation, a display not just of abasement but of a fundamental dissection of self, a being caught in the relentless tug-of-war between salvation and perdition.

Then in the deepness of night I began chanting. A deep incantation rose in a sonorous voice as I felt my skeleton itself vibrate.

My voice rose and lowered in an ancient chant, its origins a mystery even to me. The verses poured forth, in tongues that echoed the forgotten speech of civilizations long vanished, a melding of Latin's structure with the mystic tones of Aramaic, their cadence a tribute to rituals old as humanity. I envisioned myself at a sprawling music festival, seated in the lotus position just behind a DJ whose trance beats filled the air. With a microphone in hand, my chants wove through the electronic rhythms, sending out healing vibrations to the sea of dancers below. To the left, then to the right, and straight down the center, my voice carried waves of restoration and release, touching the souls of thousands. This vision of healing through sound has since visited me repeatedly, each time as vivid and inexplicable as the last. It's an extraordinary experience, one that transcends the ordinary and plunges into the depths of the mystical.

I don't know if the DJ was the budget Sam Harris, but I sure hope it was.

31.
EXODUS FROM CONFINEMENT

"We've known each other for centuries."
—TED LEVINE AS THE WARDEN TO LEONARDO
DICAPRIO IN MARTIN SCORSESE'S SHUTTER
ISLAND.

"I don't believe in astrology; I'm a Sagittarius and we're skeptical."
—ARTHUR C. CLARKE

July 25, 2023

But, you know what? I was feeling pretty good by morning. Whatever had to move through me moved through me. The medicine (Clozapine) seemed to have a soporific effect, dulling me through the next day. The drug was working its way through my system, resetting all my dopamine receptors.

I finally made it out of solitary confinement in the morning.

Vict'ria gave me my glasses back.

I winked at her.

Standing in line to get our food. I talked to that Nigerian gentleman for a long time. He had his own story that is not mine to tell.

So then, I was to begin several more days of rest and recuperation in this place.

I am quite bored in this place. I start talking to all the patients when not reading books. Speaking of books, I picked up a random one and it was called *Heartbroken*. I don't read romance novels and, even though I was heartbroken in the past, I was over it. But the story itself was quite weird. One day was told in reverse and the next day was told going forward. That seemed to have an unusual synchronicity with how I was experiencing time.

Besides reading, I think it's interesting to get to know people. And then this woman appears. She's a new patient.

A blonde, about thirty, with the kind of beauty that seemed almost out of place, like finding a Picasso in a pawn shop. She was weird. Being "weird" in a mental health spa is expected, but she's got this extra layer of "I might be a fairy or something" going on.

She busied herself with the curious task of redecorating our shared space, armed with gummy-tacky and an artist's zeal, transforming the mundane into the magical. The walls became her canvas, upon which she rearranged photos with the care of a curator in a gallery of the absurd. I documented her endeavors with my phone, capturing each moment of transformation, each new configuration that seemed to bring a semblance of order to our disordered world.

A PROJECTOR AND A MANIFESTING GENERATOR WALK INTO A BAR

She asks me what my "human design" is. I find that to be a weird question, but I do know my human design. If you don't know, human design is sort of like Myers-Briggs. I'm an INTJ there, for example. Anyway, in human design, I am a Manifesting Generator.

She's all excited. "Oh my, that is very rare! I'm a Projector!" which sounds like we're about to start a band with rather complicated album covers.

This Human Design Projector woman I met is slowly moving around the room, rearranging the "art" on the walls so they make more sense. She is on some kind of a mish of her own.

Now, this is starting to be a weird conversation.

I should note I don't know if I believe in any of this Human Design stuff. It's like if Myers-Briggs and astrology had a baby, and that baby immediately started asking you personal questions.

Then, out of nowhere, she looks me dead in the eyes and goes, "So what happened in this lifetime? Did you break her heart or did she break yours?" And I'm thinking, "Wow, we're really skipping the small talk, huh?" It's like she's trying to peer into my soul with X-ray vision. I half expected her to pull out a crystal ball next. But hey, I guess that's just how Projectors roll.

I looked down and softly said, "She broke my heart."

As this enigmatic woman gazed upon me with a sorrow that seemed to stretch back through the annals of time itself. I'm thinking, what the hell is happening with this conversation? I mean have I lived this life a hundred times and one time I break her heart and the next time she breaks mine? The intensity of the moment had me questioning whether we were trapped in some cosmic rerun, doomed to alternate roles of heartbreaker and heartbroken through the ages. Was this a scenario where, in a past life, I played the role of Osiris to her Isis, or perhaps we were the less talked-about Geb and Nut, caught in an eternal celestial drama?

And I watch her as she moves around the mental hospital. Taking down one picture and putting up another. I'm watching what she does and I find so much meaning in it.

There is another woman who I swear is an incarnation of Cruella DeVille. She has all these stuffed dogs that are always near her when she sits on her favorite couch. Cruella takes a liking to me and even gives me her favorite Lapis Lazuli necklace and bracelet because they have magical powers, so she says.

Note this is just some of the fun stuff that happens in mental institutions. By and large, it was an incredibly fun and awesome experience except for all the terror that ripped my soul apart.

Upon enduring what could only be described as an extended stay at Wellington's most exclusive (read: only) mental wellness retreat, the powers that be granted me a three-hour parole. So I go down-town to a boardgaming place and order some board games back to my home. The thought of returning to my abode to partake in these games with my companions filled me with a giddiness usually re-served for children in candy stores or adults when the Wi-Fi finally works. The mission is successful and I talk to the doctor. He says I need to keep taking the medicine for two weeks then get off it. There are some bad side effects, and my dopamine receptors should be reset by then. I was to follow the instructions over the next two weeks.

A view of the dining area in the Wellington Mental Hospital. I would sit with random people and get to know them. I asked a lot of questions… I listened. It was so beautiful to get to know people's journeys. Everyone came here for a different reason, many much darker than mine. I had so much empathy.

Then, it's time to head back to Queenstown, and they send a male nurse with me, probably to make sure I don't try to open the plane door mid-flight or something. Everything was fine.

I return and get some needed rest and have a chance to reconnect with nature and my soul. It's beautiful.

Finally, I am home. But even with all that peace, there are still tears every day, like my eyes decided to start their own cleanse. Guess it's just my way of letting all the pent-up stuff go, one drop at a time.

AUGUST-DECEMBER 2023

Note at this point, most of my wild adventures have ended, but very interesting things continue to happen to me nonetheless. I'll go through the next few months and then we'll get to my dreams that are more than dreams in many cases in Part Deux of the book. Those will not only contain some wild situations, including entities in my bed, but I will also keep bringing in interesting updates about my life that are all related to this ever-evolving situation.

VISITING TOKYO

I've come up with a good analogy for what happened to me in Scotland, at least in reference to trying to explain it to people that don't believe it. Or, rather, they believe that the experience sounds, to them, indistinguishable from a serious hallucinogenic drug trip as if I was eating an acid-soaked haggis. In some cases, these "critics" have never tried drugs at all, or they simply want to throw my experience into the same bucket as one of their own spiritual experiences.

However, no matter what anyone says, I know this was different. And, obviously, it's given me a totally new view on the structure of reality and spirituality.

So this is the analogy I came up with recently on a hike here in

New Zealand. It came after listening to these five-hundred-plus case studies of people that have also been to the spirit world and have experience with past lives, all knowing they are here on a "Mission" to Earth and this whole scene down here is a hyper-complicated "play" where we are all actors helping one another with soul-lessons.

It's not the perfect analogy, but you'll get it.

Let's say you've never heard of Japan. Really, nobody has. But I go to Tokyo for a few days, and then I come back and tell you about it. I describe all the culture, the way the people act, Mt. Fuji in the distance, the food, samurais, geishas, you name it. To you, this is a fanciful story I could have made up on a drug trip, even though I am beyond insistent that this is not the case. I was *there*.

Frustrated, I go off and do research to see if anyone else has ever visited Tokyo or any other part of Japan. I end up finding all of these hypnotized case studies from around the world where other people have gone to Tokyo. They describe the exact same things I have witnessed and experienced. Sure, one or two that may have overlap are anecdotal, but over five hundred? And, from other book references, it looks like there are well over five thousand case studies I could have chosen, and, of the authors that write about this, they have published less than 10% of their case studies.

Now, why am I such a firebrand about this? It's because I have actually figured something out that has rocked my view on reality and why we are all here. I want to shake people by the shoulders and beg, "Look, this is it!" So much of the world is caught up in fear and negative human emotions. It's so obvious to me that our task is simply to clear all these toxic traps, be of service to others, and share the simple idea that love is the answer. All of the drama and nonsense that bring people down is self-delusion because they have been listening to the wrong messages. We're all stuck in a bad reality show, thinking drama and fear are the main courses, when really, we should be passing around the love like it's the last slice of pizza at a party. It's like I was shown the cheat codes to life, not to keep them to myself, but to shout from the rooftops, "Hey, loving each other is the whole point!" I was taken and shown these things for a purpose, and that is why I put together this recommended reading list at the end. Do your own research and think for yourself and see what conclusions you come to. And be sure to pass around that last slice of pizza.

32.
AUGUST, 2023

"We must be willing to let go of the life we planned so as to have the life that is waiting for us."
—JOSEPH CAMPBELL

"I told my wife the truth. I told her I was seeing a psychiatrist. Then she told me the truth: that she was seeing a psychiatrist, two plumbers, and a bartender."
—RODNEY DANGERFIELD

As for August, I'm having a very nice time in my home and spending a lot of time in nature. I'm full of gratitude. I live in a beautiful place with plenty of trees, creeks, hills, and mountains for hiking and reflection.

I'm a low-anxiety, Zen individual, typically navigating life's ebbs and flows with a calm demeanor. Yet, like anyone else, the accumulation of everyday stresses—from relational dynamics, financial concerns, to the pressures of creative pursuits—can subtly heighten my anxiety levels. I've discovered that immersing myself in nature for at least an hour daily significantly alleviates this buildup. This practice serves as a reminder that humans are not designed for prolonged confinement or continuous digital engagement, despite my own

professional inclinations as a digital artist. While my work often en-
tails a balance between outdoor explorations and intensive digital
refinement, I ensure that my routine includes substantial time out-
doors, reconnecting with the natural world.

Returning home has been somewhat challenging due to the
spread of rumors about my experiences. Misunderstandings can
skew perceptions significantly. I even had a friend say, "Oh man, I
heard you got in a lot of trouble with drugs when you tried to cross
the border!" I was like, oh my God, if that is what you heard and
think, God knows what other people heard and think. My internal
reaction was a mix of disbelief and amusement, pondering the tele-
phone game that had transformed my narrative into a plotline one
might expect in an overly ambitious crime drama.

Such misconceptions not only distort the truth but also contribute to a broader sense of isolation, as if society decided to put me in
a bubble because they couldn't find the right label to slap on my
forehead. This societal reaction underscores the pervasive fear and
misunderstanding surrounding mental health issues. Emerging from
such experiences, individuals often confront societal apprehension
and isolation, highlighting the critical need for a supportive and understanding community to welcome them back. I was reminded of
the quote from Martin Luther King Jr.: "In the end, we will remember not the words of our enemies, but the silence of our friends."

Reflecting on my experiences, I felt a sense of empathy for those
emerging from mental health treatment only to face societal exclu-
sion and judgment. It underscored for me the vital need for a compassionate and understanding community to welcome them back
with open arms.

By December, the situation had begun to shift. My home became
a gathering place for friends, offering the warmth and connection I
had missed. Our nights were filled with deep conversations, shared
meals, and walks in nature, creating a space where my return to my
usual self was evident. Yet, the road to reconnection was long, with

the small-town penchant for rumors adding an additional layer of challenge to overcoming the stigma attached to mental health.

It is said that little people talk about other people. Big people talk about ideas.

RETURNING TO BURNING MAN?

So during August, I was mostly by myself. I did have a few friends stop over to check on me. Of course, each carrying the kind of look you'd expect if you announced you were going to juggle chainsaws for fun. Some came with a preconceived notion that I was a wild, violent drug addict and would dive right back into it like Richard Pryor hitting the crack pipe after rehab. Friends did visit, albeit with misconceptions about my state of mind. Their apprehension about my attending Burning Man, fearing a relapse into chaos, was a hurdle in our conversations. Despite the frustration this brought, I recognized their concerns stemmed from their own fears and experiences with loss due to mental health crises. This perspective allowed me to approach our interactions with understanding and patience, even in the face of doubt.

Navigating through layers of misunderstanding about Burning Man added another dimension to my challenges. The event, often misconceived by those who've never attended, is painted by the media as a frenzy of substance use, nudity, and unbridled revelry. This distorted image, fueled by sensationalism and aligned with the fears of those around me, led to a cascade of judgments about my decision to return there. It made me reevaluate the dynamics of these friendships, pondering whether a shift in my social circle might be necessary as I continue to evolve. My journey wasn't about superiority; rather, it was about seeking a resonance of love and understanding that seemed absent in these relationships.

Burning Man, for me, has always transcended the simplistic caricature presented by the media. Over eleven consecutive years of attendance, I've experienced its profound magic firsthand, even before exploring any psychoactive substances. The festival embodies a journey akin to Joseph Campbell's exploration of myth and the archetypal hero's quest, offering a space to rediscover oneself in the middle of the desert's vastness, far beyond the confines of conventional society's expectations.

On the Playa (that's what we call the desert at Burning Man), I found not the cacophony of vice but a symphony of self-exploration, a testament to the transformative power of communal experience and personal mythmaking, far removed from the expectations of a society that often feels too small to contain such dreams.

My friends were trying to get me to promise that I would not take any drugs. I understand why they thought this. They were pretty convinced that I would forever destroy myself if I did anything. I generally do not like to be controlled and I trust myself and my own path. I listen to my heart and soul and am generally quite considerate in all my decisions, even though of course, like anyone, I have occasional lapses and mistakes. In my mind, I was certainly not planning on doing any drugs, however I held out the possibility of a healing night of MDMA with loved ones and friends. I know many doctors there, and they would be good sitters and people to talk to during that time. I had just experienced so much trauma over those two weeks, and I indeed felt a need to expunge that pain, and MDMA is well-known for these healing capabilities.

Some readers will know this, but MDMA is now regularly used to treat people with PTSD, Depression, and all other sorts of painful issues. Rick Doblin and the MAPS organization currently has them in final FDA trials to be approved for prescriptions in the US. You take this beautiful medicine along with a professional psychotherapist that is with you the entire time, guiding your journey and healing. This has already been legalized for these kinds of healing treatments in other places around the world. These have proven more effective than years of traditional therapy, and it is certainly better than numbing out the population on years and years of SSRIs.

Burning Man, contrary to the uninitiated's perceptions, is something of a sanctuary for healers, shamans, and medical professionals of all stripes, many of whom I count among my circle of trust. My potential participation in the event was with an eye towards exploration of these healing avenues, a pilgrimage of the psyche rather than a hedonistic jaunt.

There's a big difference between doing drugs to get "fucked up and party" and using them on a spiritual quest for growth and consciousness. Most people do not get this. The two groups who do not get this are A) People that have never tried drugs and only get their info from the media and B) people that only use drugs to party hard and/or escape from their life.

I can recommend many books and other resources on this topic on my website at:

https://stuckincustoms.com/treys-recommendations/

A standout work is *Drug Use for Grownups* by Dr. Carl Hart, a Columbia Professor whose expertise shines in his push for decriminalizing drug use. Dr. Hart builds his case through rigorous scientific research, poignant personal accounts, and a critical analysis of drug history and societal effects. His perspective is unique: overseeing thousands of clinical trials on various drugs without personal use, he observed high-functioning, responsible adults across all professions. This led him to explore these substances later in life, a journey he embarked on with his wife, enriching both his life and marriage. Dr. Hart's candid discussion on the benefits and impacts of his experiences offers a thought-provoking view on a controversial topic.

I also have a podcast about my various adventures and stories with various drugs called "Molecules I've Ingested" at https://podcasts.treyratcliff.com/. I have somewhat of a unique background because I didn't drink or do any drugs until my early forties. My engineering background gave me an extremely structured mind so that as I got into experimenting with many molecules, I approached it in somewhat of a clinical way as I analyzed all the combinations and permutations of these substances. I tend to have a lot of "drug-geek" friends that do the same thing. We use tiny scales to make sure the dosages and timings are as perfect as possible. There are so many great resources out there such as https://www.erowid.org/ that help prepare everything. In the vast majority of my molecular adventures, I sit around with my friends and we prepare some sort of intention for the session. Now, sure, 10–20% of the time, the intention may just be to simply have a great time and dance to incredible music. There's nothing wrong with that, as dance and letting loose can be very healing. The rest of the pie chart is mostly for internal personal growth, healing, and trying my own humble best to be a more conscious and loving person.

Nevertheless, my friends' frustration was palpable when I declined their requests, tinged with an undercurrent of coercion suggesting that our friendship hinged on my compliance. This realization stung, yet I grasped the situation. Suddenly finding oneself in a friendship laden with conditions is disheartening. The sting of conditional friendship was as sharp as a Vogon's poetry critique. "Trust me, guys, I got this," I wanted to say, but it seemed my crew had voted me most likely to navigate us into a black hole. But, I'm a big boy, and I've suffered lifetimes inside this one, mostly by myself. So, in many ways I was back to that again. Not trying to sound like a martyr here; it's just how the cookie crumbled.

Toward the end of the month, I decided not to go to Burning Man after all. I was getting many signs from the universe that this was not my year and I decided I'd rather spend an extra few weeks with my family in the States. After the sort of events I had been through, I did indeed long to see my family. So I spent extra time with my ex and my amazing kids in Austin. I had more time with my stepmom and brother in Dallas. And then I went to stay with my mom and see my sister in Chicago. All that was great and also difficult in many ways.

Navigating the aftermath of my experience was akin to trying to restore order after a metaphorical upheaval. Imagine the aftermath of an Earthquake in a meticulously organized Amazon warehouse, where once neatly arranged contents are now in disarray. This imagery captures the challenge of reintegrating my thoughts and mental processes, which were further complicated by the administration of tranquilizers and other medical interventions. These experiences did not allow for a natural realignment of my cognitive landscape.

To aid in the reorganization of my mind, I found solace in solitude, meditation, and the embrace of nature. The state of my mental clarity fluctuated daily; at times, my thoughts were scattered, while at others, they found a semblance of peace. Describing the process of mental recalibration is challenging, but it might be likened to attempting to use a computer mid-defragmentation. Though operational, its performance is intermittently hindered by ongoing internal adjustments.

UNEXPECTED BODY FEEDBACK

During this period of heightened sensitivity, I became acutely aware of my physical responses and intuitions. For instance, while jogging, spontaneous hand movements would serve as nonverbal cues, guiding my actions and decisions, such as the affirmation of a positive thought for the encouragement to persist in my activity. This connection between body and mind underscored the intricate process of healing and self-discovery.

One time, I was having a pretty bad day and everything was just going to shit. You know those days. I was in Austin in the middle of a hot humid miserable Texas day. Many people think Texas is dry like in the westerns. It is over in west Texas, but Austin, Dallas, San Antonio, and Houston are thick with a wet hot humidity that makes you want to sit in a rocking chair on the porch in the breeze and drink an iced tea.

Okay, so it's a solar-flare hot day, and I'm walking across this ugly 7-11 parking lot with rubble and trash on the ground, and I just wanted to give up. The strangest thing happened. I just automatically said, "I surrender, I surrender, I surrender," and as I said this, my two eyes spun around in a clockwise way three times. I didn't do any of this consciously, but it reminded me of saying things in threes like on the big night in Scotland when I said "Love is the Answer" thrice.

Relatively unrelated and thanks to Stu, I own a piece of Scotland now, which is great because I needed somewhere to keep my collection of bagpipe music and existential thoughts. Also, I can demand people call me Lord. They can add the "& Savior" bit if they want. That's optional, but it does get them bonus points.

This experience didn't lead to an immediate shift in my circumstances, but it reinforced my belief in a universe that listens and guides that are always present. Despite the isolation we often feel in our worldly existence, disconnected from a greater source, this moment served as a reminder of the unseen support surrounding us. The notion that we navigate our journey alone is an illusion; faith reveals the presence of soul guides who offer unwavering support, patience, and love, reminding us of our connection to the whole.

33.
SEPTEMBER, 2023

"If you truly love someone, your love sees past their humanness."
—MICHAEL SINGER

"There is no point in using the word 'impossible' to describe something that has clearly happened."
—DOUGLAS ADAMS

I fly back to New Zealand and move back into my little cabin. Here at my ranch, there is the main house with about five bedrooms, and then I also have a little two-bedroom cabin on the property that I use as my art studio. I love staying here. It's great to be back. I feel so much better in the middle of nature than in the middle of all those concrete strip malls and some of the crazy stuff that happens in the U.S. I'm not anti-U.S. or anything, but I've always been sensitive to energy, and there is a very uncomfortable feeling there lately with all the unconscious activity I see. Even sitting on a domestic U.S. air flight, I just feel a lot of tension and anxiety from everyone around me. Anyway, I could talk more about that, but suffice it to say I am happy to be home.

Gayle and her children, residing in the main house, brought a lively presence to the ranch. Our evenings, filled with cooking and meaningful conversations, became a cherished routine. Gayle, a close friend of my wife's during her time here, has been a source of wonderful support. Our nightly gatherings in the movie room for entertainment and relaxation underscored the comfort and acceptance we shared. Her decision to stay, despite warnings about my return potentially heralding chaos, demonstrated a trust that dispelled the fears others harbored. This acceptance was especially comforting, considering the concern some had voiced, fearing my return might bring turmoil. Recognizing their intentions were rooted in fear, possibly influenced by their own experiences, I chose empathy over judgment, cherishing the bond we shared.

During the ensuing six weeks, I navigated through a phase of moderate depression, a not uncommon aftermath of such experiences. This period was quite challenging due to the diminished presence and support of friends and loved ones, some of whom harbored lingering fears about my state. This isolation nudged me toward hermit-like tendencies, not fully agoraphobic but veering dangerously close. Mornings became a struggle, with lethargy chaining me to my bed until the late hours, as I sought solace in the voices of podcasts, delaying the moment I had to plant my feet on the ground and confront the day.

Amidst this solitude, a few steadfast friends like Emily, a flame of warmth in my life, made their way to my side. It was Emily who, during our Christmas week together, presented me with a copy of *Journey of Souls*. This book became a catalyst for healing, offering insights that began the process of piecing together the fragmented aspects of my existence—from the transformative experience in Scotland to the trials of my divorce, the trajectory of my career, and the complexities of personal relationships. It was as if the scattered puzzle pieces of my life found their rightful place, leading me on a path towards other books I have mentioned above. This subsequent discovery bridged the gaps between my scientific curiosity, philosophical musings, and spiritual beliefs, weaving them into a cohesive understanding of the universe and my place within it. In short, it was like someone organized my sock drawer while I was out.

My esteemed friend, Dr. Tim Rigg, harbors insights into the essence of recovery, particularly the significance of community support. His initiative in Queenstown, New Zealand, to establish a community program underscores the comprehensive needs for maintaining mental well-being: nourishing food, regular physical activity, a sense of purpose, and, crucially, a nurturing, supportive network.

RONNY'S SUICIDAL THOUGHTS

During this period of healing, I reconnected with my friend Ronny Black, whose spirit is as gentle as it is resilient. Our conversations became a lifeline for him, a solitary light in his struggle with sad isolation. Ronny's ordeal in the Bellevue mental facility, enduring six harrowing weeks, is beyond my comprehension; a single night within those walls left scars on my psyche.

One heartrending day, Ronny confided in me his contemplation of suicide, considering the quietus of helium inhalation as his escape. I found myself in fervent dialogue with him, endeavoring to dissuade him from this path, emphasizing his invaluable contributions to the world and proposing that his psychological ordeal was not without deeper significance. Despite his abstention from drugs, rooted in his dedication to bodybuilding and personal health, Ronny's despair was palpable. I persisted in reaching out to him through the veil of night, clinging to hope. Eventually, he responded with a haunting image— a photograph of a helium tank, a stark symbol of his anguish.

I was so sad. I tried my best. But THEN, almost two weeks later, he sent me a message that he was back in the hospital. Thank the gods. Man, I went through a real scare there, and it added another layer of depression on top. I've recently talked to him about his whole suicide attempt. He got that tank of helium from one of those party rental places to make balloons for kids. He was on it for thirty minutes, but there was a mix of oxygen in there that wouldn't kill him in a clown's darkest nightmare. So then he decided he was gonna drive to New Jersey, where you can get a gun easily, and then check into a hotel room and kill himself. Right before that, he called 911. And before he could get out, the police came to his home to save him.

I've never thought about suicide. I'd never do that to my kids. Also, from my readings about what happens in the spirit world, your soul advisor and others don't like it when you commit suicide because they consider it a waste of a perfectly good human body. Don't get me wrong, they still love you and they are understanding, but you came here to Earth so your soul could learn some lessons. But, you let fear dominate your life and you pulled the emergency chute. That's fine, and you can stay in the spirit world for as long as you like and learn and grow, but at some point you will choose to come back into another solid body so you can learn the soul lessons you didn't make it through last time. There is no easy way out.

Anyway, I'm happy Ronny is alive n' kickin. We talk on a regular basis, not just because he doesn't have anyone else, but because I quite like the guy. I invited him out to New Zealand to spend some time in nature. Nature can be very healing.

Here's an interesting story from my personal life that happened to dovetail perfectly with what I was reading at the time.

A LILLIA STORY

Embarking on a long twenty-kilometer trek through New Zealand's majestic Southern Alps with my Brazilian friend, Lilia, a woman of vitality and humor, unveiled a serendipitous connection. Our shared experience with Anna Duggan, a practitioner of past life regression hypnosis, presented an uncanny coincidence. Lilia's session revealed a poignant narrative from a previous existence, articulated through her own voice under trance, devoid of any external interpretation.

In her past life, Lilia faced despair, leading her to end her life by hanging herself, leaving behind a witness in a young son who grappled with heart-wrenching grief and confusion. This traumatic event from her past was intricately linked to her current life. The soul that once resided in her son reincarnated as her husband in this lifetime, illustrating the fluid and interchangeable roles souls play through various incarnations within familial bonds.

In this life, Lilia's marriage, forged in her early twenties, took a sorrowful turn as her husband succumbed to a terminal illness. Her unwavering devotion during his protracted decline epitomized a profound act of karmic restitution. This journey was not merely about repaying a debt from a past misdeed but also served to test her resilience against the specter of despair. Through enduring and transcending this ordeal, Lilia cleared her karmic slate and affirmed her soul's capacity for growth and redemption.

This narrative underscores the intricate weavings of our soul's journey, where past actions shape our present challenges and opportunities for growth. It highlights the importance of understanding our soul's history through past-life regression, which can illuminate our life's purpose, the nature of our soul group, and the paths we've chosen for our spiritual evolution.

Lilia's story, a testament to the resilience of the human spirit and the transformative power of love, serves as a powerful reminder of the intricate connections that bind our past, present, and future.

Although anecdotal, this beautiful type of past-life story related to suicide I have heard repeated again and again and again. It's hard to have scientific proof (I come from a background of hard science and needing proof), but if you have enough of the same sort of stories that reinforce one another with a 100% Venn Diagram overlap, you are really on to something. Besides, it just makes sense that a loving universe that wants you to grow would implement a system like this.

MAINTAINING A SENSE OF HUMOR

Naturally, as you can tell, I have a wild sense of humor. It keeps me going. I constantly remind myself that I am lucky to be here, and you can be loving and kind while having a wicked sense of humor. I was so happy to read countless case studies of the life between lives and that our souls in the spirit world enjoy sharing humor with friends.

Here is a snippet from Case 21 from *Journey of Souls*.

> Although the next case is presented from the perspective of one group member, his superconscious mind provides an objectivity into the process of what goes on in groups…

> Some readers may find it hard to accept that souls do joke with each other about their failings, but humor is the basis upon which self-deception and hypocrisy are exposed. Ego defenses are so well understood by everyone in spiritual groups that evidence of a mastery of oneself among peers is a strong incentive for change. Spiritual "therapy" occurs because of honest peer feedback, mutual trust, and the desire to advance with others over eons of time. Souls can hurt, and they need caring entities around them. The curative power of spiritual group interaction is quite remarkable. Soul members network by the use of criticism and acclaim as each strives toward common goals. Some of the best help I am able to give my clients comes from information I receive about their soul group. Spiritual groups are a primary means of soul instruction. Learning appears to come as much from one's peers as from the skill of guides who monitor these groups.

> In the case which follows, my client has finished reliving his last past life as a Dutch artist living in Amsterdam. He died of pneumonia at a young age in 1841, about the time he was gaining recognition for his painting. We have just rejoined his spiritual group when my subject bursts out laughing.

> Dr. N: Why are you laughing?

> S: I'm back with my friends and they are giving me a hard time.

> Dr. N: Why?

S: Because I'm wearing my fancy buckled shoes and the bright green velvet jacket—with yellow piping down the sides—I'm flashing them my big floppy painter's hat.

Dr. N: They are kidding you about projecting yourself wearing these clothes?

S: You know it! I was so vain about clothes and I cut a really fine figure as an artist in Amsterdam cafe society. I enjoyed this role and played it well. I don't want it to end.

Dr. N: What happens next?

S: My old friends are around me and we are talking about the foolishness of life. We rib each other about how dramatic it all is down there on Earth and how seriously we all take our lives.

Dr. N: You and your friends don't think it is important to take life on Earth seriously?

S: Look, Earth is one big stage play—we all know that.

Dr. N: And your group is united in this feeling?

S: Sure, we see ourselves as actors in a gigantic stage production.

Dr. N: How many entities are in your particular cluster group in the spirit world?

S: (pause) Well, we work with ... some others ... but there are five of us who are close.

Dr. N: By what name do they call you?

S: L ... Lemm—no that's not right—it's Allum ... that's me.

Dr. N: All right, Allum, tell me about your close friends.

S: (laughs) Norcross ... he is the funniest ... at least he is the most boisterous.

Dr. N: Is Norcross the leader of your group?

S: No, he is just the loudest. We are all equal here, but we have our differences. Norcross is blunt and opinionated.

Dr. N: Really, then how would you characterize his Earth behavior?

S: Oh, as being rather unscrupulous—but not dangerous.

Dr. N: Who is the quietest and most unassuming member of your group?

S: (quizzical) How did you guess—it's Vilo.

Dr. N: Does this attribute make Vilo the least effective contributing member of your group?

S: Where did you get that idea? Vilo comes up with some interesting thoughts about the rest of us.

Dr. N: Give me an example.

S: In my life in Holland—the old Dutch couple who adopted me after my parents died—they had a beautiful garden. Vilo reminds me of my debt to them—that the garden triggered my painting—to see life as an artist ... and what I didn't do with my talent.

Dr. N: Does Vilo convey any other thoughts to you about this?

S: (sadly) That I should have done less drinking and strutting around and painted more. That my art was ... reaching the point of touching people ... (subject pulls his shoulders back) but I wasn't going to stay cooped up painting all the time!

Dr. N: Do you have respect for Vilo's opinions?

I put the next chunk of this dialog in a Bonus Level at the end if you want to read more. But this is enough to give you an idea. After reading this and so many other detailed and hilarious stories, I am glad humor is a big part of the universe. I knew Douglas Adams was on to something.

34.
OCTOBER & NOVEMBER, 2023

"The most precious gift we can offer anyone is our attention. When mindfulness embraces those we love, they will bloom like flowers."
—THICH NHAT HANH

"I walk around like everything is fine, but deep down, inside my shoe, my sock is sliding off."
—UNKNOWN, BUT IT SOUNDS LIKE SOMETHING I
      MIGHT HAVE SAID

I'm feeling better and better in my mind and body. I do have some very interesting things to tell you about my dreams. In fact, I would not even call them dreams. Nor are they lucid dreams. I lucid dream quite a bit, but these are about ten steps beyond those.

There have been so many that I've decided to add them to the second part of the book. There are some interesting experiences in there that I think will entertain you and blow your mind. Some may call it going to the "Other Side," a theme I've seen explored in many songs and pieces of art. Call it what you wish, but I ask you not to simply dismiss them as nutty random dreams. There is something else going on. Anyway, more on that in the final section of the book.

The rest of October and November went on without anything terribly exciting or dramatic. I popped out of my depression and started exercising regularly and meditating. I took many walks and hikes in nature. I spent almost every evening with Gayle making dinner and hanging out with her kids. We'd watch tv shows or movies late into the night. It was great.

I also came up with some interesting art projects and initiatives for the next year. Previously, I've done big art projects on occasion for corporate clients like the Ritz-Carlton or big whisky companies. I've grown tired of that, I suppose, using my art and social media base to promote big corporations. Maybe "tired" is not the right word. But after my event in Scotland, I've felt more of a direction change to focus my artistic efforts to make more of a change in the Earth and the environment. Nothing terribly self-righteous here or anything, but just do my own humble path to try to align some interesting art projects that get me excited with moving the needle a bit on the environment.

NOBLE PLANS FOR 2024?

One of the initiatives is an art project for the rainforests in the Amazon basin. One of my existing collectors happens to be Leonardo DiCaprio (sorry for the name-drop, but it's a goodie!). Anyway, it just so happens that he has a big save-the-rainforest in the Amazon effort going, so this makes a natural path for an interesting art project. The goal is to raise enough $$ to buy back some chunks of the rainforest for protection.

The ocean's preservation also beckons, with plans to embark on underwater expeditions in partnership with National Geographic. While the precise nature of this venture remains in flux, its essence revolves around exploring and highlighting the ocean's magnificence and vulnerability through art. This endeavor challenges me to conceive, plan, and execute a project that not only captivates but also catalyzes conservation efforts.

Beyond the realm of art, a healing initiative captures my attention, inspired by my transformative experience with Ibogaine in Mexico. Recognized for its impact on addiction recovery, Ibogaine addresses the underlying causes of dependency, offering a reset for the psyche. This project, distinct from my artistic pursuits, reflects a deep commitment to facilitating healing and growth, underscoring the diverse ways in which my work seeks to contribute to the world's wellbeing.

Embarking on a goal to harness the transformative power of Ibogaine for healing, I've aligned with Clare Wilkins, affectionately referred to as my "Ibogangel." As the pioneering force behind Pangea Biomedics, established in 2006, Clare has dedicated her expertise to the administration and refinement of Ibogaine treatments. Her approach, characterized by administering the substance in gradual doses over an extended period, ensures a gentle adjustment for those undergoing therapy, minimizing discomfort while maximizing effectiveness.

Clare's extensive experience, encapsulated in over seven hundred administered treatments, has elevated her status within the community and deepened our collective understanding of Ibogaine's potential in addiction treatment. Her collaborative efforts with MAPS on research focusing on Ibogaine's enduring impact post-detoxification, and her involvement in a critical ICEERS-conducted clinical trial, underscore the breadth of her contributions to the field.

In New Zealand, where Ibogaine's use is sanctioned, Clare and I envision establishing clinics aimed at providing this groundbreaking treatment. Our model seeks to balance accessibility, offering treatments at full cost to those who can afford it while ensuring free access to individuals in financial hardship. This initiative recognizes the disproportionate impact of substance abuse across socioeconomic strata, with a particular focus on communities besieged by methamphetamine and other drugs. By training therapists in the nuanced application of Ibogaine, our goal is to sow seeds of healing across society, championing a philosophy rooted in compassion and mutual aid. This endeavor reflects a commitment to fostering wellness and recovery, leveraging the unique properties of Ibogaine to offer a light of hope to many.

I'm aware that none of these projects may work out, and I can't will them to happen. I can put out the intention, and if there is enough of the right energy around it, I'm sure the universe will conspire to make them happen. If not, well, something else amazing will happen.

Embarking on the final stretch of 2023, I'm imbued with a sense of optimism and purpose. My daily regimen is a balanced blend of physical activity, wholesome nutrition, and a steadfast abstention from substances. This foundation supports my engagement in art projects that resonate deeply with my spirit, propelling me into a state of fulfillment and eager anticipation for what lies ahead.

In the solitude afforded by my current single status, I find myself with an abundance of time. This luxury allows me to dive into a myriad of learning endeavors, ranging from absorbing diverse podcast narratives to indulging in my lifelong passion for gaming. This hobby, rooted in childhood, offers me a peculiar insight into our potentially simulated existence, fostering a unique perspective on reality.

PLAYING WITH ARTIFICIAL INTELLIGENCE

"Real stupidity beats artificial intelligence every time."
—TERRY PRATCHETT

My exploration of artificial intelligence (AI) has led me to develop several GPTs, with "Trey's Photo Critique AI" emerging as a particular highlight. By feeding this AI extensive data from my blog and published works, it has learned to replicate my analytical approach to photography critique. This venture into AI not only satisfies my creative impulses but also aligns with my futuristic vision of leveraging technology for artistic expression.

Beyond that, I've gone full world-builder, using AI to craft all kinds of wild places, kind of like how a kid uses Legos to build castles, but way more advanced. These are the places I dream about, only now I'm not just visiting; I'm the creator. I think about my lucid dreams and the fanciful, beautiful, and almost impossible places I visit—you'll read about these about soon enough. It harks back to that mesmerizing moment in *Blade Runner 2049* where Ryan Gosling, operating on a Hollywood budget as opposed to mine, encounters the world-weaving wunderkind in her crystalline sanctum. I see this as a possible path for me in the future. Turning surreal and fascinating dreams into ever-evolving 3D worlds that you can explore alone or with friends.

Concluding this segment with a reflection on Artificial Intelligence, I draw a parallel to a pivotal moment in human evolution: the discovery of fire for cooking. It's kind of like the invention of the wheel, but for steaks. This innovation served as a "pre-digestion" process, an "external stomach," if you will, transforming raw ingredients into forms more readily assimilated by our bodies. This advance significantly reduced the energy our ancestors expended on digestion, energy that could then be redirected towards cerebral and creative pursuits.

In a similar vein, I view Artificial Intelligence as an "external brain," a tool that extends our cognitive capabilities. Just as cooking allows us to extract the most nourishing or flavorful parts of our food, AI can process, analyze, and synthesize vast quantities of information, presenting us with insights and solutions that might otherwise elude our grasp. This metaphorical "cooking" of data and ideas through AI enables us to conserve our mental energy for higher-level thinking, creativity, and problem-solving. Yes, AI can do all our homework while we tackle the big questions, like what cats are actually looking at.

35.
DECEMBER, 2023

"There are no coincidences in life. What person that wandered in and out of your life was there for some purpose, even if they caused you harm."
—Deepak Chopra

"Reality is an illusion created by a lack of alcohol."
—N.W. Erickson

As my journey unfolds, I find solace and connection through a wealth of literature and podcasts that echo my personal odyssey of awakening. It's comforting to recognize that my path towards enlightenment is shared by many, ensuring that I am not navigating these transformative waters in isolation.

Delving into the works of Stanislav Grof has been rather enlightening. Grof's clever contributions to the understanding of spiritual emergencies have provided me with invaluable insights. Reflecting on his expertise, I can't help but feel a sense of missed opportunity;

having someone of Grof's caliber by my side during my tumultuous time in New York could have significantly altered my experience. The initial phase of my spiritual emergence was filled with awe and wonder, yet it was abruptly disrupted by my confinement and sedation in a hospital, halting the natural progression of my awakening prematurely.

Beyond Grof, I feel like I could give a lecture on Carl Jung with my eyes closed and one hand tied behind my back.

In seeking closure and further exploration of my inner landscape, I have decided to embark on another Ayahuasca journey in Costa Rica come May 2024. It'll be my fourth ceremony, but just like every time you wake up with food poisoning to visit the toilet, it's like the first time. This decision stems from a deep-seated belief that there remains uncharted territory within my psyche, hidden traumas awaiting illumination and resolution. In the interim, my commitment to learning remains steadfast, with Carl Jung's theories providing a rich vein of knowledge that rivals formal academic study in psychiatry. This continuous quest for understanding and healing encapsulates my resolve to navigate the complex terrain of self-discovery, armed with the wisdom of those who have tread similar paths.

Over the Christmas holidays, I kinda turned into a wine enthusiast, like if Dionysus was hosting a TED talk in my living room. It was fun, you know, like riding a merry-go-round with a glass of cabernet. This had been my first foray into drinking after well over a year and my Ibogaine treatment. My holiday sesh kept my brain from doing too many somersaults because things were getting a bit overcharged up there, but after a marathon that would make Bacchus blush, I decided to tap out. My body was like, "Hey man, let's trade those grapes for some water," and I listened. The whole episode was a bit like getting lost on the way to the bathroom and finding yourself at a New Year's party instead.

I came across another interesting person who has been on a somewhat parallel path. His name is Matthew Roberts. I first took notice of him when I was watching a show and he talked about laying on his bed and he gets the feeling he is sliding off of it, and then he encounters entities. I shot off the couch like a rocket! He's also a hell of a nice guy and very credible. Matthew was a US Naval service member on board the USS Theodore Roosevelt and then he worked at the Office of Naval Intelligence in Washington D.C. He has a few YouTube interviews out there if you want to learn more.

Here's the bed where I would fall asleep, again looking beyond adorable, and I would sometimes wake up with strange triangle scabs on my thigh.

My musings on extraterrestrial beings and unidentified flying objects are subjects I reserve for deeper exploration, perhaps within the pages of my dream journal. Reflecting on my childhood, I recall mysterious mornings awakening to find a small, triangular scab on my left thigh, akin in size to a pinky thumbnail. This peculiar mark, when shown to my mother, was met with perplexity and dismissal, a reaction not uncommon in the face of the unexplained. Intriguingly, my later readings revealed that others have reported similar experiences with the exact same size and shape of red scabs. Under hypnosis, they recall their time being zipped away to an alien ship where they would be looked after and healed. In many cases, these are souls from other planets that are not used to these human bodies on Earth, so they need a few tweaks along the way. I have yet to have any hypnosis about this, so I have no idea. But, I found this all somewhat interesting!

My contemplations on the topic of aliens and UFOs extend far beyond simple curiosity. I am inclined to believe that if extraterrestrial beings are present among us, their intentions towards Earth and humanity are benevolent. The philosophical lens through which we view the myriad aspects of our reality, from politics and spirituality to the concept of extraterrestrial life, can dramatically color our interpretations. The dichotomy of "Fear and Scarcity" versus "Love and Abundance" serves as a fundamental framework for understanding these phenomena. Each perspective offers a distinct interpretation of events and entities, with one rooted in apprehension and limitation, and the other in hope and the infinite.

When it comes to the enigmatic notion of alien beings, my conviction is rooted in a universal truth: the core essence of the universe and its myriad expressions is not malevolent. The profound love that permeates the cosmos extends to our planet and its inhabitants. This belief posits that any interactions or connections with beings beyond our current sensory comprehension are underscored by a universal love for humanity. Such a perspective invites us to consider the existence of extraterrestrial entities not as a threat, but as an extension of the canvas of love and interconnectedness that binds all of existence.

In sum, I do think we're getting visitors, and they're here to spread some of that universal love, not to sign us up for an intergalactic timeshare we can't afford.

A DEEP DIVE INTO PHILIP K. DICK

I believe that PKD might have been a prophet of sorts. The saga of Philip K. Dick's metamorphosis from the fringes of sci-fi scribbling into a demigod of visionary insight is a narrative so richly bizarre, it could only belong to him—or perhaps a character in one of his own tales. I began a deeper dive on him after having lunch with the amazing Erik Davis in San Francisco. Erik wrote a nice article about me for one of my photography books that I will include at the end of the book. Erik's enthusiasm for PKD, you see, isn't mere fandom; it's akin to a scholarly devotion, a kind of intellectual hero worship that I find one part admirable and the other part charming-stalker.

Philip K. Dick's journey from a marginalized science fiction writer to a visionary figure harbors intriguing parallels to spiritual awakenings. His transfiguration began under the influence of sodium pentothal, used for anesthesia during dental surgery, which unexpectedly opened a door to experiences. Dick recounts an encounter with a nurse who wore a fish-shaped pendant, known as the Ichthys, a symbol historically associated with Christianity. This seemingly mundane moment catalyzed a series of visions and mystical insights for Dick, his own burning bush, prompting a deep dive into concepts of divine intelligence, the nature of reality, and the depths of human consciousness. This pivotal experience reshaped his literary exploration, infusing his subsequent narratives with questions of metaphysical significance and the possibility of transcendent communication. If a trip to the dentist can lead to all this, maybe I've been underestimating my dental hygiene routine.

In the labyrinthine narratives of his *VALIS* trilogy, Dick weaves a tapestry of reality's fabric that is as intricate as it is speculative, casting himself as "Horselover Fat," a nom de plume that dances between autobiography and allegory. This character's journey through the questions of existence, peppered with divine communiqués and metaphysical musings, mirrors Dick's own quest for understanding. It's a testament to the notion that enlightenment can strike in the most unexpected of places, even in the guise of dietary necessity, as Dick's lean times led him to dine on horse meat—a choice that, while perhaps unconventional, speaks to the lengths to which necessity mothers invention, or in this case, sustenance. Horse meat isn't that bad; I had quite a bit in Iceland. I also had rotten fermented shark. That was bad.

This cartoon is from R. Crumb's immortal *The Religious Experience of Philip K. Dick*. Interesting how it also reflects the past-life clarity of the writings of other authors.

Philip K. Dick really had a knack for making you question everything, like whether that chair you're sitting on is legit or just pretending.

All of his books carry certain themes that I find fascinating. One is the difference between what is real and what is fake. For example, in the *Man in the High Castle*, he plays with the concept through counterfeit items indistinguishable from their genuine counterparts, while *Do Androids Dream of Electric Sheep?*—the inspiration for the film *Blade Runner*—centers on Rick Deckard's existential dilemma over his artificial sheep and the societal pressure to own real animals. This theme extends to Deckard's mission to eliminate androids masquerading as humans, juxtaposed with his emotional entanglement with an android woman. These narratives underscore Dick's fascination with the blurred lines between reality and fabrication, challenging readers to consider the essence of identity and the constructs that define our perceptions of the world.

Philip K. Dick's disdain for the Californian landscape where he resided is palpable in his reflections on the state's urban sprawl. He lamented the omnipresence of concrete, consumerism, and superficiality that characterized his environment, feeling alienated in a reality that seemed fundamentally misaligned with his inner world. This sense of disconnection fueled his literary explorations into the fabric of reality, leading him to question the constructs of existence itself.

His hardcore dental regimen mentioned above became the catalyst for *The Exegesis of Philip K. Dick*, an extensive nine-thousand-page manuscript where he sought to decode the essence of reality, the existence of parallel dimensions, and the concept of a universal, divine intelligence (VALIS). His inquiry spanned across religious, philosophical, and metaphysical realms, incorporating Gnosticism, Christian mysticism, and Eastern philosophies to grasp the nature of his visions and the potential of transcendent, otherworldly communication.

Dick's relentless pursuit of understanding, encapsulated in his vow to "know what this pure consciousness was, 'ere I die trying…" illustrates his commitment to unraveling the mysteries that pervaded his life and work. Through this journey, he questioned the nature of the physical world and also sought to bridge the gap between the known and the unknowable, pushing the boundaries of human comprehension.

Through my nebulous spaces of existence, I've stumbled upon a curious alignment between the worlds spun by Philip K. Dick in *A Scanner Darkly* and Hunter S. Thompson in *Fear and Loathing in Las Vegas*. Both tales, though marinated in the psychedelic brine of the 1970s, carve out much more than just a chronicle of drug-induced wanderings. They navigate the murky waters of identity, reality, and the quintessence of being human, with a compass that seems to spin in all directions at once.

Hunter S. Thompson's *Fear and Loathing in Las Vegas* presents a surreal journey through the eyes of Raoul Duke and Dr. Gonzo, who, while in their psychedelic escapades, ironically find themselves in the middle of a narcotics police convention. This juxtaposition of their own drug-fueled existence against a backdrop of law enforcement's crusade against drugs serves as a rich canvas for exploring themes of contradiction, societal norms, and the absurdity of reality.

Then there's *A Scanner Darkly*, where Bob Arctor is both the spider and the fly in his own drug-fueled web. The guy's undercover, spying on himself, and the deeper he goes, the blurrier the line gets between being the observer and the observed. It's like trying to read a book about yourself, written by you, but you keep forgetting you're the author.

These literary explorations serve not just as reflections on the era's drug culture but as metaphors for the deeper, often tumultuous, journey of self-exploration. They underscore the complex interplay between external reality and internal perception, inviting readers to consider the multifaceted nature of existence. Like Dick and Thompson, I too am navigating the intricate riddle of my experiences, though my ambitions steer clear of penning a nine-thousand-page tome. Instead, I seek to connect the dots within a broader spectrum of understanding, where the pursuit of knowledge fuels my journey toward enlightenment.

My explorations into the realms of consciousness have revealed parallels with the experiences of authors like Philip K. Dick and Matthew Roberts (another author and friend I will discuss soon). Dick's encounters with a guiding female voice and Roberts' similar awakenings jibe with my own nightly journeys, albeit through a different sensory medium. While they hear female voices telling them important things when they awaken, my nights are punctuated by electric surges—tangible waves of energy coursing through my body, serving as signs to the insights I seek.

These electric pulses, akin to a tactile language of the subconscious, guide me towards areas of my life needing attention or contemplation. This unique form of communication underscores the diverse ways our deeper consciousness connects with us, offering guidance and wisdom beyond our waking understanding.

Moreover, my habit of listening to podcasts as I drift into sleep often serendipitously aligns with moments of awakening to segments that seem handpicked for my current dilemmas or curiosities. This synchronicity between the information presented in my dreams and the podcasts' timing suggests an orchestration by a part of me—or perhaps a universal intelligence—that knows exactly what I need to hear.

As we venture deeper into the mysteries of dream states and intuition in the upcoming part of this book, we'll delve into the significance of these nocturnal messages. This exploration is not just about understanding the mechanics of dream-induced insights but about embracing a broader, more interconnected view of consciousness, where the lines between the physical and the metaphysical, the personal and the universal, blur in fascinating ways.

We're not just talking about figuring out why you keep showing up to school naked in your dreams; it's about seeing the big picture, where everything in the universe is kinda holding hands, blurring the lines between what's happening inside your head and what's out there in the stars.

36.
UNDERSTANDING AN UPGRADED BODY

"The greatest discovery of my generation is that a human being can alter his life by altering his attitudes."
—WILLIAN JAMES

"I used to do drugs. I still do, but I used to, too."
—MITCH HEDBERG

Not only did something happen to my mind to enable it to see new things, my body has been similarly upgraded. I'm convinced it all happened there in Edinburgh. When that realm of transcendent light beings—which I am one of—sent me back into this body and mind, I think it came with a firmware upgrade.

It's taking me a few months to begin to notice these things. So, I am thinking about things differently while I am feeling different and new things in my body. It's a lot.

I've been feeling different, thinking different, and here's the kicker: I've got this new, intense need to dance. Sure, I've always liked dancing, usually just blending into the crowd at festivals where my dance moves were somewhere on the spectrum from "two left feet" to "occasionally groovy." I was never one to worry much about what people thought of my dancing, but I've always felt like I was missing a step, literally. But let me tell you, something's changed. I've turned into a dance machine.

This sudden evolution from a casual dancer to someone who could give a disco ball a run for its money isn't just about getting better at busting moves. It's a sign of something bigger, like my entire being got an upgrade. Now, when the music hits, it's not just my ears listening; it's my whole self. I'm not just dancing to the music; I am the music. It's as if those light beings from Edinburgh didn't just give me a tune-up; they cranked the volume and hit play on a whole new soundtrack for my life.

Ecstatic dance events offer a unique and transformative experience, akin to a communal journey of self-expression, emotional release, and spiritual connection. These gatherings are characterized by their open and accepting environments, where participants are encouraged to move freely to the rhythm of captivating music. Unlike conventional dance settings, ecstatic dance emphasizes individual movement and exploration over choreographed steps or partner dances. The experience is as much about the internal journey as it is about the communal energy, creating a shared experience of transformation and renewal. In Queenstown, these events stand as a testament to the power of dance as a form of therapy, celebration, and connection to the universal rhythms of life.

Imagine entering a space pulsating with vibrant energy, where the music acts not just as a backdrop but as a conduit for personal exploration and expression. Here, a guide—much like a yoga instructor—uses their voice to navigate the collective energy, offering prompts that encourage participants to let go of inhibitions, open their hearts, and connect with deeper emotional states. These prompts might invite attendees to release pent-up emotions, embrace vulnerability, and cultivate a sense of inner peace and joy.

In this sanctuary, the usual social norms of dance are set aside. Participants might find themselves moving with eyes closed, allowing the music to guide their bodies in fluid, spontaneous movements. Some may even find comfort and release lying on the floor, letting the vibrations move through them in waves of energy. The atmosphere is one of non-judgment and freedom, where each person's dance is a personal journey, reflective of their inner landscape and emotions.

MUSIC, MEDITATION, AND MOVEMENT

So, here I am, in a new body of sorts. Sometimes I hear a song I like come on while sitting here at my computer, and my body compels me to jump up and start dancing. I'm doing dance moves I didn't even know I knew! I just completely let go and something else takes over. My body is so happy. It's moving all over the place and doing some of the most incredible things. I'm not saying I'm a great dancer or anything, but it certainly feels good, and that is what matters. I'm sure some things look silly as hell, but I don't care. It feels great. Some stuff does look pretty freakin' sweet though. I should record this shit.

This phenomenon, where my body becomes the maestro and my consciousness the enraptured audience, might just be the universe's way of conducting an exorcism on trauma trapped within my cellular memory. The concept, as detailed in works like *The Body Keeps the Score*, suggests that our bodies hold onto the traumas of our past, often events we can't consciously recall but that influence us profoundly. It appears that Gabor Mate and the cosmos are in agreement: our bodies are not just vessels for our brains to cart around but repositories of our histories and perhaps, the keys to our liberation, one unexpected boogie at a time.

My exploration into meditation, plant medicine ceremonies, and various forms of self-inquiry over the past fifteen years has been a quest to unEarth and heal these hidden wounds. Dancing, I've discovered, acts as a powerful conduit for this healing process. It's as if the very act of moving energetically and freely allows the body to expel the "dark energy" of trauma. Each twist, turn, and leap serves to unravel and release these bound energies, facilitating a form of emotional and physical detoxification.

What's cool about dance is you don't need some fancy stage or a crowd of onlookers; it's just about getting up and letting loose. It's like having a heart-to-heart with yourself but through your feet. By just letting the body do its thing, we can shake off the shadows, kinda like cleaning your room by turning up the tunes and turning down the worries. It shows that our bodies know how to heal and talk to us, not with words but with moves, proving that sometimes the best way to deal with the tough stuff is to just dance it out, no dance floor required. It's a testament to the body's capacity for communication, healing, and ultimately, liberation.

37.
THE META-AWAKENING AND MY THEORY ON LIFE

"Who looks outside, dreams; who looks inside, awakes."
—CARL JUNG

"If I had to live my life again, I'd make the same mistakes, only sooner."
—TALLULAH BANKHEAD

In these final chapters I embark on a journey to distill my expansive thoughts and numerous speculations about the universe's intricate design. Although the breadth of this subject could easily fill countless discussions, my aim here is to encapsulate the essence succinctly, perhaps leaving room for more detailed exploration in future dialogues or podcasts.

Central to my understanding is the imperative to transcend fear. This life, as I perceive it, is a quest to elevate our vibrational frequency, a necessary evolution for those who aspire to inhabit the New Earth. You don't want to be left behind and stuck with all the other humans who are dominated by fear. That's gonna be a hot mess as those who've embraced change begin to vanish from sight. To you, they may have died or disappeared from your view cone, but, indeed, they have sublimated. Maybe you don't feel at home on this Earth, surrounded by violence and mean people. Maybe you are already tired of being surrounded by fear and negativity. If you've read this far, it's likely you've already ignited the flame of awareness within, embarking on your unique journey of transformation.

Congratulations are in order! You are brave. You are courageous. You are resilient. Your old friends or family members with negative thought patterns based on fear may indeed fall away from your life and try to pull you back to a previous identity that serves their own. Simply observe it with kindness and understanding. When you live in the light and love, you become impervious to this.

Elevating one's vibration is not an esoteric concept reserved for the spiritually elite but a practical guide for living. It encompasses acts of kindness, the nurturing of love, dietary mindfulness favoring a plant-based regime (with allowances for organic meat and fish), maintaining physical health, immersing oneself in the natural world, and fostering a grounded presence that radiates light. Meditation serves as a conduit for healing and for drawing purer energy from the universal source. It's about being a vessel of service and protecting your energy from those undeserving, thereby igniting a transformative spark in others ready to ascend to a higher frequency, readying themselves for the journey to the New Earth.

I know humans around the world are being awakened and activated in some way. "I'm on a mission from God!" Haha no, not really. Or maybe. God or The Source didn't quite tell me what the mission was. I do have faith that things will become revealed to me over time, just as I am being shown so many things lately. It reminds me of this delightful quote from Douglas Adams: "I seldom end up where I wanted to go, but almost always end up where I need to be."

MY NON-WORKSHOP DRUTHERS

Let's be clear: I'm not strutting around with a halo or drafting my own addition to holy texts. I'm more of a backstage crew member for the universe, one who's more concerned with ensuring the cosmic play runs smoothly than standing in the spotlight. My lifestyle is modest, powered by the creative fuel of my artistic endeavors, leaving me comfortably detached from the monetary treadmill.

You won't catch me hawking enlightenment seminars or peddling workshop transcendence for $99.99. Some other people do indeed do this and there is probably some good stuff out there (there's even some *great* stuff like Richard Rudd's "Gene Keys"). It's just not my bag. Or maybe my bag will change. Who knows? Either way, I've been brainstorming what to call this workshop that may never come into fruition. Here are my ideas so far:

- "Find Your Inner 5D Galaxy Within Your Chakras of Power as You Manifest Your Inner Trans Goddess or Trans God"
- "Cosmic Alchemy for Earthbound Deities: Transmuting Your Shadow into Militant Vegan Stardust"
- "Galactic Mermaid & Merman Transformation: Activating Your Atlantean DNA for Aquatic Ascension except for the Not Destroying the Earth with Vaginal Crystals Part"
- "The 9th Dimensional Dragon's Breath: Igniting Your Celestial Essence Through Mythical Meditation While Picking Organic Potatoes with Hairy Legs"
- "Dance with the Cosmos: Unlocking the Celestial Rhythms of Your Soul for Interstellar Orgasms Via the Oft-Ignored Man-Nipple"
- "From Chaos to Cosmos: Organizing Your Spiritual Closet with Intergalactic Feng Shui with Secret BDSM Area For Trauma-Fun"

- "The Galactic Gardener's Guide: Planting Seeds of Intention Across the Universe for a Bloom of Consciousness—AKA Stellar Bukkake Party"
- "Quantum Phoenix Rising: From Cosmic Ashes to Stellar Light, Embrace Your Eternal Fire or As We Call Fire In The Astral Plane: Trans-Ice"
- "Quantum Quokka Quests: Smiling Your Way Through Spiritual Realms with Happy Marsupial Guides"
- "Harnessing Hyperdimensional Hummus: Vegan Victories in the Vortex of Vitality"
- "Auric Origami: Folding Your Energy Fields into Fifth-Dimensional Figures for Fun and Non-Physical Profit"
- "Orbital Oolong Ceremony: Sipping the Stars with Spirited Space Sages"
- "Alien Ancestry Unveiled: Reconnecting with Your Extraterrestrial Lineage for Universal Harmony with Optional Rectal Crystals"
- "Stardust Soiree: Vegan Visions and Intergalactic Glitter for your Gluten-Free Nipple Pasties"
- "Celestial Cetaceans: Singing with Space Whales for Intergalactic Empathy and Echo-Friendly Echoes"
- "Astral Archeology: Digging Through the Akashic Records with Your Ethereal Soul-Shovel"
- "Zodiac Zoology: Petting the Cosmic Critters and Feeding the Astral Furries on Your Spiritual Safari"

As you can see, I'm doing my best to expand my demographic reach to the furries in addition to other key niche groups. I assume furries are pretty open-minded people, especially because their previous life was probably a rather cuddly and horny pet.

WHY DID I CHOOSE THIS LIFE?
I'm also sure I chose this life and body ahead of time. I knew what

was going to happen, but when you pop into these bodies, you have that amnesia that makes every day a bit of a surprise as you have to play the ultimate "Game of Life." And brother, let me tell you, I don't know about you, but I feel like I'm playing on the Hardest Difficulty level. From my studies, Earth is not only the hardest planet to be incarnated on, but it's the most important. If my research holds any water, Earth is essentially the final boss level in the game of existence, a place whose trials and tribulations ripple out across the cosmos, influencing far-flung galaxies and dimensions beyond our ken.

The process of awakening may not require vast numbers, but rather a critical mass of individuals, potentially gathering on platforms like Discord to devise innovative solutions, such as reactivating ancient Pyramids in a grand, game-solving adventure. It's an intriguing thought, like we're all part of this massive, universal escape room, and somewhere out there, there's a spiritual scoreboard lighting up every time we get a clue right. I bet the beings watching over us get a kick out of seeing us put the puzzle pieces together, kind of like how I feel when I see someone try to open a door that clearly says "pull" by pushing it.

Then there's this thing called the Maharishi Effect, named after a guy who was really into sitting quietly and thinking about nothing much at all. This concept, named after Maharishi Mahesh Yogi, the proponent of Transcendental Meditation (TM), posits that when a critical mass—specifically, about 1% of a population—engages in TM and its advanced techniques together, it can lead to observable improvements in societal well-being. Numerous studies have reported reductions in crime rates, decreased social unrest, and overall enhancement of quality of life in areas where such meditation groups were active.

It's an astonishing illustration of how a handful of harmoniously humming humans can indeed iron out the wrinkles in the fabric of society, making the case that perhaps, in the grand scheme of things, we're all just a big cosmic choir needing to find our pitch.

One ponders the rationale behind the awakening of seemingly

"ordinary" individuals over celebrities or influential figures like Elon Musk, Joe Rogan, or Oprah Winfrey. Despite my own unconventional path, the question arises: Why not empower those with significant achievements, influence, and resources, who have already contributed positively to our world (as each of them have in a manifold manner) and possess the skills to enact widespread change? This curiosity underscores the mysterious and democratic nature of spiritual awakening, hinting at a deeper, perhaps more personal, journey towards enlightenment and global transition. Or, maybe, they all have been activated in some way and they are all playing their role. We are all one.

Take Oprah, for example, the high priestess of daytime TV in yesteryear, who introduced the masses to the teachings of Eckhart Tolle, essentially turning living rooms into makeshift ashrams. And Joe Rogan, with his podcast pulpit, has been nudging the collective consciousness toward a gentle and fun open-mindedness one episode at a time. Then there's Elon Musk, straddling the line between saving our planet and inadvertently pitching a future where we're all part smartphone.

Yet, the spiritual alarm clock has a peculiar way of ringing. It's not about who has the loudest voice but who is ready to listen and evolve, suggesting that maybe, just maybe, awakening is a lonely and personal journey. So many lost people are not ready to listen. They are asleep. They are on their path; they are loved.

It hints of a future where change isn't a broadcast but quietly relaxed and realized within each of us, hinting at a revolution that's more about internal recalibration than external declaration. In this grand narrative, everyone's playing their part, knowingly or not, in the intricate dance of awakening, where each step, each stumble, and each leap forward is choreographed by something far greater, painting a picture of a world transformed not by the few with power but by the many with purpose.

SOME EYEWITNESS ACCOUNTS
FROM THE NEW EARTH

You may be thinking, okay Trey, what is all this "New Earth" business? This is not merely a speculative or esoteric idea but a transformative vision shared by individuals across the globe, revealed through hypnotic sessions as detailed in *The Three Waves of Volunteers and a New Earth*. This narrative isn't drawn from the imagination of science fiction enthusiasts or those deeply entrenched in metaphysical studies. Instead, it emerges from the collective unconscious of ordinary individuals—teachers, accountants, lawyers—who, under hypnosis, channel insights from a universal consciousness.

Now, the sheer volume of thousands of these accounts, echoing each other across continents without a single contradiction, is enough to make even the most skeptical hitchhiker take pause. As you delve into these narratives, you might feel a bit frightened (especially if you're concerned about what happens to the Old Earth), however a sense of recognition or truth that aligns with your innermost feelings and intuitions about the future may arise.

One thing that has become clear to me is that as we upgrade our vibration and raise our frequency, we indeed have the potential to move into an evolved reality. The best comparison I can offer is that of a radio. Just as many radio frequencies surround us all the time, allowing us to hear different things, similarly, by adjusting the frequency of our bodies, we can perceive and participate in different realities.

This will give you permission and motivation to create your own universe of love while you eschew fear from your life. Now, this is a big chunk of text, so get ready! Sometimes in books I will skip over long excerpts, but this is not one to be skipped. Wait till you get to the part about fruit on the New Earth! Sign me up!

This is from Chapter 36 of her book:

> The entity speaking through V. had a deep, gravelly voice:
>
> V: The whole idea is, we have to get people to expand just a

little bit. And we have to get this level raised just a little bit. And when we do, we can make that change, and make it easier for them. It will be the ones that we can't get to change that are going to be left behind. It's going to be horrible. We can't get them to see. We can't get them to love.

D: Then the others, the ones that will change, will go into another world? Another Earth?

V: It's like it's going to expand into another dimension. Let me see how I can explain this to you. It's like a raising, if you can understand, like we're going to raise into a different vibration. They'll be able to see what's going on, but we can't help them anymore.

D: Is it like a separation? Like two Earths, is that what you mean?

V: Oh no, no. It's a changing of dimension. We're going to go from here to here. And those that can't change will be left behind.

D: When we go into the other dimension, will it be a physical Earth?

V: It will be just like we are right now.

D: That's what I meant by two Earths.

V: Yes, yes. But they're not going to be aware of us. God help them, God help them. It's going to be so terrible for them.

D: They won't know what has happened?

V: No, they will know. That's the whole idea. They will know, but it will be too late for them to change their vibrations. They can't change it in a second. They have to change it over a period of time. We've been working on this for awhile. It has to seep in and work on your body, and it has to slowly change and raise your vibrations. And when it happens, it's going to be too late for them, but they will see it, though. They will die, but they will see it and they will learn from that.

D: That world will still exist, but it will be different?

V: Not very well, no, not very well. There won't be much left in that world. Not much.

D: Many people will die at that time?

V: Yes. But I think much of their death will be painless. I think they will live just long enough to see what's happening. And I think God will spare them the horrible traumatic pain. I pray that's what will happen.

D: But the others that do shift into the new vibration, with an identical physical world....

V: (Interrupted.) Yes, but some won't even be aware that they've made the change. Some will. Those that have been working towards it will know.

D: Will they know about the people being left behind?

V: I don't think so. There will be an awareness of a change that took place. I'm not sure if it's going to be a conscious awareness. Let me think about that. (Pause) We'll go into this dimension and we'll know. Some won't know though. They'll feel something. They'll feel a difference. Almost like a cleanness, a clearness. A crispness, a difference. I know what it is. They'll feel the difference. They'll feel the love.

D: So, even if they haven't been working toward it, they will be carried along with it.

V: Yes, because they're ready for it.

D: And the other ones won't be....

V: They're not, they're not.

D: So, they're left in the negativity? You said the whole world is going to be changed at that time.

V: Yes, those that can go on, that can move into this, will move. And those that can't, won't. And it'll be horrible for them.

D: And it will be like two worlds.

V: Yes, two worlds existing at the same time, but not always aware of each other.

[cut part and put in the Bonus Levels at the end]

More from another subject in Australia:

C: It's like a car. Imagine a car that has an old body. It's just the same old car you've been driving. And then you put a new engine in it. And suddenly that car begins to perform differently, even though it looks the same. And then you get another engine, and you replace it. And the car keeps getting faster and faster, and brighter and smarter. And then before you know it, the car is doing such good things, that the body starts to change. It's like the energy of the new engine starts to reform the body. And before you know it, the chap has turned into a sports car. A beautiful, glossy, attractive vehicle. And that's what this is about. The energies that are coming in have the ability to transform the vehicle. And it will start to be different. It's going to look different. It's going to look... well, younger comes to mind. It's going to look smarter and younger. The cells of the body, the vibration of the body is changing, and is matching the vibration of the incoming energy. And the physical changes will be next.

D: What will those physical changes be?

C: Oh! The body's going to change to be lighter. And I'm getting that it will look taller. It's not that it's going to be taller. But the energy from within is somehow going to become visible on the outside. And it will make the body seem taller, elongated, slimmer. And more transparent.

D: Transparent?

C: Yes. It's a pioneering thing.

D: Is this the way the people on Earth will be evolving? (Yes) Will everyone make the changes?

C: Yes, because the people have all been given that choice. If they want to evolve with the Earth, they will evolve into this new human being. It will look different. And that's what this experiment is about. That's why Christine and others are moving the ones who don't want to evolve with the Earth. They are going to leave. (Almost crying) And bring a lot of pain to their families. But the people who are staying must hold the light. That's a big job. To get divorced and separated from these things that are happening now. And these things are going to continue to happen until the cleansing is complete. Those who are here to stay, are taking this race of people into a very new and different civilization. Those people are being tested now, to see if they can hold the light when there is disaster, and not be sucked in. They're the people who will move ahead with this planet.

D: Almost like a last test?

C: Yes. The testing is going on right now. Whatever each being needs to test them, to see what they're capable of giving back to this program; how firm their commitment is. How willing they are to serve. That is all being tested now.

D: So each one is having their own individual test?

C: Yes. And the people who are finding it tough now are the ones who are staying. They're the ones who are going through the tests. But some of them are not coming through.

D: They're not passing the test.

C: No. There are some who are not.

D: This is what I was told by other people, that some would be left behind. (Yes) And I thought that sounded cruel.

C: No, it's not cruel because each soul is given the choice. And if they are not moving and evolving, it's because they are choosing not to. And they will reincarnate into another place of their choice. And it's all right. Because it's only a game. They'll stay in the Old Earth. The New Earth is so beautiful. You will see colors and animals and flowers you never imagined possible. You'll see fruit that is perfect food. It doesn't have to be cooked. It's just eaten as it is. And everything that the being needs to nourish them will be there. These new fruits are developing now with the help of the Star People.

D: Are these fruits and vegetables we don't have on the Earth now?

C: We don't have them. They're mutations in some ways. I'm seeing a custard apple as an example of what happened. We will have a fruit called a "custard apple." And it doesn't look like an apple. It has a rough exterior, and it's about the size of two oranges put together. And then you open it. It's like custard inside. So that's a fruit, but a food. It's not just a fruit, but another food has been introduced to it, like custard. That's an example of one of the future foods. So these foods will be delights to the senses. And nutritious and sustaining for the—I keep being stopped when I start to say "body." And I am being told to say "being." They'll be nutritious for the being. And things we now have to cook—like you'd cook custard—will be incorporated into these fruits. And it has to do with helping the planet, and cutting down on the use of electricity and energy. So the fruits are going to provide us with what we need.

D: I've heard man has done many things to the food that is not healthy for the body.

C: That's right. The organic foods are coming onto the Earth, and those organic farmers are moving with the Earth evolution program. That's why they're there. And that's why consciousness is being raised about this because people need to know how to grow properly. And the Rudolph Steiner schools are teaching children this. So, the children who are going to be with the new Earth will know this. And those children are now teaching in universities and in institutions, and they're spreading the word. So when the cleansing of the Earth occurs, much of that toxicity is going to be pushed away. You see, the new Earth is not this dimension. The new Earth is another dimension. And we will move into that new dimension. And in that new dimension, there'll be these trees that have purple and orange in their trunks. And there will be beautiful rivers and waterfalls. And the energy will be brought back. There will be energy in the streams and the water that goes over rocks and sandbanks. And it hits the Earth. It creates energy and will be straightened out in this world. Many of these streams have been changed and straightened out to make them navigable and nice. That's taking away the energy from the Earth. The Earth is going to be cleansed. I'm seeing water.

D: Does this have to occur before the Earth shifts and evolves into the new dimension?

C: I'm seeing us stepping through. (Startled) Oh! What I'm seeing is that the people who are going to the new dimensions will step through into this new world.

D: While the other one is being cleansed?

C: Yes, yes.

D: What do you see about the water that will happen with the cleansing?

C: (A big sigh) It's not going to be shown to me.

D: They don't want you to see it?

C: No, they won't show me that. What they're showing me is... an opening? And we step through. We step into, what looks like this Earth, but it's different colors. It's different textures. At first it looks the same. At first only. And then as we look around, we start to see that it's not. It's changing before our eyes. And it's so beautiful.

I cut off more of this conversation from the book here, but I have the whole thing in its entirety in the bonus section at the end.

In summarizing this dialogue, it's clear that the collective testimony of thousands worldwide not only corroborates but also deepens our understanding of this transformative concept. The idea of transitioning to a New Earth, as outlined in these sessions, bridges our deepest intuitions and the stark reality of our current existential crossroads. It's a call to action—a reminder that the journey towards a higher vibrational existence begins with the individual's commit-ment to love, compassion, and a deliberate rejection of fear.

This narrative invites us to envision a future where our collective vibrational shift can lead to a dimensional leap, separating us from the outdated constructs of the Old Earth. The descriptions of a physically identical yet vibrationally enhanced New Earth under-score the urgency of this evolutionary leap. It's a testament to the power of love as the ultimate transformative force, capable of trans-cending dimensions and birthing a reality infused with clarity, peace, and unity.

Another difficult thing for many people is the concept of Letting Go. So many people hang on to the past or ways in which they have been "wronged," blaming external things for their own peace of mind (or lack of it). Clinging to resentment and past grievances does a disservice to your soul, permitting the past and other people to wield power over you. However, when you release the grip of these burdens, life becomes significantly easier and brighter.

The shift to a New Earth isn't just some lofty bedtime story for adults; it's a blueprint for an existential makeover, an invitation to a party where love is the guest of honor, and fear gets bounced at the door.

Should these concepts stir a chord within you, igniting a spark of curiosity or resonance, I warmly invite you to delve into the com-prehensive reading list provided at this book's conclusion. Further, I encourage you to visit my website, where I share a curated selection of literature spanning an array of subjects. While it may appear that my focus leans heavily towards this specific area, rest assured, my interests are broad and diverse. Additionally, for those seeking en-tertainment or enlightenment through visual storytelling, I offer a myriad of recommendations for both movies and television shows, each selected for its potential to inspire, challenge, and enrich. These range from edgy French films to amazing romcoms. From *Schindler's List* to *Superbad*, these lists have it all.

And let's get one thing straight: getting on board with this love train doesn't mean you gotta be all serious all the time. Life's too short not to crack up at the absurdity of it all. We're basically cosmic toddlers, learning as we go, but doing it with a sense of fun. Because, at the end of the day, if we're not having a laugh, then what's the point, right? So, let's keep playing, keep laughing, and maybe, just maybe, we'll figure out this New Earth thing together—one lesson at a time, one dance at a time, and one laugh at a time.

OTHER GREAT TEACHERS—THE WISDOM OF TOLLE, SINGER, DASS, AND KRISHNAMURTI

So many teachers, so little time. Two of my favorites are Ekhardt Tolle and Michael Singer. I loved how in the beginning of his latest book, Tolle compared the idea of becoming "conscious" to the first flowers on Earth—sparse at first, then proliferating across the globe. This imagery captures the essence of awakening: a gradual but inevitable spread of awareness that transforms the landscape of human experience. His suggestion that becoming conscious is akin to Earth's first blooms is not just whimsical; it's like the moment humanity discovered coffee and realized mornings had potential. Initially rare, yet destined to proliferate, this awakening promises a global garden of enlightenment in the weeds of worldly woes. It's a vision that is hopeful, and maybe just the right soul food that signals an organic spread of awareness to help heal the current rate of global grumpiness.

Now, in the vast supermarket of spiritual guidance, with its endless aisles of wisdom, two more items stand out on the shelf: Ram Dass and Jiddu Krishnamurti. Ram Dass is like the ultimate fusion cuisine, blending Eastern mysticism with the hearty, practical bread of Western therapy, all seasoned with mindfulness, love, and a dash of meditation. Ram is like if Eastern mysticism and Western therapy had a baby, and that baby was really into mindfulness and could meditate before it could walk. Meanwhile, Krishnamurti is that dish that's not even on the menu, challenging you to cook without a recipe, inviting an unmediated quest for truth that's as liberating as finding out that clothes are optional. K-man is all about ditching the menu and cooking up your own truth, no recipes needed.

Together, these spiritual sous-chefs offer a smorgasbord of paths to enlightenment, from savoring the taste of the present moment to dissecting the very ingredients of our reality. Their teachings are a dinner invitation to step away from the fast food of superficial existence and sit down to a feast of deep, meaningful engagement with the essence of the universe. It's a journey that's both intimately personal and as universal as asking for extra fries with that, guiding us toward a consciousness that's as unbounded as the universe and as rich; with possibilities that seem impossible to us now. And let me tell you, in this banquet of the beyond, there's always room for dessert.

38.
WHAT HAPPENS AFTER YOU DIE?
...AND A FINAL MESSAGE

"When you die, you're not going to have to put up with everlasting non-existence, because that's not an experience. A lot of people are afraid that when they die, they're going to be locked up in a dark room forever, - Try and imagine what it would be like to go to sleep and never wake up. And if you think long enough about that...it will pose the next question. What was it like to wake up after never having gone to sleep? That was when you were born...you see...you...you can't have an experience of nothing so after you're dead the only thing that can happen is the same experience or the same sort of experience as when you were born."
—ALAN WATTS

"Do not take life too seriously. You will never get out of it alive."
—ELBERT HUBBARD

About ten years ago I made a video that went viral and got over a million views called "Life From Above and Beyond." It used that quote above from Alan Watts. It carried a message, an echo of wisdom that I had yet to fully grasp. It was not until the mists of Scotland enfolded me that the true weight of those words settled upon my shoulders.

We are all luminous beings, temporarily donning the cloak of physicality. Our true essence, that of pure consciousness and radiant spirit, hails from realms far beyond the mundane confines of Earthly life. It is from this exalted state that we make the deliberate choice to embark on the human journey, encapsulating ourselves within the bounds of flesh and bone, to experience, learn, and evolve. It is with intent and purpose that we descend into this land of tactile wonders, to touch, to err, to grow.

So after you die, you return to this beautiful spirit world that will be so familiar to you. You can stay there as long as you want or come back. Many souls do choose to come back to Earth and give it a different run in a new body so their soul can learn new lessons. But the time in between lives is beyond epic.

Death, often shrouded in mystery and fear, marks not an end but a transcendental return to our origin—the spirit world—a glorious sea of unfathomable bliss and understanding. It is here, in the afterglow of physical existence, that the soul experiences an ineffable reunion with the Source, a sensation akin to the ecstatic liberation I encountered during my transformative journey in Scotland.

In Scotland's embrace, I found a mirror to this truth. Death, that elusive thief, often cloaked in dread and sorrow, in truth, is but a door—a portal back to the ineffable wonder of our beginnings. The spirit world awaits with open arms, a domain of serenity and revelation. And it was there, in the heart of ancient lands, that I tasted a freedom so complete, it was as if my very soul had found its way back to the shores of its primeval sea.

Awaiting is a celestial homecoming adorned with the vibrant hues of love, as each being radiates a unique light, a spectral signature of their essence. You recognize all of them as your eternal friends and family and they recognize you. There is no judgment. There is only a torrent of love and excitement upon your triumphant return. Everyone is beyond excited to see their timeless friends and there is nothing but love.

A pivotal moment in this journey is the passage through a luminous cascade, a celestial ablution that purifies the soul of worldly burdens. This light-shower, a metaphysical cleanse, washes away the residues of pain, sorrow, and suffering, allowing the spirit to bask in purity and peace. It's a process of unburdening, of shedding the weights that tethered the soul to the physical plane, preparing it for the next phase of its voyage. It's like, "Hey, let's rinse off all that Earthy grime and get you sparkling for the next round." Kinda makes me wish they had one of these light-showers at Burning Man, but with less waiting in line.

DEFENDING YOUR LIFE.
ALBERT BROOKS IS YOUR LAWYER.

You then go through a debriefing with your soul guide. This reminds me of a hilarious movie with Meryl Streep and Albert Brooks called *Defending Your Life*. Every soul seems to have the same guide from lifetime to lifetime and in between. They are wise. They do not judge. They are loving. But there is no punishment, only love, support, and understanding. After all, they know everything.

This debriefing session is like watching the 3D director's cut of your life, complete with the ability to pause, rewind, and explore those tantalizing "what if" scenarios. For a good description of this, read the sequel to the Dr. Michael Newton book I mentioned earlier called, *Destiny of Souls*. The guide reminds you of your purpose and goals in the previous life and there is a discussion as to any progress made to correct patterns of a previous incarnation. Imagine being able to ask, "What if I had taken that job in Toledo?" and actually getting to see the answer unfold. Spoiler alert, you would have had an empty life in Toledo and had boring friends that would have held you back from being your true self. That's in the Toledo immigration brochure, by the way, so you should have known.

In the Bonus Level section of the book, there's a poignant story set in the late 1800s about a sixteen-year-old girl faced with an unimaginable dilemma. Pregnant and bereft upon learning of her husband's death, she chooses to end her life in a lake, seeing no viable future amidst the harsh judgments of her village or the bleak prospects of London. In the aftermath, within the spirit world, she engages in a profound review of her life alongside her soul advisor. Through a vivid, three-dimensional, interface they explore not only the tragedy of her decision but also alternative paths filled with hope and redemption, including the potential life of her beautiful daughter in a nurturing environment. There are countless transcripts of this "Life Review" process in the life between lives in the spirit world. Personally, I can't wait to go through my personal life Netflix documentary and see what would have happened had I made other choices. It sounds fascinating.

I'm reminded of this quote from Søren Kierkegaard: "Life can only be understood backwards; but it must be lived forwards."

This time round, a cycle both liberating and daunting, underscores the grand design in which we are all threads interwoven. Our journeys, divergent as they may seem, are united by the cosmic loom that weaves us into the fabric of all that is. And as we traverse the varied landscapes of human endeavor, let us hold in our hearts the remembrance of our stardust lineage and the sublime odyssey that beckons us when we shed our temporal shells—a voyage that sails us homeward, toward the welcoming shores of the universal expanse, to the cradle of infinity.

And here's the kicker: if you manage to sort out all your soul's to-do list (with the biggest to-do being not letting fear dominate your thoughts and govern your decisions) there's no more coming back to Earth to relearn how to parallel park. You graduate to becoming one of the universe's helpers, showing the rookies how to navigate the interstellar rave without stepping on too many toes. It's like reaching that level in a video game where you've unlocked all the achievements and now you're just cruising, helping others find the Easter eggs and hidden levels of dharma.

TIME TO LEARN AND PARTY AND TRAVEL THE UNIVERSE!

What do you do after the big welcome home party that is thrown for you, after your debriefing with your Soul Advisor who showed up at every one of your games and always thinks you're the MVP? It's more like what *can't* you do? Because you can do pretty much anything. Want to fly back down to Earth as an invisible soul and see what is going on or comfort people? Go for it! Want to grab a group of friends and go visit another planet or space station to see what kind of crazy stuff is going on? Go for it! Want to go to a learning planet with a master that can teach you how to use energy to create anything from plants to fish to crazy animals? Go for it! Want to go to the university that is like Hogwarts of the Heavens and study all your past lives and the collected knowledge of the universe under the guidance of a teacher and guest galactic TED teachers? Go for it!

As far as studying and growing, there are countless accounts of this. You go to something that seems to be described as a sort of university to help your soul move along to even further enlightenment. There seem to be even locations like libraries, structures like a class of friends, leaders that are teachers from a higher level that come in from time to time and guide you. Even your teachers have their own teachers. There appear to be many levels of learning. Although none of these structures seem to have the negative connotations of many educational systems down here. There is no power-structure or hierarchy in the manner with which we are familiar. For example, I never really liked school, but these schools sound amazing.

To make it clear, your life is so much more than what is in your body right now. That stirs an excitement within me. The anticipation of what lies beyond the veil does not hasten my steps toward its threshold; rather, it infuses each moment here on Earth with purpose and passion. I am anchored by the belief that my mission here is not yet complete, that there are still chapters to be written, love to be shared, and hope to be sown.

Furthermore, it gives me an amazing release of grieving for people that have died. Not only are they in a better place, they are feeling a freedom of light and love they could never feel in this body. When someone dies now that is close to me, I no longer feel sorry for them. I may feel sorry for myself a bit because I will miss their presence and love. But I don't feel sorry for them. They are truly free. They've left behind the heaviness and pain and problems of this life and are now light and free. Happy beyond happy. They are being showered with more affection and love than was humanly possible on this mortal coil.

My soul guide, that timeless buddy of mine, deserves a galaxy's worth of gratitude. They're the unsung hero behind the scenes, meticulously planning my Earth-escapades and ensuring I get the most out of this universal field trip. It's a partnership forged in the stars, with love and growth as the guiding principles, proving that even in the vast, seemingly indifferent, cosmos personal attention to each soul's journey is a top priority. So, here's to the cosmic guides, the celestial mentors who help us navigate the maze of existence, always reminding us to choose the path of love over fear, even when the universe throws us a curveball.

As I sit here and write this, I cry because I think about my three kids, and how their three soul guides helped to choose me and their mom as their parents. I thank them so much. Because, honestly, I know everyone totally loves and adores their kids and thinks they are special. But this is next-level stuff. Their soul guides, in their infinite wisdom, have woven our spirits together, choosing us to embark on the sacred journey of parenthood. For this, my gratitude knows no bounds, for within their gaze, I glimpse the light glowing beyond their beings, so pure and profound. I pray they have a life full of as little (or zero) suffering as possible. May they learn the things they need to in this life without all the pain their parents and their grandparents and their entire lineage had to endure.

And in the quiet moments, when the world retreats into hushed reverence, I am reminded of the universal truth that binds us all—love. It is the answer whispered by the winds, reflected in the stars, and echoed in the stillness of the night. Love is the answer, the key to unlocking the highest potential within our souls. Love is the glow that guides us home, the warmth that thaws the winters of our discontent. In love, and through love, we find our way, we heal, we become whole. Love, now and always, is the answer.

I love my family very much and wish the best for their souls without suffering. May they be safe, may they be happy, may they be healthy.

I love you very much and wish the best for your souls without suffering. May you be safe, may you be happy, may you be healthy.

Love is the answer. Love is the answer. Love is the answer.

– END OF BOOK ONE –

BONUS LEVEL:
A DEEPER DIVE INTO THE AUTHOR

"Light Falls Like Bits" by Erik Davis

Moonrise Kingdom

Infinity of Tokyo

Gypsy

Three images from Trey Ratcliff's copious online portfolio: A thin waterfall spills toward the sands of a rocky cove, forming a jet of silver fluid that appears at once solid and gaseous, like diaphanous alabaster. There is something unreal about the scene. The foam of an ominously green sea dissipates like a cloud, the sand inlets glow as if they were getting hit with invisible stage lights, even as the dark sky behind the distant Monterey pines lets you know that deep evening has arrived. Two questions come to mind: Where is this variegated light coming from? And: What is this amazing place? With characteristic generosity, Ratcliff—I admit it feels strange to call such an intimately mediated man as Trey by his last name—gives you the name of the falls in his comments, as well as the app (his own, Stuck on Earth) he used to source it. The magic light, of course, is Ratcliff's own algorithmic mise-en-scène. He'll give you tips, but he also knows that, even in the Information Age, magic still requires a bit of mystery.

A dense conglomeration of low-slung urban dwellings fills the frame, with clusters of looming high-rises on the far horizon. There are no visible billboards or neon signs, but you know without reading the caption that we are looking at a neighborhood in Tokyo. Light is coming from everywhere: the sky is glowing purple and gray, the tall buildings in the distance are all lit up, and each of the hundred-odd buildings in the foreground sends forth its own peculiarly tinted shade—yellow, burnt orange, turquoise, lime green, dusty pink. Ratcliff titled the shot Infinity of Tokyo, but the picture is the opposite of the blazing signage and crowded streets that usually define the photography of that city. There are no people, and only a couple of trees, but somehow the luminescent warren feels organic, almost tranquil, with each glowing structure settling into its own unique slot in the crazy quilt of made space.

A begoggled woman casually rests her arm on a couch inside what looks to be a ramshackle gypsy caravan, outfitted with brocade fabrics, pillows, Persian carpets, and delicate Islamic woodwork. She is wearing the stuff of scruffy romance: an oddball hat, a fur vest, an orange skirt, purple patterned leggings, and dusty boots. The shot is slanted, like on the old *Batman* TV show, and through the open windows in the structure we see an oblique nighttime horizon line glowing with distant structures that could be moon pods or a gathering of luminescent undersea creatures. Light is popping out from unexpected places: a hanging Moroccan brass star lamp casts multicolored light across the ceiling, orange glowing shapes peek in through one window, the horizon light is a cool blue, and the woman seems to hold a glowing stick in her lap. Most viewers can tell that this is Burning Man, an art event and one of Ratcliff's paradigmatic places. But the shot also reminds us that Burning Man is not simply a specific place and time—it is also a nexus of other worlds, a hub of marvels. As Ratcliff notes in his comments, the windows of the gypsy hut became "outward portal-glances to worlds and times that whizzed by."

Ratcliff's photographs work like that, too. Day after day, year after year, Ratcliff posts a single shot to his travel photography web-log Stuck in Customs, photos of worlds and times that whiz by. There are shots from Chinese mountains, Patagonian plains, Icelandic lakes, and New York streets. Many online photographers travel and shoot the world, of course, and some opt for the bold and hyper-detailed pictures that are Ratcliff's forte. But in Ratcliff's case, the world has really started to pay attention. As of last count, Ratcliff had thirteen million followers on his blog and the various social networking sites he enthusiastically haunts. As arguably the leading travel photo-blogger, Ratcliff and his generous images help mediate the world to the world—or, more specifically, the planet to the Internet. But his globe-trotting communiqués are a far cry from the rough-and-tumble reportage of camera-wielding journalists beholden to raw and brawny dictates of photo-realism. Instead, he presents what I would call "photographic hyperrealism": an intensely vibrant and dramatic aesthetic saturated with the light and detail of reality, but intensified into wondrous slices of time and space that peel off from that reality to hover somewhere—and somewhen—between memory, dream, and the CGI screen. The fact that these images resonate with so many people tells us something about the way we see the world currently, and at the heart of that contemporary seeing is the convulsive and now-dominant presence of digital media. Before he became known as a photographer, Ratcliff worked as an online entrepreneur, technology patent holder, and web-based game designer. He is a digital native—a geek, in other words—and the production, circulation, and consumption of his photographs must be seen in the light of a new technological reality that's blurring the boundaries between culture and computation. Ratcliff has always shot digital. He never experienced his own photography as an analog process that results in a physical artifact—the photo—that manifests a chemically mediated trace of the world's photons. Instead, his photos have always started out as what he has called "a pile of bits"—the quantized output of the sensors that digital cameras use to splinter "the seen" into a matrix of numbers. But piles also imply disorder, or perhaps the unfinished. In other words, the numbers that constitute digital images are almost demanding to be tweaked and processed after the fact—especially if you are a geek. From this perspective, the tools of post-processing are not so much the imposition of special effects on a pure image, but protocols that allow the original light to unfold its own potentials—potentials that have as much to do with fabulation as fidelity.

At the heart of Ratcliff's technical process is High Dynamic Range (HDR) photography. Whether you are talking digital cameras or vinyl LPs or the eyeballs of vampire bats, dynamic range refers to the amount of territory that stretches between the faintest and the strongest values capable of being registered or reproduced by a given system. The impulse for HDR photography derives from the yawning gap between the dynamic range of the camera lens and the far greater and more sensitive spread of the human visual system. The basic idea is to take multiple exposures of the same scene at different shutter speeds (or stops), and then to seamlessly overlap those images into a single picture that now includes a far greater range between light values. While not a natively digital process, HDR has been aided and abetted by digital cameras and increasingly sophisticated software packages that allow photographers to manipulate the cornucopia of data that results from the process. At the heart of this post-production phase is tone-mapping, which involves the controlled stepping down of the information in the full HDR image into the more limited dynamic ranges of, for example, digital screens. Rather than simply losing all that additional data, the tone-mapping options in programs such as Photomatix—which Ratcliff uses and heartily recommends to fans—give HDR photographers a wide range of operators that can algorithmically massage the visual data in a wide variety of ways. Despite this variability, a recognizable "HDR aesthetic" is emerging, one that includes elements like intense saturation, crisp detail, localized high contrast, and sometimes overtly artificial or "painterly" values.

Through the popularity of his images and his commitment to an "open source" sharing of his technical insights and working methods, Ratcliff is actively helping to shape this emerging and increasingly infectious aesthetic. He also continues to push the possibilities of the technology, exploring modes of post-processing that are too time-consuming for most HDR photographers. For example, after massaging individual sectors of the image with local operators, Ratcliff then applies a number of algorithms to the entire picture plane. He saves the various resulting images, and then uses Photoshop to recombine the best areas of those multiple drafts into a final image. Ratcliff's photographs are therefore more like collages than they might at first appear. Indeed, part of the curious effect of Ratcliff's more arresting photographs derives from the playful tension between the single composed scene, rooted in wondrous actuality, and the various differently processed layers that suggest the superposition of different worlds, times, and perspectives. Some describe these arresting images as "surreal"; that term, while capturing the dreamlike sheen of many of these photographs, puts too much weight on distortion or warp. I prefer the term "hyperreal": an algorithmic intensification of reality that exceeds reality.

HDR has its detractors, of course, and their voices are worth hearing (It's all about contrast, right?). Like many powerful techniques that get packaged into accessible software sliders and controls, HDR tone-mapping is very easy to do thoughtlessly. The Internet (not to mention much commercial photography) is full of oversaturated, garish HDR images that, critics complain, take us too far from realism, and therefore override, in the quest for special effects, photography's capacity to be intimate with the actual world. HDR photography is, in a word often bounced around HDR comment threads online, unnatural. One irony with this notion, which is pointed out by many defenders, is that the higher dynamic range of these photographs makes them, at least in principle, closer to the human body's natural visual experience. But I'm not sure what nature has to do with HDR in either case. Photographers have always been tweaking and manipulating their images, even in the quest to frame reality as it is. The question is: What reality is being framed?

The appeal of photo-realism relies, in part, on an analog logic that ties the photographic artifact to the real world. The physical existence of the picture, an absolutely necessary product of the photochemical technical process, becomes a satisfying symbolic stand-in for moments of space-time that are, as we all know, always slipping into oblivion. In that sense, photo-realism reassures us about the existence of the real world. But what happens to this equation, then, when the camera transcodes photons into numbers, and the materiality of the photograph evaporates into the bitstream? Rather than metonymically standing in for a vanished physical reality, the digital photograph—which can easily spend its entire existence circulating as data through circuits, wavelengths, and LED screens—stands in for something else: not the actual world, but the provisional, constructed, and ever-shifting run-throughs of that world that make up memory, perception, and media itself. One ironic example of this self-referential trend is the use of filters on Instagram, which lend digital snapshots an emotional aura and mnemonic depth by vampirically simulating the visual artifacts of older analog photography.

Ratcliff is not interested in that sort of false nostalgia, though he is certainly willing to raid the history of media—and particularly, cinema—in order to intensify his images. Instead, he wants to explore uniquely digital computational possibilities, not to further distance ourselves from a vanishing analog world, but to revivify moments of wonder within our current mediascape. One of Ratcliff's reasons for embracing the Baroque possibilities of algorithmic post-processing is that these "artificial" techniques can paradoxically simulate the marvelous unfoldings of the world we occasionally experience, those magic moments, in perception or memory, where the world is more than itself. These moments are often associated with the sorts of epic natural landscapes that Ratcliff so often shoots, with big weather, subtle gradations of unnameable colors, and absurdly picturesque topographies. Everyone knows that even highly realistic photographs of such places are—for those who were there—often shallow and disappointing. Instead, Ratcliff subjects those scenes to a hyperrealistic intensification that mirrors or extends the capacity for enchanted perception that lies in our own nervous systems. Of course, these moments of powerful perceptual feeling also have long been the bread and butter of epic filmmaking, an additional layer of mediation that Ratcliff invites into his photos, as he unabashedly intensifies a single photographic slice of space-time into the crescendo heights of a *Lawrence of Arabia* or *Lord of the Rings*.

For postmodern critics such as Jean Baudrillard and Umberto Eco, the hyperreal was associated somewhat apocalyptically with the notion of a model or simulation of reality that no longer has any actual relationship to reality but is still experienced or consumed as if it does. Ratcliff's photos share something of this desire to provide a vision of reality that exceeds reality. At the same time, however, his hyperreal images are not free-floating postmodern bric-a-brac. Part of their popularity and their life derive from how they are embedded in, and mediated by, Ratcliff's own online presence as well as the stories, comments, and conversations that surround the shots. In other words, his photos arrive on our monitors or smartphone screens already situated within Ratcliff's world—the ongoing tale of his travels, the notes he appends and the comments he responds to, and the technical discussions his images spark. In other words, the community of fans, followers, hobbyists, and pros that has grown up around his work is now part of the substance of the work itself. Though Ratcliff's photos have more to do with the mythic than the mundane, they are part of a larger online flow of communication that brings them down to Earth by both humanizing them and exposing their technological constitution.

Another reason that so many people respond to Ratcliff's photos is that the world itself is becoming increasingly hyperreal. The physical environment is exceedingly penetrated by screens and cameras, while within the mediascape itself special effects and professional production values are competing for the scarce resource of our eyeball time. This turn also helps to explain Ratcliff's attraction to Burning Man, the annual gathering of artists, freaks, makers, and geeks who, over the course of a few weeks, construct and dismantle a surreal city in an immense salt flat in northwestern Nevada. The 50,000-plus attendees are strongly encouraged to become participants, to co-create the experience, and to reward the attention of others by going generously over the top in any number of ways. People become avatars, vehicles become art, shelters become theme parks, dance clubs become dreams. At once an intensification of, and escape from, current technological reality, Burning Man can be seen as a (paradoxically gritty) celebration of the hyperreal: a bacchanal of DIY special effects, intoxicating distortions, noncommercial machineries, and sometimes mind-bending, high-tech tweaks of the human visual system. The visual experience of the festival alone is staggering, and over the years, the entire human history of luminescence has been represented: lasers and LEDs, neon signs and zoetropes, Tesla coils and glow sticks, dream machines and UV. And hovering over it all is the original "artificial" light: controlled (and sometimes not-so-controlled) fire.

For photographers, Burning Man presents a bit of a conundrum. The festival features an endless series of marvels, juxtapositions, and colorful, half-nude human beings, but the inevitable gap between experience and the photographic document seems heightened here. Indeed, anyone with even a cursory interest in the festival has already seen more Burning Man photographs than they'll ever need. For the most ambitious photographers out there, the goal is not just to record the wonders, but to channel and express the vibe of the event itself as it strikes the minds and imagination of its participants. Here, Ratcliff's hyperrealistic aesthetic—with its dreamlike taste for

narrative fragments, unusual technical details, and brazen luminescence—is, again, paradoxically naturalistic. Rather than document-
ing the festival, his strongest playa photographs share in and intensify the exuberance of the event itself, whose participants are constantly striving for the gloriously absurd, the interdimensional, the
larger- (or weirder-) than-life.

At the same time, Burning Man is not an infinite spectacle. The
event constantly reminds you that people and their creative relationships are behind all the marvels. It's no accident that Ratcliff shoots
a lot of people when he is at Burning Man, because it's a tribe in
which he can recognize himself—despite his mild-mannered, un-
pierced personal style. Like many of the geeks and Internet entrepre-
neurs who flock to the event, Ratcliff acknowledges that Burning
Man is not just an amazing party. It's also an experimental model
for the emergence of a new kind of cultural and political economy,
one in which generosity, open-source know-how, and spectacular
gifts are part of a larger circulation of general abundance that exceeds
cash and consumerism.

And indeed, some of this ethic fuels the success of Stuck in Customs. Ratcliff approaches HDR photography like a maker rather
than a "professional" or even an "artist," and this spirit of technical
transparency and can-do creativity makes people feel welcome at his
site, and encouraged to become makers and photographers themselves. He presents himself as a dedicated hobbyist rather than an
aesthetic master. Of course, Ratcliff is a professional, and a very successful one at that. Some of his visitors order his limited-edition
prints, others license those images for commercial purposes, and still
others partake of his e-books, apps, and other offerings. But
Ratcliff's online success is directly connected to the fact that, like a
good Burner, he is also unfailingly generous to his fans and followers. To the ire of many online pros who feel he is setting a bad example, Ratcliff refuses to watermark his images. He also makes mas-
sive-resolution copies of his images available under a creative

commons license that only restricts their commercial use. As a digital native, Ratcliff recognizes that the photograph is no longer a scarce object at the heart of a gallery or magazine system, but a screen event at the heart of a liquid network—a network that is better to approach with, as he himself puts it, an attitude of love rather than fear. This abundant optimism animates the generosity of the images themselves, which show a planet, urban and wild, exceeding its already considerable wonders.

Erik Davis is an author, award-winning journalist, and lecturer based in San Francisco. His wide-ranging work focuses on the intersection of alternative religion, media, and the popular imagination. He is the author of four books, and his essays on music, technoculture, and spirituality have appeared in dozens of books. Davis has contributed to scores of publications, and has been interviewed by CNN, the BBC, NPR, and the New York Times. He explores the "cultures of consciousness" on his weekly podcast Expanding Mind. He graduated from Yale University in 1988, and is currently earning his PhD in religious studies at Rice University.

FASCINATING CASE STUDIES

In this serpentine section, I seek to compile some of my favorite transcripts so as to compel you to read the whole books recommended. I've taken giant chunks of some case studies so that you may see them in their entirety. If you've read this far, you must be somewhat interested as I leave more breadcrumbs for you to join me in this beautiful warren of rabbit holes.

I'll share these case studies from various authors from all around the world. One of the most prolific is Dolores Cannon. She's the one I have a fruit-date with on the New Earth! Here's one of her videos so you can get a sense of her.

https://youtu.be/liGPDc2d4mw?si=Od-rMik92XM0Jb1fY&t=2642

BONUS LEVEL: THE 1860 SUICIDE OF A SIXTEEN-YEAR-OLD GIRL

This first transcript is from Dr. Michael Newton's book *Destiny of Souls*, the sequel to *Journey of Souls* that both corroborates reports from his first book and ventures into some rather fascinating uncharted territory. I have read many of these sorts of accounts of people that have died and then can spend days, weeks, and months reviewing their life in the library and seeing the results of various alternative choices. Apparently, whenever you make a choice, another "version" of you actually lives out the other choice and you get to see what happens. Fascinating.

While watching, you can just observe like a 3D Netflix show of sorts, or you can become yourself in the third person. Or, even more interesting, you can "become" anyone in the scene. There are accounts of bullies that see themselves in grade school throwing rocks at a smaller kid, and then they can change perspective and be the smaller kid as well.

This is one of many cases I have studied and read about that involve suicide. Apparently, on the other side, even though there is no judgment, they don't like it very much when you commit suicide.

Unfortunately, you'll need to be incarnated again to pay off that negative karma, because every suicide really hurts people around you. Besides that, you are bailing out on your mission here on Earth to learn the lessons your soul needed to learn. In the spirit world, they believe suicide is a waste of a perfectly good human body. There are always other choices you can make, as you can see in the story below.

CASE 29 FROM *DESTINY OF SOULS*

Everything below is directly from the book, perhaps with a few omissions to make it read quicker without any of the context or meaning being lost:

> Amy had recently returned to the spirit world from a small farming village in England where she killed herself in 1860, at age sixteen. This soul would wait another hundred years before coming back due to her self-doubts about handling adversity. Amy drowned herself in a local pond because she was two months pregnant and unmarried. Her lover, Thomas, had been killed the week before in a fall off a thatched roof he was repairing. I learned the two were deeply in love and intended to marry.

> Amy told me during her past life review that she thought when Thomas was killed, her life was over. She said she did not want to bring disgrace upon her family from the gossip of local villagers. Tearfully, this client said, "I knew they would call me a whore, and if I ran off to London, that is exactly what a poor girl with child would become."

> In suicide cases, the soul's guide might offer seclusion, aggressive energy regeneration, a quick return, or some combination of these things. When Amy crossed over after killing herself, her guide, Likiko, and the soul of Thomas were there to comfort her for a while. Soon she was alone with Likiko in a beautiful garden setting. Amy sensed the disappointment in Likiko's manner and she expected to be scolded for her lack of courage. Angrily, she asked her guide why the life didn't go as planned in the beginning. She had not seen the possibility of suicide before her incarnation. Amy thought she was supposed to marry Thomas, have children, and live happily in her village to old age. Someone, she felt, had pulled the rug out from under her.

Likiko explained that Thomas' death was one of the alternatives in this life cycle and that she had the freedom to make better choices than killing herself. Amy learned that for Thomas, his choice to go up on a high, steep, and dangerously slippery roof was a probable one—more probable because his soul mind had already considered this "accident" as a test for her. Later, I was to learn Thomas came very close to not accepting the roof job because of "internal forces pulling him the other way." Apparently, everyone in this soul group saw that Amy's capacity for survival was greater than she gave herself credit for, although she had shown tenuous behavior in her earlier lives.

Once on the other side, Amy thought the whole exercise was cruel and unnecessary. Likiko reminded Amy that she had a history of self-flagellation and that if she was ever going to help others with their survival, she must get past this failing in herself. When Amy responded that she had little choice but to kill herself, given the circumstances of Victorian England, she found herself in the following library scene.

Dr. N: Where are you now?

S: (somewhat disoriented) I'm in a place of study... it looks Gothic... stone walls... long marble tables...

Dr. N: Why do you think you are in this sort of building?

S: (pause) In one of my lives, I lived as a monk in Europe (in the twelfth century). I loved the old church cloister as a place for quiet study. But I know where I am now. It is the library of great books... the records.

Dr. N: Many people call them Life Books. Is this the same thing?

S: Yes, we all use them... (pause, subject is distracted) There is a worrisome-looking old man in a white robe coming toward me... fluttering around me.

Dr. N: What's he doing, Amy?

S: Well, he's carrying a set of scrolls, rolls of charts. He is muttering and shaking his head at me.

Dr. N: Do you have any idea why?

S: He is the librarian. He says to me, "You are here early."

Dr. N: What do you think he means?

S: (pause) That... I did not have compelling reasons for arriving back here early.

Dr. N: Compelling reasons... ?

S: (breaking in) Oh... being in terrible pain—not able to function in life.

Dr. N: I see. Tell me what this librarian does next.

S: There is a huge open space where I see many souls at long desks with books everywhere but I'm not going to that room now. The old man takes me to one of the small private rooms off to the side where we can talk without disturbing the others.

Dr. N: How do you feel about this?

S: (shakes head in resignation) I guess I need special treatment right now. The room is very plain with a single table and chair. The old man brings in a large book and it is set up in front of me like a TV viewing screen.

Dr. N: What are you supposed to do?

S: (abruptly) Pay attention to him! He sets his scroll in front of me first and opens it. Then he points to a series of lines representing my life.

Dr. N: Please go slowly here and explain what these lines mean to you, Amy.

S: They are life lines—my lines. The thick, widely spaced lines represent the prominent experiences in our life and the age they will most likely occur. The thinner ones bisect the main lines and represent a variety of other... circumstances.

Dr. N: I have heard these less prominent lines are possibilities of action as opposed to the probabilities. Is that what you are saying?

S: (pause) That's right.

Dr. N: What else can you tell me about the thick versus thin lines?

S: Well, the thick line is like the trunk of a tree and the smaller ones are the branches. I know the thick one was my main path. The old man is pointing at that line and scolding me a bit about taking a dead-end branch.

Dr. N: You know, Amy, despite this Archivist fussing about these lines, they do represent a series of your choices. From a karmic standpoint, all of us have taken a wrong fork in the road from time to time.

S: (heatedly) Yes, but this is serious. I did not just make a small mistake in his eyes. I know he cares about what I do. (there is a pause and then loudly) I WANT TO HIT HIM OVER THE HEAD WITH HIS DAMN SCROLL. I TELL HIM, "YOU GO TRY MY LIFE FOR A WHILE!"

Note: At this point, Amy tells me that the old man's face softens and he leaves the room for a few minutes. She thinks he is giving her time to collect herself, but then he brings back another book. This book is opened to a page where Amy can see the Archivist as a young man being torn apart by lions in an ancient Roman arena for his religious convictions. He then puts this book aside and opens Amy's book. I ask her what she sees next.

S: It comes alive in three-dimensional color. He shows me the first page with a universe of millions of galaxies. Then the Milky Way... and our solar system... so I will remember where I came from—as if I could forget. Then, more pages are turned.

Dr. N: I like this perspective, Amy. Then, what do you see?

S: Ahh... crystal prisms... dark and light depending upon what thoughts are sent. Now, I remember I have done this before. More lines... and pictures... which I can move forward and backward in time with my mind. But the old man is helping me anyway.

Note: I have been told these lines form vibrational sequences representing timeline alignments.

Dr. N: How would you interpret the meaning of the lines?

S: They form the patterns for the life pictures in the order you wish to look at—that you need to look at.

Dr. N: I don't want to get ahead of you, Amy. Just tell me what the old man does with you now.

S: Okay. He flips to a page and I see myself onscreen in the village I just left. It isn't really a picture—it's so real—it's alive. I'm there.

Dr. N: Are you actually in the scene or are you simply observing the scene?

S: We can do both, but right now I am supposed to just watch the scenes.

Dr. N: That's fine, Amy. Let's go through the scene as the old man is presenting it to you. Explain what is going on.

S: Oh... we are going to look at... other choices. After seeing what I actually did at the pond where I took my life—the next scene has me back at the pond on the bank, (pause) This time I don't wade in and drown myself. I walk back to the village, (laughs for the first time) I'm still pregnant.

Dr. N: (laughing with her) Okay, turn the page. Now what?

S: I'm with my mother, Iris. I tell her I am carrying Thomas' baby. She is not as shocked as I thought she would be. She is angry, though. I get a lecture. Then... she is crying with me and holding me. (subject now breaks down while tearfully continuing to talk) I tell her I am a good girl, but I was in love.

Dr. N: Does Iris tell your father?

S: That is one alternative on the screen.

Dr. N: Follow that alternative path for me.

S: (pause) We all move to another village and everyone there is told I am a widow. Years later, I will marry an older man. These are very hard times. My father lost a lot when we moved and we were even poorer than before. But we stay together as a family and life eventually becomes good. (crying again) My little girl was beautiful.

Dr. N: Is that the only alternative course of action you study right now?

S: (with resignation) Oh, no. Now, I look at another choice. I come back from the pond and admit I am pregnant. My parents scream at me and then fight with each other about who is to blame. I am told they do not want to give up our small farm they worked so hard for and leave the village because I am disgraced. They give me a little money to get to London so I can try to find work as a serving girl.

Dr. N: And how does this work out?

S: (bitterly) Just what I expected. London would not have been good. I wind up in the streets, sleeping with other men. (shudders) I die kind of young and the baby is a foundling who eventually dies too. Horrible...

Dr. N: Well, at least you tried to survive in that alternative life. Are any other choices shown to you?

S: I'm growing tired. The old man shows me one last choice. There are others, I think, but he will stop here because I ask him to. In this scene, my parents still believe I should go away from them, but we wait until a traveling peddler comes to our village. He agrees to take me in his cart after my father pays him something. We do not go to London but rather to other villages in the district. I finally find work with a family. I tell them my husband was killed. The peddler gave me a brass ring to wear and backs up my story. I'm not sure they believe me. It doesn't matter. I settle in the town. I never marry, but my child grows up healthy.

Dr. N: After you are finished turning these pages with the old man and have contemplated some of the alternatives to suicide, what are your conclusions?

S: (sadly) It was a waste to kill myself. I know it now. I think I knew it all along. Right after I died, I said to myself, "God, that was a stupid thing to do, now I'm going to have to do it all over again!" When I went before my council, they asked if I would like to be retested soon. I said, "Let me think about it awhile."

After this session, my client discussed some of the choices she has had to make in her current life involving courage. As a teen-ager, she became pregnant and dealt with this difficulty through the help of a school counselor and finally her mother, who was Iris in her life as Amy. They encouraged her to stand up for herself regardless of the opinions of others. In our session together, my subject learned her soul has a tendency to prejudge serious events in her life in a negative manner. In many past lives, there was always a nagging thought that whatever decision she made in a crisis would be the wrong one.

Although Amy was reluctant to return to Earth again, today she is a woman of much greater confidence. She spent the hundred years between lives reflecting on her suicide and decisions made in the centuries before this life. Amy is a musical soul and she said at one point:

"Because I wasted the body assigned to me, I am doing a kind of penance. During recreation, I can't go to the music room, which I love to do, because I need to be alone in the library. I use the screens to review my past actions involving choices where I have hurt myself and those around me."

When a client uses the word "screen" to describe how they view events, the setting is relevant. Small conference rooms and the library appear to have tables with a variety of TV-size books. These so-called books have three-dimensional illuminated viewing screens. One client echoed the thoughts of most subjects when she said, "These records give the illusion of books with pages, but they are sheets of energy which vibrate and form live picture-patterns of events."

The size of these screens depends upon usage within a given setting. For instance, in the life selection rooms we use just before our next incarnation, the screens are much larger than seen in spiritual libraries and classrooms. Souls are given the option of entering these life-sized screens. The huge, shimmering screens usually encircle the soul and they have been called the Ring of Destiny. I will discuss the Ring further in chapter 9.

Despite the impressive size of the screens in future-life selection rooms, souls spend far more time looking at scenes in the library. The function of the smaller library screens is for monitoring past and current time on Earth on a continuing basis. All screens, large or small, have been described to me as sheets of film which look like waterfalls that can be entered while part of our energy stays in the room.

All cosmic viewing screens are multidimensional, with coordinates to record spacetime avenues of occurrence. These are often referred to as timelines and they can be manipulated by thought scanning. There may be other directors of this process not seen by the soul. Quite often a subject will employ mechanical contrivances in their scanning descriptions such as panels, levers, and dials. Apparently, these are all illusions created for souls who incarnate on Earth.

Regardless of screen size, the length, width, and depth in each frame allows the soul to become part of a procession of cause and effect sequences. Can souls enter the smaller screens associated with books in the same way as with the larger screens found in the Ring [of Destiny]?[5] While there are no restrictions for time travel study, most of my subjects appear to use the smaller screens more for observing past events in which they once participated. Souls take a portion of their energy, leaving the rest at the console, and enter the screens in one of two ways:

○ As observers moving as unseen ghosts through scenes on Earth with no influence on events. I see this as working with virtual reality.

○ As participants where they will assume roles in the

---

[5] Trey's comment: This is the commonly used place-name where people get to choose from a selection of bodies and lives for their next mission.

action of the scene, even to the extent of altering reality from the original by re-creations.

Once reviewed, everything returns to what it was since the constant reality of a past event on a physical world remains the same from the perspective of the soul who took part in the original event.

BONUS LEVEL: THE DUTCH PAINTER

This is more from the case study 21 that was mentioned earlier in the book from Dr. Michael Newton's *Journey of Souls*. There is quite a bit more as well in the book, and I think all the case studies are quite fascinating.

Although the next case is presented from the perspective of one group member, his superconscious mind provides an objectivity into the process of what goes on in groups...

Some readers may find it hard to accept that souls do joke with each other about their failings, but humor is the basis upon which self-deception and hypocrisy are exposed. Ego defenses are so well understood by everyone in spiritual groups that evidence of a mastery of oneself among peers is a strong incentive for change. Spiritual "therapy" occurs because of honest peer feedback, mutual trust, and the desire to advance with others over eons of time. Souls can hurt, and they need caring entities around them. The curative power of spiritual group interaction is quite remarkable. Soul members network by the use of criticism and acclaim as each strives toward common goals. Some of the best help I am able to give my clients comes from information I receive about their soul group. Spiritual groups are a primary means of soul instruction. Learning appears to come as much from one's peers as from the skill of guides who monitor these groups.

In the case which follows, my client has finished reliving his last past life as a Dutch artist living in Amsterdam. He died of pneumonia at a young age in 1841, about the time he was gaining recognition for his painting. We have just rejoined his spiritual group when my subject bursts out laughing.

Dr. N: Why are you laughing?

S: I'm back with my friends and they are giving me a hard time.

Dr. N: Why?

S: Because I'm wearing my fancy buckled shoes and the bright green velvet jacket—with yellow piping down the sides—I'm flashing them my big floppy painter's hat.

Dr. N: They are kidding you about projecting yourself wearing these clothes?

S: You know it! I was so vain about clothes and I cut a really fine figure as an artist in Amsterdam cafe society. I enjoyed this role and played it well. I don't want it to end.

Dr. N: What happens next?

S: My old friends are around me and we are talking about the foolishness of life. We rib each other about how dramatic it all is down there on Earth and how seriously we all take our lives.

Dr. N: You and your friends don't think it is important to take life on Earth seriously?

S: Look, Earth is one big stage play—we all know that.

Dr. N: And your group is united in this feeling?

S: Sure, we see ourselves as actors in a gigantic stage production.

Dr. N: How many entities are in your particular cluster group in the spirit world?

S: (pause) Well, we work with ... some others ... but there are five of us who are close.

Dr. N: By what name do they call you?

S: L ... Lemm—no that's not right—it's Allum ... that's me.

Dr. N: All right, Allum, tell me about your close friends.

S: (laughs) Norcross ... he is the funniest ... at least he is the most boisterous.

Dr. N: Is Norcross the leader of your group?

S: No, he is just the loudest. We are all equal here, but we have our differences. Norcross is blunt and opinionated.

Dr. N: Really, then how would you characterize his Earth be-havior?

S: Oh, as being rather unscrupulous—but not dangerous.

Dr. N: Who is the quietest and most unassuming member of your group?

S: (quizzical) How did you guess—it's Vilo.

Dr. N: Does this attribute make Vilo the least effective contrib-uting member of your group?

S: Where did you get that idea? Vilo comes up with some inter-esting thoughts about the rest of us.

Dr. N: Give me an example.

S: In my life in Holland—the old Dutch couple who adopted me after my parents died—they had a beautiful garden. Vilo reminds me of my debt to them—that the garden triggered my painting—to see life as an artist ... and what I didn't do with my talent.

Dr. N: Does Vilo convey any other thoughts to you about this?

S: (sadly) That I should have done less drinking and strutting around and painted more. That my art was ... reaching the point of touching people ... (subject pulls his shoulders back) but I wasn't going to stay cooped up painting all the time!

Dr. N: Do you have respect for Vilo's opinions?

S: (with a deep sigh) Yes, we know he is our conscience.

Dr. N: So, what do you say to him?

S: I say, "Innkeeper, mind your own business—you were having fun, too."

Dr. N: Vilo was an innkeeper?

S: Yes, in Holland. Engaged in a business for profit, I might add.

Dr. N: Do you feel this was wrong of Vilo?

S: (contrite) No ... not really ... we all know he took losses to help those poor people on the road who needed food and shelter. His life was beneficial to others.

Dr. N: I would guess telepathic communication makes it hard to sustain your arguments when the complete truth is known by everyone?

S: Yes, we all know Vilo is progressing—damn!

Dr. N: Does it bother you that Vilo may be advancing faster than the rest of you?

S: Yes ... we have had such fun ... (subject then recalls an earlier life with Vilo where they traveled together as brothers in India)

Dr. N: What will happen to Vilo?

S: He is going to leave us soon—we all know that—to have associations with the others who have also gone.

Dr. N: How many souls have left your original group, Allum?

S: (A long pause, and then ruefully) Oh ... a couple have moved on ... we will eventually catch up to them ... but not for a while. They haven't disappeared—we just don't see their energy as much.

Dr. N: Name the others of your immediate group for me besides Vilo and Norcross.

S: (brightening) Dubri and Trinian—now those two know how to have a good time!

Dr. N: What is the most obvious identifying characteristic of your group?

S: (with relish) Adventure! Excitement! We have some real pioneer types around here. (subject rushes on happily) Dubri just came off a wild life as a sea captain. Norcross was a free-wheeling trading merchant. We live life to its fullest because we are talented at taking what life has to offer.

Dr. N: I'm hearing a lot of self-gratification here, Allum.

S: (defensively) And what's wrong with that? Our group is not made up of shrinking violets, you know!

Dr. N: What's the story on Trinian's last life?

S: (reacts boisterously) He was a Bishop! Can you believe it? What hypocrisy.

Dr. N: In what way?

S: What self-deception! Norcross, Dubri, and I tell Trinian his choice to be a churchman had nothing to do with goodness, charity, or spirituality.

Dr. N: And what does Trinian's soul mentally project to you in self-defense?

S: He tells us he gave solace to many people.

Dr. N: What do you, Norcross and Dubri, tell him in response?

S: That he is going soft. Norcross tells him he wanted money or otherwise he would have been a simple priest. Ha—that's telling him—and I'm saying the same thing. You can guess what Dubri thinks about all this!

Dr. N: No, tell me.

S: Humph—that Trinian picked a large city with a rich cathedral—spilling a ton of money into Trinian's fat pockets.

Dr. N: And what do you tell Trinian yourself?

S: Oh, I'm attracted to the fancy robes he wore—bright red—the finest of cloth—his Bishop's ring which he loved—and all the gold and silver around. I also mention his desire to bask in adulation from his flock. Trinian can hide nothing from us—he wanted an easy, cushy life where he was well-fed.

Dr. N: Does he try to explain his motivations for choosing this life?

S: Yes, but Norcross reproaches him. He confronts Trinian on seducing a young girl in the vestry. (jovially) Yes, it actually happened! ... So much for providing solace to parishioners. We know Trinian for who he really is—an outright rogue!

Dr. N: Does Trinian offer any excuses to the group for his conduct?

S: (subject becomes quieter) Oh, the usual. He got carried away with the girl's need for him—she had no family—he was lonely in his choice of a celibate church life. He says he was trying to get away from the customary lives we all choose by going into the church—that he fell in love with the girl.

Dr. N: And how do you, Norcross and Dubri, feel about Trinian now?

S: (severely) We think he is trying to follow Vilo (as an advancing soul), but he failed. His pious intentions just didn't work for him.

Dr. N: Allum, you sound rather cynical about Trinian's attempts to improve himself and make changes. Tell me honestly, how do you feel about Trinian?

S: Oh, we are just teasing him ... after all...

Dr. N: Your amusement sounds as if you are scornful over what may have been Trinian's good intentions.

S: (sadly) You're right ... and we all know that ... but, you see ... Norcross, Dubri, and I ... well, we don't want to lose him from the group, too ...

Dr. N: What does Vilo say about Trinian?

S: He defends Trinian's original good intentions and tells him that he fell into a trap of self-gratification during this life in the church. Trinian wants too much admiration and attention.

Dr. N: Forgive me for passing judgment on your group, Allum, but it seems to me this is something you all want, except perhaps Vilo?

S: Hey, Vilo can be pretty smug. Let me tell you, his problem is conceit and Dubri tells him that in no uncertain terms.

Dr. N: And does Vilo deny it?

S: No, he doesn't ... he says at least he is working on it.

Dr. N: Who among you is the most sensitive to criticism?

S: (pause) Oh, I guess it would be Norcross, but it's hard for all of us to accept our faults.

Dr. N: Level with me, Allum. Does it bother the members of your soul group when things can't be hidden from the others—

when all your shortcomings in a past life are revealed?

S: (pause) We are sensitive about it—but not morbid. There is great understanding here among us. I wanted to give artistic pleasure to people and grow through the meaning of art. So, what did I do? I ran around the Amsterdam canals a lot at night and got caught up in the fun and games. My original purpose was pushed aside.

Dr. N: If you admit all this to the group, what kind of feedback do you get? For example, how do you and Norcross regard each other?

S: Norcross often points out I hate to take responsibility for myself and others. With Norcross it's wealth ... he loves power ... but we are both selfish ... except that I am more vain. Neither of us gets many gold stars.

Dr. N: How does Dubri fit into your group with his faults?

S: He enjoys controlling others by leadership. He is a natural leader, more than the rest of us. He was a sea captain—a pirate—one tough individual. You wouldn't want to cross him.

Dr. N: Was he cruel?

S: No, just hard. He was respected as a captain. Dubri was merciless against his opponents in sea battles, but he took care of his own men.

Dr. N: You have told me that Vilo assisted people who were in need on the road, but you haven't said much about the positive side of your lives. Is anyone in your group given any gold stars for unselfish acts?

S: (intently) There is something else about Dubri ...

Dr. N: What is that?

S: He did one outstanding thing. Once, during heavy seas, a sailor fell off the mast into the ocean and was drowning. Dubri tied a line around his waist and dove off the deck. He risked his life and saved a shipmate.

Dr. N: When this incident is discussed in your group, how do you all respond to Dubri?

S: We praise him for what he did with admiration in our minds. We came to the same conclusion that none of us could match this single act of courage in our last lives.

Dr. N: I see. Yet, Vilo's life at the inn, feeding and housing people who could not pay him, may represent acts of unselfishness for a longer term and therefore is more praiseworthy?

S: Granted, and we give him that. (laughs) He gets more gold stars than Dubri.

Dr. N: Do you get any strokes from the group for your last life?

S: (pause) I had to scramble for patrons to survive as a painter, but I was good to people ... it wasn't much ... I enjoyed giving pleasure. My group recognizes I had a good heart.

Every one of my clients has special attachments to their soul group, regardless of character makeup. People tend to think of souls in the free state as being without human deficiencies. Actually, I think there are many similarities between groups of souls close to each other and human family systems. For instance, I see Norcross as the rebellious scapegoat for this group of souls, while he and Allum are the inventory takers for everyone's shortcomings. Allum said Norcross is usually the first to openly scrutinize any rationalizations or self-serving justifications of past life failures offered by the other members. He appears to have the least self-doubt and emotional investment over standards of conduct. This may define his own insecurity, because Norcross is probably fighting the hardest to keep up with the advancing group.

I suspect Allum himself could be the group's mascot (often the youngest child in human families), with all his clowning around, preening, and making light of serious issues. Some souls in spiritual groups do seem to me to be more fragile and protected than other group members. Vilo's conduct demonstrates he is the current hero (or eldest family member), with his drive for excellence. I have the impression from Allum that Vilo is the least defiant of the group, partly because he has the best record of achievement in recent past lives. Just as in human family systems, the roles of spiritual group members can be switched around, but I was told Vilo's kinetic energy is turning pink, signaling his growth into Level II.

I attach human labels on ethereal spirits because, after all, souls who come to Earth do show themselves through human characteristics. However, I don't see hatred, suspicion, and disrespect in soul groups. In a climate of compassion, there are no power struggles for control among these peer groups whose members are unable to manipulate each other or keep secrets. Souls distrust themselves, not each other. I do see fortitude, desire, and the will to keep trying in their new physical lives. In an effort to confirm some of my observations about the social dynamics among spiritual group members in this case, I ask Allum a few more questions.

Dr. N: Allum, do you believe your criticism of each other is always constructive?

S: Sure, there is no real hostility. We have fun at each other's expense—I admit that—but it's just a form of ... acknowledgement of who we really are, and where we should be going.

Dr. N: Is any member of your soul group ever made to feel shame or guilt about a past life?

S: Those are ... human weapons ... and too narrow for what we feel.

Dr. N: Well, let me approach your feelings as a soul in another way. Do you feel safer getting feedback from one of your group members more than another?

S: No, I don't. We all respect each other immensely. The greatest criticism comes from within ourselves.

Dr. N: Do you have any regrets for your conduct in any past life?

S: (long pause) Yes ... I feel sorry if I have hurt someone ... and ... then have everyone here know all about my mistakes. But we learn.

Dr. N: And what do you do about this knowledge?

S: Talk among ourselves ... and try to make amends the next time.

Dr. N: From what you told me earlier, I had the idea that you, Norcross, and Dubri might be releasing some pent-up feelings over your own shortcomings by dumping on each other.

S: (thoughtfully) We make cynical remarks, but it's not like being human anymore. Without our bodies we take criticism a little differently. We see each other for who we are without resentment or jealousy.

Dr. N: I don't want to put words in your mouth, but I just wondered if all this flamboyance exhibited by your group might indicate underlying feelings of unworthiness?

S: Oh, that's something else again. Yes, we do get discouraged as souls, and feel unworthy about our abilities ... to meet the confidence placed in us to improve.

Dr. N: So, while you have self-doubts about yourselves, it's okay to make cynical remarks about each other's motivations?

S: Of course, but we want to be recognized by one another for being sincere in working on our individual programs. Sometimes self-pride gets in the way and we use each other to move past this.

BONUS LEVEL: A DISCUSSION OF THE NEW EARTH

Note that I have now read over thirty case studies where different people from all walks of life, all around the world, from an array of differing religions from hardcore Catholic to atheist, and all stories not only overlap but reinforce one another.

This particular one is from Chapter 36 in *The Three Waves of Volunteers for a New Earth* by Dolores Cannon. Check my suggested reading list and you will read more and more transcripts like this:

The entity speaking through V. had a deep, gravelly voice:

V: The whole idea is, we have to get people to expand just a little bit. And we have to get this level raised just a little bit. And when we do, we can make that change, and make it easier for them. It will be the ones that we can't get to change that are going to be left behind. It's going to be horrible. We can't get them to see. We can't get them to love.

D: Then the others, the ones that will change, will go into another world? Another Earth?

V: It's like it's going to expand into another dimension. Let me see how I can explain this to you. It's like a raising, if you can understand, like we're going to raise into a different vibration. They'll be able to see what's going on, but we can't help them anymore.

D: Is it like a separation? Like two Earths, is that what you mean?

V: Oh no, no. It's a changing of dimension. We're going to go from here to here. And those that can't change will be left behind.

D: When we go into the other dimension, will it be a physical Earth?

V: It will be just like we are right now.

D: That's what I meant by two Earths.

V: Yes, yes. But they're not going to be aware of us. God help them, God help them. It's going to be so terrible for them.

D: They won't know what has happened?

V: No, they will know. That's the whole idea. They will know, but it will be too late for them to change their vibrations. They can't change it in a second. They have to change it over a period of time. We've been working on this for awhile. It has to seep in and work on your body, and it has to slowly change and raise your vibrations. And when it happens, it's going to be too late for them, but they will see it, though. They will die, but they will see it and they will learn from that.

D: That world will still exist, but it will be different?

V: Not very well, no, not very well. There won't be much left in that world. Not much.

D: Many people will die at that time?

V: Yes. But I think much of their death will be painless. I think they will live just long enough to see what's happening. And I think God will spare them the horrible traumatic pain. I pray that's what will happen.

D: But the others that do shift into the new vibration, with an identical physical world....

V: (Interrupted.) Yes, but some won't even be aware that they've made the change. Some will. Those that have been working towards it will know.

D: Will they know about the people being left behind?

V: I don't think so. There will be an awareness of a change that took place. I'm not sure if it's going to be a conscious awareness. Let me think about that. (Pause) We'll go into this dimension and we'll know. Some won't know though. They'll feel something. They'll feel a difference. Almost like a cleanness, a clearness. A crispness, a difference. I know what it is. They'll feel the difference. They'll feel the love.

D: So, even if they haven't been working toward it, they will be carried along with it.

V: Yes, because they're ready for it.

D: And the other ones won't be....

V: They're not, they're not.

D: So, they're left in the negativity? You said the whole world is going to be changed at that time.

V: Yes, those that can go on, that can move into this, will move. And those that can't, won't. And it'll be horrible for them.

D: And it will be like two worlds.

V: Yes, two worlds existing at the same time, but not always aware of each other.

D: I know when you're in a different dimension, you're not always aware of the other one. But that's the message you want to get across is that we should spread this information about love while we still can, to bring as many as possible along.

V: Love is the key. Because God is love. And love is God. And love is the supreme power. And that's what we need to feel in our lives. What we need to give to each other and feel for each other.

D: Yes, love has always been the key. So, they're trying to tell as many people, so they can bring them along. That's what the urgency is.

V: The urgency is that we've run out of time. Just be prepared. Uh, what? Tell her what?

She was listening to someone else. There were mumbling sounds, then the deep gravelly voice returned.

V: Tell you... ready. Ready for the change coming soon. Soon now. Ready... She's not a good vehicle. She's not done this before. I can't get my ideas through her to convey to you. I must work on it. Let's cleanse this vehicle. Oh, yes! Uh... there. That's better.

D: What is it you want to tell me?

V: Must help all mankind. Tell them what is to come soon. Changes, dimensional shift. Those that can hear you will hear you. They'll be ready for that dimensional shift. (Her normal voice returned.) Those that can't, will not accept it anyway, so (Laugh) they'll think we're crazy. But the others, they may not know it, but it will touch a spark in them. When it happens, they'll be ready and they can make that shift. They may not know it's coming, but something inside will be ready for it and they'll be able to make it. It's those that don't know it's coming, but if we tell them, it's inside them. Then when it happens, it'll come out and they'll be ready for it.

D: Those of us that do make the shift, will we continue to live our lives the way we have?

V: No, no, better. Different. Longer.

D: Will we continue physical lives?

V: Oh, physical in that dimension, yes. But physical in this dimension, no.

D: But I mean, if we make the shift, will we....

V: (Interrupted) You mean, will you live or die?

D: Will we continue lives as we know it?

V: Yes, some will not even be aware. You see, that little thing that we plant in their head, will help them make the dimensional shift and they may not even know it. But they'll know there's destruction. They'll see destruction. They'll see what's taking place and they'll see the dead bodies, but they won't know that they've made that shift. They won't be aware of the fact that the reason they're not down there dead is because they made that shift and that change didn't affect them.

D: You said something about the things that are put in the head. Do you mean the implants?

V: No, no, no. I mean a seed, a thought. They don't know it consciously, but inside, that will help them. It's like a spark that, when the time comes, their mind would have accepted it subconsciously, already.

D: I have heard that we will live longer?

V: Longer, better. Learn. Things will be so much better. People will learn more, after a little while. They'll know more. They'll become more aware of things. The way things are. They may not know when they make the shift, but then they'll learn about it. They'll realize after a while what's happened.

D: And the ones that are not ready will be left on the other Earth.

V: Yes, they'll be gone.

D: And many on both places won't even realize that something dramatic has occurred.

V: The ones on the other place will. They'll be dead. But they'll know because that's the lesson they've learned. Once they die, they will know. They will see the truth. And they will see what opportunity they missed, but they will learn from that.

D: I have also been told that when they reincarnate, if they have negativity, karma, to repay, they will no longer come to Earth because the Earth will have changed so much.

V: They will not be allowed to come back here until they've made the switch. They've made the change.

D: I've heard they will go somewhere else to work out their karma because they have missed the opportunity.

V: Yes. Some will. And some may be given an opportunity to come back. But it will be a while, a long, long while.

D: But in the meantime, we will be going forward and learning new things and making progress in a whole new world.

V: What a beautiful world. A world of light and peace. Where people can live together and love one another.

D: But it will still be a physical world with our families and houses like we have now.

V: Just a smarter world.

D: (Laugh) That, I can understand.

Another subject who was experiencing unexplained physical symptoms, described the new body in this way:

S: She is identifying more with her future body. It's not really settled in yet, but it's there. And this future body takes her essence, or portions of her. And merges it or pulls it up so she will get used to this future body.

D: Will the body physically change?

S: Some, yes. It will be stronger, and younger. This body that she is in now, it could be healed and redone, but she needs the future body. It will be lighter. More capable. She is feeling this now, her essence has been merging with this future body and pulled up.

D: So this body she has now will be changed?

S: It will be essentially left behind. It's going to be transformed and parts of it that aren't needed will be dropped away.

D: So it's not like leaving one body and going into another.

S: No. Gradually the newer body and the older body will be mostly merged together. But there will be certain parts of the older body that won't be necessary, so they will be left behind. It will just disintegrate.

It will probably be so gradual that we will not even notice the difference. Except for the physical symptoms that some are experiencing as the body makes the adjustments. I have been told that the older generation may be more aware that something is happening in the body. Yet it does no good to worry about it, since it is a natural process that is occurring now to everyone as part of the evolution of the new Earth.

More from another subject in Australia:

C: It's like a car. Imagine a car that has an old body. It's just the same old car you've been driving. And then you put a new engine in it. And suddenly that car begins to perform differently, even though it looks the same. And then you get another engine, and you replace it. And the car keeps getting faster and faster, and brighter and smarter. And then before you know it, the car is doing such good things, that the body starts to change. It's like the energy of the new engine starts to reform the body. And before you know it, the chap has turned into a sport's car. A beautiful, glossy, attractive vehicle. And that's what this is about. The energies that are coming in have the ability to transform the vehicle. And it will start to be different. It's going to look different. It's going to look... well, younger comes to mind. It's going to look smarter and younger. The cells of the body, the vibration of the body is changing, and is matching the vibration of the incoming energy. And the physical changes will be next.

D: What will those physical changes be?

C: Oh! The body's going to change to be lighter. And I'm getting that it will look taller. It's not that it's going to be taller. But the energy from within is somehow going to become visible on the outside. And it will make the body seem taller, elongated, slimmer. And more transparent.

D: Transparent?

C: Yes. It's a pioneering thing.

D: Is this the way the people on Earth will be evolving? (Yes) Will everyone make the changes?

C: Yes, because the people have all been given that choice. If they want to evolve with the Earth, they will evolve into this new human being. It will look different. And that's what this experiment is about. That's why Christine and others are moving the ones who don't want to evolve with the Earth. They are going to leave. (Almost crying) And bring a lot of pain to their families. But the people who are staying must hold the light. That's a big job. To get divorced and separated from these things that are happening now. And these things are going to continue to happen until the cleansing is complete. Those who are here to stay, are taking this race of people into a very new and different civilization. Those people are being tested now, to see if they can hold the light when there is disaster, and not be sucked in. They're the people who will move ahead with this planet.

D: Almost like a last test?

C: Yes. The testing is going on right now. Whatever each being needs to test them, to see what they're capable of giving back to this program; how firm their commitment is. How willing they are to serve. That is all being tested now.

D: So each one is having their own individual test?

C: Yes. And the people who are finding it tough now are the ones who are staying. They're the ones who are going through the tests. But some of them are not coming through.

D: They're not passing the test.

C: No. There are some who are not.

D: This is what I was told by other people, that some would be left behind. (Yes) And I thought that sounded cruel.

C: No, it's not cruel because each soul is given the choice. And if they are not moving and evolving, it's because they are choosing not to. And they will reincarnate into another place of their choice. And it's all right. Because it's only a game. They'll stay in the Old Earth. The New Earth is so beautiful. You will see colors and animals and flowers you never imagined possible. You'll see fruit that is perfect food. It doesn't have to be cooked. It's just eaten as it is. And everything that the being needs to nourish them will be there. These new fruits are developing now with the help of the Star People.

D: Are these fruits and vegetables we don't have on the Earth now?

C: We don't have them. They're mutations in some ways. I'm seeing a custard apple as an example of what happened. We will have a fruit called a "custard apple." And it doesn't look like an apple. It has a rough exterior, and it's about the size of two oranges put together. And then you open it. It's like custard inside. So that's a fruit, but a food. It's not just a fruit, but another food has been introduced to it, like custard. That's an example of one of the future foods. So these foods will be delights to the senses. And nutritious and sustaining for the—I keep being stopped when I start to say "body." And I am being told to say "being." They'll be nutritious for the being. And things we now have to cook—like you'd cook custard—will be incorporated into these fruits. And it has to do with helping the planet, and cutting down on the use of electricity and energy. So the fruits are going to provide us with what we need.

D: I've heard man has done many things to the food that is not healthy for the body.

C: That's right. The organic foods are coming onto the Earth, and those organic farmers are moving with the Earth evolution program. That's why they're there. And that's why consciousness is being raised about this because people need to know how to grow properly. And the Rudolph Steiner schools are teaching children this. So, the children who are going to be with the new Earth will know this. And those children are now teaching in universities and in institutions, and they're spreading the word. So when the cleansing of the Earth occurs, much of that toxicity is going to be pushed away. You see, the new Earth is not this dimension. The new Earth is another dimension. And we will move into that new dimension. And in that new dimension, there'll be these trees that have purple and orange in their trunks. And there will be beautiful rivers and waterfalls. And the energy will be brought back. There will be energy in the streams and the water that goes over rocks and sandbanks. And it hits the Earth. It creates energy and will be straightened out in this world. Many of these streams have been changed and straightened out to make them navigable and nice. That's taking away the energy from the Earth. The Earth is going to be cleansed. I'm seeing water.

D: Does this have to occur before the Earth shifts and evolves into the new dimension?

C: I'm seeing us stepping through. (Startled) Oh! What I'm seeing is that the people who are going to the new dimensions will step through into this new world.

D: While the other one is being cleansed?

C: Yes, yes.

D: What do you see about the water that will happen with the cleansing?

C: (A big sigh) It's not going to be shown to me.

D: They don't want you to see it?

C: No, they won't show me that. What they're showing me is... an opening? And we step through. We step into, what looks like this Earth, but it's different colors. It's different textures. At first it looks the same. At first only. And then as we look around, we start to see that it's not. It's changing before our eyes. And it's so beautiful.

D: But this is not the spirit side? Because the spirit side is described as being very beautiful also.

C: No, it's the new Earth. It's not the spirit side. It's the fifth dimensional Earth. Some people will pass through before others. I'm being told to tell you now that Christine has been there several times. There's a group going to go through now. And she'll be bringing more through. And they'll be coming and going a bit until they go for good.

D: Then the others will be left on the old Earth?

C: Yes, the ones that are choosing to stay will stay.

D: They'll be undergoing a lot of hardships, won't they?

C: Yes, the whole planet. (Startled) I just saw the whole planet explode. That's horrible, isn't it?

D: What do you think that means?

C: I don't know. I just saw it explode. But I saw the new Earth. There's this beautiful fifth dimensional place with harmony and peace.

D: When they showed you the planet exploding, is that just symbolic? As though that Earth will no longer exist for the ones who cross over?

C: Well, the people who have crossed over are watching what's happening. They can see. Now, is it going to explode? They're saying to me, "Don't get caught up with what's going to happen because you've got to focus on the light." And that's the challenge for these people who are going to be in the new Earth. The challenge for them is to not get caught up in anything that's going to happen because that's what pulls us back into the third dimension. And that's what's happened to many people who were on a path forward. They've been pulled back because they got caught up in the fear and the sadness and regret and the black stuff. So they're saying, "You don't need to know because it wouldn't serve anybody if it were known." So really what they are saying is, "Focus on the good stuff." Focus on the fact that there is going to be this beautiful new existence, new dimension, that many people on the Earth are going to be moving into. Who are already moving into.

D: I was told whenever you cross over, you will be in the same physical body that you have now. You will just be changed.

C: Yes, you will still be in the same body, but it is going to change.

D: So it can be done without dying or leaving the body. It's a different thing altogether.

C: Yes, we just walk across. Christine's done it before, and she knows how to do it. She's done it and understands it.

D: But it will be sad because there will be so many people that won't understand what's happening. It's so hard with so many—I want to say "ordinary"—people who have no idea of anything except the religion they've been taught. They don't know that this other is possible.

C: Yes, but they're not ordinary. They only seem ordinary. It's a mask they're wearing. They're changing.

D: But there still are many people who haven't even thought about these things.

C: Yes, but they'll be choosing not to awaken, and that is their choice. We have to respect that. They have been given the choice like everybody on the Earth, and they have made that choice. And that's okay. It's all right. It's fine.

D: So, if they have to go to another place to work out the negative karma, that's part of their evolvement. (Yes.) But do you see a majority of people evolving to the next dimension?

C: No. Not the majority. And the numbers, to some extent, are not important because what will be, will be. And the more people that can awaken and take that journey, the more people there'll be. That's why so many of you are doing this work. To help people open up to the journey, and let go of the fear. And step into that void where anything is possible. Where the blackness is residing. That's what you people are all doing. And you need to do it. And everybody you speak to, then goes out and does it as well. You may not be aware of it, but you're acting like Christ. Everyone you speak to becomes a disciple, and they go out, and they in turn awaken other people. So it's working. And it's soon. It's all happening soon.

D: Do you have any idea of a time period?

C: The next few years will be the—I'm getting the word "decision point." It will be the "cut-off" point. I think it means that those who have not decided by then, will be left behind. It's critical.

D: But there are some entire countries in the world that are not ready for this. That's why I am thinking there are many people that won't make the crossover.

C: There's more happening than people know about. I'm seeing some countries where people are being persecuted. The reason that's happening is to awaken spirituality because persecution causes it. When people are persecuted or when they're facing death, or when they're facing huge human feats. That is a trigger that awakens people. And that's the purpose of much of the persecution that's occurring at the moment; to make sure that these people are awakened. So that's the positive side of it.

D: Is there something that triggers it or precipitates it?

C: It's like the curtain drops. And I'm not allowed to see. I'm just being told that it will be the end of one and the beginning of another.

D: They're trying to lead us into war at this time. (2002) Do you think it has something to do with that?

C: (Big sigh) I'm afraid that's the test. I said that many people were being tested. And I didn't realize it then, but I do now, that's all part of the test, if we can keep ourselves separated from that. It's like we have to create our own... it's like each one of us is the universe. All parts of the universe are held here (placed her hand on her body). And if we keep this universe here....

D: This body?

C: Yes. If we keep it at peace, and we keep it in balance, then we are passing the test. Then we can withstand anything. And those things that are happening in the world are really to test the whole; all of us.

D: You mean to not get caught up into the fear.

C: Yes. Turn the TV off. Don't listen to it. Don't read the paper. Don't get caught up in it. Your world is what you create here. (Touched her body again.)

D: In your own body.

C: Yes. In your own space here. This is your own universe here. If every person creates peace and harmony in their own universe, then that's the universe they're creating in that fifth dimensional Earth. The more people who can create peace and harmony in this body universe, the more people who will be in that fifth dimensional new Earth. The ones who can't create peace and harmony in this body universe, are not passing the test. That's the test.

D: We're trying to do this to keep the war from happening, or to lessen it anyway.

C: I'm being told that it doesn't matter what happens because it's all a game. It's all a play. And the things that are happening are there for a reason. And the reason at the moment is to test each human being to find out where they are in their own evolution. And so if we hold peace and light here (the body), we don't have to worry about whether there's a war or not. It's only an illusion anyway.

D: But right now it seems very real, and it could have some very disastrous consequences.

C: Yes, but that's fear for each individual. Our job is to help each individual find peace here (the body). And then, of course, as you bring more people together, who have peace and harmony within their own body universe, then instead of the blackness spreading, that spreads. And that creates this whole new world. If you'd been given all that information back in the beginning of your work, you would have been overloaded. It's the same reason why they're saying, "We're not going to tell you exactly what's going to happen." We don't know exactly what's going to happen. But we're not going to tell you what we know because you don't need to know. All you need to do is focus here (the body) creating your heaven on Earth. Each human being creating their own heaven on Earth. That's all you have to do. And coming together with others who are creating their own heaven on Earth. And then expanding that energy out. And before you know it, you've changed the world. You don't even think about the world. What you focus on is what you create. Think about peace. The main thing people have to understand is that, what they focus on expands. So if they focus on, if they can replace predictions with something that is wonderful that they want, and expand that. Then they can create their own heaven on Earth. And I'm being shown in your book The Convoluted Universe (Book One), you give a description of thought. I'm being told to remind you about this. You talk about an energy ball the size of a grapefruit. And that ball has energy strands. And I'm changing this as I go. Energy strands which go over each other and transverse each other. And those energy strands can do anything they like. They can split, and they can become four energy strands. They can weave. They can multiply. They can go backwards. They can zip up. They can do absolutely anything. And this is the ball of possibility. When you think a thought, it doesn't just disappear. It becomes an energy strand. It becomes energy. It moves into that ball of possibility. So, imagine your thought becoming energy. And the more energy you give it, the stronger that becomes. And then it manifests, and it becomes real. It becomes physical. If you send a thought out that there's going to be peace. And then you follow it with, "Oh, but that war is getting worse," or "Those politicians are making a mistake." You weaken the energy: the positive strand you brought out. So we have to teach people to send out the positive thought, and then to reinforce it with more positive thoughts, and more positive thoughts. And we have to teach them that when one of those negative thoughts comes into their mind, not to just let it go, but to replace it with a positive thought. So that they're adding to that energy ball of possibility. They're contributing to it. We have to teach them to do that. They do not know how to do that. And I'm being told to tell you to reinforce that the illusion—I don't know why I'm being told to tell you this. But they're saying that if we could get people to think of this conflict that's occurring in the Middle East as a movie, it would help people. The other thing I'm being told to tell you is that for every action, they can make an opposite reaction. Where there's birth, there's death. And everybody must let go of any greed, any domination, materialism. Any of those issues that are stopping them from doing this work, must be let go. Because these issues are not going to serve anybody in the new Earth. There's not going to be the need for money, as such. So why would you bother about it? Those who are working for the Earth, for the universe, are being provided for, and will continue to be. What you need will come to you. So it's time now to let go of that ethic of working to get the money. You're working to change the Earth. You're working to save this situation. That's where the driving force must be. It must come from love and service. And that's the only way we will maximize this effort. It must come from love and service, not from greed.

D: I've been told love is the most powerful emotion.

C: Yes, love heals.

BONUS LEVEL:
THE HEALING OF ANN

This case study comes from Chapter 37 of book four of *The*

Convoluted Universe by Dolores Cannon. I included this for a few reasons. For one, it is a great example of the 500+ case studies I have researched. You can see the amount of depth in each of these case studies and how thorough Dolores is in her questioning and research. Again, one of these stories may indeed be anecdotal, but when you read countless accounts like this from different people and different authors that overlap, well, it's pretty compelling stuff.

This particular one brought me solace because I have been seeing so many patterns and symbols after my event. My own Book 2 goes into more detail about the symbols and patterns I see while I sleep or astral project. I see everything from mathematical formulas to symbols that could be anything from hieroglyphics to ancient Hebrew or ancient Aramaic. I've always wondered why these symbols are flashing in front of my eyes, and when I read accounts like this, it makes more sense. Well, kinda.

I also included this one because it's not just a fascinating catch-all case study, but it also has a little bit of alien spice in it! Note that I have yet to see an alien (that I can remember!), but after reading so many accounts like this, I certainly believe. And it's good to hear after considering many case studies about this that aliens are very friendly and here to help us all. There's nothing to be scared of. One day, if they make themselves known to us, there is nothing to be afraid of. However, of course, many people will indeed be afraid. That's a whole different discussion, but for now, let's move on with this case study. Enjoy!

ANN HAD WRITTEN TO ME, but the letter was so similar to many others I receive I did not pay much attention to it. Besides, I was busy traveling and lecturing. Then she called and said she had met my friend, Nina, and had a strange experience at her house, and Nina thought she ought to see me. I normally don't let anyone come to my house for sessions, but my car was completely shot and I was going to have to buy a new one. So I couldn't drive to Fayetteville and have the session at Nina's house. So finally I agreed that they could come to my home. (This was before I opened my office in town in 2003.) My daughter

Nancy and I were also leaving for Europe in a few weeks, so I definitely didn't want to get involved with a local person at this time. I agreed out of courtesy to Nina because of our long friendship, but I did not think anything would come of seeing Ann.

On the phone Ann gave the impression of someone who had absolutely no knowledge of metaphysics, UFOs, or anything of that nature. That was why her experience with Nina was so strange. It had frightened her so much that she was sitting on the floor in her kitchen crying just before she decided to call me out of desperation. I could tell by asking her questions that she did not even have the basic understanding of the paranormal. Nina agreed to come with her to my house in October, 1999, and when they arrived we had a discussion at the dining room table while eating lunch.

Ann had several physical problems. She was an insulin dependent diabetic, was on heart medication (even though she was only in her early forties), and had been diagnosed with the early stages of throat cancer. The doctors had performed a biopsy and wanted to operate. She was also involved in a bad marriage.

Ann tried to describe what had happened that had triggered the unusual event. It occurred in September, just a month before. Nina is a practitioner of an energy work called "gentle touch," where she acts as a conduit for energy to help the person release any blockages in order to promote wellness. It is similar to Reiki and is done on a massage table. Ann had gone to Nina's house to visit and discuss her problems, including marriage troubles. During the conversation Nina offered to help her relax, and Ann was on the massage table when the incident occurred. All of this was totally new to Ann and she didn't even know what Reiki was. She was expecting to relax and maybe fall asleep because this often happens with any type of energy or massage work. Ann had had a hard day at work in the hospital emergency room where she worked as an aide, and was ready to relax. The room was totally dark except for the faint glow of a candle, to further induce relaxation.

Ann described what happened next, "I was relaxing because this was going to be like a massage, and all of a sudden I wasn't there anymore. I was, but I wasn't. Let me explain this to you. I knew that Nina was still around me, but at that same time I was also in another room somewhere else where these beings were all around me. And every one of the beings were touching me, on my arms or my legs. I wasn't really afraid of them. It was kind of a sense of ... curiosity. I was as curious about them, as they were about me. And I remembered that I was still on Nina's table, and I was able to tell Nina, 'Nina, remember everything I describe to you.' For an instance I was able to see Nina, but after I said that, Nina was gone. I was at two places at one time."

Ann then did her best to describe the beings she saw around her. "Their faces were all around me. They were like orange gel. Real thick, thick, thick gel. There was almost like a holographic-type face in there as well. It wasn't a real face. They never opened a mouth to talk to me, but I knew what they were saying. I don't know how to tell you. In my head I heard the voice, but no-body's lips were moving. Their faces were very warm. But this gel ... I remember I kept wanting to put my hand in it."

D: To see if it were solid or liquid?

A: I don't know. It just looked inviting. It looked fun, actually. (Laugh) But I was also skeptical and afraid. I wanted to, but I didn't. They kept telling me that they needed to remember love emotions. That I had an abundance of compassion, and they really enjoyed me. There were a whole bunch of them. There was a main person—not a person, a being—that was by my head. And there was all this machinery behind them. I really couldn't focus in on it, but I remember seeing there were knobs, there was color, there were buttons. And the light that was above my head was huge. It was massive, and perfectly round. It was up there like a surgery light, but even brighter. It didn't bother my eyes, I could look right into it. They told me to look into that light, and it would not hurt me. They would never hurt me, is what they told me. I was looking into the light, and all of a sudden, a strobe starting going off really fast. And I didn't like that at all. It scared me because as I was lying there I thought they were trying to steal my emotions from me. And they were trying to steal my love, and that I would never have it again. They didn't say that, but I thought they were going to do that.

This is similar to the investigator in The Custodians, who thought they were going to steal her memories when they put a machine on her head onboard a craft. She found out it was actually like a duplicating machine. It was only recording, not removing them. This may have been what was happening to Ann.

A: They were adamant to make it known that they would never hurt me. And in fact, now I would fear humans more than I would them. Seriously, I feel that humans are more scarier monsters than they are. There are more communications we had, where they just flashed so much stuff in front of me. And it's so fast. And I can see quick formulas even in my mind's eye right now as I'm talking to you. I could almost write some of it down, but I can't put the whole thing down because it comes too fast. But I can see numbers, I can see signs.

I have heard this many times in the last few years, that people all over the world are receiving information on a subconscious level. Most of the time it appears as geometric symbols or strange signs that have no conscious meaning to them. They are receiving these in many unusual ways. Some say they are relaxing lying on a couch in their living room when a beam of light comes through the window aimed at their forehead. And they see symbols moving down the light into their mind. Others are expressing this by a strange compulsion to spend hours drawing unusual symbols. In my work with the ETs, they say this is the transfer of information into the subconscious mind through the use of symbols because symbols contain entire blocks of information. The information is being subtly transferred to the brain on a cellular level. It is information the individual will need in the future as the Earth and mankind goes through the coming transformation. They will have the information when they need it, and they will not even be aware of where it came from. I was told, and this has been written in some of my other books, that this is the meaning of the Crop Circles. The symbols designed in the grain fields contain blocks of information that is transferred into the minds of anyone who sees the symbol. They do not have to be physically in the circles to receive the information, all they have to do is see the symbol.

Some of the information Ann was receiving she thought might be formulas. She had a limited education, leaving school after only the tenth grade and getting her GED later. So she had no conscious knowledge of chemistry. She served a few years in the Coast Guard as a paramedic.

We returned our attention to the experience, and she attempted to describe their appearance. "All of them looked just alike. Their hands were nothing like ours. There were four fingers, but not really a thumb. Yet their maneuverability with their fingers was very good. They could do anything with them. They were really touchy. Their fingers were not set like ours. If we could have taken our forefingers and spread them out a little bit more. If one of these came out more to the side. I'll never forget their hands. And they were all over me, so I will remember the hands. And their arms and their legs are very thin and skinny."

I wanted to understand this because some of the description did not fit any other aliens that my subjects have described. The idea of orange gelatin faces mystified me. She said she didn't think it was a mask, gelatin was the only thing that fit the description. "Thick, thick, thick, thick, real thick. But in that gel effect you could actually see almost a face, but not quite a face. And the rest of them is green. I hate saying this. I really do. It's my green aliens. It was caterpillar pea ugly green with radiances of a yellowish green around them on their skin. The skin itself was kind of a caterpillar greenish." She laughed at the absurdity of the mental picture. She didn't know how tall they were because she was lying down.

Ann explained that the beings were going through the same hand motions that Nina was when she was giving Ann energy on the massage table. Maybe they were imitating, or learning.

I didn't want to tell Ann too much about other cases I had examined, and Nina also was not saying much. We did not want to influence her. I knew she had not done any reading about this type of thing, and I wanted the information to be spontaneous when we had the session.

After the discussion we all went to the bedroom for the session. When Ann was in trance I took her back to the date when the event occurred at Nina's house. She returned immediately to the night, and repeated the conversation she was having with Nina and her husband Tom as they sat around the dining room table. Nina was nodding to indicate the situation was correct. To speed the events up I had her move forward in time.

A: We're walking. And we went through the garage, and into

another small room. Smells like horses.

D: Why does it smell like horses?

A: (Laugh) Because there are horses. I can hear them.

Nina lives in the country and has a small stable next to the garage. Her workroom is next to the two. Nina had Ann get on her massage table so she could help her relax. Nina began to work on her head area, and then Ann appeared to be watching something. Then she asked very softly, almost in a whisper, "What is that?"

D: What do you see?

A: Ummm. A bunch of them ... several. No, they're not people. They're beings.

D: How do you know they're not people?

A: Because they don't look like us. They look different. They are much different. They're over here, touching my hands and my arms. They're on my legs.

D: Can you feel it as they touch you? (Oh, yes.) If you can feel them touching you, they must be physical. Is that right?

A: Oh, yes! (Carefully, as though she wanted to say it correctly.) They are touching me. And I am letting them touch me. I'm telling Nina to watch. I don't think she can see these people. I have to tell her what they look like.

D: Tell me, what do they look like?

A: Ooooh, they got spongy faces. Jelloey, spongy, orangey faces. They got eyes in there.

D: What do their eyes look like?

A: Kind of dark bubbly. Bubbles. Two bubbles. One on one

side and one on the other. Dark. Not quite black.

D: But you said the faces are kind of spongy?

A: Well, in your understanding it would be spongy. Jello. Sort of smooth with a glimmer now and then of a rippling effect.

D: Does their whole body look like that?

A: No. Just the face. I can't see their whole body. The head is a greenish color ... and it has a strange yellowish-grayish color mixed in with it. They have long arms. Plastic looking. And they're just constantly feeling.

D: Are they wearing anything?

A: No. There's no man, there's no woman. There are no clothes. They don't need them. Their skin is protection. They're telling me they're not going to hurt me. They're telling me that I have emotion. Strong emotion, and they're learning from me.

D: What are they learning from you?

A: Love. They don't understand our love.

D: Can you ask them some questions? (Yes) Tell them we're curious. Why don't they understand these emotions?

A: (Pause, as though listening.) They're from a different universe that is technological, mechanical. It is on a higher vibrational level. They don't hurt each other. We hurt each other.

D: Did they ever have emotions?

A: Yes. Not like ours. Not like we understand. Theirs were completely different. Their emotion was in the understanding of education, progression, strength, until progression and strength got in the way. And through their generation growth pattern they put it to the back, and gained the strength and the growth, then the technology. And they forgot emotion because the generation pattern changed their molecular structure.

D: Generation pattern? What do you mean? Somewhere in here the voice changed (as it always does) and I knew I was speaking to someone other than Ann. When this happens I always know I will be able to obtain answers that she could not possibly know.

A: Molecular structure. You don't understand, I have to change the words for you.

This meant that the entity would have to search through Ann's vocabulary to find the words nearest to what it was trying to convey. This is often difficult because many concepts are hard to explain using our understanding. They have told me many times that our language is insufficient. Often they have to resort to analogies or examples. The word "molecular" was pronounced a little differently.

D: Do you mean molecular structure?

A: Yes. Is that how you say it there?

D: We say "molecular." It has to do with the molecules? Is that correct?

A: Yes. It changes the brain wave patterns. It changes the sensors in the body. The chemistry in the body, to where it becomes more mechanical. It's very difficult to explain from this universe. Generation patterns. The generations as they progressed, their bodies changed. I am trying hard to explain this to you. You need to ask me better.

D: All right. I'm trying to phrase the questions because Ann would like to know also. Why are you interacting with Ann in that room?

A: Because she's very open. (Softly) Oh, wow! There are two at the same time, (Ann apparently was interjecting.)

D: You can tell me so I can understand.

A: Do you understand mental telepathy?

D: Yes, I do.

A: All right. We will speak to you through mental telepathy.

D: I would rather have it in words. Is that all right?

A: If it can be defined.

D: If you can define it, or if you can give me analogies. Do you know what analogies are?

A: Oh, yes. You live off this very much.

D: You may not realize it, but I have a little black box here. Do you know what it is? It's a recorder that records words.

These entities have often referred to my tape recorder as my little black box, so I used their terminology. They find it amusing that we have to resort to such primitive devices.

A: We record through light.

D: Yes, and you people are always asking, "Why do I need a box to record the words?" We can't remember like you can. So we have to put the information in the box so I can play it back later.

A: It is your lower technology.

D: Yes, that's why I have to use words, instead of mental telepathy. So you can understand I have to have analogies. What do you mean, you record through light?

A: We record and retain through light. Energy and pigmentation and light. It is penetrated into our body, and we put it in our remembrance. And that is where it is stored.

D: Can you recall it any time you want?

A: Oh, yes. We can magnify it at any time we want.

D: But with me I have to have it in words because we are still in the lower ....

A: I'll give them to you in words.

D: I would appreciate that. So you chose to interact with Ann at that time because she is open? Is that what you said?

A: Very much so.

D: And you said you are communicating with her with mental telepathy?

A: Very much so.

D: Have you ever had contact with her before this night. (No) Did you just choose her at that time?

A: She is excellent to our abilities.

D: And you said you have come from another vibrational frequency?

A: Yes. I am from the seventh plane. Which is a created universe from the seventh plane.

D: That's why it's invisible to us, isn't it?

A: Completely.

D: Then as you are interacting with her, is she actually in two places at once? (Yes) Can you explain how that is done?

A: Through change of vibration. It is a—I don't know how to choose your words.

D: Try. (Pause) All we have is our language. We don't have your abilities.

A: I am looking for the correct analogy. Your sleep pattern would be the closest thing we could relate to on this level. You are sleeping, you are here. As you sleep you would travel. This is the same as we use with her in her sleep pattern.

D: Although she is not asleep at the time she is in that room. (No) It's also not a dream, either. (No) But can you interact with her physical body even though she is in ....

A: (Interrupted) Mental.

D: You're working with the mental body?

A: Correct.

D: Do you have any idea who I am and what I do?

A: You're a teacher.

D: Well, I have worked with many of your kind. Maybe not exactly your kind ....

A: Yes, we know this.

D: And they've allowed me to have knowledge when I've asked for it.

A: Yes, we know this.

D: But I have never met your type of being before.

A: We know this. It has been many, many, many days. Much time has gone by. Your understanding of time is much different than ours. You are at a time frame and a level right now that you will be called. You are drawing near to many universes at this time. You are calling us, and we are coming.

D: Because I have interacted with many other types, but not one that fits your description.

A: I know this.

D: But you're positive, aren't you? (Oh, yes.) Because I wouldn't want anything to do with negative.

A: This is true. Your planet has had so much negative energy that it is very difficult for us to penetrate to your planet, to your universe. You have distracted this universe something terrible. You will be on a high destruction plane. We are looking for people at this time in your plane and in your universe that we can penetrate and help. We come not to harm.

Ever since this voice began it became more gravely sounding, deeper and rougher than Ann's normal voice. An old sound.

D: Are you speaking from onboard a craft, or are you on a planet?

A: I am on a plane level. Not a planet, but a plane. Your understanding of craftship is much different than our understanding of the concept of travel.

D: She said she could see some machinery in the background.

A: Yes, we had to take her to a level close to her understanding, where she would not be .... Oh, I don't know the word for your language. She would not be afraid.

D: Does this happen often, that people think they are onboard a craft, and actually they aren't?

A: Yes, quite often.

D: Is your world that you come from a physical world, as we think of physical?

A: Not as you understand the physical. In a sense, where we come from, we can gather as one unit if needed to be. Let me explain this a little bit further. If there are several of us that need to combine and join together for a further understanding, we can join into one body.

D: I'm thinking of a group mind.

A: Correct.

D: But you can combine into one single entity?

A: Correct. That is the unity.

D: Would the entity appear similar to the way you do now, or would it be larger or ....

A: No, no. There is no visual sight to it as you understand visual sight.

D: Then why are you appearing to her with the orange faces and the green bodies?

A: This is her understanding of us.

D: Do you really appear that way?

A: We can appear in any shape form that we need to appear to the individual.

D: What is your normal appearance?

A: We are an energy mass.

D: That's what I was thinking it sounded like. Then on the place that you come from, you don't need physical things.

A: Correct.

D: But yet you did say you evolved technologically.

A: Correct. There are many planets in each universal level and planes. Each one of these planets has their own beam structure. We have to manifest to that beam structure for their understanding. Without our technology, understanding you at times would not be able to progress. You are a species, a being that is very low. You hurt one another. You inflict pain on one another. We are trying to help you.

D: But you know it is not all of us.

A: Correct. But there are so few of you that do understand that enlightened side.

D: I'm trying to understand. You said you don't have the emotions anymore because you went in the other direction through technology.

A: Yes. As a combined unit we can understand emotion.

D: But if you had technology, I am thinking of physical things.

A: Yes. That is your understanding. Technology is in the consumption of energy. The break up and split up of energy combined to a mass source.

D: Did you at one time have a physical body?

A: Yes, when we were at a lower plane. We evolved beyond that through our technology.

D: But this was not the correct way to go? (No) If you had had a choice, which way would you have gone?

A: That's a personal decision. Each entity has that choice.

D: But I meant, if you had not gone to technology and become what you are, could you have gone in another direction?

A: Yes, there are several choices to choose from.

D: When you had a physical body, how did that appear?

A: There is no one form of physical being. It is a choice.

D: So you could all look different? (Yes) I'm so limited by what we think of as physical.

A: Yes, you are. Your senses of touch, smell, hear and sight are very limited.

D: That's why I am always trying to expand my understanding.

A: I will try to help you. You are trying to think in a physical formation, and we are trying to project in an emotional.

D: Is this one of the reasons you contacted Ann because you wanted to know how the emotions of the human being works? (Yes, yes.) It's complex, isn't it? (Oh, yes.) But we are a complex being.

A: You are a funny being.

D: (Chuckle) What do you mean?

A: You beings, you find humor in the strangest ways.

D: You have humor, too, don't you?

A: Umm, not on your level of understanding.

D: Well, what do you think is humorous?

A: You beings.

D: (Laugh) Observing us?

A: Yes. We observe you as a whole unit.

D: Yes, but yet we are not a group mind.

A: (Suddenly) It is cold here.

D: On our world, you mean?

A: It is cold.

A: Some. We have given her pieces and bits of information. As time goes on we I didn't know if Ann was feeling cold in her physical body, or if the entity was experiencing cold from our world. I decided to play it safe and alleviate any physical symptoms. I then covered Ann with a blanket.

D: Where you come from, can you control the temperatures better?

A: There is not a temperature change as you have here.

D: Well, if you communicate and work with Ann, the main thing is we do not want any harm to come to her.

A: Never harm any being. We are here to help you. There is time for your information and knowledge. At this time it is not meant for you to have all information and knowledge. We have shared with Ann some information and knowledge. And there are certain times that we will increase that information and knowledge.

D: I was told one time that all of my questions would never be answered because some knowledge was as poison rather than medicine.

A: That is correct. You beings do not know how to put information into perspective to make a unity. I think I'm saying that word wrong.

D: I think I understand what you mean, though. But they've told me if I ask the questions in the proper way they would try to answer.

A: This is correct. What are you wanting to know?

D: Ann said she was having many things flooding into her mind lately. (Yes) Although it frightened her at first, she said she seems to be getting formulas.

A: Yes, that is correct. There are many formulas that are giving. Not all formulas are directed to a specific item, as you would say on your planet.

D: What are the formulas to be used for?

A: You have a lot of problems that you concentrate on. Illness.

D: Yes, that seems to be a strange word to you.

A: Yes. You do not know how to surpass this.

D: We're trying.

A: Yes, but you don't.

D: Do the formulas you're giving her in her mind have to do with this illness?

A: Some. We have given her pieces and bits of information. As time goes on we will tie it together. We cannot change the force of your world. We will not inflict that change on your force. You have to invite us for that change. It has to be a mass invitation.

D: But couldn't she use the information to help others?

A: They have to ask for the help.

D: We know people that might be able to turn the formulas into medicine. (Yes, yes.) Would you be able to tell us some of these formulas so we can have them for the little black box?

A: I can write them down for you. You do not understand my language. I have to write in yours.

I had the pen and notebook ready, and I uncovered Ann's hands. Then I placed the notebook in her hand. For several seconds she felt the paper, especially the metal spiral binding, as though it was an unusual object. "You have strange articles."

D: (Laugh) Yes, it is. A piece of paper, and here's a pen. This is a writing instrument that we use.

I put it in her other hand. She found the pen curious, and kept feeling both the pen and paper.

D: That is a writing instrument, and this is what we write upon. It's called "paper." What do you think? Can you do this?

A: You in your language have a formula.

Ann wrote on the notebook without opening her eyes. The entity explained that the formula dealt with chemistry, and someone familiar with chemistry would understand it. She then stopped abruptly.

A: This is the beginning simple basis, a curing all (carrying?) element that penetrates to the red blood system of your species. It would enlarge the white blood cells so they would work in unity with the red blood cells that are ulcerated in cancered cells in your body. They would then be replenished to help.

D: Would this be a formula for a medicine of some kind? (Yes) A liquid?

A: No. It is a mass.

D: Like a tablet?

A: Tablet? I don't know tablet.

D: A small thing that you would take through the mouth. (Yes) And a chemist looking at this could understand it.

A: Some. Not all people are advanced. This will be researched.

D: Do you have another formula?

A: Not at this time.

I was taking the notebook and pen away from Ann, so I could cover her up again. She held it a little longer while feeling the spiral binding again. I explained, "That is metal that holds the pages together. It is a spiral on the edge."

A: I want to feel it.

D: It holds the pages together so we can turn them. Write on one side and then the other.

A: Why do you need to do this?

D: We have to have something we can look at.

A: Why do you not use your mind?

D: We haven't gotten to the point we can go mind to mind.

A: (Interrupted) Why?

D: We're not advanced enough yet, I guess.

A: You will be. It is very cold here on your planet.

D: Let's cover you up again. Don't worry, we won't keep you here too long. We will try to be as kind as we can because we do appreciate your help. Is it cold in this vibration? Is that what you mean?

A: I am shaking. Yes, it's cold.

I started to give suggestions for her comfort, so she (and it) wouldn't feel the cold, but she interrupted just as I began. "It is gone. I read it."

D: You read it?

A: It is gone.

D: The feeling of cold was in the body that we are communicating through.

A: Correct.

D: Are these the main things that you want to give her, the formulas for illness?

A: Some. We want to learn from your people.

D: What would the other formulas deal with that you want to give her?

A: Craft. You call "aircraft." Your aircraft is polluting our system.

D: Polluting your system?

A: Your universe. And it is leaking into other universes. And we must put a stop to this.

D: What do you mean? Our airplanes?

A: Your .... I will try to find the words that you use. Your fuel.

D: The fuel we use to power our machinery?

A: Yes. Correct. You have resources here on your planet, as we speak, but you choose not to use them. These resources were given to you from our same creator, our same God, our same energy force. And your people have chosen not to use them.

D: But you know we are just a small piece of the whole of humanity.

A: You don't have much time.

D: We don't have much say, though.

A: Yes, you have all say. You have all choice.

D: But we are not the ones in power.

A: Yes, you are.

D: I mean, we are not the ones that make the decisions for the world.

A: Yes, you are. You are not working as a unit.

D: That's true. We are all individuals.

A: Correct. You separate your energies, your powers.

D: That's why what we say isn't going to affect the ones in power. The ones that .... (He interrupted: Yes.)

It was obvious that it would be impossible to argue with a being that was used to operating as a unit to accomplish what they wanted. He could not understand our limitations due to functioning as single units. Of course, he had a point. I have found this in my work (especially with Nostradamus), that when people cooperate together, their mind power is enormously increased. But how do you get this across to the average person, that they have such latent power?

D: But you said the fuel is leaking into the other universes?

A: (Emphatically) Yes! It dissipates into the air, which breaks into our molecular system, which is traveled through time and space.

D: I guess we don't think of....

A: No, you don't.

D: You're talking about the other dimensions? (Yes) But what can we do about it?

A: You can fix it. You have natural resources that are planted in your Earth's soils. You have plantation in your Earth's soils at this given time, that is also used for your medical medicine, as well. And you choose not to use these resources.

D: A plant, you said?

A: Yes. I do not know the name.

D: What does it look like?

A: It is ... (Pause) I do not know how to describe it in your language. How do you describe something if you don't know the words and their meanings? The other entities have taken the information from my subject's brain and vocabulary. This entity seemed to have difficulty finding the proper comparisons.

D: We have to know what it is before we know how to use it.

A: It is pointy, quite pointy.

D: The leaves?

A: Yes. There are several sprout as the phalanges.

D: Does it have a flower?

A: It at times will. It has a strong odor. There are some of you who use this plant now, but you do not use it in a unit sense for your whole planet.

D: What do we use it for?

A: You intake it into your body. You breathe it.

D: If it has a flower at times, what color is the flower? That might help us identify it.

A: I don't know what you mean by color of your flower.

D: (How do I explain this?) Ah. Well, the flower is the part that will usually make some seeds later. It has petals. We have colors like red, yellow, white. Do you have any colors in your spectrum where you live?

A: We have spectrums, yes.

D: You don't have colors like that?

A: Not in your level of understanding.

D: Because I'll have to have more information before we can understand what kind of a plant it is.

A: Again, I will draw this for you.

D: That's very good. Just give me a moment, and I'll get my archaic writing instruments out again. Because we can't look into your mind to get the picture.

I got the notebook and pen out again and put them in Ann's hands.

A: I enjoy this.

He again was fingering the materials as though they were un-known and unfamiliar objects.

D: What does it feel like to you?

A: I cannot describe. (He began drawing a picture of a plant.) It feels different. I am not used to this substance.

D: That does have pointy leaves. That's what we would call the "leaves." Are the points sharp?

A: They do not hurt or inflict pain on you. They will help you. I did tell you this.

D: Can you draw the flower?

A: The flower?

D: Yes, can you draw what that looks like? That will help us identify it. You said you don't know colors.

A: The flower. (She was drawing it.)

D: It has many petals. Is this a tall plant?

A: Oh, yes, very tall. Much taller than you as a human.

D: Then we're not looking for something low to the ground.

A: No, it starts low. It grows tall. It is a very majestic plant. Although your people have trampled it.

D: We don't know its value?

A: Yes, some of your people do know its value. But many of your people fight.

D: So this is the plant that we can use for medicine, and we can also use for fuel?

A: Yes. Your resources are very limited. This is a plant structure that is not limited. It is plentiful all over your planet. And you do not choose to use so.

D: We probably don't know it's useful.

A: Yes, you have ones that do know. We have seen them and talked to them.

D: So what part of the plant would be used for the fuel?

A: The stem and the leaf. It will replenish itself. It was given to you.

D: For that purpose?

A: Correct. You have what you call ... your sight? To see. It is very good for one's sight to see. It is very good for many of your illnesses that you have created in your own planet, due to your resources that you have chosen to use. You are a planet of self-destruction and illness.

D: We have caused these illnesses ourselves?

A: Correct.

D: I was thinking as I looked at this drawing. It's not a tree, is it? Because trees are taller than we are.

A: No, it is a plant. We understand your tree life. This will grow in a ... how do you put it? Cluster form. We will give Ann the knowledge and the sight. This is what you call her, Ann?

D: Yes. That's her name that we call her.

A: We will associate that.

D: We have to have names and labels.

A: Yes, we realize that. —The one you call Ann, you have to strengthen her.

D: That's what I was going to ask you about. She is experiencing some physical ailments.

A: She has not come to us and asked for healing.

D: What are you doing?

D: Can you work with her? (Yes) Would it be all right if I told you that it is permissible to work with her body?

A: No. She has to. We cannot force change any of your structures without your permission.

D: What about going down her list? We want her to be completely healthy, don't we?

A: Correct.

D: What about the diabetes? (Pause) Do you know that word? (No) It has to do with sweet things that cause problems in the body. It makes the body go out of order.

A: Sweet?

D: Sweet. Sugar?

A: This is a substance.

D: It's a substance, and it sometimes causes an imbalance in the body.

A: One moment. (Long pause) She will no longer have that.

D: Can you make it go away?

A: She has already asked.

D: Because she has to give herself injections. Do you know what that is?

A: She will no longer.

D: Because no one likes to keep taking injections.

A: She will no longer.

D: You can bring that part into balance?

A: It has already been done so.

D: What if she doesn't realize this and still keeps taking the injections?

A: You do not work as a whole unit on this universe.

D: Will the doctors, the medical people, be able to see she no longer needs the injections?

A: You will.

D: Because the doctors say that if she stops the injections she will hurt herself.

A: Correct. The one that you call "Ann".... One moment. (Long pause)

D: What are you doing?

A: I'm trying to become one with what you call "Ann."

D: But no harm.

A: We never inflict harm on your kind.

D: And only a temporary fusing, so you can find out what's wrong with the body. Is that right?

A: One moment. (Long pause) This that you call "pain" in the body that you mentioned. —It is gone. —Many of her physical problems are caused by putting wrong substances into her living body. Fuel intake.

D: What she's eating or drinking?

A: Correct.

D: Can you show her what to eat?

A: We do not eat substances as you do. It is up to her substance intake. What you call "fuel source."

D: What is she taking as a substance intake that she shouldn't?

A: One moment. (Long pause) This is very difficult to describe this.

D: Does she eat it or drink it?

A: It is a "eat." It is a substance. I cannot describe the substance. It is brown in color, of your color. I am understanding your spectrum.

D: You can see the spectrum now.

A: Correct. It is brown. A dark substance. It's a fleshy substance. It is of your animal. It is quite large to your proportion. It has ... four walking vessels. You use wrong chemicals. You chemicalize your flesh.

D: And this is causing problems in her body?

A: Correct.

D: I think I know what it is you're talking about. It's a kind of an animal that we do eat.

A: Yes, many of you do.

D: Would it be correct to say it's a cow?

A: I do not understand cow.

D: A cow is a large animal. It has rather smooth skin. Sometimes they're brown, sometimes they're black. But they are large. (Yes) And we eat their meat. (Yes) This is the one she should stay away from? (Yes) Very good. Because I think she can do that and substitute other things. (Yes) I think this is going to help her a lot.

A: She is helping us.

D: Yes, and in return you want her to stay healthy.

A: Correct.

D: Then can you help her with these problems with her throat?

I thought I had better try to help with all of her ailments since it was working so well.

A: One moment. (A very Long Pause)

D: What's happening?

A: It is done.

D: Very good. Very good. Is it gone immediately, or will it be a gradual ....

A: (Interrupted) Yes. It is gone.

D: Then the body is returning to its proper state of complete balance and harmony, isn't it?

A: Correct. You, you, as a human race, do not do this together.

D: We try to do it in small groups sometimes.

A: Hmmm. Very little. It takes much more.

D: But we try to show people that their minds can control their bodies.

A: Correct. —This one that you call "Ann," she can call upon us—in what your time structure, you say "daily." What is daily?

D: Well, it's a little hard to explain. We have days because our planet revolves....

A: (Interrupted) Are you speaking of Sun and moons?

D: Yes. It goes around the Sun. During the day is when it's light....

A: (Interrupted) She can call us upon every Sun that comes to the bright side of your moon, in your words.

Ann's voice had been so gravelly that it didn't sound anything like her normal voice.

D: That's daily.

A: Correct.

D: When it becomes night, that's when the planet turns away from the Sun.

A: Correct.

D: Yes. But the main thing is, she has to live a life on this plane. So we don't want to do anything to interfere with that. We have to live in this physical world.

A: We have come, not to interfere, but to assist you. We do not come to harm.

D: She was afraid at first that you were going to take something away from her.

A: That was never.

D: Do you know that sometimes I use this information that I write about it?

A: You are a teacher.

D: Is it all right if I use the information that you tell me?

A: Correct.

D: This way more people will know about it.

A: It is very good for your people to know and to learn to unite. You are a teacher. But you do not ask all the right questions.

D: I don't have them in my mind yet. They have always told me the questions are more important than the answers.

A: Correct.

D: So just be patient with me.

I then asked the entity to recede back to the seventh plane where he said he was from.

When Ann awakened she had absolutely no memory of the session. We attempted to explain what had happened, especially the parts about her physical condition. When she looked at the drawing of the plant she thought it looked like cannabis or marijuana. It has been said that this plant has many more uses and value than we recognize, especially since the government has classified it as a drug.

I told Ann that I would never tell anyone to stop taking medication, especially to stop insulin injections. But if they were correct and the diabetes condition had been removed, would it harm her to take shots if her body no longer needed them? I really did not want that responsibility. I needn't have worried because Ann said that she had to take her blood sugar reading every morning to indicate how much insulin she gave herself. Her blood sugar had been running around 300.

An amazing thing happened when she called me a few days later. When she took her blood sugar reading the next day it had dropped to the 80s. She did not give herself a shot. All day her husband kept asking her when she was going to take the injection. Her response was, "I don't need it anymore." That was a very important statement because it showed that her mental attitude had changed, and her belief system had clicked in. She believed that she no longer needed it.

Since she had been scheduled for throat surgery, she went back to her doctors at the VA hospital, and told them to take all the tests again, and to not ask her why. Later all of the tests came back negative. There was no sign of throat cancer, and her heart condition had improved to the point that she no longer needed medication. It has now been twelve years (in 2011) since we conducted this session. She has never had another insulin injection. Her blood sugar dropped from 300 to 80 and has never risen. Of course, the doctors have no answers. They wrote across her medical records, "We have no explanation for this case." She now tells everyone, "I used to be an insulin dependent diabetic."

Another thing happened that may have influenced her cure and would be more in line with my therapy work with the subconscious. Ann was in a bad marriage and this was causing her much stress. One of the main causes of diabetes that I have found is the lack of sweetness. Psychologically, the lack of love in the person's life. This would also account for the heart problems, the heart being the seat of the emotions. And the throat problems, being unable to express her feelings to the most important people in her life. Shortly after this session Ann got a divorce, and she and her son have been living on their own. I know this was a very important contributing factor to the cure.

This was one of the most dramatic cases I had worked on at that time in 1999. Most of the cures that occur now during my work come from the intercession of the subject's subconscious mind when the subject understands the reason for the illness or physical symptoms. In Ann's case it was done through the intercession of an entity from another dimension. Yet it was bound by regulations. It could not interfere, but only performed the physical cures when it asked Ann's permission. So the entity from the seventh plane was also bound by the restriction of noninterference, and had to be sure that Ann really wanted to let the illnesses go. When it had her permission, the cures were instantaneous.

BONUS LEVEL: BOOK AND MEDIA RECOMMENDATIONS

If you consume everything on this list, you will really level up our friendship. I started this list during my lonely Covid solitary homeparty and then I continue to add and modify it over time as I attempt to decrease the entropy of the panoply of options to consume…

Check my always updated list online on my website for the book at https://stuckincustoms.com/treys-recommendations/

BOOKS ABOUT REALITY AND SPIRITUALITY
Do you feel like reality is a bit weird and you don't feel quite right here on Earth? Or maybe you have a feeling of awakening? Dig in. Go in the order below if you wish and enjoy!

- *Three Waves of Volunteers for the New Earth* by Dolores Cannon—my #1 non-fiction book! This explains a system of the universe and life that makes sense to me after not only all my studies in science and philosophy but also from some things I have experienced in the spirit world.

It pairs well with the next book. Also, the audiobook has wonderful readers.

- *Journey of Souls* by Dr. Michael Newton—Twenty-nine amazing case studies of people that were hypnotized and not only discuss fascinating past lives, but they spend a lot of time talking about the time between lives with their soul friends as they choose their next mission to Earth.
- *Many Lives Many Masters* by Dr. Brian Weiss—Another great non-fiction book about a doctor who gets healed by his patient as much as heals her. Together, with the above two books, these form an alloy of the truth of the nature of consciousness, souls, and why we are all here.
- *Journeys Out of the Body* by Robert Monroe—An amazing book by a skeptic like me where he details story after story of how he learned to leave his body and have the most incredible experiences.
- *The Alchemist* by Paulo Coelho—A fiction book filled with the truth
- *The Convoluted Universe* a series of books by Dolores Cannon. Case study after case study of people that have experienced not only past lives here, but on other planets. The level of detail and the overlapping accounts from different people from all walks of life all around the world form a web of stories that reinforce one another without any contradictions. Truly fascinating.
- *Destiny of Souls*—The incredible sequel to the above book by Dr. Michael Newton. There are about sixty new case studies that build on different aspects of the first book. Mind-blowage.
- *Seth Speaks*—This rather amazing book by Jane Roberts is a remarkable series of channelings where one of their friends from the great beyond dictates an entire book. It touches on many of the same aspects as the Dr. Michael

Newton and Dolores Cannon books, even though it pre-dated them when it was published in 1971. The audio book is quite nice too.

- *The Untethered Soul* by Michael Singer—I may like this even better than Ekhardt Tolle, and that's saying a lot...
- Eckhardt Tolle books A New Earth + The Power of Now
- *The Holographic Universe: The Revolutionary Theory of Reality* by Michael Talbot—an amazing look at quantum physics that is understandable even if you are not a hardcore science nerd
- *In My Own Way* by Alan Watts—I love all of Alan's books and this one is a great entryway!

OTHER GREAT BOOKS

I have a lot more books to add... just a quick amuse-bouche for ya there!

- *The Name of the Wind* by Patrick Rothfuss—my #1 fiction book... read this and we can really be besties :) There will be more books, but for now, just two in the series. The second one is *The Wise Man's Fear.*
- *The Almanack of Naval Ravikant: A Guide to Wealth and Happiness* by Naval. It's by far one of my favorite books... he has some of the most lucid thinking I've ever encountered.
- Yuval Noah Harari books—*Sapiens* + *Homo Deus*
- Matt Ridley books—start with The Origins of Virtue and The Red Queen or Genome
- *Sex at Dawn* by Christopher Ryan and Cacilda Jetha. A fascinating book about the sexual history of humans.
- How to Change Your Mind: What the New Science of Psychedelics Teaches Us about Consciousness, Dying,

Addiction, Depression, and Transcendence by Michael Pollan (also a great Netflix series!)
- Neal Stephenson books: Ananthem + Cryptonomicon + Snow Crash
- *The Etymologicon* by Mark Forsyth—if you love words like I do, this book is like nothing I've ever come across.
- *Mistborn* by Brandon Sanderson—A gripping fantasy series set in a world where certain people can ingest metals to gain magical powers.
- *The Martian* by Andy Weir—A gripping and scientifically accurate tale of an astronaut stranded on Mars, fighting for survival.
- *Project Hail Mary* by Andy Weir—the audio version is great with the alien voices
- *Guns, Germs, and Steel* by Jared Diamond—A thought-provoking analysis of the factors that contributed to the rise and fall of various civilizations throughout history.
- *Drug Use for Grown-ups* by Dr. Carl Hart—a Columbia Professor whose expertise shines in his push for decriminalizing drug use.
- *The Art of War* by Sun Tzu—An ancient Chinese treatise on military strategy, still relevant today for understanding conflict and competition in various aspects of life.
- *The War of Art* by Steven Pressfield—The War of Art identifies the enemy that every one of us must face, outlines a battle plan to conquer this internal foe, then pinpoints just how to achieve the greatest success.
- *Daemon* by Daniel Suarez—An amazing adventure about a near-future with augmented reality
- *Ready Player One* by Ernest Cline—a great adventure book about VR gaming in the future with some real twists... the book is way better than the movie.

PODCASTS

- <u>My Podcasts</u>—Seems strange to recommend my own pod? Maybe not. I have several types... from psychedelic experiences to 360 video interviews around the world.
- <u>Gabi Kovalenko</u>—An amazing lady who is full of inspiration and will make you think a bit differently about yourself and the world.
- <u>Lex Fridman</u>—**A must-go-to...**
- *The* <u>*Tim Dillon Show*</u>—**By far one of the funniest podcasts out there.**
- <u>Duncan Trussell Family Hour</u>—I think Duncan is hilarious and has incredible insights... a hilarious psychonaut (also the guy behind Midnight Gospel)
- Joe Rogan - of course! So many interesting guests... love to you Joe!
- <u>Jordan Peterson</u>—I love this guy... What a dude. Such clarity of thought and he's helped so many people get their lives back together.
- <u>*Next Level Soul*</u>—Another wonderful podcast that will help you think about a reality that is bigger than you just being stuck in your body.
- <u>Sam Harris *Making Sense*</u>—**Everything from science to consciousness. He's the dude.**
- <u>*Hardcore History* with Dan Carlin</u>—**Amazing dude who is so passionate about history details that will blow your mind.**
- <u>Always Sunny Podcast</u>—They do one episode where they break down each episode of each season—suggest the YouTube version
- Michael Singer Podcast—Writer of a favorite book *The Untethered Soul.*
- Bledsoe Said So—Great podcast about everything from

the afterlife to aliens to conspiracy theories. But solid stuff for sure.

- <u>Offbook the Improvised Musical Comedy</u>—Hilarious... god so funny.
- *<u>My Dad Wrote a Porno</u>*—**Too funny.**
- <u>Bankless</u>—**A top pod on crypto.**
- <u>The Dollop</u>—Funny podcast with two guys where one guy goes through a crazy historical situation while the other guy makes jokes.
- <u>Naval</u>—Very smart 1–2-minute podcast episodes, often business or consciousness-related.
- *<u>The Happiness Lab</u>* with <u>Dr. Laurie Santos</u>
- <u>The Dream</u>—Start with Season 1 episode 1... just great storytelling
- <u>Tim Ferris</u>—**Has some good ones...**
- <u>Aubrey Marcus</u>—Lots of good gems in there even though Aubrey has an amazing ability to talk about himself a lot during the interviews.
- *<u>Conan O'Brien Needs a Friend</u>*—**Funny stuff.**

TV SHOWS—COMEDIES

- *Fleabag* [on Amazon Prime Video]—If you don't watch this, our nascent friendship is over...
- *It's Always Sunny in Philadelphia* [on Hulu]—Probably my favorite funny show of all time... If you're really into it like me, you'll love the podcast about the show
- *Curb Your Enthusiasm* [on HBO Max]—From the creator of Seinfeld. No need to watch in order... start with any season as they are all great. I recommend season 6 and beyond because the first few seasons look like they were shot on Betamax...

- *Succession* [on HBO Max]—While not specifically a comedy, it's a drama that is fucking funny... so I have it listed below in drama as well... a show about a media empire gone wrong, with a power struggle among the family members. Also the same great writer (Jesse Armstrong) as *Peep Show.*
- *Rick & Morty* [on HBO Max]—Too funny whether you are sober, drunk, or high
- *Southpark* [on HBO Max]—of course
- *Flight of the Conchords* [on HBO Max]—Musical comedy from New Zealand... one of many reasons I moved here.
- *Arrested Development*—One of my favorite, well-written shows of all time
- *What We Do in Shadows* [on Hulu]—TV show based on the vampire mockumentary
- *Our Flag Means Death* [on HBO Max]—Another great Taika mockumentary about pirates
- *Peep Show* [on Amazon Prime Video]—Hilarious British show about two roommates and their internal dialogs. It's about 15 years old but the humor is just as good as ever—written by Jesse Armstrong, the same writer that does the great *Succession.*
- *30 Rock* [on Hulu]—Hilarious Tina Fey creation
- *The Office*—the Ricky Gervais one [on Netflix] AND the US one with Steve Carrell [on Peacock]
- *Silicon Valley* [on HBO Max]—Funny show about tech companies
- *Life's Too Short* [on HBO Max]—another Ricky Gervais vehicle
- *Schitt's Creek* [on Netflix]—Start season 2
- *Extras* [on HBO Max]—Ricky Gervais Comedy
- *Portlandia* [on Netflix]—Hilarious Fred Armisen vehicle
- *Unbreakable Kimmy Schmidt* [on Netflix]—Funny

relax-on-the-couch show and giggle... written by Tina Fey... about a woman who was brainwashed in a bunker for most of her life then has to navigate a wild and hilarious life in New York City.

- *The Good Place* [on Netflix]—Fantastic and funny show with lots of twists and turns about the afterlife where people think they are in heaven.
- *Twin Peaks* [on Showtime, Hulu with Showtime add-on, or Netflix for the original series]—the old and new series from David Lynch—not really a comedy, but the first surrealist drama on TV
- *Conan without Borders* [on Netflix]—Hilarious travel show
- *Sex Education* [on Netflix]—Hilarious British show about a sex therapist mom and son
- *Comedians in Cars Getting Coffee* [on Netflix]—Seinfeld gets a coffee with a new comedian every episode
- *Toast of London* [on Netflix]—a VERY silly show about a voice actor with Matt Berry
- *Last Man on Earth* [on Hulu]—Like it sounds
- *Brooklyn Nine-Nine* [on Hulu]—More funny Andy Samberg

TV SHOWS—DRAMAS

- *Succession* [on HBO Max]—A drama and dark comedy show about a media empire gone wrong, with a power struggle among the family members. Also the same great writer (Jesse Armstrong) as Peep Show.
- *Chernobyl* [on HBO Max]—Amazing gripping drama (kind of a documentary)
- *Sherlock* [on Netflix]—The BBC one that launched

Benedict Cumberbatch. Also Martin Freeman and the great Andrew Scott.

- *Ozark* [on Netflix]—Intense show with Jason Bateman—Spoiler alert which is the same spoiler for every drama: Something bad happens.
- *House of Cards* [on Netflix]—Presidential drama with Kevin Spacey—some of his best work
- *Barry*—Great show from Bill Hader... He plays an ex-Marine with a dark past trying to turn his life around and become an actor in a quirky... oh man this show is hard to describe. But it's great!
- *Goliath* [on Amazon Prime Video]—Mystery show with Billy Bob Thornton
- *Ted Lasso* [Apple TV+]—such a sweet tale...
- *Billions* [on Showtime]—Great drama about billionaires
- *Yellowstone* [on Paramount Network]—I got so sick of people telling me to watch it that I am watching this and it's quite excellent.
- *The Queen's Gambit* [on Netflix]—A broken genius
- *Mr. Robot* [on Amazon Prime Video]—Great show with Rami Malik about a hacker with multiple personalities that takes down the system
- *After Life* [on Netflix]—Funny/Sad show with Ricky Gervais
- *Breaking Bad* [on Netflix]—A high school chemistry teacher turned methamphetamine manufacturer faces the dark side of the drug world.
- *Atlanta* [on Hulu]—*Curb your Enthusiasm* with the genius Danny Glover
- *Fargo* [on Hulu]—Billy Bob Thornton and Martin Freeman in a murder drama—Season 1 is the best

TV SHOWS—SCI-FI & FANTASY

- *Black Mirror* [on Netflix]—Watch every one! The first one may be too intense but stick with it... each episode stands alone—my faves are San Junipero and Nosedive
- *Picard* [on Paramount+]—I was a huge TNG fan and this series is surprisingly amazing... just loved it.
- *Devs* [on Hulu]—Great Sci-Fi show from the creator of *Ex Machina*
- *Attack on Titan*—My favorite Japanese anime set in a dystopian medieval future where giant titanic "humans" are attacking the villages.
- *The Boys* [on Amazon Prime]—A dark, satirical take on the superhero genre, exploring the consequences of unchecked power and celebrity.
- *Westworld* [on HBO Max]—Great Sci-Fi show. A bit difficult to follow but that makes it interesting in a way.
- *The Peripheral* [on Amazon Prime]—from the same makers as *Westworld* above
- *The Mandalorian* [on Disney+]—Even if you don't like *Star Wars*, you'll like this series
- *Boba Fett* [on Disney+]—Another great Star Wars series
- *Firefly* [on Hulu]—Only one season but great characters and fun!
- *His Dark Materials* [on HBO Max]—based on a favorite Philip Pullman series of books

MOVIES—SCI-FI & FANTASY

- *The Matrix*—groundbreaking film that blends cyberpunk aesthetics with philosophical inquiries into reality, freedom, and identity
- Chris Nolan movies with Hans Zimmer Soundtracks:

Inception [on Netflix] + *Interstellar* [on Amazon Prime Video] + *Momento* [on Peacock] + *The Dark Knight* [on HBO Max]

- Joaquin Phoenix movies: *Her* [on Netflix] + *Joker* [on HBO Max]
- *Ex Machina*—AI Robot thriller from Alex Garland [on Netflix]
- *Blade Runner 2049*—Pure cinematic genius from director Denis Villeneuve
- 2001: A Space Odyssey—A classic.
- *Minority Report*—A sci-fi thriller about a future where crimes are prevented before they happen.
- *Dune*—Another winner from Villeneuve
- *Fight Club*—A film that critiques consumer culture and identity, known for its twist ending and philosophical underpinnings.
- *12 Monkeys*—A time-travel thriller that explores themes of memory, madness, and fate.
- *Parasite*—A dark comedy thriller that delves into class disparity, family dynamics, and social commentary in contemporary South Park. Sorry I mean South Korea.
- *The Platform* [on Netflix]—Dark weird movie that is quite gripping
- *Crouching Tiger Hidden Dragon*—beautiful movie [on Netflix]
- *Defending Your Life* [on HBO Max]—Albert Brooks + Meryl Streep romance about people stuck in purgatory who have to defend their life decisions
- *Spiderman: Into the Spider-Verse* [on Netflix]—some of the best art in a decade and incredible on ketamine
- *Mad Max: Fury Road* [on HBO Max]—genius cinematography

MOVIES—ARTSY

- All Wes Anderson Movies: Any order is fine... I recommend: *Moonrise Kingdom* [on Peacock] then *The Darjeeling Limited* [on HBO Max] then *The Fantastic Mr. Fox* [on Disney+] then *The Grand Budapest Hotel* [on HBO Max]
- Tarantino Movies: *Pulp Fiction* [on Netflix] then *Django Unchained* [on Netflix] then *Once Upon a Time in Hollywood* [on Starz] then *Inglorious Basterds* [on Peacock]
- Woody Allen Movies: *Midnight in Paris* [on Netflix] then *Vicky Cristina Barcelona* [on Hulu]
- Chris Nolan movies with Hans Zimmer Soundtracks: *Inception* [on Netflix] + *Interstellar* [on Amazon Prime Video] + *Momento* [on Peacock] + *The Dark Knight* [on HBO Max]
- Taika movies: *Jojo Rabbit* [on HBO Max] and *What We Do in Shadows* [on Kanopy]
- Joaquin Phoenix movies: *Her* [on Netflix] + *Joker* [on HBO Max] + *Walk the Line* [on Starz]
- Christopher Guest movies: *Best in Show* [on HBO Max], *Spinal Tap* [on HBO Max], *A Mighty Wind* [on HBO Max]
- DDL Movies: *There Will be Blood* [on Netflix] + *My Left Foot* [on HBO Max] + *Gangs of New York* [on Netflix]
- *Samsara* [on Amazon Prime Video]—While not technically a documentary, it's one of the most beautiful and interesting things you'll ever see. If you like this, also see the prequel *Baraka*, which is the "movie" that got me into my life as an artist.
- *Ex Machina*—AI Robot thriller from Alex Garland [on Netflix]
- *Jojo Rabbit*—Great Taika movie about a boy and Hitler

[on HBO Max]

- *The Platform* [on Netflix]—Dark weird movie that is quite gripping
- Crouching Tiger, Hidden Dragon—beautiful movie [on Netflix]
- *Lost in Translation*—Bill Murray + Scarlett Johannson [on Peacock]
- *Spiderman: Into the Spider-Verse* [on Netflix]—some of the best art in a decade and incredible on ketamine
- Jim Carrey Movies: *Eternal Sunshine of the Spotless Mind* [on Peacock] + *The Truman Show*—[on Amazon Prime Video]
- *A Star is Born* [on HBO Max]—that Bradley Cooper can do anything
- *Amelie* [on HBO Max]—a classic French film
- *Chinatown* [on Amazon Prime Video]—Genius Roman Polanski Movie
- *Call Me By Your Name* [on Starz]—Great and touching movie

MOVIES—COMEDY

- Woody Allen Movies: *Midnight in Paris* [on Netflix] then *Vicky Cristina Barcelona* [on Hulu]
- Taika movies: *Jojo Rabbit* [on HBO Max] and *What We Do in Shadows* [on Kanopy]
- Christopher Guest movies: *Best in Show* [on HBO Max], *Spinal Tap* [on HBO Max], *A Mighty Wind* [on HBO Max]
- Will Ferrell movies: *Anchorman* [on Netflix] + *Blades of Glory* [on Hulu] + *Stepbrothers* [on Hulu] + *Talladega Nights* [on Hulu]

- Sacha Baron Cohen vehicles: Borat: Cultural Learnings of America for Make Benefit Glorious Nation of Kazakhstan [on Amazon Prime Video] + The Dictator [on Netflix]
- *7 Days in Hell*—Tennis mockumentary with Andy Sanberg [on HBO Max]
- *Tropic Thunder*—Hilarious Vietnam War movie with Robert Downey Jr and Ben Stiller [on Amazon Prime Video]
- *Wedding Crashers*—Everyone loves it. Owen Wilson + Vince Vaughn [on HBO Max]
- *Team America: World Police*—Hilarious movie from the South Park creators [on Showtime]
- *Lost in Translation*—Bill Murray + Scarlett Johannson [on Peacock]
- *Defending Your Life* [on HBO Max]—Albert Brooks + Meryl Streep romance about people stuck in purgatory that have to defend their life decisions
- *Bad Santa* [on Starz] —Billy Bob Thornton... like most suggestions here, not family-friendly
- *SuperBad*—Oh man... how did I miss this one... I have so many more comedies to add but my OCD is running out of steam...
- *The Whale*—Just kidding this is defo not a comedy... I cried my eyes out... it's in the next movies category of...

MOVIES—ACTION/DRAMA

- Tarantino Movies: *Pulp Fiction* [on Netflix] then *Django Unchained* [on Netflix] then *Once Upon a Time in Hollywood* [on Starz] then *Inglorious Basterds* [on Peacock]
- Chris Nolan movies with Hans Zimmer Soundtracks: *Inception* [on Netflix] + *Interstellar* [on Amazon Prime

Video] + *Momento* [on Peacock] + *The Dark Knight* [on HBO Max]

- Ed Norton Movies: *Fight Club* [on Hulu] + *American History X* [on HBO Max]
- Leo DiCap movies: *The Revenant* [on FXNow] + *The Wolf of Wall Street* [on Hulu] + *Titanic* [on Paramount+] + *The Aviator* [on HBO Max] + *Catch Me if You Can* [on Showtime]
- Joaquin Phoenix movies: *Her* [on Netflix] + *Joker* [on HBO Max] + *Walk the Line* [on Starz]
- Christian Bale Movies: *American Psycho* [on Hulu] + *The Machinist* [on Tubi] + *The Prestige* [on Disney+]
- DDL Movies: *There Will be Blood* [on Netflix] + *My Left Foot* [on HBO Max] + *Gangs of New York* [on Netflix]
- *Ex Machina*—AI Robot thriller from Alex Garland [on Netflix]
- *The Whale*—An award-winning movie with Brandon Fraser directed by the great Darren Aronofsky
- *Jojo Rabbit*—Great Taika movie about a boy and Hitler [on HBO Max]
- *Gladiator*—when I first fell in love with Hans' music [on Starz]
- *Unforgiven*—Great Clint Eastwood flick [on HBO Max]
- *Tombstone*—Speaking of Westerns, this one may be in my top three [on Hulu]
- *The Social Network*—About the founding of Facebook [on Netflix]
- Crouching Tiger, Hidden Dragon—beautiful movie [on Netflix]
- *Lost in Translation*—Bill Murray + Scarlett Johannson [on Peacock]
- *Top Gun: Maverick*—I thought this would be stupid but I was really entertained

- *Mad Max: Fury Road* [on HBO Max]—genius cinematography
- Jim Carrey Movies: *Eternal Sunshine of the Spotless Mind* [on Peacock] + *The Truman Show* [on Amazon Prime Video]
- *A Star is Born* [on HBO Max]—that Bradley Cooper can do anything
- *Amelie* [on HBO Max]—a classic French film [on HBO Max]
- *Chinatown* [on Amazon Prime Video]—Genius Roman Polanski Movie
- *Call me By Your Name* [on Starz]—Great and touching movie

DOCUMENTARIES

- *Samsara* [on Amazon Prime Video]—While not technically a documentary, it's one of the most beautiful and interesting things you'll ever see. If you like this, also see the "prequel" *Baraka*, which is the "movie" that got me into my life as an artist.
- *Exit Through the Gift Shop* [on Amazon Prime Video]—Surprise doco about Banksy...
- *Jim & Andy* [on Netflix]—Jim Carrey gets lost in his portrayal of Andy Kaufman
- *Jiro Dreams of Sushi* [on Netflix]—A beautifully crafted documentary about an 85-year-old sushi master and his relentless pursuit of perfection.
- *Won't You Be My Neighbor?* [on HBO Max]—A heartwarming documentary about the life and legacy of Fred Rogers, the beloved host of the children's television show, Mister Rogers' Neighborhood.

- How to Change Your Mind: What the New Science of Psychedelics Teaches Us about Consciousness, Dying, Addiction, Depression, and Transcendence by Michael Pollan (also a great book below).
- *Free Solo* [on Disney+]—A stunning documentary about professional rock climber Alex Honnold as he attempts to climb El Capitan without a rope.
- *Searching for Sugar Man* [on Amazon Prime Video]—A fascinating documentary about two fans who set out to discover what happened to their favorite musician, Rodriguez, who mysteriously disappeared from the public eye.
- *Fyre: The Greatest Party That Never Happened* [on Netflix]—A behind-the-scenes look at the infamous Fyre Festival, which was sold as a luxury event but turned out to be a disaster.
- *Helvetica* [on Amazon Prime Video]—A design documentary that focuses on the ubiquitous typeface, Helvetica, and its impact on our visual culture.
- *Tales from the Tour Bus* [on Cinemax]—Hilarious animated real stories of touring rock bands from Mike Judge
- *Seven Days till Air*—Great doco on the creation of a Southpark episode (on YouTube)
- *Struggle* [on Netflix]—A doco about an amazing artist you've never heard of
- *Inside Bill's Brain* [on Netflix]—3-part interesting doco about Bill Gates
- *Chef's Table* [on Netflix]—The most beautiful food show you'll ever see
- *Abstract* [on Netflix]—Incredible doco about creativity
- *Fantastic Fungi* [on Apple TV and Google Play]—About the magic of mushrooms
- Running With the Devil: The Wild World of John McAfee [on Showtime]—what a wild story

- *George Carlin's American Dream* [on HBO]—two doco part from Judd Apatow—I love docos about comedians because I see a lot of my own life in them... in that we are really solo performers, constantly putting ourselves out there and getting more rejection than acceptance, which most people don't realize.
- *Some Kind of Monster* [on Amazon Prime Video]—amazing doco about Metallica
- *Trafficked* [on National Geographic]—Great doco about what happens behind-the-scenes in various black markets
- *Robin Williams: Come Inside My Mind* [on HBO]—A documentary about the life and career of the late comedian Robin Williams.
- *What is a Woman*—About trans stuff—I have a feeling trans people don't like it (Note: I couldn't find the exact streaming service for this documentary; it might not be available on popular platforms)
- *Tiger King; Murder Mayhem Madness* [on Netflix]—Crazy doco about a guy that collects big cats
- *ZZ Top Texas* [on Netflix]—Cool doco about the band
- *Goop Lab* [on Netflix]—Only episode 1 about mushrooms is good. The rest are dumb.
- *Behind the Curve* [on Netflix]—Debunks those silly flat-Earthers
- *Have a Good Trip–Adventures on Psychedelics* [on Netflix]—Hilarious stories about famous people doing LSD/Acid
- *Going Clear* [on HBO]—Scientology
- *Icarus* [on Netflix]—Russian Doping Scandal
- *McEnroe* [on HBO]—Doco on John
- *Last Dance* [on Netflix]—Multipart series about Michael Jordan
- *The Zen Diaries of Garry Shandling* [on HBO]—A

documentary about the life and career of the late comedian Garry Shandling.

TREY'S MUSICAL LOVES

- Machine Elf Long Mix Playlist—This is a collection of
  one to five-hour mixes of some favorite genres of music
  mixed with my visual fractals to enjoy
- Trey's Burning Man Afternoon Songs—For those
  shoulder times when you are gathering your wits but still
  wanna groove a bit
- Trey's Party Bangers—**A short list of high-energy
  songs**
- Trey's Feelin' Rene Swank—**A fun playlist I made that
  makes me think of my bestie Rene**
- Trey's 80s Playlist—**I grew up then... Well, in truth, I
  still haven't**
- Trey's French Accordion Music—**to make you feel like
  you're sitting in a cafe in Paris**
- Trey's Boogies—**When you feel a need for Abba n'
  stuff**
- Trey's Groovy Vegan Salad—**Just as it sounds**
- Trey's Molly Serotonin Explosion—A lot of songs may
  not show up because I downloaded from Soundcloud...
- Trey's Mindful List—**Something when you want a
  calm mind**
- Trey's Oldies—**but goodies**
- Trey's Zimmery—**just as it sounds**
- Guided Psilocybin Journey—for that heroic 5 gram
  mushie dose or something in that ethereal realm—cu-
  rated by Jon Hopkins and Imperial College London
- Terra Clara—another playlist I listened to during my

ibogaine ceremony from my friend Claire Wilkins
- <u>Meditacao</u>—A great Ayahuasca playlist that will almost make you forget about your bucket-of-nightmares

MASTERCLASS.COM—FAVE CLASSES

- Warner Herzog teaches documentary making
- Hans Zimmer teaches film music
- Chris Voss teaches Negotiation
- David Lynch teaches directing

MEDITATION & YOGA

- Sam Harris Waking Up App—It costs $$ but if you can't afford it, contact them and they'll make it FREE for you because Sam's a dude!
- Yoga Nidra—Use these to go to sleep... they work magic... a bunch on YouTube... I like the 1-hour ones because sometimes it's hard to sleep... but it works 100% of the time. Unless I'm on molly.
- <u>Machine Elf Playlist—very calming videos made by yours truly!</u>
- *Yoga With Adriene*—She's a fun gal in Austin with a lot of beginner-focused yoga.

BOOK TWO:
SUBSEQUENT AWAKENINGS

This part of our saga ventures into territories that even the boldest of cartographers would hesitate to map. We're talking about a cocktail of experiences that include, but are not limited to, ancient visions, nightly visits from otherworldly beings in my bed, astral jaunts across the cosmos, and unexpected detours through alternate realities. It's a segment where my bed becomes a portal, my dreams a gateway, and my waking life a series of footnotes to these bedtime adventures. These also include waking reflections and other significant things that have happened in my life as I continue this rather unusual rollercoaster after those events in Scotland.

I hope you smile and laugh and are amazed and blown away as I have been.

To get a free PDF copy of Book Two, join our community at https://www.facebook.com/groups/treyratcliffsreadingnook/ and sign up for the free newsletter at https://stuckincustoms.com/stucknewsletter/

Can't wait to hang with you in the community. See you soon! :)

ABOUT THE AUTHOR

Trey Ratcliff is an acclaimed photographer, artist, and writer whose work has been recognized by institutions such as the Smithsonian, featured in *National Geographic*, and even auctioned at Sotheby's. Beyond his artistic accolades, Trey is the creative mind behind StuckInCustoms.com, the leading travel photography blog that captured the imaginations of millions with its stunning visuals from every corner of the globe.

Renowned for introducing the art world to High Dynamic Range (HDR) photography, Trey's innovative approach has not just earned him the title of a "pioneer" by TED's Chris Anderson but has also brought the technique into mainstream appreciation. His art, celebrated for its vibrant and emotive qualities, appeals to a wide audience, and patrons of his fine art masterpieces have found their way into the collections of knights, professional athletes, and esteemed celebrities like Edward Norton and Leonardo DiCaprio.

In an act of clairvoyance or perhaps just exceptionally good taste, Trey relocated to Queenstown, New Zealand, in 2012, inadvertently setting the trend for doomsday preppers seeking picturesque landscapes to backdrop their apocalypse rehearsals.

With a mission to inspire mindfulness and a deeper appreciation for our world through his lens, Trey has traversed all seven continents, sharing over 140 billion views of his work on Google and cultivated a social media following of more than 6 million. His adventures and the stories he tells through his photography remind us of the joy found in exploration and the profound impact of viewing our world through a compassionate, artistic gaze.

Printed in Great Britain
by Amazon

46845472R00303